ELEMENTAL THEOLOGY

DOCTRINAL AND
CONSERVATIVE

ELEMENTAL THEOLOGY

Doctrinal and Conservative

Written and Edited
by

EMERY H. BANCROFT, D.D.

Late professor of Bible Doctrine
and Systematic Theology
At the Baptist Bible Seminary
Johnson City, New York

ZONDERVAN PUBLISHING HOUSE
GRAND RAPIDS, MICHIGAN

First Zondervan printing 1955
Second printing. 1960
Third printing 1963
Fourth printing. 1965
Fifth printing. 1966
Sixth printing 1967
Seventh printing 1968
Eighth printing. 1970
Ninth printing. 1971

Printed by special arrangement
with the
Baptist Bible Seminary
Johnson City, New York

Printed in the United States of America

INTRODUCTION

This is the third edition of *Elemental Theology, Doctrinal and Conservative*, by Dr. Emery H. Bancroft. It is being sent forth with the assurance that many will find hereby the clarity and depth of the great doctrines of the Word of God.

These doctrinal studies are approached with a strong Biblical, rather than a philosophical emphasis. Therefore, this volume provides a vital contribution to our churches that are loyal to the Bible. In a day when philosophical errors are confusing all Christendom, it is refreshing to find a volume that sets forth lucidly a Biblical theology. Here the appeal for authority is not to historians, theologians, or the Church Fathers, but to the Word of God.

Because of the organization of this book it is especially suitable for use as a text in Bible schools, colleges and seminaries. It is in constant, widespread demand for this purpose by many schools. Pastors find this volume invaluable for their personal study and for use in Bible classes. Many individuals use this book with great benefit for personal Bible study, because it sets forth the great truths in clear, simple language. The teaching herein is fortified by a wealth of Scripture quotations and references.

Dr. Bancroft, with the Lord since 1944, was a man of great faith and spiritual discernment. His personal ministry was an unmeasured blessing to a host of students including those in Baptist Bible Seminary, which he helped to establish. Now his written ministry in this book, and the companion volume, *Christian Theology, Systematic and Biblical*, continues to bring blessing to thousands of students of the Word of God.

Johnson City, New York   PAUL R. JACKSON, D.D.

PREFACE TO THIRD EDITION

During the last several months of Dr. Emery H. Bancroft's ministry, it was my privilege to be closely associated with him as his assistant. The discussion of the material with him and the conducting of the classes afforded rich spiritual blessing.

When Dr. Bancroft went home to be with the Lord in 1944, I succeeded him as instructor in Elemental Theology, which I consider a high and holy privilege. Each year as I have taught through this book, I have received fresh blessing and learned something new. Of course, we never can exhaust the riches of God's Word.

In making some revisions for this third edition it has not been my purpose to change the theological position which was delineated so well by the first Dean of the Seminary. I have sought rather to make certain that Scripture references are correct and pertinent; to correct some typographical errors; and to make some additions in order to amplify statements which have always been a part of the book. It is my prayer that these changes may enhance the effectiveness of this volume which already has been a means of rich blessing to so many during the past quarter century.

Baptist Bible Seminary
Johnson City, New York   MEAD C. ARMSTRONG, LITT.M.

SYMBOLS USED

D.S.....................Doctrinal Statement
A.V.....................Authorized Version
R.V.....................Revised Version
M.T.....................Moffatt's Translation
W.T.....................Weymouth's Translation
S.F. ....See Further
S.A.....................See Also
f.c......................First Clause
l.c......................Last Clause
i.e......................that is
e.g. ....for example
viz ....namely

TABLE OF CONTENTS

CHAPTER ONE

THE DOCTRINE OF THE SCRIPTURES

CHAPTER TWO

THE DOCTRINE OF GOD

CHAPTER THREE

THE DOCTRINE OF JESUS CHRIST

CHAPTER FOUR

THE DOCTRINE OF THE HOLY SPIRIT

CHAPTER FIVE

THE DOCTRINE OF MAN

CHAPTER SIX

THE DOCTRINE OF SIN

CHAPTER SEVEN

THE DOCTRINES OF SALVATION

CHAPTER EIGHT

THE DOCTRINE OF THE CHURCH

CHAPTER NINE

THE DOCTRINE OF ANGELS

CHAPTER TEN

THE DOCTRINE OF LAST THINGS

ELEMENTAL THEOLOGY

**Doctrinal and
Conservative**

CHAPTER ONE

THE DOCTRINE OF THE SCRIPTURES

(BIBLIOLOGY)

"The sacred Scriptures form the most remarkable book the world has ever seen. They are of high antiquity. They contain a record of events of the deepest interest. The history of their influence is the history of civilization. The wisest and best of mankind have borne witness to their power as an instrument of enlightenment and of holiness; and having been prepared by men who 'spake from God, being moved by the Holy Ghost,' to reveal 'the only true God and Him Whom He did send, even Jesus Christ,' they have on this ground the strongest claims upon our attentive and reverential regard."—ANGUS-GREEN.

The attitude taken toward the Scriptures themselves governs in a large measure the conceptions and conclusions drawn from their teachings. If they are regarded as fully authoritative upon the subjects with which they deal, then their positive statements constitute the sole foundation for Christian doctrine.

A. Their Canonicity or Genuineness.

I. The Meaning of It.

By the canonicity of the Scriptures is meant that, according to certain and fixed standards, the books included in them are regarded as parts of a complete and divine revelation, which is therefore authoritative and binding in relation to both faith and practice.

The word "canon" is of Christian origin, from the Greek word "kanon," which in turn was probably borrowed from the Hebrew word "kaneh," meaning a reed or measuring rod; hence, a norm or rule. Later it came to mean a rule of faith, and eventually a catalogue or list. Gal. 6:16.

"It should be understood, however, that the canonization of a book does not mean that the Jewish nation, in the one case, or the Christian church, in the other, gave to that book its authority; but rather that its authority, being already established on other and sufficient grounds, it was in consequence recognized as properly belonging to the Canon and so declared to be."—GRAY.

"It is to be recognized that each of the canonical books possesses a quality which determined its acceptance. It was accepted because first perceived to be of Divine origin." To canonize a book meant: (1) The recognition that its teaching was, in a unique sense, Divine; (2) The consequent ascription to it of a religious authority by a community or its leaders.—ANGUS-GREEN.

1

II. The Proofs of It.

The Scriptures do not demand blind credulity on the part of those who approach them for their study, but an intelligent belief resting upon the basis of credible facts.

1. The Old Testament Canon.

"The Old Testament contains no record of the canonization of any book or collection of books, but everywhere recognizes the books as of canonical authority."

"All theories are at fault which consider the canonization of the O.T. books as the work of the people. Canonical authority and the recognition of it are two distinct things. That the decision of the people was not the cause of the canonicity is proven by three considerations.

1. Authority in those times was not conceived of as coming from the people but from God. This critical theory would force into ancient times the principle of modern civilization. The books must have possessed canonical authority before they were recognized by Israel, or Israel would not have recognized them. They were canonical because Divinely inspired, and possessed Divine authority from their first promulgation.

2. The two accounts of so-called canonization are not really such. The so-called canonization of the book of Deuteronomy in the time of Josiah is not canonization at all. The book was recognized as already authoritative by all who read it. Hilkiah said to Shaphan: "I have found the book of the law in the house of the Lord." (II Kings 22:8) Shaphan read the book before Josiah the King. The King immediately rent his clothes and commanded that inquiry be made of the Lord concerning the words of the book saying: "Great is the wrath of the Lord that is kindled against us, because our fathers have not hearkened unto the words of the book to do according unto all that which is written concerning us." Josiah gathered the people together and read the book to them. (II Kings 23:1, 2).

Likewise the record of Nehemiah 8 is not that of the canonization of a book. Ezra evidently considered the book as already canonical, or he would not have taken such pains to read it at the solemn assembly of the people. The people had the same idea of it for they asked Ezra to read it (Neh. 8:1-3) "and when he opened it all the people stood up" as an evidence of this authority. Their acceptance was but the recognition of previously existing authority. The reading was for the instruction of the people.

3. There is no record in the O T. of the formal acceptance by the people of any of the books of the second and third divisions of the canon. Yet these books were evidently considered canonical. If either the acceptance by the people or the official endorsement by the scribes made the books canonical, the recording of that act would be an important part of each book, or at least of each division of the canon. Yet no such record exists. The explanation is obvious that the books were recognized as canonical from the first."—RAVEN. The Old Testament Scriptures are spoken of, among other titles, as "The Law and the Prophets" (Matt. 22:40; Acts 13:15; Rom. 3:21).

(1) The Law.

    a. Acceptance shown by place assigned in the temple.

    (a) Tables of the law preserved in the ark of the covenant.

Deut. 10:5—And I turned myself and came down from the mount, and put the tables in the ark which I had made; and there they·be, as the Lord commanded me.

(b) Book of the law kept by Levites at the side of the ark.

Deut. 31:24-26, R.V.—And it came to pass, when Moses had made an end of writing the words of this law in a book, until they were finished, that Moses commanded the Levites, that bear the ark of the covenant of Jehovah, saying, Take this book of the law, and put it by the side of the ark of the covenant of Jehovah your God, that it may be there for a witness against thee.

(c) Scriptures found in Temple in days of Josiah.

II Kings 22:8—And Hilkiah, the high priest, said unto Shaphan the scribe, I have found the book of the law in the house of the Lord. And Hilkiah gave the book to Shaphan, and he read it.

b. Acceptance shown by their recognition as authoritative.

(a) Law to be read in presence of the people every seven years.

Deut. 31:10-13—And Moses commanded them, saying, At the end of every seven years, in the solemnity of the year of release, in the feast of the tabernacles, when all Israel is come to appear before the Lord thy God in the place which he shall choose, thou shalt read this law before all Israel in their hearing. Gather the people together, men, and women, and children, and thy stranger that is within thy gates, that they may hear, and that they may learn, and fear the Lord your God, and observe to do all the words of this law: and that their children, which have not known anything, may hear, and learn to fear the Lord your God, as long as ye live in the land whither ye go over Jordan to possess it.

(b) Obedience to them urged upon the people.

II Chron. 17:9—And they taught in Judah, and had the book of the law of the Lord with them, and went about throughout all the cities of Judah, and taught the people.

(c) King to have copy by which to regulate his decisions.

Deut. 17:18-20—And it shall be, when he sitteth upon the throne of his kingdom, that he shall write him a copy of this law in a book out of that which is before the priests the Levites: And it shall be with him, and he shall read therein all the days of his life: that he may learn to fear the Lord his God to keep all the words of this law and these statutes, to do them. That his heart be not lifted up above his brethren, and that he turn not aside from the commandment, to the right hand, or to the left: to the end that he may prolong his days in his kingdom, he, and his children, in the midst of Israel.

(d) Joshua obligated to read them.

Josh. 1:8—This book of the law shall not depart out of thy mouth; but thou shalt meditate therein day and night, that thou mayest observe to do according to all that is written therein: For then thou shalt make thy way prosperous, and then thou shalt have good success.

(e) Basis of God's judgment of the kings.

I Kings 11:38—And it shall be, if thou wilt hearken unto all that I command thee, and will walk in my ways, and do that is right in my sight, to keep my statutes and my commandments, as David my servant did; that I

3

will be with thee, and build thee a sure house, as I built for David and will give Israel unto thee.

(f) The captivity of Israel and Judah caused by disobedience to them.

Neh. 1:7–9—We have dealt very corruptly against thee, and have not kept the commandments, nor the statutes, nor the judgments, which thou commandedst thy servant Moses. Remember, I beseech thee, the word that thou commandedst thy servant Moses, saying, if ye transgress, I will scatter you abroad among the nations. But if ye turn unto me, and keep my commandments, and do them; though there were of you cast out unto the uttermost part of the heaven, yet will I gather them from thence, and will bring them unto the place that I have chosen to set my name there.

(g) Recognized by returning captives.

Ezra 3:2—Then stood up Joshua the son of Jozadak, and his brethren the priests, and Zerubbabel the son of Shealtiel, and his brethren, and builded the altar unto the God of Israel, to offer burnt offerings thereon unto the Lord, as it is written in the law of Moses, the man of God.

(2) The Prophets.

a. Acceptance shown by the Prophets being placed on equality with the Law. "The prophets emphasized the Law (Isa. 1:10), but considered their own words equally binding. Disobedience to the prophets was equally punishable (II Kings 17:13)."—RAVEN.

b.. Acceptance shown by Daniel's reference to prophetic utterances preserved in books.

Dan. 9:2—In the first year of his reign I Daniel understood by books the number of the years, whereof the word of the Lord came to Jeremiah the prophet, that he would accomplish seventy years in the desolation of Jerusalem.

(3) Supplementary proof from the New Testament.

a. Christ's reference to the Scriptures as existent and authoritative.

Matt. 22:29—Jesus answered and said unto them, Ye do err, not knowing the Scriptures, nor the power of God.

S. F. John 5:39; John 10:35; Matt. 23:35; Luke 24:44.

b. The Apostles' reference to the Scriptures as of Divine origin and authority.

II Tim. 3:16—All Scripture is given by inspiration of God, and is profitable for doctrine, for reproof, for correction, for instruction in righteousness.

S.A. II Peter 1:20, 21.

2. New Testament Canon.

(1) Composed of books written by Apostles or received as of Divine authority in the apostolic age.

John 16:12–15—I have yet many things to say unto you, but ye cannot bear them now. Howbeit when He, the Spirit of truth, is come, he will guide you into all truth: for he shall not speak of himself; but whatsoever he shall hear, that shall he speak: and he will shew you things to come. He shall glorify me: for he shall receive of mine, and shall shew it unto you. All things that the Father hath are mine: therefore said I, that he shall take of mine, and shall shew it unto you.

S. F. II Peter 3:15, 16; John 14:26.

4

(2) Composed of books standing on a plane of authority not shared by any other books.

I Thes. 2:13—For this cause also thank we God without ceasing, because, when ye received the word of God which ye heard of us, ye received it not as the word of men, but, as it is in truth, the word of God, which effectually worketh also in you that believe.

(3) Composed of books which bore evidence of their own origin.

Col. 1:1, 2—Paul, an Apostle of Jesus Christ by the will of God, and Timotheus our brother, to the saints and faithful brethren in Christ which are at Colosse: Grace be unto you, and peace, from God our Father and the Lord Jesus Christ.

S. F. Rom. 1:1, 7.

(4) Composed of books endorsed and approved by the universal Christian consciousness.

(5) Composed of books concerning which the church was given spiritual discernment to enable her to discriminate the false from the true.

"It was some considerable time after our Lord's ascension before any of the books contained in the New Testament canon were actually written.

"The first and most important work of the Apostles was to deliver a personal testimony to the chief facts of the Gospel history. Their teaching was at first oral, but in the course of time many endeavored to commit to writing this oral Gospel. So long as the apostles were still living, the necessity for written records of the words and actions of our Lord was not so pressing. But when the time came for their removal from the world, it became extremely important that authoritative records should be put forth. Thus the Gospels came into existence. "Founders of churches, often unable to visit them personally, desired to communicate with their converts for purposes of counsel, reproof, and instruction. Thus arose the Epistles.

"The persecution of Diocletian (302 A.D.) brought to the front the question of the sacred literature of the church. The persecutors demanded that the Scriptures should be given up. This the Christians refused to do. Hence the question became urgent. What books are Apostolic? The answer lies in our New Testament. Careful, prayerful, and deliberate examinations proved which were genuine and which were false. Thus arose the New Testament Canon."—EVANS.

D. S. The books of the Old and New Testament Scriptures as we have them today are shown to have been accepted by the Church throughout the Christian era as comprising the complete revelation from God and as having been written by the human authors to whom they are accredited.

B. Their Credibility or Trustworthiness.
I. The Meaning of It.

By the credibility of the Scriptures is meant that their records are true and are thus to be relied upon as the statements of the facts.

The canonical character of the Scriptures, including the genuineness of their authorship, is thus shown to have been established, but the question of their truthfulness remains yet to be corroborated. A book may be genuine as to its authorship, and yet not credible as to its contents. For example, among the works of fiction we have those of Dickens, Shakespeare, and Stevenson with indisputable evidence of their authorship. No one with intelligence, however, would attempt

5

to establish the credibility of their narratives. They are universally recognized as fiction. Is this the case with the Bible, or is it both genuine and true?

II. The Proofs of It.

The truthfulness of any statement or series of statements may be tested by comparison with facts, if such facts are available. The truthfulness of Scriptural statements may be and has been tested by the facts discovered by scientific investigation and historical research.

1. Established by Negative Considerations.

(1) Not contradictory to any well-established facts of science.

When rightly interpreted, its statements harmonize with all the known facts concerning the physical constitution of the universe and the mystery of planetary and stellar worlds: the constitution of man and his complex nature and being; of the lower animals, and their various ranks in the scale of being; of plants, and the mystery of vegetable life; and the constitution of the earth with its material forms and forces.

The question is often raised as to the scientific accuracy of the Biblical statements, and it is sometimes disposed of by saying that the Bible is not a scientific book. While it is true that it does not make such a secondary question as natural science its subject, but is rather a history of redemption, yet it does include within its scope every realm of science. In all its statements therefore, it must and does speak with accuracy.

(2) Not contradictory to the generally supported philosophic conclusions concerning the facts of the universe.

The Bible opposes and refutes a number of false philosophic conceptions of the world such as atheism, polytheism, materialism, pantheism, and the eternity of matter (Gen. 1:1), but has no conflict or quarrel with those views which have proved themselves to be scientifically sound.

2. Established by Positive Considerations.

(1) Topographical and geographical trustworthiness.

Archeological discoveries prove that the peoples, places and events mentioned in Scriptures are found just where the Scripture locates them, in the exact locality and under the exact geographical circumstances described in the Bible.

Dr. Kyle says that travellers need no other guide than the Bible when following down the coast of the Red Sea, along the line of the Exodus, where the topography corresponds exactly to that given in the Biblical account.

"Sir William Ramsay, who started his explorations in Asia Minor as a person who doubted the historicity of Acts, bears testimony to this marvelous accuracy about points of geography and knowledge of political conditions which only a person living at that time and present on the spot could possibly have known. He was so impressed with these facts that he became an ardent advocate of the historicity of Acts."—HAMILTON.

(2) Ethnological or racial trustworthiness.

All Scriptural statements concerning the races with which they deal are shown to be in harmony with the ethnological facts as revealed by archeology.

"It is a fact well established by archeological research that wherever any peoples

6

are mentioned in the Scripture, or any statement is made about their kinship, origin, customs, whether they rule over others or serve other nations, or any other fact about them whatsoever, these statements can be depended upon to be in exact accordance as revealed by archeology. Hence the only theory that a historian can hold for a minute in the face of such facts is that the author of the table of nations in Genesis 10, must have had original sources of the first rank before him when he was writing these words."—HAMILTON.

(3) Chronological trustworthiness

The Scriptural identification of people, places, and events with the period of their occurrence is corroborated by Syrian chronology and the facts revealed by archeology.

The Bible has a real system in which the period to which the events referred is shown to be correct, the order of events is the order of their occurrence, and the accompanying circumstances are correctly timed and arranged. The first elements of trustworthy history are found in the Bible documents. The places where the events are said to happen are accurately located, the people who are said to be in such and such localities are actually there, and the time of the events recorded is the exact time when they must have happened. This furnishes the framework for the whole of Old Testament history.

(4) Historical trustworthiness.

The Scriptural record of the names and titles of the kings are in complete harmony with the secular records as brought to light by archeological discovery.

Dr. R. D. Wilson, professor Semitic languages, says that the names of forty-one of the kings mentioned by name in the Old Testament from the time of Abraham to the end of the Old Testament period, are also found in contemporary documents and inscriptions written in the time and usually under the direction of these kings themselves, in their own languages.

(5) Canonical trustworthiness.

The acceptance of the books included in the Scriptures of today by the church in all the Christian era carries with it the indorsement of their credibility.

a. Agreement of the printed copies of the Old and New Testaments dated 1488 and 1516 A.D. with the present printed copies of the Scriptures.

"These printed copies, on being compared, agree in the main with the printed copies of the Scriptures we possess today, and thus prove, by a single step, the Old and New Testament, in the form we have them now, to have existed four hundred years ago."—EVANS.

b. Acceptance upon the evidence of 2000 Biblical manuscripts possessed by scholars in the 15th century compared with the acceptance of secular writings upon the evidence of 10 or 20 copies.

"At the time these Bibles were printed, there were in possession of a certain scholar over 2000 manuscripts. Kennicott collected 630, and DeRossi 743 more, for the critical edition of the Hebrew Bible. Upwards of 600 more were collected for the edition of the Greek Testament. This was certainly a sufficient number to establish the genuineness and authenticity of the sacred text. They have served the purpose of restoring the text to its original purity, and also give us assured certainty and protection against future corruption.

"Most of these manuscripts were written between 1000 and 1500 A.D. Some date as far back as the eighth and ninth centuries. A few go as far back as the fourth century. That they date no earlier than the fourth century is doubtless accounted for by the fact that in the year A.D. 302 the Emperor Diocletian ordered the wholesale destruction of the sacred books."—EVANS.

> c. Attestation of four-oldest Bibles dated between 300 and 400 A.D. written in different parts of the world together containing the Scriptures as we have them today.

D. S. The truthful content of the Scriptures has been fully proved by an appeal to secular records and to actual facts revealed by scientific research.

C. Their Inspiration or Divine Authority.

I. The Meaning of It.

By the inspiration of the Scriptures is meant that the writers were so empowered and controlled by the Holy Spirit in the production of the Scriptures as to give them divine and infallible authority.

The claim for inspiration differs from that of credibility. In reference to the former, the Scriptures are affirmed to be the Word of God in such a sense that its words, though written by men and having indelibly impressed on them the marks of their human authorship, were written, nevertheless, under such an influence of the Holy Ghost as to be also the words of God, the adequate and infallible expression of His mind and will for us. Although the Holy Spirit did not select the words for the writers, it is evident that He did select them through the writers.

> "Thus while the credibility of the Bible means only that it takes its place with the best histories of human production, the inspiration of the Bible implies that, however it may resemble such histories, it belongs to an entirely different category; that, as no other writings are, it is not only generally reliable, but errorless and incapable of error; and that it is this because it differs absolutely from all other books in being itself, even as to its words, the very Word of God."—GREEN.

II. The Proofs of It.

The marks of the Divine are always distinguishable in that they evidence that which is above the natural. Thus the Scriptures are distinguishable from all human productions in that they possess characteristics which made necessary their classification as supernatural and divine.

1. The Testimony of Archeology—Corroborative Evidence of the Pick and Spade to the Accuracy of the Scriptures.

The testimony of archeology to the truthfulness or credibility of the Scriptures may also be regarded as corroborative evidence of their inspiration. If the Scriptures are to be relied upon as the statement of truth with no admixture of error, then their witness to their own inspiration may be accepted as trustworthy. The following are illustrative of archeology's testimony to the accuracy of the Scriptural records.

> "The story of Abraham has been referred to as no more to be believed than the story of Achilles, or Aeneas, or King Arthur, but as a matter of fact, documents, written in the time of Abraham and in the land in which he was reared, are now brought to the light of day. His birthplace has been discovered, the details of his sojourn in Egypt are now known to bear every evidence of his-

8

toricity, and we have similar confirmatory proof concerning his famous battle with the confederate kings, mentioned in Gen. 14. Even Melchizedek, whom he met, is not the mystery he was, as is proved from the Tel el-Amarna tablets."—GRAY.

"The treasure city of Pithon, built for Rameses II, by the Hebrews during the time of their hard bondage in Egypt (Exod. 1:11), has recently been unearthed near Tel-el-Kebir; and the walls of the houses were found to be made of sunbaked bricks, some with straw and some without straw, exactly in accordance with Exod. 5:7, written 3,500 years ago, 'Ye shall no more give the people straw to make bricks, as heretofore.' "—COLLETT.

"Recent explorations have made clear several important matters concerning the journeyings in the wilderness. For example, the point of crossing at the Red Sea; the real character of the desert; the location of the giving of the law; of Kadesh-Barnea, and other important places. Great light has been thrown upon the history and character of several of the peoples who inhabited the land of Canaan notably Hittites and Amorites, revealing the reason of God's anger against them for their gross iniquity, and showing the necessity for supernatural intervention if the Israelites were to triumph over them."—GRAY.

Another case is that of the mention in the book of Daniel of Belshazzar as King of the Chaldeans. Until quite recently there was no such name to be found in all Chaldean or other ancient history, although there existed an apparently complete list of the Babylonian kings, leaving no gap for the insertion of any other. This list gave the name of the king—Nabonidus—who was actually reigning at the very time when the Bible accounted that Belshazzar was king.

In 1854 Sir Henry Rawlinson discovered in Ur of the Chaldees some terracotta cylinders containing an inscription by the above named Nabonidus, in which he makes mention of "Belshazzar, my eldest son." But there still remained the difficulty, How could he be King of the Chaldeans, while every ancient record showed that his father Nabonidus was the last reigning monarch?

"In 1876 Sir Henry Rawlinson's workmen were excavating on an ancient part of Babylon when they came upon some jars filled with more than two thousand cuneiform tablets. One of these was found to contain an official account, by no less personage than Cyrus, King of Persia, of the invasion of Babylon, in which, after stating that Nabonidus first fled and then was taken prisoner, he adds that on a certain night the king died. Now seeing that Nabonidus, who was taken prisoner, lived for a considerable time after the fall of Babylon, this 'King' could have been none other than Belshazzar, of whom the old discredited Bible recorded long ago that 'in the night was Belshazzar, King of the Chaldeans, slain.' It is evident that Belshazzar was acting as regent during his father's absence. The fact which has thus come to light, that Nabonidus and Belshazzar his son were both reigning at the same time, explains, as nothing could Belshazzar's offer to make Daniel the third ruler in the Kingdom (Dan. 5:16), Nabonidus being the first, and Belshazzar, the regent, the second."—COLLETT.

Many illustrations similar to these are to be found.

2. The Testimony of the Bible—Internal Proofs of Its Divine Origin.

(1) The unity of it.

"The unity of the Bible is unique. Never elsewhere have so many different treatises, historical, biographical, ethical, prophetical, and poetical, been combined together, making one book, as all the hewn stone and timber make one building, or better still, as all the bones, muscles and ligaments combine in one body. This again, while indisputable as a fact, is unparalleled in literature, all the conditions being, humanly speaking, not only unfavorable, but fatal to such combination.

"There are sixty-six books, written by forty different men, coming from various conditions and circumstances in life, possessing varying degrees of culture from the shepherd to the statesman. These books were written in three different languages, during a period covering over sixteen centuries. The subjects on which they wrote were diverse and varied, and yet there is a doctrinal and structural unity pervading the whole. Notwithstanding all the divergent elements, they have produced essentially one book. Not only is the Bible as a whole an unrivalled phenomenon, but its features are all phenomenal, and none more so than this convergence of contents like rays toward one common focal point.

"Great cathedrals, like those of Milan and Cologne, occupied centuries in building. Hundreds and thousands of workmen wrought upon them. Surely no one needs to be told that behind and beyond these builders there must have been some one architect who built the temple in his own mind before the cornerstone was laid, who, first of all, drew the plans and furnished even the minute specifications; so that such a structure owes its matchless symmetry, not to the men of brawn that worked on it, but to that one man of brain that thought out the cathedral in its completeness.

"The Bible is a stately cathedral. Many human builders have in turn wrought on the structure. Who is the architect? What one mind is that which planned and saw the whole building, before Moses wrote those first words of Genesis, which by no accident, as though to carve the architect's name on the vestibule, are these: 'In the beginning God'."—PIERSON.

(2) The unique representations of it.

"What the Scripture has to say on all its leading themes is so contrary to the thoughts and ideas of all classes of men, that we are obliged to conclude that it is impossible that the human mind invented them."—PINK.

a. In relation to God, as infinite, sovereign, triune, holy, and loving.

Isa. 6:1–3—In the year that king Uzziah died I saw also the Lord sitting upon a throne, high and lifted up, and his train filled the temple. Above it stood the seraphims: each one had six wings; with twain he covered his face, and with twain he covered his feet and with twain he did fly. And one cried unto another, and said, Holy, holy, holy, is the Lord of hosts: the whole earth is full of his glory.

S. F. Dan. 4:35; Heb. 1:10–12; II Cor. 13:14.

"This conception altogether transcends the grasp of the finite intellect, and therefore could not have had its birth there. No man and no number of men ever invented such a God as this."—PINK.

b. In relation to man—condemnable as debased in character and sinful in conduct.

Rom. 3:10–12—As it is written, There is none righteous, no not one: There is none that understandeth, there is none that seeketh after God. They are all gone out of the way, they are together become unprofitable: there is none that doeth good, no, not one.

S. F. Jer. 17:9.

S. A. Eph. 4:18.

10

Unlike every other book in the world the Bible condemns man and all his doings. Such a description of fallen human nature was never invented by the human mind. Man would never paint such an uncomplimentary picture of himself.

c. In relation to the world (world system) as evil and opposed to God.

I John 2:15-17—Love not the world, neither the things that are in the world. If any man love the world, the love of the Father is not in him. For all that is in the world, the lust of the flesh, and the lust of the eyes, and the pride of life, is not of the Father, but is of the world. And the world passeth away, and the lust thereof: but he that doeth the will of God abideth for ever.

S. F. Gen. 6:5; Jas. 1:13-15.

"Men regard sin as a misfortune and ever seek to minimize its enormity. Unlike all other books, the Bible strips man of every excuse and emphasizes his culpability."—PINK.

d. In relation to the punishment of sin—as proportionate to its heinousness and guilt.

Ezek. 18:4—Behold, all souls are mine; as the soul of the father, so also the soul of the son is mine: the soul that sinneth, it shall die.

S. F. Rom. 6:23; Luke 12:47, 48; Psa. 62:12; Jer. 25:14; Rom. 2:6.

"What sinning man or men ever invented such an indescribably frightful doom as the Bible declares is awaiting every Christ-rejector? And the fact that Eternal Punishment is taught in the Bible, taught plainly and prominently, is another of the many evidences of its super-human origin and authorship."—PINK.

e. In relation to salvation from sin—as absolutely independent of human merit and solely based upon the merits of Christ.

Rom. 3:20, 24—Therefore by the deeds of the law there shall no flesh be justified in his sight: for by the law is the knowledge of sin. Being justified freely by his grace through the redemption that is in Christ Jesus.

S. F. Gal. 2:16; Titus 3:5; Eph. 2:8, 9.

The independence and self-righteousness of man would disincline him from setting forth such a conception of salvation as that contained in the Scriptures, namely, by grace through a divinely provided atonement.

(3) Prophecy and its fulfillment.

"No one but God can foretell the future with certainty; therefore, if it can be shown that the Bible contains numerous predictions that have been literally fulfilled, we at least cannot doubt that the Book came from God."—BODDIS.

a. Regarding the Jews.

II Ki. 21:11-15 (see especially v. 14):—And I will forsake the remnant of mine inheritance, and deliver them into the hand of their enemies; and they shall become a prey and a spoil to all their enemies.

II Chron. 36:6—Against him came up Nebuchadnezzar king of Babylon and bound him in fetters, to carry him to Babylon. Nebuchadnezzar also carried off the vessels of the house of the Lord to Babylon and put them in his temple at Babylon.

S. F. Matt. 24: 34-35.

"The entire Jewish history bears witness to the truth of the sacred Scriptures. Their continued existence as a separate people proves that the prophecies concerning them were really given by God. Read the Scriptures in connection with any standard history of the Jews and you will find that the prophecy and the history fit each other as the glove fits the hand for which it was made."—BODDIS. This is true of current history as well as of that of the past.

b. Regarding the Gentiles.

Daniel 2:—Colossal image—partially fulfilled in history of Babylon, Medo-Persia, Greece and Rome.

S. F. Joel 3:12; Matt. 25:31, 32.

Trustworthy Bible students have believed that the history of the first three of these empires mentioned has been the enfolding and fulfillment of the above prophetic picture. A partial fulfillment of the prophecy concerning the last empire is also historically true, but a larger part of this prophecy awaits a future and larger realization.

Of Rome Dr Boddis says: "Could the wisest of prophets have guessed that a comparatively insignificant community on the banks of the Tiber would become the m ghty empire of iron whose power would break the earth in pieces? Could he unaided by divine power, have foreseen that this great empire would eventually divide into east and west, never to be again united? What man, living even in the days of Antiochus, could have known that in its last stage, it would consist of several kingdoms, in which democracy and imperial power should be united? The prophecy has been literally fulfilled to the present hour, only one part being future, the final manifestation of the ten toes and the smiting of the image by the stone."

c. Regarding our Lord.

"The Old Testament is full of Jesus. All prophecy has Him as its theme. The Scriptures give us the line of Messiah's descent. He is to be of the seed of the woman, of the race of Shem, of the line of Abraham, through Isaac and Jacob, not Ishmael and Esau, of the tribe of Judah and the family of David.

"We also find predicted his entire life and ministry. His birthplace, His miraculous birth of a virgin, the sojourn into Egypt, His forerunner, the character of His ministry, His riding into Jerusalem upon an ass, His betrayal, trial and crucifixion, death, burial, resurrection and ascension, His second coming and reign—all these are predicted in unmistakable terms from Genesis to Malachi.

"It has been estimated by Bible students that more than three hundred details of prophecy have been fulfilled in Christ. Those which still remained unfulfilled concern His second coming and reign, which is still future.

"Could this great array of Messianic prophecy have found its fulfillment in one person, had it not come from God? How true are the words of Scripture, Prophecy came not in old time by the will of man; but Holy men of God spake as they were moved by the Holy Ghost.' "—BODDIS.

(4) The asserted claims of it.

II Tim. 3·16—All scripture is given by inspiration of God, and is profitable for doctrine, for reproof, for correction, for instruction in righteousness.

S. F. II Sam. 23.1, 2; II Pet. 1:20, 21.

The Bible whose genuineness has been established and credibility proved declares its own inspiration and divine authority.

3. The Testimony of Christ—Confirmatory Evidence to the Claims of Scripture by Him and Through Him.

The entire life and ministry of Jesus, together with His resurrection, set their seal to the divine inspiration and authority of the Scriptures.

(1) Of His words.

Luke 24:44, 45—And he said unto them, These are the words which I spake unto you, while I was yet with you, that all things must be fulfilled, which were written in the law of Moses, and in the prophets, and in the psalms, concerning me. Then opened he their understanding, that they might understand the scriptures.

S. F. Luke 24:25–27; John 10:35; Matt. 15:3, 6; Matt. 5:18.

"Whenever our Lord referred to the Scriptures, He invariably did so in terms calculated to inspire the utmost confidence in every word. And the whole record of His life fails to furnish one single exception to this rule."—COLLETT.

He spoke of the Old Testament books as "the Scriptures" which "cannot be broken." He also spoke of the truth "yet to be revealed," and gave instructions concerning the Holy Spirit by whom that revelation was to be given. (John 16:13, 14.)

(2) Of His works.

Matt. 11:4, 5—Jesus answered and said unto them, Go and shew John again those things which ye do hear and see. The blind receive their sight, and the lame walk, the lepers are cleansed, and the deaf hear, the dead are raised up, and the poor have the gospel preached to them.

Isa. 61:1 — The Spirit of the Lord God is upon me, because the Lord hath anointed me to preach good tidings unto the meek: he hath sent me to bind up the brokenhearted, to proclaim liberty to the captives, and the opening of the prison to them that are bound.

S. A. John 14:11; John 10:41.

The testimony of the words of Jesus to the inspiration of the Scriptures are supported and supplemented by the testimony of His works. The claims He made for their divine authority were substantiated by these credentials of His divine power.

Revelation, as distinguished from the manifestation of God in the course of nature, and the ordinary doings of Providence, is in its very idea miraculous. The fact of the presence and more immediate agency of God in connection with Christian doctrine is signified to the senses by works of supernatural power. These works corroborate the evidence furnished by the doctrine itself, as seen in its fruitage. Miracles are aids to faith. They come in with decisive effect to convince those who are impressed by the moral evidence. They were so regarded by Jesus. Miracles and doctrine are mutually supporting species of proof.

(3) Of His resurrection.

Acts 17:31—Because he hath appointed a day, in the which he will judge the

13

world in righteousness by that man whom he hath ordained whereof he hath given assurance unto all men, in that he hath raised him from the dead.

S. A. Psa. 16:10, 11; Rom. 1:4; I Pet. 1:21.

In the resurrection of Christ, we have the outstanding miracle of the New Testament, and its evidential value is most marked. It furnishes positive proof that Jesus Christ was what he claimed to be. He was thus marked off to be the Son of God with power. It also furnishes endorsement for everything that Christ endorsed, substantiating and corroborating all His claims and teachings concerning Himself and the Scriptures. If, therefore, Christ taught that the Scriptures were inspired, and He did, then His resurrection established the truth of that teaching.

4. The Testimony of Transformed Lives—Their Influence Upon Character and Conduct.

The purpose of God in redemption as revealed in the Scriptures is to restore men to God from whom He has become estranged through sin, not only judicially but experimentally, to give man not only a righteous standing but also a righteous state,—"To redeem them from all iniquity and purify unto himself a peculiar people, zealous of good works." Has this been done? The history of the Christian church replies in the affirmative. Saul, the persecutor, became Paul, the apostle. John Bunyon, John Newton, Wesley, and Spurgeon, of the past, and Colonel Clark, Jerry McCauley, and S. H. Hadley of our own generation, men in whose lives the grace of God has embodied and expressed itself, show this to be true. This achievement of the avowed purpose of the Scriptures proves their inspiration.

D. S. That the Scriptures have a divine origin, being authoritatively inspired of God, is shown by the combined witness of archaeology and the Scriptures, including the recorded testimony of Christ and evidenced by the transformation of human lives.

Study Questions on the Doctrine of the Scriptures

1. Define Canonicity and give the derivation of the word "canon."
2. Discuss the three proofs that canonization did not rest with the people. Outline proofs for the Canonicity of the Law; of the Prophets. Give supplementary proof from the N.T.
3. Give the five-fold proof for the genuineness of the New Testament Canon.
4. Give D. S. under Canonicity.
5. Define the credibility of the Scriptures.
6. May a book be genuine as to its authorship and yet not be credible as to its contents? Illustrate.
7. What negative considerations establish the credibility of the Scriptures? Discuss.
8. Discuss fully the five-fold positive proof of the credibility of the Scriptures.
9. Define the inspiration of the Scriptures.
10. Distinguish between inspiration and credibility.

11. Discuss the testimony of archaeology to the inspiration of the Scriptures and cite three illustrations of the accuracy of the Biblical record.
12. Discuss the unity of the Bible as an internal proof of its divine origin.
13. Discuss five representations of Scripture which because of their uniqueness could not have been of human origin.
14. Discuss prophecy and its fulfillment as an internal proof of inspiration.
15. Quote one passage in which the Bible declares its own inspiration.
16. Discuss the testimony of Christ to the divine origin of the Scriptures.
17. Discuss the testimony of transformed lives to the inspiration of the Scriptures.
18. Give D. S. under the Inspiration of the Scriptures.

CHAPTER TWO

THE DOCTRINE OF GOD

(THEOLOGY)

A. The Fact of God.

"Whether or not there is a supreme personal intelligence, infinite and eternal, omnipotent, omniscient and omnipresent, the Creator, Upholder and Ruler of the universe, immanent in and yet transcending all things, gracious and merciful, the Father and Redeemer of mankind, is surely the profoundest problem that can agitate the human mind. Lying as it does at the foundation of all man's religious beliefs, it is bound up with, not alone the temporal and eternal happiness of the individual, but also the welfare and progress of the race."—WHITELAW.

The fact of God is assumed by the Scriptures without giving any argument to establish or prove it. Therefore, our chief ground of belief in the reality of God is found within the pages of the Bible. The Bible, therefore, is not intended for the atheist, who denies the existence of God, nor for the confirmed agnostic who denies the possibility of knowing whether there is a God or not. Neither does it have value for the infidel who rejects the revelation of God and hence the God of revelation. The atheist rejects the idea of God because he is not able to discover Him in the material universe. But God as Spirit does not belong in the category of matter, and, therefore, is not discoverable by merely natural or material investigation.

"Before one can positively assert that there is no God, he must presumptuously assume for himself the wisdom and omnipresence of God. He must explore the entire circuit of the universe to be sure that no God is there. He must have interrogated all the generations of mankind and all the hierarchies of heaven to be certain they had never heard of a God."—CHALMERS.

The word "agnosticism" is derived from the Greek negative "A," "not," and the Greek term, "ginosko," "to know," thus meaning "not knowing." It was coined by Professor Huxley to express his own attitude. It was likely suggested by the name given to an early sect (the Gnostics), who pretended to special knowledge.

17

Infidelity unreasonably rejects any possibility of a divine revelation, for it is evident to the unbiased mind that the God of nature is also the God of revelation, because many proofs of the one can be offered for the other. The infidel, however, rejects the Bible as a divine revelation, and, therefore, rejects that which it reveals and thus refuses to believe in the God of the Bible.

I. Established by Reason.

There are a number of arguments which, though they may not be accepted as conclusive proofs of God's existence, still may be regarded as corroborative proofs of His existence.

1. The Argument from Universal Belief.

Rom. 1:19-21, 28—Because that which may be known of God is manifest in them; for God hath shewed it unto them. For the invisible things of him from the creation of the world are clearly seen, being understood by the things that are made, even his eternal power and Godhead; so that they are without excuse; Because that, when they knew God, they glorified Him not as God, neither were thankful; but became vain in their imaginations, and their foolish heart was darkened. And even as they did not like to retain God in their knowledge, God gave them over to a reprobate mind, to do those things which are not convenient.

S. F. Job 32:8; Acts 17:28-29; Rom. 2:15; Rom. 1:32.

This argument from universal belief cannot be overlooked.

"Man everywhere believes in the existence of a Supreme Being or Beings to whom he is morally responsible and to whom propitiation needs to be made. Such belief may be crudely, even grotesquely stated and manifested, but the reality of the fact is no more invalidated by such crudeness than the existence of a father is invalidated by the crude attempts of a child to draw a picture of its father."—EVANS.

2. The Argument from Cause and Effect.

It is accepted principle that every effect must have an adequate cause. All elements therefore which are possessed by any effect must reside at least potentially within the cause. There are certain elements which are characteristic of the material universe which argue for the existence of God as we know Him through the medium of Divine Revelation.

"When Galen, a celebrated physician, but atheistically inclined, had anatomized the human body, and carefully surveyed the frame of it, viewed the fitness and usefulness of every part of it and the several intentions of every little vein, bone and muscle, and the beauty of the whole, a spirit of devotion came upon him and he wrote a hymn to his Creator. A man must be a fool, indeed, who after fully studying his own body can remain an atheist."—ARVINE.

(1) The Element of Intelligence or Purposeful Tendency.

Order and harmony are marks of intelligence. By this is meant that order and harmony are invariably conjoined with intelligence. If this be true, and these are found in nature, then the existence of intelligence in nature is proved beyond all peradventure. As an illustration of this an example in chemistry might be cited. Every molecule of matter of every possible variety is a definite mass of electrons built together with the most exact arithmetical and geometrical relations. There is vastly more order in the construction of a molecule than of a mansion.

(2) The Element of Personality.

Man, possessed of personal being, argues for the existence of God as a personal Being.

"We know that we exist. We cannot rationally doubt that fact, for the knowledge is immediate and carries with it its own certificate of certainty. From this the next step is inescapable. The fact is almost forced upon us that we are not self-caused. We know that we did not produce our own souls. This immediately brings with it the correlative truth that we must have been caused by someone other than ourselves who must have had sufficient power to produce our souls, which are the observed effect. Either we were caused by a personal agency or by an agency that was not personal. There is no other alternative. Here we appeal to the axiomatic truth of the reason, that the cause must be adequate to produce the observed effect."—HAMILTON.

(3) The Element of Power.

The heavens and the earth and man himself are the witnessing results of a power that is both superhuman and supernatural. This is evidenced in their origination and also in their preservation. All nature bears impressive witness to a universal and wonderful creation and maintenance.

(4) (The Argument from) The Mental, Moral and Emotional Nature of Man.

Man is possessed of mentality and morality. Therefore these qualities must be included in the cause which produced him.

"Man has an intellectual and moral nature, hence his Creator must be an intellectual and moral Being, a Judge, and Lawgiver. Man has an emotional nature; only a Being of goodness, power, love, wisdom and holiness could satisfy such a nature, and these things denote the existence of a personal God. Conscience in man says: 'Thou shalt,' and 'Thou shalt not,' 'I ought,' and 'I ought not.' These mandates are not self-imposed. They imply the existence of a Moral Governor to Whom we are responsible. Conscience, there it is in the breast of man, an ideal Moses thundering from an invisible Sinai Law of a holy Judge. Said Cardinal Newman 'Were it not for the voice speaking so clearly in my conscience and my heart, I should be an atheist, or a pantheist, when I looked into the world.' Some things are wrong, others right: love is right, hatred is wrong. Nor is a thing right because it pleases, or wrong because it displeases. Where did we get this standard of right and wrong? Morality is obligatory, not optional. Who made it obligatory? We must believe that there is a God, or believe that the very root of our nature is a lie."—EVANS.

3. The Argument from Evident Harmony of Belief in God with Existing Facts.

When we come to consider the earth in itself, that is, apart from the other members of the solar system, we find no escape from the conviction that a creative hand fashioned it. How else could the things, which only the wilfully blind can fail to observe, be accounted for?

Some one has well said that if there were no God we would find it necessary to create one.

From all that we can learn through astronomical investigation that which is obviously true of the earth, in the way of purposeful tendency, is also true of other planets and systems which have come under telescopic observation. Belief in a self-existent, personal God is in harmony with the facts of the phenomena of the natural world.

"If God exists, a universal belief in his existence is natural enough; the irresistible impulse to ask for a first cause is accounted for; our religious nature has an object; the uniformity of natural law finds an adequate explanation, and human history is vindicated from the charge of being a vast imposture."— PENDLETON.

II. Established by Revelation.

The argument from divine revelation is drawn from the content of the Scriptures themselves.

"From the commencement of modern science apparent inconsistencies between nature and revelation have been constantly emerging, which, for the time, have occasioned great offense to zealous believers, but in every instance, without exception, the error has been found to exist either in the too hasty generalizations of science from imperfect knowledge of the facts, or from a prejudiced interpretation of the Scriptures, and invariably matured science has been found not only to harmonize perfectly with the letter of the Word properly interpreted, but, moreover, gloriously to illustrate the grand moral principles and doctrines therein revealed."—HODGE.

"A great deal of our knowledge rests upon the testimony of others. Now the Bible is competent testimony. If the testimony of travelers is enough to satisfy us as to the habits, customs and manners of the peoples of the countries they visit, and which we have never seen, why is not the Bible, if it is authentic history, enough to satisfy us with its evidence as to the existence of God?"— EVANS.

B. The Nature of God (Revealed by His Attributes)

Since time began, man has sought to picture or portray God by imagery, painting, and word description, but has always fallen far short. For how can finiteness ever hope to comprehend and express infinity? God's own chosen people tried to present measurements and descriptions of Him to their fellowmen and so made idols of metal and said, "These be thy gods, O Israel, which brought thee up out of the land of Egypt" (Ex. 32:4). But they failed utterly to get the faintest conception of God into their molten images, as is seen by the depth of depravity into which their substitution of idols in place of the true Jehovah worship sank them. Nor have modern attempts through science and philosophy been more successful, for our God is not to be measured nor pictured nor "found out unto perfection."

The nature of God is best revealed by His attributes. We must be careful not to think of them as abstract but as vital mediums through which His nature is revealed.

"The term 'attribute,' in its application to persons or things, means something belonging to persons or things. It may be defined as an essential, permanent, and distinguishing quality or characteristic which may be affirmed of a subject, as the color or fragrance of a rose. The attributes of a thing are so essential to it that without them it could not be what it is; and this is equally true of the attributes of a person. If a man were divested of the attributes belonging to

20

him, he would cease to be a man, for these attributes are inherent in that which constitutes him a human being. If we transfer these ideas to God, we shall find that His attributes belong inalienably to Him, and therefore what He is now He must ever be."—PENDLETON.

The attributes of God, then, are those essential, permanent and distinguishing characteristics which may be affirmed of His Being. His attributes are His perfections, inseparable from His nature and conditioning His character.

There have been many attempts made by theologians to arrange the attributes of God in classes. They have been styled natural and moral attributes, communicable and incommunicable, positive and negative, absolute and relative. To all these divisions and epithets of designation objections can, no doubt, be made. Possibly the classification of natural and moral attributes in God is as good as any. These have been defined thus:

"The natural attributes of God are all those which pertain to His existence as an infinite, rational Spirit; . . . . . the moral are those additional attributes which belong to Him as an infinite, righteous Spirit."—PENDLETON.

I. Natural Attributes.

1. The Life of God.

(1) The Meaning of "life."

Life may be regarded as that form of existence, spoken of as the animate as distinguished from the inanimate, embracing a force and a condition, the force of which is the determining factor of all relations caused and sustained, both internal and external, the condition of which is that constituted by these relations, so caused and sustained.

This difference in the use or application of the word "life" is too often overlooked, and much confusion of thought is the result. It cannot be too well understood that this word "life" has two important uses. As to the first, Professor Drummond remarks: "To say that life is a correspondence is only to express the partial truth. There is something behind it. Life manifests itself in correspondences, but what determines them? The organism exhibits a variety of correspondences. What organizes them? As in the natural so in the spiritual, there is a Principle of Life! We cannot get rid of that term, however clumsy, however provisional, however much a mere cloak for ignorance it may seem. Science, as yet, is unable to dispense with the idea of the principle of life." Professor Drummond further says, concerning this Principle of Life, "It is a potter which works in the protoplasm . . . a potter which works in the protoplasm of all animate things or beings in this world: plant, tree, bird, beast and man, each having its own potter or form of life, working upon precisely the same plasmic matter, composed of carbon, hydrogen, oxygen and nitrogen, and each following its own plan, builds up a plant, a reptile, an eagle, an elephant or a man. This life is the immediate cause of all organisms. The plant life makes the plant, the bird life the bird, the man life the man"; and, carrying out his line of thought, natural law in the spiritual world, he contends with great clearness and force that the Christ life makes the Christian.

Our second use of the word "life" has reference to a condition of existence, so called. This is the most common use. Indeed, it is believed that too many know no other use of the term. This is the service Paul makes it render in I Cor. 15:19: "If in this life (condition of existence) only we have hope in Christ, we are of all men most miserable."

21

Webster says that life is that state of being alive; that condition in which animals and plants exist, as distinguished from inorganic substance and dead organisms. The three principal distinctions are: (1) the power of growth, (2) reproduction, (3) automatic or internally initiated adaptations to changes in the environment.

Mr. Munger thus defines life: "Life, as we see it, is a functional play of something—we know not what—set in a favorable relation to an environment and ending when the relations become unfavorable."

Standard Encyclopedia says: "Life may be defined as the internal and external activity of an organism in relation to its environment."

Herbert Spencer, the scientist, gave this definition of life: "Life is the definite combination of heterogeneous changes, both simultaneous and successive in correspondence with external co-existences and sequence"; or more briefly, "The continuous adjustments of internal relations to external relations."

This definition is doubtless true as far as it goes, but this, like many others, deals only with life as a condition of existence, while the subtle actor, which no man hath yet seen, or can see, remains unknown, save by his works, and is still undefined.

"Life is a term which cannot be fully defined. Science defines it as correspondence between organ and environment. But it must mean far more as applied to God, since God has no environment. The life of God is His activity of thought, feeling and will. It is the total inward movement of His Being which enables Him to form wise, holy and loving purposes and to execute them."— MULLINS.

The two factors of life in general, force and condition, when used of God, are to be regarded as possessed by Him in an infinite degree.

(2) The Scriptural Fact of Life as a Divine Attribute.

John 5:26—For as the Father hath life in himself; so hath he given to the Son to have life in himself.

S. F. Jer. 10:10; Acts 14:15; II Chron. 16:9; Psa. 94:9–10.

D. S. God has life; He hears, sees, feels, acts, and therefore is a Living Being.

(3) The Life of God Illustrated and Demonstrated in the Scriptures.

I Thes. 1:9 M. T.—People tell us of their own accord about the visit we paid to you, and how you turned to God from idols, to serve a living and a real God.

S. F. Jer. 10:10–16; Hab. 2:18–20.

These passages present a number of striking contrasts:

True God	falsehood
Living	no breath in them
Made the earth by His power	work of errors
Former of all things	graven image, molten image
Everlasting King	they shall perish
Living and True God	idols

D. S. By the sharp distinctions drawn in the Scriptures between the gods of the heathen and the true God, the fact of life as a divine attribute is clearly shown.

2. The Spirituality of God.

This truth opposes the false teaching of materialism, that the facts of experience are all to be explained by referring them to the realities, activities and laws of physical or material substance. Materialism ignores the distinction between mind and matter, and refers all the phenomena of the world (that which is apparent) to the functions of matter.

Professor Tyndall, in his famous Belfast address, made the oft-quoted assertion: "By an intellectual necessity I cross the boundary of experimental evidence and discern in matter the promise and potency of all terrestrial life."

Spirituality is fundamental to the Being of God. It is the mode of God's complete and triune existence. Says Dr. Farr: "God is something more than a condition of being, like space or time. He acts as well as exists. He is an agent, an actor, a living Being and Spirit life."

The truth of the spirituality of God is revealed in our spiritual being. God is not only our Creator but the father of our spirits. We are His offspring (John 4:24; Acts 17:28, 29). All the essential characteristics of our spirits may be ascribed to Him in an infinite degree for "He is a rational being who distinguishes with infinite precision between the true and the false; He is a moral being who distinguishes between the right and the wrong, and He is a free agent whose action is self-determined by His own will."—A. A. Hodge.

The term "spirit" may be regarded in general contrast to "matter." The two substances embrace all the objects to be found in the realm of knowledge. There is no substance of which it can be said that it is neither matter nor spirit. The world of matter is all around us. We see it in the earth and its productions, in the sea and its treasure, in the sun and the planets revolving around it. Our senses bring us into contact with the universe of material nature, and we hear, see, smell, touch and taste. It is manifest, too, that matter is capable of great changes. It may be fashioned into many forms, and taken through many processes of refinement. Gold may be purified seven times—that is, purified to perfection—till every particle of dross is taken from it; and the diamond may, by laborious and persevering effort, be fitted to sparkle in a monarch's crown; but no operation performed on matter, can endow it with thought, will or reflection. These are peculiarities of mind and spirit.

(1) The meaning of it.

God as Spirit is incorporeal, invisible, without material substance, without physical parts or passions, and therefore free from all temporal limitations.

From the foregoing, it is seen that God as Spirit is to be apprehended not by the senses of the body, but by the faculties of the soul, quickened and illumined by the Holy Spirit (I Cor. 2:14; Col. 1:15–17).

(2) The Scriptural fact established.

John 4:24—God is a Spirit; and they that worship him must worship him in spirit and in truth.

"God is a Spirit." The indefinite article is not found in the Greek text but has been supplied by the translators. There is no indefinite article in the Greek language. "God is Spirit." This seems consistent with the succeeding clause, "they that worship him must worship him in spirit and in truth." No article is supplied.

D. S. God is spiritual in nature, i.e., in His essential Being God is Spirit.

(3) The Scriptural fact illuminated.

a. By Old Testament teaching.

Deut. 4:15–20, 23—Take ye therefore good heed unto yourselves, for ye saw no manner of similitude on the day that the Lord spake unto you in Horeb out of the midst of the fire. Lest ye corrupt yourselves, and make you a graven image, the similitude of any figure, the likeness of male or female, the likeness of any beast that is on the earth, the likeness of any winged fowl that flieth in the air, the likeness of anything that creepeth on the ground, the likeness of any fish that is in the waters beneath the earth; And lest thou lift up thine eyes unto heaven, and when thou seest the sun, and the moon, and the stars, even all the host of heaven, shouldest be driven to worship them, and serve them, which the Lord thy God hath divided -unto all nations under the whole heaven. But the Lord hath taken you, and brought you forth out of the iron furnace, even out of Egypt, to be unto him a people of inheritance, as ye are this day. Take heed unto yourselves, lest ye forget the covenant of the Lord your God, which he made with you, and make you a graven image, or the likeness of anything, which the Lord thy God hath forbidden thee.

S. F. Isa. 40:25.

The worship of God through the medium of images and things temporal was forbidden because no one had ever seen God, and therefore could not know how He looked; neither was there any resemblance between the material things of earth and God who is Spirit (Ex. 20:4).

D. S. From the teaching of the Old Testament, it is made clear that God in His essential being is spirit, and as spirit is immaterial and hence cannot be seen by the material eye nor represented by material things.

b. By New Testament teaching.

Lk. 24:39—Behold my hands and my feet, that it is I myself; handle me, and see; for a spirit hath not flesh and bones, as ye see me have.

S. F. I Tim. 1:17; Col. 1:15; Acts 17:22–29; Acts 14:8–18.

Physical eyes see only objects of the material world, but God is not of the nature of the material world; hence, He cannot be seen with the material eye.

D. S. From the teaching of the New Testament it is evident that God is spirit, without flesh and bones, and therefore does not come within the scope of physical vision, neither is He capable of correct material representation, because of His essentially spiritual nature.

(4) The Scriptural fact interrogated.

a. What is meant by the statement that man was made in the image of God?

Answer: There are a number of things that may be included in the image and likeness of God in its relation to man.

(a) Man was made in the personal image and likeness of God. Both are personal beings.

(b) It may refer to a triune image and likeness. God possesses a triunity of persons; Father, Son and Holy Spirit. Man possesses a tri-unity of parts; spirit, soul and body.

I Thes. 5:23—And the very God of peace sanctify you wholly; and I pray God your whole spirit and soul and body be preserved blameless unto the coming of our Lord Jesus Christ.

(c) It certainly refers to the intellectual and moral likeness.

Col. 3:10—And have put on the new man, which is renewed in knowledge after the image of him that created him.

Eph. 4:24—And that ye put on the new man, which after God is created in righteousness and true holiness.

b. What is meant by the physical terms which are applied to God as though He were a man?

See, for example, Ps. 102:25; Nahum. 1:6; I Kings 8:42; Job 34:21; I Pet. 3:12.

Answer: Such anthropomorphic expressions are to be understood only in the sense of being human terms used in order to bring the infinite within the comprehension of the finite, to enable man to know God.

"It is important to remember that human language is the crystallization of human experience. Hence, all the terms it has at command are terms which are in a sense vitiated for its purpose by the radical limitation. For how can any terms which have been created to express human experience, and which have human associations clinging to them, be adequate to set forth the inner life of the Divine, which has no analogy in human experience and therefore no terminology in human language."—A. S. PEAKE.

"Though God would not have man believe Him to be corporeal, yet He judged it expedient to give some prenotices of that divine incarnation which He had promised."—CHARNOCK.

c. How are the passages which state that men saw God to be reconciled with those which declare that God has not been and cannot be seen?

Examples of former:	Examples of latter:
Ex. 24:10; Jud. 13:22.	Ex. 33:20; Col. 1:15.
Ex. 33:18–19, 21–23; Isa. 6:7.	John 1:18

Answer: There is no real contradiction between these passages. The first group refers to the manifestations of God, while the other refers to God in the invisible essence of His being, which is spirit.

To illustrate: "A man may see the reflection of his face in a glass. It would be true for the man to say, 'I saw my face,' and also true to say 'I never saw my face.' So men have seen a manifestation of God, and it is perfectly true to say that those men saw God. No man ever saw God as He is in His invisible essence and so it is perfectly true to say, 'No man has seen God at any time.' "—TORREY.

(a) That which is spirit is capable of manifesting itself in visible form.

John 1:32—And John bare record, saying, I saw the Spirit descending from heaven like a dove, and it abode upon him.

S. F. Judges 6:34; Acts 2:1–4.

(b) The Scriptural record shows that God has manifested Himself in visible form. "The Angel of the Lord" in the Old Testament is a manifestation of Deity. Clear distinction is drawn in the Bible between "an Angel of the Lord" and "the Angel of the Lord." This distinction is preserved only in the Revised Version.

25

Note some examples in which "The Angel of the Lord" is shown to be a manifestation of Deity.

aa. In the experience of Hagar and Ishmael.

Gen. 16:7–10, 13. "The Angel of the Lord" in verse 10 is clearly identified with the "Lord" (Jehovah) in verse 13.

S. F. Gen. 21:17–18.

bb. In the experience of Abraham and Isaac.

Gen. 22:11–12. Here "The Angel of the Lord" in verse 11 is identified with God in verse 12.

cc. In the experience of Abraham in the plains of Mamre.

Gen. 18:1–24. In these verses, one of the three clearly identifies himself with the Lord Jehovah. In Gen. 19:1 only two came to Sodom, one had remained behind with Abraham; who this one was, appears in verses 17, 18, 22 and 23 of chapter 18.

S. A. Gen. 19:27; John 8:56.

dd. In the experience of Joshua and Israel at Bochim.

Judges 2:1–2. Here the "Angel of the Lord" says distinctly "I did" what Jehovah did.

d. Which one of the persons of the Trinity was manifested in "The Angel of the Lord"?

Answer: "The Angel of the Lord" is clearly a manifestation of Deity in the Old Testament, and is identified with the Second Person of the Trinity, the Lord Jesus Christ. "The Angel of the Lord" was God the Son before His permanent incarnation (Judges 13:18 R. V. compared with Isa. 9:6). In Judges 13:18 the Hebrew word for "secret" is practically the same as in Isaiah where it is given as "Wonderful," the name of the Coming Christ.

S. A. Mal. 3:1 and John 8:56.

"The Angel of the Lord" does not appear after the birth of Christ. The expression occurs in the A. V., but it is always a mistranslation as the R. V. shows.

Luke 2:9, R. V.—And an angel of the Lord stood by them and the glory of the Lord shone round about them: and they were sore afraid.

S. F. Matt. 1:20, R. V.; Matt. 28:2, R. V.; Acts 8:26, R. V.; Acts 12:7, R. V.; Acts 12:23, R. V.

3. The Personality of God.

This is the truth that opposes the error of Pantheism, which teaches that God is everything and everything is God; that the universe is God, and God is the universe; that he has no separate and distinct existence. The idea is that the aggregate of individual things is God. It may as well be said that the contents of a man's consciousness, at any one time, were the man himself; or that the waves of the ocean were the ocean itself. Pantheism denies the distinction between matter and mind, between the Infinite and the finite. There is according to this theory but one substance, but one real Being; hence the doctrine is called Monism, or "The All One Doctrine." It makes the world of matter therefore, not only con-substantial, but co-eternal with God. This of course precludes the idea of creation; except as an eternal and necessary process. It denies that the Infinite and Absolute Being in Himself has intelligence, consciousness or will. The Infinite comes into existence in the finite. The whole life, consciousness, intelligence, and knowledge of God is the life, consciousness, intelligence, and knowledge of matter. Pantheism, therefore, denies the personality of God, for personality, as well as consciousness, implies a distinction between the self and the not-self; and such distinction, according to Pantheism, is a limitation inconsistent with the nature of the infinite God, who, therefore, is not a person who can say "I," and who can be addressed as "Thou."

Any conception of the Divine personality which does not take into account our own, is for us impossible. It does not follow that our own must be the measure of the Divine. "The great objection," as Dr. Peake states, "urged against the doctrine of a personal God, is that personality implies limitation." To this Lotze seems to have given the true answer: "We argue that personality implies limitation, because we argue from personality as we possess it. But really the limitation, of which we are conscious, is not due to the fact that we possess personality, but that we possess it so imperfectly It is only the Absolute who possesses perfect personality." Still, there may be a likeness between the former, with its finite powers, and the latter, with its infinite perfections, which is helpful to a better understanding of the Divine. There is a real truth in the record of our creation in the image and likeness of God, and personality is the deepest truth of that image and likeness. Those proofs which establish the existence of God may also be adduced to establish His personality. Thus universal belief which argues for God's existence is belief in a personal God. The argument from cause and effect does the same. Man, as a personal effect, demands a personal God as an adequate cause of himself. And so is it with the argument from intelligence in nature. So far as we know rational intelligence has no existence apart from personality; hence that which argues for an intelligent cause of the universe demands that the cause be personal.

(1) The meaning of it.

Personality may be defined as existence possessed of self-consciousness and the power of self-determination.

Personality is not to be confused with corporeity or existence in a material body, but rather, when properly defined, personality embraces the collective properties and qualities which characterize personal existence as distinguished from impersonal existence and animal life; for we regard animals as possessing natures rather than personalities. Personality, therefore, represents the sum total of traits necessary to describe what it is to be a person.

In respect to these personal traits there must not only be consciousness—for the beast has that—but self-consciousness, and there must not only be determination—for the beast has that also—but self-determination, the power by which man from an act of his own free will determines his acts.

The constituent elements of personality are three: intellect, or the power of thinking; sensibility, or the power of feeling; and volition, or the power of willing. Associated with these are conscience and the freedom of choice. If it can be proved that to God are ascribed operations of intellect, sensibility and will, then we may affirm His personality.

(2) The Scriptural Fact of God's Personality Established:

　　a. **By names which are given to God which reveal personality.**

One of the important names by which God has made Himself known is

27

"Jehovah." It is this name and its many combinations through which He has revealed Himself in the various relations which He sustains to men. Jehovah was revealed to Israel at the time when they were called to trust God in a new and covenant relationship.

All that the name of Jesus means to us, "Jehovah" meant to ancient Israel. It meant to them everything in the way of salvation and blessing. Elohim is God as Creator of all things, but Jehovah is the same God in covenant relation with those whom He has created. Jehovah means the eternal, the immutable One, He, Who was, and is, and is to come. He is the God of Israel and the God of those who are redeemed, and thus now "in Christ" we can say "Jehovah is our God."

The name "Jehovah" is combined with other words, which form what are known as the "Jehovah titles."

(a) "I AM."

Ex. 3:14—And God said unto Moses, I AM THAT I AM: and he said, Thus shalt thou say unto the children of Israel, I AM hath sent me unto you. S. F. John 8:58.

This name reveals self-consciousness.

"I AM THAT I AM" is the thought behind the name "Jehovah." Three things are involved: the self-sufficiency of God, His absolute sovereignty and His unchangeableness.

The whole history of the children of Israel gathers round the covenant that God made with them at Sinai. That covenant consisted of two terms: first, "I will be your God," and then, "Ye shall be my people." Their subsequent history is simply a record of how they came to know who Jehovah was and what He was willing to be to them and what they ought to be as His people. Every need of Israel was met in Jehovah their God.

(b) "Jehovah-Jireh" (The Lord will provide).

Gen. 22:13–14—And Abraham lifted up his eyes, and looked, and behold behind him a ram caught in the thicket by his horns; and Abraham went and took the ram, and offered him up for a burnt offering in the stead of his son. And Abraham called the name of that place Jehovah-Jireh: as it is said to this day. In the mount of the Lord it shall be seen.

This name reveals personal provision.

This was the name given by Abraham to the place where he had sacrificed a ram provided by God instead of his son, Isaac. The Lord sees and provides for the necessities of His servants.

(c) "Jehovah-Nissi" (The Lord Our Banner).

Ex. 17:15—And Moses built an altar, and called the name of it Jehovah-Nissi. S. A. Josh. 5:13–14; Ps. 20:7.

This name reveals personal leadership.

This name Moses gave to the altar which he reared to signalize the defeat of the Amalekites by Israel under Joshua at Rephidim. God is here shown as the Lord who leads us against the enemy and in whose name we are more than conquerors. The suggestion is that the people should rally round God as an army gathers round its standard.

(d) Jehovah-Rapha (The Lord that healeth).

Ex. 15:26—And said, if thou wilt diligently hearken to the voice of the Lord thy God, and wilt do that which is right in his sight, and wilt give ear to his commandments, and keep all his statutes, I will put none of these diseases upon thee, which I have brought upon the Egyptians; for I am the Lord that healeth thee.

This name reveals personal preservation.

The word means to mend as a garment is mended, to repair as a building is reconstructed, and to cure as a diseased person is restored to health. All healing both direct and indirect is from God. He is our saving health.

(e) "Jehovah-Shalom" (The Lord Our Peace).

Jud. 6:24—Then Gideon built an altar there unto the Lord, and called it Jehovah-Shalom; unto this day it is yet in Ophrah of the Abiezrites. Eph. 2:14–15.

This name reveals God as personal peace-giver.

This was the name given by Gideon to the altar he built at Ophrah alluding to the word spoken to him by the Lord, "Peace be unto thee."

This title might be rendered, "The Lord who is the peace of His people." Combining faith in the divine provision with reliance on "Jehovah" for victory in every circumstance, we find the secret of peace.

(f) "Jehovah-Raah" (The Lord, my Shepherd).

Ps. 23:1—The Lord is my Shepherd; I shall not want.
S. F. Ps. 95:7.

This name reveals personal guidance, guarding and goodness.

All that the shepherds were to their flocks and more, God is willing to be to His own.

(g) "Jehovah-Tsidkenu" (The Lord Our Righteousness).

Jer. 23:6—In his days Judah shall be saved, and Israel shall dwell safely; and this is his name whereby he shall be called, THE LORD OUR RIGHTEOUSNESS.

S. A. I Cor. 1:30.

This name reveals God as imputed personal righteousness in meeting our personal obligations and requirements to Himself.

Israel had no righteousness of her own; she was a wayward and rebellious people; so God revealed himself to her not only as Jehovah, but as Jehovah-Tsidkenu—"The Lord our Righteousness." This relationship had to be entered into before Jehovah could be experienced in the various capacities.

(h) "Jehovah-Sabaoth" (Jehovah of Hosts).

I Sam. 1:3—And this man went up out of this city yearly to worship and to sacrifice unto the Lord of hosts in Shiloh. And the two sons of Eli, Hophni and Phinehas, the priests of the Lord, were there.

This name reveals personal headship and control.

In Hebrew usage, "host" might mean an army of men, or the stars and the angels, which apart or in conjunction, made up the host of heaven. So Israel is called the host of Jehovah. The general meaning of the term is well expressed in the term "Lord Omnipotent." With the acceptance of the idea of divine omnipotence, the heavenly forces were regarded as united into a confederacy under the dominion of the one God, the Lord of Hosts.

(i) "Jehovah-Shammah" (The Lord is present).

Ezek. 48:35—It was round about eighteen thousand measures; and the name of the city from that day shall be, The Lord is there.

This name reveals personal presence.

This is the name to be given to the new Jerusalem restored and glorified, as seen in the vision of Ezekiel. Jehovah returns to the temple which He had forsaken, and from that time forward the fact of supreme importance is that, "He is there," dwelling in the midst of His people.

(j) "Jehovah-Elyon" (The Lord Most High).

Ps. 97:9—For thou, Lord, art high above all the earth; thou art exalted far above all gods.

S. F. Ps. 7:17; Ps. 47:2; Isa. 6:1.

This name reveals personal pre-eminence.

God is spoken of as the God of gods, is presented as sitting on a throne, high and lifted up. Such expressions, together with this name, are simply the assertions of the supremacy and absolute sovereignty of God. He is the Transcendent One.

(k) "Jehovah-Mkaddishkim" (The Lord that sanctifieth thee).

Ex. 31:13—Speak thou also unto the children of Israel, saying, Verily my sabbaths ye shall keep; for it is a sign between me and you throughout your generations; that ye may know that I am the Lord that doth sanctify you.

This name reveals personal purification.

This name suggests God in the subjective aspect of His saving or redeeming work. He is the God who separates from sin and to Himself those whom He saves.

D. S. The names which are used of God in the Scriptures imply personal relations and actions and these signify personality.

b. By the personal pronouns used of God.

(a) Thee and Thou.

John 17:3—And this is life eternal, that they might know thee the only true God, and Jesus Christ, whom thou hast sent.

(b) He and Him.

Ps. 116:1–2—I love the Lord, because he hath heard my voice and my supplications. Because he hath inclined his ear unto me, therefore will I call upon him as long as I live.

If God were a mere force or principle then the pronouns representing Him would of necessity be neuter, but such is not the case as is seen by these and other passages. The personal pronouns which are used of God represent Him as a person, always being masculine gender.

D. S. The personal pronouns which are used of God imply and prove His personality.

c. By the characteristics and properties of personality ascribed to God.

(a) Grief.

Gen. 6:6—And it repented the Lord that he had made man on the earth, and it grieved him at his heart.

Grief is a personal emotion which is here ascribed to God due to the personal attitude and actions of men. Grief argues for personality.

(b) Anger.

I Kings 11:9—And the Lord was angry with Solomon, because his heart was turned from the Lord God of Israel, which had appeared unto him twice.

The anger here is the personal, though holy, resentment of God which he felt towards Solomon because of his perfidy and faithlessness after he had been so highly favored and honored. Only a person could be capable of such resentment.

(c) Jealousy.

Deut. 6:15—(For the Lord thy God is a jealous God among you) lest the anger of the Lord thy God be kindled against thee, and destroy thee from off the face of the earth.

The jealousy of God, not like that of man, is holy. It is simply His regard for His holy name, will, and government. It is, however, a personal element and reveals personality in its possessor.

(d) Love.

Rev. 3:19—As many as I love, I rebuke and chasten: be zealous therefore, and repent.

Love involves three essential elements of personality, namely, intellect, sensibility and will.

God therefore must be personal for love is personal.

(e) Hatred.

Prov. 6:16—These six things doth the Lord hate: yea, seven are an abomination unto him.

That which is impersonal is incapable of hating anyone or anything. Only personality is capable of hatred.

D. S. God possesses the characteristics and properties of personality and, therefore, of necessity must be a person.

d. By the relations which God sustains to the universe and to men.

The God of the Bible is not only to be distinguished from the God of the Pantheist, who has no existence separate from His creation, but also from the God of the Deist, who has created the world and put into it all the necessary powers of self-action and development and set it going and left it to go of itself. Says Wallace, the co-labourer of Darwin: "I believe that the universe is so constituted as to be self-regulating. Why should we suppose the machine too complicated, which was so designed by the Creator as to work out harmonious results? The theory of continual interference is a limitation of the Creator's power."

If the fact is conceded that God was interested enough in the world to create it, we can in no way account for his immediate loss of interest in it. Any theory which fairly and honestly admits God as Creator cannot deny His continuous agency. God is personally and actively present in the affairs of the universe.

(a) As Creator of all things.

Gen. 1:1—In the beginning God created the heaven and the earth.

S. F. Gen. 1:26; John 1:1-3; Rev. 4:11.

In thinking of God as Creator we must attribute to Him infinite and eternal power. This power must have existed before it was exerted and manifested in creation. As everything before creation is eternal, it follows that the creative power was eternal. Nor is this power impersonal. The simplest idea of power is that of ability to do something, and this is always connected with the thought of the personal. Hence, there is not power apart from those who possess and use it. Genesis ascribes all the works of creation to the living God. There is no room for evolution without a flat denial of Divine revelation. There is growth and development within but no passing or evolving from one sphere to another, for all God's works are perfect. He is presented as distinct from nature as its creator, and comments upon it and commends it as good.

Some writers see a gross discrepancy between the account of creation as found in Genesis and the indications suggested by the geological strata of the earth. According to these indications the material universe is of great age, just how great no one seems to know of a certainty. There is a diversity of opinion as shown by the following:

Prof. Ramsay makes it fully 10,000 million years. Eugene Dubois makes it about 1,000 million years. Goodchild makes it about 700 million years. Darwin makes it more than 300 millions years. Sir Oliver Lodge makes it more than 100 million years. Prof. Sollas makes it about 55 million years. Dr. Croll makes it at almost 20 million years. Prof. Tait makes it at almost 10 million years.

It is true in this, as in other instances, that there is no conflict between the Bible when correctly interpreted and the established facts of science. The six days, commonly known as days of creation, were probably not such at all, but days of reconstruction. We have the record of the original creation in Gen. 1:1, while Gen. 1:2 described a chaotic condition which came about subsequent to the creation of the material universe. How long after, we do not know. It may have been a period as great or greater than the longest of the above estimates. This reads in the A. V., "And the earth was without form and void," but it may with equal authority be translated, "The earth became without form and void." Rotheram renders it, "Now the earth had become waste."

"In Isa. 45:18, we read, 'Thus saith the Lord that created the heavens; God Himself that formed the earth and made it, He created it not in vain'—so our Authorized Version has it; but the original word translated 'in vain' is exactly the same as that translated in Gen. 1:2 'without form,' and is rendered in both places in the R. V. 'waste'; perhaps 'desolation' better conveys the true meaning. In any case, we have here God's own statement that Gen. 1:2 does not describe the original condition of the earth, for when He first created it 'He created it not waste (or desolation).' On the other hand, we read in Job 38:4-7, when God first 'laid the foundations of the earth,' which would appear to correspond with Gen. 1:1, the conditions were such that 'the morning stars sang together and all the sons of God shouted for joy,' indicating that perfect state of blessedness which we should naturally expect to find as coming fresh from the hand of God. Indeed, Dr. Bullinger has pointed out that the Hebrew word for creation 'implies that the creation was a perfect work, in perfect and beautiful order.' As to how and why this earth, once so beautiful, ever became 'waste and void' we cannot speak with certainty. It is, however, a striking fact that there are only two other places in the Bible where the words translated in Gen. 1:2 'without form' and 'void' occur together—viz., Isa. 34:11, translated 'confusion' and 'emptiness,' and Jer. 4:23. In both these cases the expressions are used in connection with destruction caused by God's judgment on account of sin."—SIDNEY COLLETT.

32

Therefore, we may legitimately infer that a cataclysmic judgment fell upon the earth and its inhabitants, leaving it in the waste condition described. As to the identity of these inhabitants we cannot be sure. It has been thought that the demons are the representatives of this race and that their disembodiment is a part of their punishment for some unknown sin.

D. S. The creation of the universe and of man proves the personality of the Creator—God.

(b) As Preserver of all things.

Heb. 1:3—Who being the brightness of his glory, and the express image of his person, and upholding all things by the word of his power, when he had by himself purged our sins, sat down on the right hand of the Majesty on high.

S. F. Col. 1:15–17.

As creation has to do with the origin of things, so preservation has to do with their continuance. God sustains a continuous personal relation to his creation. The Deists deny this by saying that God withdrew after his work of creation and left the universe to a process of self-development and self-action. The most strenuous objection to this is that it denies to God interference according to His divine wisdom, as seen in incarnation, in redemption, in providential intervenings and in answered prayer. The divine power operates through the order of natural law which God has established, yet He carries on a special continuous activity in the upholding of the universe. This activity is that of Christ, the immanent God by Whom all things consist or hold together, who "upholdeth all things by the word of his power."

D. S. The preservation of the universe and all its parts in orderly relations demands and proves the personality of God.

(c) As Benefactor of all life.

Matt. 10:29–30—Are not two sparrows sold for a farthing? and one of them shall not fall on the ground without your Father. But the very hairs of your head are all numbered.

S. F. Ps. 104:27–30; Matt. 6:26; I Kings 19:5–7.

Life in all of its aspects is God's gift to His creatures. That of which He is the Author, He is also the Sustainer. The Bible accredits God with the sustenance of all living creatures. Of men, Paul says, "In him we live and move and have our being." James declares that "Every good gift and every perfect gift is from above, and cometh down from the Father of Lights." David ascribes the provision of creature food to God. "These wait all upon Thee; that thou mayest give them their meat in due season. That thou givest them they gather." Jesus depicted the Father's loving provision for birds and men, saying, "Your heavenly Father feedeth them."

D. S. The personality of God is revealed in the universal and adapted supply of all His creatures' needs.

(d) As the Ruler and Over-Ruler in the affairs of men.

Rom. 8:28—And we know that all things work together for good to them that love God, to them who are the called according to his purpose.

S. F. Ps. 76:10; Gen. 39:21; Dan. 1:9; Gen. 50:20; Ps. 75:5–7.

Victor Hugo, recognizing the over-ruling divine hand, said, "Waterloo was

God." God in the exercise of his infinite wisdom and power, so personally affects and controls the free actions of men as to determine all things in accordance with His eternal purpose and their best welfare.

Wordsworth says, "God foresees evil deeds, but never forces them."

The Scriptures teach that this providential governing of God is universal, including all the actions of all God's creatures; that it is powerful, being the rule of omnipotence; that it is wise, as the outworking of God's infinite wisdom; and that it is holy, as is demanded by His moral excellency.

> *"Careless seems the great avenger;*
> *History's pages but record*
> *One death grapple in the darkness,*
> *Twixt old systems and the Word.*
> *Truth forever on the scaffold;*
> *Wrong forever on the throne;*
> *But that scaffold sways the Future;*
> *And, behind the dim unknown*
> *Standeth God, within the shadow,*
> *Keeping watch above His own."*
> —LOWELL.

D. S. God has a hand in human history; sustains a personal relation to the affairs of men and nations, and therefore is a Person.

(e) As the Father of His children.

Gal. 3:26—For ye are all the children of God by faith in Christ Jesus.

S. F. Heb. 12:5–11; John 1:11–13.

The Fatherhood of God is really a New Testament revelation, for the Old Testament reveals but little of the Sonship of Jesus Christ. It makes only a few references to the Messiah as being the Son of Jehovah, and these could not be thoroughly understood until Christ came and made their meaning clear. Therefore, until Christ was revealed as Son, God could not be known or understood as Father, for Fatherhood, apart from Sonship, is inconceivable and unthinkable. Hence it became the mission of Jesus Christ to make God known as Father. And accordingly, in His prayer in John 17, He says: "And now, O Father, glorify thou me with thine own self with the glory which I had with thee before the world was. I have manifested thy name (i.e. the name of Father) unto the men which thou gavest me out of the world."

The Fatherhood of God, therefore, is the infinite and eternal relationship which God sustains to Jesus Christ, His eternal Son, and is also applied to the redemptive and filial relationship, which God sustains to the repentant, believing sinner, through the merit of the atoning death of Christ. And as it is true that the Fatherhood of God cannot be known except as it is revealed in the Sonship of Jesus Christ, Matt. 11:27, so is it also true that that Fatherhood cannot be possessed or experienced by man, save through the mediation of Jesus Christ. Otherwise, it is absolutely inaccessible. "No man," said Jesus, "cometh unto the Father but by me." A Father God is of necessity a Personal God. To admit the Fatherhood of God, therefore, is inevitably to acknowledge His Personality.

D. S. We are the children of God through faith in Christ Jesus. God's personality is revealed in His Fatherhood.

34

4. The Tri-unity of God.

This word is derived from two Latin words "tres" and "unitas," "three" and "unity," which states the doctrine of three in one, or Trinity.

This is the truth which opposes the following errors:

Sabellianism, or a modal trinity, which holds that there are but three aspects or manifestations of one person.

Swedenborgianism, which holds that "the Father, Son and Holy Spirit are three essentials or elements of one God," which make one, just as the spirit, soul, and body make one man.

Tritheism holds that there are three Gods rather than the three personal distinctions in the one God. The persons in the God-head taken to mean three, as though they were three deified beings is not a trinity at all, but a triad.

The trinity of God is well stated in the Athanasian Creed which reads, "We worship one God in trinity and trinity in unity, neither confounding the persons nor dividing the substance."

"The Trinity is therefore three eternally inter-constituted, inter-related, inter-existent, and therefore inseparable Persons within One Being and of One Substance or Essence."—CHAMPION.

(1) Unity of Being.

This truth opposes the error of Polytheism—the doctrine of many gods. "No other truth of the Scripture, particularly of the Old Testament, receives more prominence than that of the Unity of God," says Dr. Evans. The prevailing conception of God in the patriarchal age was that of almightiness, or, better still, all-sufficiency. "I appeared to your fathers as El Shaddai—God Almighty." This is to give increased potency to the simple idea of might, which seems to carry with it the exclusion of other powers or deities and to lead directly to the conception of the unity of God.

a. The meaning of it.

By the unity of God is meant, not that He is possessed of a single personality, but of oneness of essence and being as the one and only Deity.

It is to be noted that while the unity of God is a real and true unity, yet it is a compound rather than a simple or single unity. Thus while the Scriptures compel belief in the oneness of being in God, they admit the tri-unity of the personality within that being, hence the unity of God becomes the basal truth in the doctrine of the Trinity.

b. The Scriptural fact of the Divine Unity established.

(a) By reason.

In proof of the Divine Unity one might refer to the system of nature as indivisible, bearing the impress of one Almighty agent in all its wide realm, from the revelations of the telescope to the wonders of the microscope, with all intervening displays of oneness of design. Among all the planets, constellations, systems and galaxies of systems which fill the vast spaces surrounding our earth, there is a marvelous co-ordination and co-operation, which show that they are all parts of a complete whole, and it is God who unites them and makes them such. It is the unity of God which saves all of these from being a "multiverse" and causes them to be a universe.

"The application of this term to God is designed to teach that there is one, and but one, God. The doctrine of God's unity is involved in His self-existence and in the eternity of His Being. It is evident that there is need of only one self-existent being in the universe, for self-sufficiency and sovereignty are allied to self-existence. That is to say, a self-existent being must be a self-sufficient being, able to do whatever he chooses to do. One self-existent being forever supersedes the necessity of another; and not only so, but renders the existence of another impossible. There cannot be two self-existent beings for the very good reason that self-existence implies the possession of all perfection. If, then, there could be two such beings, they would each possess all perfections, and would therefore be essentially one and the same. They would fill one and the same sphere—a thing impossible if they were two and not one. The existence of more than one God does not come within the limits of possibility. The attribute of self-existence establishes this position, and the attribute of eternity fortifies it. For if one God has existed from eternity, there has been no place for another. The eternity of God is a conclusive proof of His unity."— PENDLETON.

(b) By revelation.

Deut. 6:4—Hear, O Israel; The Lord our God is one Lord:

S. F. Isa. 43:10, 11; Isa. 44:6; Isa. 45:5; I Tim. 2:5; Mark 10:18; Mark 12:29; Deut. 4:35.

D. S. Reason and revelation both clearly establish the truth of the oneness of God.

(2) Trinity of Personality.

While the Bible teaches the unity of God—that there is one and only one God —it also teaches that in the one Godhead there is a distinction of person which is threefold,—Father, Son and the Holy Spirit. This does not mean that the three Divine Persons are three in the sense in which they are one, or that they are one in the sense in which they are three. "The one indivisible divine essence, as a whole, exists eternally as Father and as Son and as Holy Spirit, so that each person possesses the whole essence, and is constituted a distinct person by certain incommunicable properties—not possessed in common with the others."—A. A. HODGE. Personal distinctions between these three are seen by the use of the personal pronouns I, Thou, He; a consultation among them and a distinct order of operation.

"The word Person in its Trinitarian sense is not wholly free from objection, but it seems to be understood by orthodox writers that there is no better word. The objection is that it cannot be used in its common acceptation as applied to human beings. It needs modification. For example, Person in the ordinary use of the term means a distinct and independent being, so that one person is one being, and a hundred persons are a hundred beings. But in the Godhead there are three persons and one Being. The dissimilarity in the two instances is manifest."—PENDLETON.

"Originally this term 'person' meant a mask; hence, the phrase 'three persons' originally bore the significance, that Father, Son and Spirit were terms expressing three different aspects of the one Being. The sense of the term has shifted, so that now three persons in common language would imply, not the same individual in three aspects, but three distinct individuals; but we cannot apply that to the doctrine of the Trinity, otherwise we fall over at once into tritheism. We may say that the truth lies between the sense of person as aspect and its sense as individual, but how we are to combine the distinction with the unity

36

is a problem wholly beyond the wit of man, because we have no analogy in our experience to qualify us for understanding it. For us, persons are mutually exclusive individuals; the persons in the Godhead are mutually inclusive; there is a mutual indwelling of each in the others."—PEAKE.

a. The meaning of it.

By the trinity of God is meant that He is one in being and substance, possessed of three personal distinctions, revealed to us as Father, Son and Holy Spirit.

b. The Scriptural fact of the Trinity.

The objection sometimes raised that neither the word "Trinity" nor any explicit statement concerning it are found in the Bible, can be equally true of other truths and terms of theology, such as the personality of God, free agency, or substitution; but the realities which they denote are here. Dr. Harris says: "The fact that a truth of God is revealed in its practical relations rather than in formula does not make it any less a truth. It does not become a human invention any more than the law of gravitation is a human invention because it formulates the result of scientific thought. The law of gravitation is not formulated in nature any more than is the doctrine of the Trinity in the Bible."

Pendleton says: "I receive the fact that the Trinity exists, simply because I believe that the Scriptures reveal it. And if the Scriptures do reveal the fact that there are three Persons in the Godhead, that there is a distinction which affords grounds for the respective appellations of Father, Son, and Holy Spirit; which lays the foundation for the application of the personal pronouns, I, Thou, He; which renders it proper to speak of sending and being sent; to speak of Christ as being with God, being in His bosom, and of other things of the like nature in the like way, and yet to hold that divine nature equally belongs to each—then it is, like every fact revealed, to be received simply on the credit of divine revelation."

(a) As taught in the Old Testament.

It is taught in the Old Testament by implication and intimation rather than by direct statement.

The theological conception of the Trinity does not endanger the truth of the Unity of God. The burden of the message of the Old Testament seems to be the Divine Unity. Yet the Trinity is plainly intimated in a six-fold way:

aa. By the Hebrew name for God which is found most frequently in the plural form, "Elohim."

See, for example, Gen. 1:1. It expresses the divine nature in its essential completeness as embodying a plurality of personalities.

"The plural Elohim is not a survival from a polytheistic stage, but expresses the divine nature in the manifoldness of its fulnesses and perfections, rather than in the abstract unity of its being."—MACCLAREN.

bb. By the use of the Hebrew word "one."

The Hebrew word for "one" in the absolute sense as used in such expressions as "the only one" is "yacheed" and is never used in the Hebrew to express the unity of the Godhead. On the contrary, the word "echad" which denotes compound unity is used for that purpose. See for examples I Tim. 2:5; Mark 12:29.

"The plural word was used for the one God, in spite of the intense monotheism of the Jews, because there is a plurality of persons in the one Godhead."—TORREY.

cc. By the plural personal pronouns used for God.

37

Gen. 1:26 compared with Isa. 40:14 and Gen. 1:27.

S. F. Isa. 6:8; Gen. 11:7.

Some would say that the "us" in Gen. 1:26, "Let us make man," refers to God's consultation with the angels with whom He takes counsel before He does anything of importance; but Isa. 40:14, "With whom took he counsel?" shows that such is not the case; and Gen. 1:27 contradicts this idea for it repeats the statement "in the image of God," not in the image of angels, also that God created man in His own image, "in the image of God (not angels) created he him." The proper translation of this verse should not be "let us make," but, "we will make," indicating the language of resolve rather than that of consultation.

dd. By intimations in such passages as:

Ps. 2:6–9—Yet have I set my king upon my holy hill of Zion. I will declare the decree; the Lord hath said unto me; Thou art my Son; this day have I begotten thee. Ask of me, and I shall give thee the heathen for thine inheritance, and the uttermost parts of the earth for thy possession. Thou shalt break them with a rod of iron; thou shalt dash them in pieces like a potter's vessel.

S. F. Zech. 2:10, 11; Acts 13:33.

God and His King Who is His Son are here presented.

In the passage in Zechariah, One Who is called the Lord is sent by the Lord of Hosts to dwell in the midst of Israel.

ee. By allusions to the Holy Spirit and His work.

Gen. 1:2—And the earth was without form and void; and darkness was upon the face of the deep. And the Spirit of God moved upon the face of the waters.

ff. By the theophanies or appearings of Deity, especially that of "the angel of the Lord," Who is distinguished from, and at the same time identified with God.

Gen. 22:11–12—And the angel of the Lord called unto him out of heaven, and said, Abraham, Abraham; and he said, Here am I. And he said, Lay not thine hand upon the lad, neither do thou any thing unto him; for now I know that thou fearest God, seeing thou hast not withheld thy son, thine only son from me.

S. F. Gen. 21:17–18; Gen. 16:7–10, 13.

gg. By direct statement. Isa. 48:16; 61:1, 2.

D. S. By the Hebrew name for God, the Hebrew word for one, by the use of the plural personal pronouns, by the theophanies, by allusions to the Holy Spirit and suggestions of Father and Son Who are regarded as Divine persons, the doctrine of the trinity is intimated and implied in the Old Testament.

(b) As taught in the New Testament.

It is clearly taught here not by implication nor intimation but by explicit declaration, or demonstration as follows:

aa. In the Apostolic Commission.

Matt. 28:19–20—Go ye therefore, and teach all nations, baptizing them in the name of the Father and of the Son and of the Holy Ghost. Teaching them to observe all things whatsoever I have commanded you; and, lo I am with you alway, even unto the end of the world.

In these parting instructions which Jesus gave to his disciples we find Him bearing definite testimony to the truth of the Trinity. He gives us here the Baptismal formula, thus making provision for keeping the doctrine of the Trinity constantly before the church. Every Christian is baptized in the name of the Father and of the Son and of the Holy Ghost. Thus he is shown to be in covenant relation, with each of the Persons of the Godhead as named. The language implies that each name represents a person and that the persons are equal.

bb. In the Apostolic Benediction.

II Cor. 13:14—The grace of the Lord Jesus Christ, and the love of God, and the communion of the Holy Ghost, be with you all.

The personality and divinity of each of the persons of the Godhead are recognized every time this benediction is pronounced. The grace of the Lord Jesus Christ and the communion of the Holy Spirit are invoked in immediate connection with the love of the Father showing that the three persons are the same in substance, i.e., Deity, and equal in power and glory.

cc. At the baptism of Jesus.

Matt. 3:16-17—And Jesus, when He was baptized, went up straightway out of the water; and, lo, the heavens were opened unto him, and he saw the Spirit of God descending like a dove, and lighting upon him; And lo a voice from heaven, saying, This is My beloved Son, in whom I am well pleased.

The Father spoke from Heaven, the Son was being baptized in the Jordan, and the Spirit descended in the form of a dove.

dd. In the teaching of Jesus.

John 14:16—And I will pray the Father, and he shall give you another Comforter, that he may abide with you forever.

S. A. John 16:7-10.

The Trinity is taught by Jesus, who, having been sent by His Father, now promises to send the Spirit, as a Paraclete, to take His place; to comfort, instruct and strengthen those whom He was leaving.

ee. In the Pauline teaching with regard to the gifts of the Spirit in relation to the church.

I Cor. 12:4-6—Now there are diversities of gifts, but the same Spirit. And there are differences of administration, but the same Lord. And there are diversities of operations, but it is the same God which worketh all in all.

S. A. Acts 20:28.

The doctrine of the trinity has been held down through the centuries of the Christian era as evidenced in its creeds and hymns: e.g., Apostles' Creed, Gloria Patria, and the Doxology.

D. S. By the threefold divine manifestation at the baptism of Jesus, the threefold reference in the apostolic benediction, the mention of three divine persons, the teaching of Christ and of Paul, the doctrine of the trinity is plainly and positively taught in the New Testament.

Summary of New Testament Teaching.

39

1. A Father Who Is God.

Rom. 1:7—To all that be in Rome, beloved of God, called to be saints; Grace to you and peace from God our Father, and the Lord Jesus Christ.

2. A Son Who Is God.

Heb. 1:8—But unto the Son he saith, Thy throne, O God, is for ever and ever; a sceptre of righteousness is the sceptre of thy kingdom.

3. A Holy Spirit Who Is God.

Acts 5:3-4—But Peter said, Ananias, why hath Satan filled thine heart to lie to the Holy Ghost, and to keep back part of the price of the land? Whiles it remained, was it not thine own? and after it was sold, was it not in thine own power? why hast thou conceived this thing in thine heart? thou hast not lied unto men, but unto God.

Boardman says: "The Father is all the fulness of the Godhead invisible, the Son, of the Godhead manifested, and the Spirit, of the Godhead acting immediately upon the creature."

c. The Trinity illustrated.

"A skeptic had questioned the possibility of the Trinity. 'Tell me how the candle burns,' asked a believer. 'The tallow, the cotton and the atmospheric air produce the light,' answered the skeptic. 'But they make one light, do they not?' 'Yes,' was the reply of the one convinced."—NEW TESTAMENT ANECDOTES.

The following further illustrations have been suggested:

The fountain, stream and river; the cloud, rain, and rising mist; colour, shape and size; the three dimensions of space; the spirit, soul, and body in man; and the legislative, judicial and executive functions of government.

While these analogies show the possibility of Trinity in unity, yet they are all imperfect analogies of the Divine. The distinctions in all of them are impersonal, while those in the Godhead are personal. In these it is a trinity of parts or aspects or functions while in the Being of God it is a trinity of persons. They are of value when used to illustrate the possibility of tri-unity, but not to prove the doctrine of the divine Trinity.

"Light is composed of three parts, one visible and two invisible; first, illuminative rays which affect our vision; second, chemical rays, which cause growth and give the results of photography; third, the principle called heat, and separate from either. So there are three persons in one God, one visible and two invisible."—BISHOP WARREN.

There are no perfect analogies of the Trinity for it is above finite comprehension and beyond human reason to understand. Many analogies have been advanced, which, though each falls short in some particular, aid us in understanding trinity in unity.

5. The Self-Existence of God.

Some have attempted to define this attribute by saying that God is the cause of Himself. Lactantius says, "God before all things was procreated from Himself. God, of His own power, made Himself. He is of Himself; therefore He is such as He willed Himself to be." Jerome says, "God is the origin of Himself and the cause of His own substance."

This error springs primarily from assuming that the existence of God must be accounted for on the principle that every beginning must have a cause; and that this necessitates finding a cause for God. This is not so, for God never began to be. Such false thinking leads to the old doctrine that God is pure action.

We might say, however, that the ground or reason (rather than the cause) of God's existence is His own immanent perfection, i. e., it is a perfection of God to be uncaused.

(1) The meaning of it.

It means that God is absolutely independent of all else than Himself for the continuity and perpetuity of His Being.

"This, of course, means that the causes of His existence are in Himself. The life is inherent. Unlike the life of creatures, it comes from no external source. If there were no creatures in the universe, their non-existence would not in the least affect the existence of God. It did not affect His existence before He performed the work of creation. He had 'life in Himself' when there was life nowhere else. In the total absence of life outside of Himself all the possibilities of life were in Himself. We are never to forget that in Him creatures 'live and move and have their being,' and are dependent on Him for life, motion and existence; but His self-existence makes Him absolutely independent. The causes of their existence not being in themselves, creatures are of necessity dependent on the Creator, to whose will the reasons of their existence are traceable. The reason of God's existence is in Himself alone, and His self-existence is an inalienable attribute of His nature. When He interposes His oath to confirm His word He swears by Himself, saying, 'As I live,' leaving His oath to rest on the immutable basis of His self-existence. In the boundless range of human and angelic thought there will never be found a deeper mystery than the self-existence of God. It defies finite comprehension. God alone knows how He exists, why He has always existed, and why He will exist forever."—PENDLETON.

(2) The fact of it.

John 5:26—For as the Father hath life in Himself, so hath he given to the Son to have life in Himself.

S. F. Acts 17:24–28; I Tim. 6:15–16, W. T.

"God is. His name is evermore, I AM (Ex. 3:14). It certainly can be no limitation of God that He is absolutely unlimited and independent, that He is uncreated and eternal, endowed from all eternity with all possible perfection as the Absolute Spirit."—HARRIS.

D. S. God is self-sustaining and has been from all eternity. His self-existence is an essential attribute of Himself. It is in His nature to exist.

6. The Eternity of God.

The attribute of self-existence suggests that of eternity, or it may be said that the two attributes are suggestive of each other. For if the causes of God's existence are in Himself, reason will admit that those causes have been in operation from eternity; and if He is an Eternal Being, then He must be self-existent. There is no past, present, or future with God so far as His knowledge is concerned, but an eternal "now."

God had no beginning and will have no end. He knows events as taking place in time, but He is not limited by time in any way. He recognizes some events as past, and others as future in relation to present events. But past, present, and

41

future are equally known to Him. We tell of events one by one as they occur. God sees all events in a connected whole as if they were one.

(1) The meaning of it.

Eternity is infinite duration, i.e., duration without beginning or end. "Punctum stans" expresses it—an ever-abiding present. Eternity is limited in our thinking by time and space. He that "inhabited eternity" is beyond our finite comprehension. In reality God's thoughts, purposes and acts are inseparable and without succession. Wordsworth says, "Our noisy years seem moments in the being of the eternal silence." The word "eternal" is sometimes used in three senses:

    a. **Figurative meaning**, such as "eternal mountains," "eternal hills," "the eternal snows," denoting antiquity or indefinitely long duration.

    b. **Limited meaning**, as denoting an existence having a beginning, but which will have no end, such as that of the angels and the souls of men, and the punishment of the wicked.

    c. **Literal meaning**, as denoting an existence which has neither beginning nor end, like that of God. Time has past, present and future; God has not.

A poet has written:

> *"Eternity transcends all finite bounds of Time,*
> *Knows nothing of Duration, with successive years,*
> *Before Thy vision, panoramic and sublime*
> *Past, present, future, at one glance appears,*
> *Unnumbered cycles pass before Thy view,*
> *The new is as the old, the old is as the new."*

"One of the deaf and dumb inmates of an institute in Paris, being asked to express his idea of the Eternity of the Deity, wrote: 'It is duration, without beginning or end; existence, without bounds or dimension; present, without past or future. His eternity is youth without infancy or old age; life without birth or death; today, without yesterday or tomorrow.' "—ARVINE.

"The God of the Bible is the only Being who is absolutely eternal, His existence having neither beginning nor end. In this sense eternity is an attribute peculiarly His own, and on the throne which is 'forever and ever' He must ever sit in majestic isolation. There is no being like Jehovah."—PENDLETON.

(2) The fact of it.

Gen. 21:32–34—Thus they made a covenant at Beersheba; then Abimelech rose up, and Phichol the chief captain of his host, and they returned into the land of the Philistines. And Abraham planted a grove in Beersheba, and called there on the name of the Lord, the everlasting God. And Abraham sojourned in the Philistines' land many days.

S. F. Ex. 3:14; Deut. 33:27; Ps. 90:2; Ps. 102:24–27; Heb. 1:12; Rev. 1:8; Ps. 93:2.

S. A. Isa. 44:6 and Isa. 57:15.

D. S. The Bible asserts the fact that God is eternal; His existence had no beginning and will have no ending; He always was, always is, and always will be.

7. The Immutability of God.

The self-existence and eternity of God may be considered arguments for His immutability. As an infinite Being, absolutely independent and eternal, God is above the possibility of change.

"Creatures change, everything earthly changes, but God changes not. He is and must be eternally the same, for He is infinitely perfect, and infinite perfection prevents and precludes change. There can be no change which does not imply imperfection.

"It is needless to say that imperfection is implied in a change for the worse, for such a change would indicate imperfection before, and greater imperfection after, its occurrence. It is also true that a change for the better denotes previous imperfection, for such a change is toward perfection. Now, God, whether we consider Him as possessing natural or moral attributes, is absolutely perfect. There can be no addition to the number of His natural attributes, and there can be no increase of their capacity and power. It would be absurd to suppose that God can be more Self-existent, more eternal or more omnipotent than He is. It is equally absurd to suppose that His natural attributes can be alienated from Him, or that He can lose them in any way.

"As to the moral attributes of the Divine Character, they also are unchangeable. They bear the stamp of perfection. If God, however, could change in His moral attributes it would imply imperfection in His moral character. If, for example, He could become a better Being than He is, it would imply that He is not perfect in goodness. If He could be more just, then justice has not reached its climax in Him. If He could be more faithful to His word, His veracity would not be perfect. If He could be more holy, it follows that He is not infinitely holy now. God in His moral as well as in His natural attributes is immutable, and therefore His character is unchangeable."—PENDLETON.

"Swift to its close ebbs out life's little day;
Earth's joys grow dim, its glories pass away,
Change and decay in all around I see;
O, Thou who changest not, abide with me."
—LYTE.

(1) The meaning of it.

By "immutability," as used in relation to God, we mean that God in His nature, attributes and counsels is unchanging; for these, as belonging to an Infinite Being, are absolutely perfect and therefore admit of no possible variation.

Immutability does not imply inactivity or immobility for God is Infinite in power and energy. Nor does it imply lack of feeling, for God is capable of Infinite sympathy and suffering and of great indignation against iniquity. It does not imply that God is incapable of making free choices for to God belongs the inalienable right to choose ends and the means of attaining them. Nor does it prohibit God from progressively unfolding and carrying out His plans and purposes.

"We might sum up the meaning of God's immutability by saying, it is His moral personal self-consistency in all His dealings with His creatures. The tune of a simple song like 'Home, Sweet Home' may be played on an instrument with variations. But through all variations the tune runs in self-consistent unity to the end. God's immutability is like the tune. It is His self-consistency manifesting itself in endless variations of method."—MULLINS.

(2) The fact of it.

Mal. 3:6—For I am the Lord, I change not; therefore ye sons of Jacob are not consumed.

S. F. I Sam. 15:29 and Ps. 102:26–27; Jas. 1:17; Heb. 13:8.

S. A. Num. 23:19 and Heb. 6:17–18.

D. S. The Scriptures clearly teach that God is immutable, that He remains forever the same and unchangeable.

(3) Objections to the doctrine.

a. Objection One:

Jonah 3:10—And God saw their works, that they turned from their evil way; and God repented of the evil, that he had said that he would do unto them; and he did it not.

This passage states that God repented. How is this to be reconciled with His immutability?

Answer:

The word "repent" here means "a change of mind," or "a changed mind." When applied to God, the word is used phenomenally, or apparently, according to Old Testament custom. God seems to change His mind because He changes His method. The phenomena are such as, in the case of a man, would indicate a change of mind. It is part of the difficulty with which Deity must deal in attempting to explain Himself to finite minds.

"God remained the same in character, infinitely hating sin, and in His purpose to visit sin with judgment; but as Nineveh changed in its attitude toward sin, God necessarily changed in His attitude towards Nineveh. His character remains the same, but His dealings with men change as they change from a position that is hateful to His unchangeable hatred of sin to one that is pleasing to His unchangeable love of righteousness."—TORREY.

"A boat rows against the stream; the current resists it. So is a nation violating a law of God; it is subject to a judgment. The boat turns and goes with the stream; the current assists it. So is a nation which has repented and put itself into harmony with God's law; it is subject to a blessing. But the current is the same; it has not changed, only the boat has changed its relationship to the current. Neither does God change—we change; and the same law which executed itself in punishment now expresses itself in blessing."—BROCHE.

b. Objection Two:

Gen. 6:6—And it repented the Lord that he had made man on the earth, and it grieved him at his heart.

This passage says not only that God repented, but that He was grieved at heart. How is this to be explained in the light of His immutability?

(a) Answer One.

"Man's wickedness was so great and so abhorrent that His very creation was an object of great grief to God. This does not necessarily imply that God wished, all things considered, that He had not created man, but only, just as it said, that He grieved that He had. Many things that we do are a grief to us, and yet everything considered, we do not wish that we had not done them."—TORREY.

(b) Answer Two.

By God's repenting that He had made man is meant, as the context clearly shows, that He turned from His creative dealings with man to dealings in judgment and destruction.

8. The Omniscience of God.

"Like every other attribute we have considered, the omniscience of God defies our comprehension. We know very little, and while in this world will probably not turn over the first page of the book of knowledge. How impossible, then, to take in the idea of universal knowledge. The little knowledge we acquire is usually gained by laborious study. We learn one thing, and infer from it another, and thus we proceed, drawing conclusions which we lay down as premises from which to draw other conclusions. How, then, can we comprehend the Infinite Mind, which knows all things by intuition? God's knowledge is not successive, but perfectly simultaneous. "The theory which some hold concerning the omniscience of God is an absurdity, namely, that as God's omnipotence is His ability to do all things He pleases to do, but He does not please to do all things, so His omniscience is His ability to know all things, but He does not choose to know all things. To refute this theory it is only necessary to say that, even in accordance with it, God must first know all things before He could decide which to know and which not to know."—Pendleton.

(1) The meaning of it.

The word "omniscience" comes from two Latin words, "omnis," signifying all, and "sciens," signifying knowledge. God is a Spirit and as such has knowledge. He is a perfect Spirit and as such has perfect knowledge.

This term denotes the infinite intelligence of God—His knowledge of all things. Calvin defined "omniscience" as "that attribute whereby God knows Himself and all other things in one Eternal and most simple act." Wisdom may be classified under omniscience; it is that whereby God produces the best possible results by the best possible means. Wisdom also seems to include moral principle as well as intellectual capacity, as seen in Job and Proverbs, where it embraces the pre-eminent qualities of an ideal man combining in itself all moral and intellectual excellences. Wisdom is a quality of God's nature and a mode of His activity.

(2) The fact of it.

Rom. 11:33—O the depth of the riches both of the wisdom and knowledge of God! how unsearchable are his judgments, and his ways past finding out!

S. F. Job. 11:7–8; Isa. 40:28; Ps. 147:5; Deut. 29:29.

S. A. Ps. 139:2, 11, 13; I Kings 8:39; Jer. 16:17; Luke 16:15; Rom. 8:27; Heb. 4:13; Isa. 42:9; Job. 37:16; Ex. 3:19; Jer. 1:5; I Sam. 23:10–13.

The universe as the expression of God's thought and plan suggests His omniscience.

"He who cannot see the workings of a Divine wisdom in the order of the heavens, the change of the seasons, the flowing of the tides, the operations of the wind and other elements, the structure of the human body, the circulation of the blood through a variety of vessels wonderfully arranged and conducted, the instinct of beasts, their tempers and dispositions, and the growth of plants; he who cannot see all these and many other things as the evident contrivance of a Divine wisdom is sottishly blind, and unworthy of the name of man."—William Jones.

D. S. The Scriptures teach that God is omniscient; His understanding is infinite; His intelligence is perfect.

(3) The application of it.

a. To things in general.

45

(a) God's omniscience is all inclusive; His knowledge is universal, including all things knowable.

I John 3:20—For if our heart condemn us, God is greater than our heart, and knoweth all things.

"God's omniscience should indeed make us ashamed to commit sin: but it should embolden us to confess it. We can tell our secrets to a friend that does not know them; how much more should we do it to Him that knows them already! God's knowledge outruns our confessions, and anticipates what we have to say."

"God's knowledge is universal. It is unlimited in space, time or quantity. This is the characteristic of His knowledge corresponding to His immensity, eternity, and plenitude, and implied in them. God's knowledge as universal is also His knowledge of all that is possible in any imaginable universe, and of all that is actual in Himself and the existing universe."—HARRIS.

(b) God knows from all eternity that which shall be to all eternity.

Acts 15:18—Known unto God are all his works from the beginning of the world.

S. F. Isa. 46:9–10.

"God's knowledge of the actual includes His eternal knowledge of the actions of free agents. The Bible teaches that God not only preknows, but in many cases has foretold the actions of men; yet He recognizes the freedom and responsibility of the agents fulfilling the prophecies. And God is revealed in the Bible as not only preknowing and foretelling the actions of free agents (Acts 2:23), but also as knowing what, under different circumstances, they would have done but never did (I Sam. 23:12)."—HARRIS, Vol. 1.

(c) God knows the whole plan of the ages, and each man's part in it.

Eph. 1:9–12—Having made known unto us the mystery of his will, according to his good pleasure which he hath purposed in himself; That in the dispensation of the fulness of times he might gather together in one all things in Christ, both which are in heaven, and which are on earth; even in Him: In whom also we have obtained an inheritance, being predestinated according to the purpose of him who worketh all things after the counsel of his own will: That we should be to the praise of his glory, who first trusted in Christ.

S. F. Rom. 8:28–30; Col. 1:25–26; Eph. 3:4–9; Prov. 5:21.

(d) God knows all that occurs in every place; the good and evil.

Prov. 15:3 R. V.—The eyes of Jehovah are in every place, keeping watch upon the evil and the good.

S. F. Mal. 3:16.

God is cognizant of conditions which obtain in every home and heart of man. God notices the actions, words and thoughts of every member of every family in this and in every place.

(e) God knows all the sons of men, their ways and works.

Prov. 5:21—For the ways of man are before the eyes of the Lord, and he pondereth all his goings.

S. F. Ps. 33:13–15.

S. A. Matt. 20:17–19; Ex. 3:19 R. V.; Acts 3:17–18; II Kings 7:1, 2; Ps. 41:9; Gal. 1:15–16; I Peter 1:2.

46

Compare I Peter 1:20 R. V. with Mark 13:32.

Man's habits and practices are subjects of divine scrutiny. They are constantly under His observation.

"The Divine Reason is not an empty capacity or power of knowing which fills itself by acquiring knowledge. It is the eternal fulness of knowledge."

    b. To things in particular.

    (a) Everything in nature, every star and every sparrow.

Ps. 147:4—He telleth the number of the stars; he calleth them all by their names.

Matt. 10:29—Are not two sparrows sold for a farthing? and one of them shall not fall on the ground without your Father.

    (b) Everything in the realm of human experience.

"There is not a city, there is not a village, not a house, on which the eye of God is not fixed. There is not a single emotion or impulse of which He has no knowledge. He knows every occurrence or adventure, involving joy or sorrow, pain or pleasure, adversity, or prosperity, success or failure, victory or defeat.

> "God nothing does nor suffers to be done
> But thou wouldst do thyself if thou couldst see
> The end of all things here as well as He."
> —SELECTED.

    aa. Man's deeds and actions.

Ps. 139:2-3—Thou knowest my downsitting and mine uprising, thou understandest my thought afar off. Thou compassest my path and my lying down, and art acquainted with all my ways.

    bb. Man's words.

Ps. 139:4—For there is not a word in my tongue, but, lo, O Lord, thou knowest it altogether.

    cc. Man's thoughts and imaginations.

Ps. 139:1, 2—O Lord, thou has searched me, and known me. Thou knowest my downsitting and mine uprising, thou understandest my thought afar off.

I Chron. 28:9—And thou, Solomon my son, know thou the God of thy father, and serve him with a perfect heart and with a willing mind; for the Lord searchest all hearts, and understandeth all the imaginations of the thoughts; if thou seek him, he will be found of thee; but if thou forsake him, he will cast thee off for ever.

    dd. Man's sorrows.

Ex. 3:7—And the Lord said, I have surely seen the affliction of my people which are in Egypt, and have heard their cry by reason of their taskmasters; for I know their sorrows.

D. S. God's knowledge reaches from everlasting to everlasting, comprehends all things in all places to the minutest detail.

"There are certain problems which arise in connection with the doctrine of the omniscience of God. How the Divine intelligence can comprehend so vast a multitudinous and exhaustless a number of things must forever surpass our comprehension. 'O the depth of the riches both of the wisdom and knowledge

of God! How unsearchable are His judgments, and His ways past finding out!'
Rom. 11:33. There is no searching of His understanding; it is beyond human
computation. God looks to the bottom and spring of actions—not only the
matter but the principle, just as a gardener knows what roots are in the ground
long before they appear, and what fruits they will produce.

"A man that stands by a river in a place can only see that part of the river that
passes by; but he that is aloft in the air, in a higher place, may see the whole
course, where it rises and how it runs. So God at one view sees the beginning,
rise and ending of actions; whatever we think, speak or do, He sees it altogether."—MANTON.

We must expect, therefore, to stand amazed in the presence of such matchless
wisdom, and find problems in connection there-with which must for the time, at
least, remain unsolved. Again, we must not confound the preknowledge of God
with His foreordination. The two things are, in a sense, distinct. The fact that
God preknows a thing makes a thing certain, but not necessary.

"Preknowledge is not the cause of the things that are preknown; for it doth
not, because it was known, come to pass, but because it was to come to pass,
therefore it was preknown; and bare knowledge is no more the cause of any
event, which, because it is known, must infallibly be, than my seeing a man
run is the cause of his running, which, because I do see, is infallibly so."—
TILLOTSON.

God's foreordination is in harmony with His preknowledge. Pharaoh was responsible for the hardening of his heart even though that hardening process was
preknown and foretold by God. The actions of men are considered certain, but
not necessary, by reason of the divine knowledge.

9. The Omnipotence of God.

"Finite beings can form nothing more than a feeble conception of this attribute They exercise what power they have in contracted spheres and under
necessary limitation. It is a secondary power derived from God, the Source of
Supreme power. Accustomed to manifest actions of imperfect power among
men, we are amazed in contemplating the almighty power of God. His omnipotence, however, is conceded by all who believe in his existence."—PENDLETON.

God's power is unconditioned and unlimited by any one or anything outside
of Himself. Power, or the efficiency to bring things to pass, is an attribute of God.
God is the originating cause of the universe and His power is always operative in it.

"All power is His, He sits on the throne, sways a universal sceptre, controls all
things, and exercises His omnipotence in behalf of those who trust in Him."—
PENDLETON.

(1) The meaning of it.

The word "omnipotence" comes from two Latin words "omnis" and "potens,"
signifying "all power." By this attribute of God is meant His unlimited power,
His power to do whatever He chooses to do. The omnipotence of God is that
attribute by which He can bring to pass anything which He wills. God's declaration of His intention is the pledge of its accomplishment.

God's omnipotence does not mean the exercise of His power in doing that which
is inconsistent with the nature of things, such as making of a past event to have
not occurred; the drawing of a shorter than a straight line between two given

48

points. It is impossible for God to lie, to sin, to die, to make wrong to be right, or hatred of Himself to be blessed. To do such things would not imply power, but impotence. God has all the power that is consistent with infinite perfection —all power to do what is worthy of Himself.

"God's creative power is primarily the efficiency of his will. It has no analogy to the exertion of muscular strength. It is rather analogous to man's moving his arm by a volition. The opening lines of the eighth book of the Iliad are often quoted as exemplifying the sublime. Jupiter forbids the gods under direct penalties to aid either the Greeks or the Trojans. To remind them of his resistless might he challenges them to hang a golden chain from heaven, and all of them, both gods and goddesses, to lay hold of it; and he warns them that, striving to their utmost, they would be unable to drag him down. But he would grasp the chain and swing them all, with the earth and sea besides; and then would fasten the chain around the summit of Olympus and leave them all dangling in mid-air. Here is nothing but muscular strength, a sort of athletic contest. How immeasurably more sublime are the scriptural representations: 'Let light be, and light was.' 'He spake, and it was done; he commanded and it stood fast.' "—HARRIS, Vol. 1.

"God has infinite volitional power by virtue of which he is able through his free self-determination to accomplish whatever is properly an object of power. The Bible declares that God cannot do certain things, but this usually expresses an inability arising not from want of executive power or energy but of purpose. The works referred to are contradictory to His character, and hence to His will."—PEPPER.

(2) The fact of it.

Matt. 19:26—But Jesus beheld them, and said unto them, with men this is impossible; but with God all things are possible.

S. F. Job 42:2; Gen. 18:14; Ps. 93:3–4; Jer. 32:17; Ps. 115:3.

S. A. Gen. 17:1; Ex. 6:3.

D. S. God can do all things—nothing is too hard for Him; all things are possible with Him—God is Omnipotent.

(3) The application of it.

a. In the realm of nature.

Gen. 1:1–3—In the beginning God created the heaven and the earth. And the earth was without form, and void; and darkness was upon the face of the deep. And the Spirit of God moved upon the face of the waters. And God said, Let there be light; and there was light.

S. F. Ps. 107:25–29; Nah. 1:3–6; Ps. 33:6–9.

"The universe as we know it is the supreme evidence of God's Omnipotence. In creating, sustaining, and guiding it, God exhibits ability to limit or restrain himself. He chose to make it as it is rather than otherwise. He chose to make man free and leave him so. The universe does not exhaust God. There are always in Him reserves of wisdom and power."—MULLINS.

"It is as easy for God to supply thy greatest as thy smallest wants, even as it was within His power to form a system or an atom, to create a blazing sun as to kindle the fire-fly's lamp."—THOMAS GUTHRIE.

D. S. All nature is subject to the divine direction and control.

49

b. In the realm of human experience as illustrated by:

(a) Joseph—Gen. 39:2, 3, 21.

God manifested His power with Joseph by turning his foes into friends and bringing about those circumstances which made for his exaltation and prosperity.

(b) Nebuchadnezzar—Dan. 4:19–37.

God's power was manifested in the case of Nebuchadnezzar by subjugating his pride and arrogance and compelling his confession of the sovereignty and supremacy of God in the affairs of heaven and earth.

(c) Daniel—Dan. 1:9.

God's power is seen in relation to Daniel by giving him favor with the Prince of the eunuchs and with the King himself and also by his miraculous preservation in the lion's den.

(d) Pharaoh—Ex. 7:1-5.

God demonstrated the supremacy of His power over the gods of Egypt by the ten plagues sent upon the Egyptians and by the great deliverance which He gave to the children of Israel by the hand of Moses.

(e) Men in general.

Ps. 75:6–7—For promotion cometh neither from the east, nor from the west, nor from the south. But God is the judge: he putteth down one, and setteth up another.

S. F. John 17:2; Ps. 76:10.

S. A. Acts 17:28; Luke 12:13–21; James 4:12–15.

"God's Omnipotence is manifested in many ways. There is no obstacle which He cannot overcome in the carrying out of His purposes or in the use of means. He can also act directly without means in the pursuit of His ends."—MULLINS.

"King Canute, a Danish conqueror of Britain, was one day flattered by his courtiers on account of his power. Then he ordered his throne to be placed by the seaside. The tide was rolling in, and threatened to drown him. He commanded the waves to stop. Of course they did not. Then he said to his flatterers, 'Behold, how small is the might of kings!' "—FOSTER.

D. S. All human actions, whether present or future are dependent upon the will and power of God and are subject to His Word.

c. In the heavenly realms.

Dan. 4:35—And all the inhabitants of the earth are reputed as nothing: and he doeth according to his will in the army of heaven, among the inhabitants of the earth: and none can stay his hand, or say unto him, What doest thou?

S. F. Heb. 1:13–14.

D. S. Holy angels are under the Divine control and subject to the will of God.

d. In the realm of evil spirits.

Job 1:12—And the Lord said unto Satan, Behold, all that he hath is in thy power; only upon himself put not forth thine hand. So Satan went forth from the presence of the Lord.

S. F. James 4:7; Rev. 20:2; Job 2:6; Luke 22:31, 32.

"When Antigonus was ready to engage in a sea fight with Ptolemy's armada, and the pilot· cried out, 'How many are they more than we?' the courageous king replied, ' 'Tis true, if you count their numbers, they surpass us; but for how many do you value me?' Our God is sufficient against all the combined forces of earth and hell."—SPENCER.

Satan has no power over any of God's children saving as God permits him to have. God can set a bar to the malignity of Satan, just as He can set a bar to the waves of the sea.

D. S. The powers of evil—the devil, demons and fallen angels—are subject to God's will and word.

10. The Omnipresence of God.

This attribute is closely connected with the omnipotence and omniscience of God, for God is everywhere present. He is everywhere active and possesses full knowledge of all that transpires in every place. This does not mean that God is everywhere present in a bodily sense; His presence is a spiritual, not a material presence, yet it is a real personal presence.

Children sometimes ask: "If God is everywhere, how is there any room for us?" And the only answer is that God is not a material but a spiritual Being, whose presence does not exclude finite or material existence.

Jesus taught: "Neither in this mountain, nor in Jerusalem, shall ye worship the father. God is a Spirit, and they that worship Him must worship Him in spirit and in truth." Our Lord's mysterious comings and goings after His resurrection were intended to teach His disciples how He could and would be with them "always even unto the end of the age." The omnipresence of Jesus demonstrates the omnipresence of God.

"All that God is in one place He is in· all places. All there is of God is in every place. Indeed, His presence has no dependence on space or matter. All the boundless glory of the Godhead is essentially present at every spot in His creation, however various may be the manifestations of this glory at different times and places."—ALEXANDER.

"What a comfort to be told that, with all our seeming separation, we are still inmates of the same house—the house of God. That is just what the Psalmist says. He says that absolute separation between two souls is an impossibility, that the wings of the morning can never lift us outside the gates of God."—MATHESON.

"To the Hebrews, the external universe is just a black screen concealing God. All things are full of, yet all distinct from Him. The cloud on the mountains is His covering; the muttering from the chambers of the thunder is His voice; the sound on the top of the mulberry tree is His 'going'; in that wind, which bends the forest or curls the clouds, He is walking; that sun is His still commanding eye. Whither can they go from His spirit? whither can they flee from His presence? At every step and in every circumstance they feel themselves God-enclosed, God-filled, God-breathing men, with a spiritual presence lowering or smiling on them from the sky, sounding in wild tempest, or creeping in panic stillness across the surface of the earth; and, if they turn within, lo! it is there also—an 'eye' hung in the central darkness of their own hearts."—GILFILLAN.

(1) The meaning of it.

The word "omnipresence" comes from the two Latin words "omnis" meaning "all," and "praesen" — "to be at hand or present." The Scriptures represent God as filling immensity; He is present everywhere and there is no point in the universe where He is not.

"A heathen philosopher once asked a Christian, 'Where is God?' The Christian answered, 'Let me first ask you, Where is He not?' "—ARROWSMITH.

There is a distinction between the omnipresence of God and His immensity. Concerning this distinction, Dick says: "When we call His essence immense, we mean that it has no limits; when we say that it is omnipresent, we signify that it is wherever creatures are, for there God is, but we are more concerned with His omnipresence which bears a personal relation to us."

(2) The fact of it.

Ps. 139:7–10—Whither shall I go from thy Spirit? or whither shall I flee from thy presence? If I ascend up into heaven, thou art there: if I make my bed in hell, behold, thou art there. If I take the wings of the morning, and dwell in the uttermost parts of the sea; Even there shall thy hand lead me, and thy right hand shall hold me.

S. F. Acts 17:24–28; Matt. 18:20; Jer. 23:23–24.

"A certain man went to a dervish, and proposed three questions: 'First, why do they say that God is omnipresent? I do not see Him in any place: show me where He is. Secondly, Why is man punished for his crimes, since whatever he does proceeds from God? Man has no free will, for he cannot do anything contrary to the will of God; and, if he had power, he would do everything for his own good. Thirdly, How can God punish Satan in hell-fire, since he is formed of that element? and what impression can fire make on itself?' The dervish took up a large clod of earth, and struck him on the head with it. The man went to the cadi, and said, 'I proposed three questions to a dervish, who flung such a clod of earth at me as has made my head ache.' The cadi, having sent for the dervish, asked, 'Why did you throw a clod of earth at his head, instead of answering his questions? The dervish replied, 'The clod of earth was an answer to his speech. He says he has a pain in his head: let him show me the pain, and I will make God visible to him. And why does he exhibit a complaint to you against me? Whatever I did was the act of God. I did not strike him without the will of God, and what power do I possess? And as he is compounded of earth how can he suffer pain from that element?' The man was confounded, and the cadi highly pleased, with the dervish's answer."
—J. H. VINCENT.

D. S. God is our nearest environment. His center is everywhere; His circumference is nowhere: God is Omnipresent.

(3) The qualification of it.

God is not everywhere in the same sense, i.e., He is manifestly present in some places in a sense in which He is not in other places; in heaven as His dwelling place and the place of His throne. This is the place where at the present time the presence and glory of God is especially and visibly manifested.

John 20:17—"Jesus saith unto her, Touch me not; for I am not yet ascended to My Father; but go to my brethren, and say unto them, I ascend unto my Father, and your Father; and to my God, and your God."

S. F. I Kings 8:30; John 14:28; Eph. 1:20.

52

S. A. Rev. 21:2, 3, 10, 22, 23; Rev. 22:1, 3.

"God the Father is especially manifested in heaven (Mark 1:9-11). God the Son has been especially manifested on earth (John 3:13) and is now in heaven (Acts 7:56; Eph. 1:20). God the Holy Spirit is manifested everywhere. (a) In nature (Gen. 1:2; Ps. 104:30); (b) In all believers (John 14:16, 17; Rom. 8:9); (c) With unbelievers (John 16:7-11). Through the Spirit, the Father and the Son dwell in the believer (John 14:17, 19, 20, 23)." —TORREY.

D. S. God the Father is especially manifested in heaven; God the Son has been especially manifested on the earth; God the Holy Spirit is manifested everywhere, in nature, with unbelievers and in all believers.

(4) The application of it to human life and experience.

    a. It is protective truth and should bring comfort and encouragement to the hearts of all believers. The unfailing presence of God is their glorious portion and possession.

"When I walk by the wayside, He is along with me; when I enter into company amid all my forgetfulness of Him, He never forgets me; in the silent watches of the night, when my eyelids have closed, and my spirit has sunk into unconsciousness, the observant eye of Him, who never slumbers, is upon me; I cannot flee from His presence, go where I will; He leads me, and watches me, and cares for me; and the same Being who is now at work in the remotest domains of nature and of Providence, is also at my hand, to eke out to me every moment of my being, and to uphold me in the exercise of all my feelings, and of all my faculties."—CHALMERS.

"It is impossible to conceive of any thought more appalling than this would be, did this unseen and ever-present Being regard us with unfriendly feelings . . . . . And it is difficult to conceive of all the agony which would accrue to us from the consciousness that an enemy unseen by us, attended all our steps; that his eye was upon us by night and by day . . . . . His invisibility would render us unable to defend ourselves from his assaults, were we otherwise capable of doing so; and leaving us ignorant of his intentions and movements, would keep us in a state of torturing suspense, ever-fearing, and not knowing how soon he might gratify his enmity by involving us in ruin. What cause for gratitude have we that a thought which might be so fraught with horror may prove to all of us the source of unfailing consolation! The character of God is such that the man is sadly wrong who derives no comfort from the consciousness of His presence."—LANDELS.

    "Lord of all being; throned afar
    Thy glory flames from sun and star;
    Centre and soul of ev'ry sphere
    Yet to each loving heart, how near."—SELECTED.

    "For God is never so far off as even to be near.
    He is within. Our spirit is the home He holds most dear.
    To think of Him as by our side is almost as untrue,
    As to remove His shrine beyond those skies of starry blue,
    So all the while I thought myself, homeless, forlorn and
    weary.
    Missing my joy, I walked the earth, myself God's sanctuary."
    —FABER.

b. It is detective truth.

As in the Roman Empire the whole world was one great prison to a malefactor, and in his flight to the most distant lands, the emperor could track him; so under the government of God no sinner can escape the eye of the Judge of all the earth. "Thou God seest me" should serve as a warning to keep us from sin.

"Let the consideration that all things are naked and opened unto the eyes of Him with Whom we have to do, have its proper influence upon us."—PRESTON.

II. The Moral Attributes.

1. The Holiness of God (including Righteousness and Justice).

(1) The Holiness of God (proper).

God's Holiness is His most exalted and emphasized attribute, expressing the majesty of His moral nature and character.

a. The importance of the doctrine.

This might well be called the emphatic moral attribute of God. If there is any difference in importance between the moral attributes, that of God's holiness seems to occupy the first place. In the visions which God granted to men in the Old Testament era the thing that stood out the most prominently was the divine holiness. See as illustrations of this the visions of Moses, Job, and Isaiah.

Some thirty times does the Prophet Isaiah speak of Jehovah as the "Holy One," thus indicating the features of those beatific visions which had impressed him the most forcibly. It is by His holiness that God desires to be known pre-eminently, that being the attribute by which He is the most greatly glorified. Superficial views of God and His holiness will produce superficial views of sin and the need of atonement.

> (a) As revealed in the Scriptures, in which God's holiness is not only most constantly and powerfully impressed upon the attention of man, but is declared to be the chief subject of rejoicing and adoration in heaven.

I Peter 1:16, R.V.—Because it is written, Ye shall be holy, for I am holy.

S. F. Rev. 4:8; Luke 5:8; Heb. 12:14; Isa. 6:3.

The Scriptures declare the holiness of God in loud and solemn tones: "Holy and reverend is His name." The perfection of holiness in God is the supreme reason for the worship to be ascribed to Him.

> (b) As evidenced by our own moral constitution, in which conscience asserts its supremacy over every impulse and affection of our nature. For example, we may be kind, but we must be righteous; so God, in whose image we are made, may be merciful, but must be holy.

Rom. 2:14–16—For when the Gentiles, which have not the law, do by nature the things contained in the law, these, having not the law, are a law unto themselves; Which shew the work of the law written in their hearts, their conscience also bearing witness, and their thoughts meanwhile accusing or else excusing one another; In the day when God shall judge the secrets of men by Jesus Christ according to my gospel.

S. F. II Pet. 2:4, 5, 9.

(c) As seen in the actual dealings of God, in which Holiness conditions and limits the exercise of other attributes. Thus, for example, in Christ's redeeming work, though love makes the atonement, it is violated holiness that requires it; and in the eternal punishment of the wicked, the demand of holiness for self-vindication overbears the pleading of love for the sufferers. Psa. 85:10.

Phil. 1:9—And this I pray, that your love may abound yet more and more in knowledge and in all judgment.

Love cannot be the fundamental attribute of God, because love always requires a standard, and this standard is found only in holiness. That, therefore, which conditions all is highest of all.

"At the railway switching grounds east of Rochester, there is a man whose duty is to move a bar of iron two or three inches to the left or to the right. So he determines whether a train shall go toward New York or toward Washington, toward New Orleans or San Francisco."—Strong.

That bar is the medium by which the direction and course of the trains is regulated and governed. Thus holiness is the regulative attribute of God by which the exercise of all other attributes is governed and directed.

(d) As shown in God's redemptive purpose and provision, in which justice and mercy are reconciled only through the foreseen and predetermined sacrifice of Christ. The declaration that Christ is "the Lamb of God slain from the foundation of the world" implies the existence of a principle in the divine nature which requires satisfaction before God can enter upon the work of redemption. That principle can be none other than holiness.

Rom. 3:26—To declare, I say, at this time his righteousness; that he might be just, and the justifier of him which believeth in Jesus.

S. F. Ps. 85:10.

b. The meaning of Holiness as applied to God. Two things by way of definition may be inferred from the Scriptures:

(a) Negatively—that God is entirely apart from all that is evil, and from that which defiles, both in Himself and in relation to all His creatures.

Lev. 11:43-45—Ye shall not make yourselves abominable with any creeping thing that creepeth, neither shall ye make yourselves unclean with them, that ye should be defiled thereby. For I am the Lord your God; Ye shall therefore sanctify yourselves; and ye shall be holy; for I am holy: neither shall ye defile yourselves with any manner of creeping thing that creepeth upon the earth. For I am the Lord that bringeth you up out of the land of Egypt, to be your God; ye shall therefore be holy, for I am holy.

S. F. Deut. 23:14.

We do not merely say that God wills to be separated from that which defiles, making holiness a matter of mere will, but that he is separate from all that is sinful in being. It is a characteristic of His being. Job said (34:10): "Therefore hearken unto me, ye men of understanding: far be it from God, that he should do wickedness; and from the Almighty, that he should commit iniquity."

"An evil God, one that could commit evil, would be a contradiction in terms, an impossible, inconceivable idea. Job seemed to doubt that the principle on which the universe was conducted was one of absolute equity. He must know that God is free from all evil-doing. However hidden the meaning of His dealings, He is always just. God never did, never will do wrong to any of His creatures."—EVANS.

(b) Positively—that by the holiness of God is meant the consummate perfection, purity, and absolute integrity of His nature and character.

I John 1:5—This then is the message which we have heard of him, and declare unto you, that God is light, and in him is no darkness at all.

"Holiness is not a dead-white purity, the perfection of the faultless marble statue. Life, as well as purity, enters into the idea of holiness. They who are 'without fault before the throne' are they who 'follow the Lamb whithersoever He goeth'—holy activity attending and expressing their holy state."— A. J. GORDON.

c. The Scriptural fact of it.

Ps. 99:9—Exalt the Lord our God, and worship at his holy hill; for the Lord our God is holy.

S. F. Isa. 57:15; Hab. 1:13; I Peter 1:15, 16.

(a) God the Father is called "Holy Father."

John 17:11—And now I am no more in the world, but these are in the world, and I come to thee. Holy Father, keep through thine own name those whom thou hast given me, that they may be one, as we are.

(b) God the Son is called "The Holy One."

Acts 3:14—But ye denied the Holy One and the Just, and desired a murderer to be granted unto you.

S. A. Isa. 41:14.

(c) God the Spirit is called the "Holy Spirit."

Eph. 4:30—And Grieve not the Holy Spirit of God, whereby ye are sealed unto the day of redemption.

D. S. The Scriptures emphasize the fact that God is Holy; His essential moral nature is Holiness.

d. The manifestation of God's Holiness as shown:

(a) In a hatred of sin.

Hab. 1:13—Thou art of purer eyes than to behold evil, and canst not look on iniquity; wherefore lookest thou upon them that deal treacherously, and holdest thy tongue when the wicked devoureth the man that is more righteous than he?

S. F. Gen. 6:5–6; Prov. 15:9, 26; Deut. 25:16; Prov. 6:16–19.

"The entire Mosaic system of washing; divisions of the tabernacle; divisions of the people into ordinary Israelites, Levites, Priests and High Priests, who were permitted different degrees of approach to God, under strictly defined conditions; the insisting upon sacrifice as a necessary medium of approach to God; God's directions to Moses in Ex. 3:5; to Joshua in Josh. 5:15, the punishment of Uzziah in II Chron. 26:16–23, the strict orders to Israel in regard to approaching Sinai upon which Jehovah came down; the doom of

56

Korah, Dathan, and Abiram in Num. 16:1-33; and the destruction of Nadab and Abihu in Lev. 10:1-3; all these were intended to teach, emphasize and burn into the minds and hearts of the Israelites the fundamental truth that God is Holy, unapproachably holy. The truth that God is Holy is the fundamental truth of the Bible, of the Old Testament and the New Testament, of the Jewish Religion, and the Christian Religion."—Torrey.

(b) In a delight in that which is holy and righteous.

Prov. 15:9—The way of the wicked is an abomination unto the Lord; but he loveth him that followeth after righteousness.

S. F. Lev. 20:26; Lev. 19:2.

(c) In the separation of the sinner from Himself.

Isa. 59:1-2—Behold, the Lord's hand is not shortened, that it cannot save; neither his ear heavy, that it cannot hear; But your iniquities have separated between you and your God, and your sins have hid his face from you, that he will not hear.

S. F. Eph. 2:13; John 14:6.

(d) In making provision for man's freedom from sin and the fruitage of a holy life.

I Peter 2:24—Who his own self bare our sins in his own body on the tree, that we, being dead to sins, should live unto righteousness; by whose stripes ye were healed.

S. F. Rom. 8:1-4; Rom. 6:22.

D. S. God's holiness is manifested in His hatred of sin and delight in righteousness; in His separation from those living in sin, and making provision for man to become holy in character and conduct.

e. The application of it.

(a) The realization of God's Holiness begets reverence and awe in the heart of those who come into His conscious Presence, unless they are hardened in sin.

Heb. 12:28-29—Wherefore we receiving a kingdom which cannot be moved, le' us have grace, whereby we may serve God acceptably with reverenc and godly fear: For our God is a consuming fire.

S. F. Isa. 6:1-3; Ex. 3:4-6.

"The one aim of Christianity is personal holiness. But personal holiness wil' be the one absorbing and attainable aim of man, only as he recognizes it t be the one pre-eminent attribute of God."—E. G. Robinson.

(b) The pure light of God's holiness reveals the blackness of our sin.

Job 42:5, 6—I have heard of thee by the hearing of the ear; but now mine eye seeth thee. Wherefore I abhor myself and repent in dust and ashes.

S. F. Isa. 6:5.

If any man think well of himself, he has never met God. Nothing will demolish self-righteousness like one real sight of God. The self-righteous person needs to get into the consciousness of the holy presence of God.

(c) There is no forgiveness without atonement. Sin must be covered from the holy gaze of God, and nothing can do this but blood—the blood of Christ. Heb. 9:22; Heb. 10:19.

Eph. 1:7—In whom we have redemption through his blood, the forgiveness of sins, according to the riches of his grace.

"All approach to God is on the ground of shed blood. The atonement has its deepest demand in the holiness of God. Any doctrine of the atonement that sees its need only in the necessities of governmental expediency does not go to the root of things. The first and fundamental reason why 'without shedding of blood there is no remission' is because God is holy and sin must be covered before there can be fellowship between God and the sinner."—STRONG.

(d) The holiness of God magnifies His grace and redeeming love, in providing for the acceptance of those who are sinners and ungodly.

Rom. 5:6-8—For when we were yet without strength, in due time Christ died for the ungodly. For scarcely for a righteous man will one die; yet peradventure for a good man some would even dare to die. But God commendeth his love toward us, in that, while we were yet sinners, Christ died for us.

S. F. John 3:16.

"How marvellous is God's love! It would be no wonder if an unholy God could love unholy men; but that the God whose name is holy, the Infinitely Holy God, could love beings so utterly sinful as we are, that is the wonder of the Eternities. There are many deep mysteries in the Bible, but no other so profound as this."—TORREY.

(2) The Righteousness and Justice of God.

These attributes are in reality the manifestations of God's holiness in his relations with men, but are dealt with separately for the sake of convenience and emphasis. Holiness, however, has to do more particularly with the character of God, while in righteousness and justice that character is expressed in the dealings of God with men.

"Justice and righteousness are simply holiness exercised toward creatures. The same holiness which exists in God in eternity past manifests itself as justice and righteousness, so soon as intelligent creatures come into being."—STRONG.

"God moves on a track of absolute and perfect equity and holiness, and the same qualities that insure that you would be borne safely into the eternal ages if connected with God, make it sure that you would be ground to powder if you place yourself before the wheels of judgment."—A. T. PIERSON.

a. The Righteousness of God.

(a) The meaning of it.

The Righteousness of God is the imposing of righteous laws and demands; this may be called legislative holiness. In this attribute we have revealed God's love of holiness, which always leads Him to do right, and to demand that which is right.

(b) The Scriptural fact of it.

Ps. 145:17—The Lord is righteous in all his ways, and holy in all his works.

S. F. Jer. 12:1; John 17:25; Ps. 116:5; Ezra 9:15.

D. S. All of God's requirements of men are absolutely righteous in character.

b. The Justice of God.

"Justice is the execution of righteousness."

(a) **The meaning of It.**

The justice of God is the execution of the penalty attached to His laws; this may be called judicial holiness. In this attribute we have revealed His hatred of sin, which, devoid of all passion or caprice, always leads Him to be just, and to demand that which is just.

(b) **The Scriptural fact of it.**

Zeph. 3:5—The just Lord is in the midst thereof; he will not do iniquity: every morning doth he bring his judgment to light, he faileth not; but the unjust knoweth no shame.

S. F. Deut. 32:4; Micah 6:8.

D. S. All of God's dealings with men are upon the basis of absolute justice.

c. The Manifestation of God's Righteousness and Justice.

(a) **In His loving righteousness and hating iniquity.**

Ps. 11:4-7—The Lord is in his holy temple, the Lord's throne is in heaven; his eyes behold, his eyelids try, the children of men. The Lord trieth the righteous; but the wicked and him that loveth violence his soul hateth. Upon the wicked he shall rain snares, fire and brimstone, and an horrible tempest: this shall be the portion of their cup. For the righteous Lord loveth righteousness; his countenance doth behold the upright.

"Goodness and severity are elements of a perfect character even among men. Without goodness, the character is stern and inflexible; it repels instead of winning. On the other hand, without severity goodness degenerates into weakness; into that moral pliancy which, under the name of good-nature has often made men consent easily to the enticement of sinners. In a perfect character, if such existed among men, you would see the counter-balancing powers of goodness and severity held in exact equilibrium. And such, the Word of God assures us, is the character of Him with whom we have to do—'Behold, therefore, the goodness and severity of God.' "—GOULBURN.

Dr. Arnold of Rugby was never sure of a boy who only loved good; till the boy also began to hate evil, Dr. Arnold did not feel that he was safe.

(b) **In the punishment of the wicked and unrighteous.**

Dan. 9:12, 14—And he hath confirmed his words, which he spake against us, and against our judges that judged us, by bringing upon us a great evil: for under the whole heaven hath not been done as hath been done upon Jerusalem. Therefore hath the Lord watched upon the evil, and brought it upon us: for the Lord our God is righteous in all his works which he doeth: for we obeyed not his voice.

S. F. Ex. 9:23-27; Ex. 34:6, 7; Ps. 5:4-6; Gen. 6:5, 7.

S. A. II Chron. 12:5-6; Rev. 16:5-6.

"The Law is obligated to punish the transgressor as much as the transgressor is obliged to obey the law—law has no option. Justice has but one function. The necessity of penalty is as great as the necessity of obligation. The law itself is under law; that is, it is under the necessity of its own nature; and therefore the only possible way whereby a transgressor can escape the penalty of the law is for the substitute to endure it for him. The deep substrata and base of all God's ethical attributes are termed law and impartial justice."—SHEDD.

(c) In forgiving the sins of the penitent believer for whom atonement has been made by Christ.

I John 1:9, R.V.—If we confess our sins, he is faithful and righteous to forgive us our sins, and to cleanse us from all unrighteousness.

(d) In keeping His Word and promises to His own.

Neh. 9:7, 8—Thou art the Lord the God who didst choose Abram, and broughtest him forth out of Ur of the Chaldees, and gavest him the name of Abraham; and foundest his heart faithful before thee, and madest a covenant with him to give the land of the Canaanites, the Hittites, the Amorites, and the Perizzites, and the Jebusites, and the Girgashites, to give it, I say, to his seed, and hast performed thy words; for thou art righteous.

God's righteousness is the guarantee of the fulfillment of His promises.

(e) In delivering and vindicating His people.

Ps. 103:6—The Lord executeth righteousness and judgment for all that are oppressed.

S. F. Ps. 129:1-4.

(f) In the rewarding of the righteous.

Heb. 6:10—For God is not unrighteous to forget your work and labour of love, which ye have shewed toward his name, in that ye have ministered to the saints, and do minister.

S. F. II Tim. 4:8.

No creature can claim anything for his obedience. If God rewards, He rewards in virtue of His goodness and faithfulness, not in virtue of His justice and righteousness. What a creature cannot claim, however, Christ can claim and the rewards which are goodness to the creature are righteousness to Christ. God rewards Christ's work for us and in us. God rewards not on account of man's works, but "according to his works." Reward is thus seen to be in Scripture a matter of grace to the creature; only to Christ who works for us in atonement, and in us in regeneration and sanctification is reward a matter of debt, or a righteous action. (See also John 6:29; II John 8; I Cor. 3:11-15; Luke 17:10.)

(g) In providing a propitiation for sin passed over and in justifying him that has faith in the substitute.

Rom. 3:24-26—Being justified freely by his grace through the redemption that is in Christ Jesus: Whom God hath set forth to be a propitiation through faith in his blood, to declare his righteousness for the remission of sins that are past, through the forbearance of God. To declare, I say, at this time his righteousness: that he might be just, and the justifier of him which believeth in Jesus.

"God is kind; but within the limits of inexorable law. He is good, but you can take no liberties with Him; for back of His pity and kindness is the righteousness that is so exact, and that must be satisfied to the uttermost farthing."—J. R. Paxton.

Therefore all His dealings with the Old Testament saints in mercy and forbearance were upon the just ground of the substitutionary sacrifice which Christ was to make as a propitiation for sins.

D. S. God has made practical manifestations of His righteousness and justice in all of His dealings with men, both the just and the unjust.

2. The Love of God, (including Mercy and Grace).

Christianity is really the only religion that sets forth the Supreme Being as Love. The gods of the heathen are angry, hateful beings, and are in constant need of being appeased. But not so our God. His love like a bridge spans the gulf of time. It has held up under the heaviest pressure. At different times, such has been the weight of human sins, that the best of men have feared that the bridge would give way beneath the burden. But it has borne all things, and "suffered long" even until now. In the time of Noah, the Bridge of Love suffered such depression under the weight of the world's iniquity, that for a brief season it disappeared beneath the flood; still it stood unbroken in the rushing torrent, and ever since it has been reflected in the heavens in the "bow of the covenant," the pledge and promise of the abiding character of that which it mirrors forth.

"God's love is more abundant than the atmosphere. The air reaches out beyond the earth some thirty miles, while the love of God reaches up to heaven itself and fills the universe."—CHAMPION.

(1) The Love of God (proper).

a. The meaning of it.

Love is that attribute of God by which He is inclined to seek the highest good for His creatures and the communication of Himself to them regardless of the sacrifice involved; or to give an alternate definition, God's love is His desire for and delight in the welfare of those loved. It is His loving interest in them.

I John 3:16–17—"Hereby perceive we the love of God, because he laid down his life for us; and we ought to lay down our lives for the brethren. But whoso hath this world's goods, and seeth his brother have need, and shutteth up his bowels of compassion from him, how dwelleth the love of God in him?"

S. F. I John 4:8, 16; Matt. 5:44, 45.

S. A. I John 4:7.

Love in its highest form is a relation between personal, intelligent beings. The love of a dog will always be animal love. But when we come into the human realm we see mother love containing the mother element. Rising still higher we see God's love containing the divine element. The character of the one loving gives character to the love. Because God is perfect, His love is perfect; because He is holy, His love is holy and pure. He seeks by His love to arouse a responsive love in man.

"Love between God and man means their complete and unrestrained self-giving to each other, and the complete possession of each by the other."—MULLINS.

"All the love in all women's hearts together, compared to the love of His heart, is as a glow-worm's torch compared to the sun at noontide."—MEYER.

b. The Scriptural fact of it.

I John 4:16—And we have known and believed the love that God hath to us.

61

God is love; and he that dwelleth in love dwelleth in God, and God in him.

S. F. I John 4:8; John 3:16.

As there is a higher mind than our mind, so there is a greater heart than our heart. God is not simply the loving One; He is also the Love that is loved. There is an infinite life of sensibility and affection in God. God has feeling and in an infinite degree. But feeling alone is not love. Love implies not merely receiving but giving, not merely emotion but impartation. So the love of God is shown in His eternal giving (James 1:5): "God who giveth," or "the giving God." Giving is not an episode in His being; it is His nature to give. Not only to give, but to give Himself. This He does eternally in the self-communications of the Trinity; this He does also in His relations with men, in His giving of Himself for us in Christ, and to us in the Holy Spirit.

"To me this is the profoundest of all truths—that the whole of the life of God is the sacrifice of self. God is love: love involves sacrifice—to give rather than to receive—the blessedness of self-giving. If the life of God were not such, it would be a falsehood to say that God is love; for, even in our human nature, that which seeks to enjoy all, instead of giving all, is known by a very different name from that of love. All the life of God is a flow of this divine self-giving love."—F. W. ROBERTSON.

c. The objects of it.

(a) God loves His Son as the original, unique and eternal object of His affection.

"If God is eternal love, that love must have an eternal object. There must, then, because of a necessity in the Divine Being Himself, be a multiplicity of persons in the Godhead."—TORREY.

Matt. 3:17—And lo a voice from heaven, saying, This is my beloved Son, in whom I am well pleased.

S. F. Luke 20:13; John 17:24; Matt. 17:5.

(b) God loves those who are united to His Son by faith.

John 16:27—For the Father himself loveth you, because ye have loved me, and have believed that I came out from God.

S. F. John 14:21, 23.

God loves all men, but He has a peculiar love for those in Christ (John 17:23). Their love for God is the result of His love for them. "We love him because He first loved us." (I John 4:19.)

(c) God loves the world, i.e. the whole human race, and each member of it.

John 3:16—For God so loved the world, that He gave His only begotten Son, that whosoever believeth in Him should not perish, but have everlasting life.

S. F. I Tim. 2:3–4; II Peter 3:9.

(d) God loves sinners, the ungodly, those who are dead in sin.

This does not mean that He loves them in that capacity, but rather as His creatures who have become such. It does mean, however, that He loves His creatures in spite of their ungodliness and sin.

Rom. 5:6–8—For when we were yet without strength, in due time Christ died for the ungodly. For scarcely for a righteous man will one die: yet peradventure for a good man some would even dare to die. But God commendeth his love toward us, in that, while we were yet sinners, Christ died for us.

S. F. Ezek. 33:11; Eph. 2:4, 5.

D. S. God loves the world, the ungodly and sinners; He has a unique love for His Son, and a peculiar love for those who are united to Him in faith and love.

d. The Manifestation of it as shown:

(a) In making infinite sacrifice for the salvation of the lost whom He loves.

John 3:16—For God so loved the world, that He gave His only begotten Son, that whosoever believeth in Him should not perish, but have everlasting life.

S. F. I John 4:9–10.

"No man has ever manifested such love as this. In a few instances one man has been willing to sacrifice his life for a friend; and not a few fathers and mothers have been willing to endanger their lives for the welfare of a son or daughter. But the instance has never yet occurred where a man was willing to give his own life or the life of a child, for an enemy. No monarch on the throne, has ever thought of giving the heir to his crown to die for a traitor, or a rebellious province. . . The nearest approach of which I have ever heard to anything like this feeling was in the pathetic wish of David that he had himself been permitted to die in the place of a rebellious and ungrateful son. "O my son Absalom, my son, my son Absalom, would God I had died for thee." Strong was that love which would lead a monarch and a father to be willing to die for such a son, but how far removed still from the love which would lead to the sacrifice of a son for the guilty and the vile."—BARNES

(b) In bestowing full and complete pardon upon penitent believers.

Isa. 55:7—Let the wicked forsake his way, and the unrighteous man his thoughts; and let him return unto the Lord, and he will have mercy upon him; and to our God, for he will abundantly pardon.

(c) In ministering to those He loves, and protecting them from evil.

Deut. 32:9–12—For the Lord's portion is his people; Jacob is the lot of his inheritance. He found him in a desert land, and in the waste howling wilderness; he led him about, he instructed him, he kept him as the apple of his eye. As an eagle stirreth up her nest, fluttereth over her young, spreadeth abroad her wings, taketh them, beareth them on her wings: So the Lord alone did lead him, and there was no strange god with him.

S. F. Deut. 33:3, 12; Isa. 48:14, 20, 21.

(d) In chastening and scourging His children for their profit.

Heb. 12:6–11—For whom the Lord loveth he chasteneth, and scourgeth every son whom he receiveth. If ye endure chastening, God dealeth with you as with sons; for what son is he whom the father chasteneth not? But if ye be without chastisement, whereof all are partakers, then are ye bastards, and not sons. Furthermore we have had fathers of our flesh which corrected us, and we gave them reverence: shall we not much rather be in subjection unto the Father of Spirits, and live? For they verily for a few days chastened us after their own pleasure, but he for our profit, that we might be partakers of his holiness. Now no chastening for the present seemeth to be joyous, but grievous: nevertheless afterward it yieldeth the peaceable fruit of righteousness unto them which are exercised thereby.

(e) In being afflicted when His loved ones are afflicted and remembering them in all of their experiences.

Isa. 63:9—In all their affliction he was afflicted, and the angel of his presence saved them: in his love and in his pity he redeemed them; and he bare them and carried them all the days of old.

S. F. Isa. 49:15–16.

D. S. God's love is manifested in the sacrificial work of Christ; in pardoning of penitent believers; and in making provisions for all their needs.

e. Various aspects of it.

God's love manifests itself by various qualities and characteristics. A number of terms have been employed to express this variety.

(a) When God's love terminates upon an object that meets His approval, it is the love of complacency.

Zeph. 3:17—The Lord thy God in the midst of thee is mighty; he will save, he will rejoice over thee with joy; he will rest in his love, he will joy over thee with singing.

S. F. Matt. 17:5.

(b) When its object is in distress, it is the love of compassion.

Isa. 63:9—In all their affliction he was afflicted, and the angel of his presence saved them: in his love and in his pity he redeemed them; and he bare them, and carried them all the days of old.

(c) When there is a relation of special intimacy between God's love and its object, it is the love of affection.

John 17:23—I in them and thou in me, that they may be made perfect in one; and that the world may know that thou hast sent me, and hast loved them, as thou hast loved me.

(d) When it takes the form of goodness toward all creatures, regardless of moral character, it is the love of benevolence.

Luke 6:35—But love ye your enemies, and do good, and lend, hoping for nothing again; and your reward shall be great, and ye shall be the children of the Highest; for he is kind unto the unthankful and to the evil.

(e) When it goes out toward the guilty it takes the form of mercy.

Isa. 55:7—Let the wicked forsake his way, and the unrighteous man his thoughts; and let him return unto the Lord, and he will have mercy upon him; and to our God, for he will abundantly pardon.

S. F. Ps. 32:10; Ps. 86:5.

"God's mercy is His pity to the needy; it reveals His attitude to those who are in need. He saw that there was no Saviour; and knowing man's need, He pitied man—that is His mercy."—THOMAS.

64

D. S. Complacency, compassion, affection, benevolence, and mercy are various aspects of the one attribute of Divine love.

(2) The Mercy and Grace of God.

While mercy and grace perhaps cannot be classified in distinctive and separate eras such as those of the Old and New Testaments, yet in their Biblical usage this is quite largely done. The term "mercy" finds its most frequent use in the Old Testament while that of "grace" is most often found in the New Testament. Mercy is often used in connection with the term "loving kindness," the one being largely negative and the other positive. The significance of both terms taken together would seem to be the equivalent for the word "grace" in the New Testament, which contains both the negative and positive aspects.

a. The Mercy of God.

It has been previously suggested that this term is largely negative in its Old Testament usage. It may also be said that it is used principally in connection with those who are in distress or misery, whether it be the distress and misery caused by sinning or suffering. Mercy has to do with the withdrawal or removal of the cause in either case.

"He is rich in mercy, abundant in goodness and truth. Thy sins are like a spark of fire that falls into the ocean of God's mercy. There is not more water in the sea than there is mercy in God."—MANTON.

Concerning suffering Lawrence Sterne has said, "God tempers the wind to the shorn lamb."

(a) The meaning of it.

The mercy of God is that principle and quality which describes His disposition and action in relation to the sinful and suffering, withholding merited penalty and relieving distress.

"God's mercy is a holy mercy, which knows how to pardon sin, not to protect it; it is a sanctuary for the penitent, not for the presumptuous."—BISHOP REYNOLDS.

"Let us take heed, for mercy is like a rainbow, which God set in the clouds to remember mankind: it shines here as long as it is not hindered; but we must never look for it after it is night, and it shines not in the other world. If we refuse mercy here, we shall have justice there."—JEREMY TAYLOR.

(b) The Scriptural fact of it.

Ps. 103:8—The Lord is merciful and gracious, slow to anger, and plenteous in mercy.

S. F. Ps. 145:8; Ps. 86:15; Ps. 62:12; Deut. 4:31.

"It is harder to get sin felt by the creature, than the burden, when felt, removed, by the hand of a forgiving God. Never was tender-hearted surgeon more willing to take up the vein, and bind up the wound of his fainting patient, than God is by His pardoning mercy to ease the troubled spirit of a mourning penitent."—GURNALL.

> "There's a wideness in God's mercy,
> Like the wideness of the sea,
> There's a kindness in His justice,
> Which is more than liberty.

65

> *There is welcome for the sinner,*
> *And more graces for the good,*
> *There is mercy with the Saviour,*
> *There is healing in His blood."*

—Faber

D. S. The Scriptures lay great emphasis upon the mercy of God; they clearly establish it as a fact in the being of God.

b. The Grace of God.

(a) The meaning of it.

Grace has been said to be an indefinable term and yet there have been many attempts to define it. This is seen by the following:

"Grace is something in God which is at the heart of all His redeeming activities, the downward stoop and reach of God, bending from the heights of His majesty, to touch and grasp our insignificance and poverty."—Phillips.

"Grace is love which passes beyond all claims to love. It is love which after fulfilling the obligations imposed by law, has an unexhausted wealth of kindness."—Dale.

"Grace—what is that? The word means, first, love in exercise to those who are below the lover, or who deserve something else; stooping love that condescends, and patient love that forgives. Then it means the gifts which such love bestows; and then it means the effect of these gifts in the beauties of character and conduct developed in the receivers."—Maclaren.

"Grace is energy. Grace is love-energy. Grace is a redeeming love-energy ministering in the unlovely, and endowing the unlovely with its own loveliness."—Jowett.

"Love has no limit or law such as Grace has. Love may exist between equals, or it may arise to those above us, or flow down to those in any way beneath us. But Grace, from its nature, has only one direction it can take. Grace always flows downward."—Alexander Whyte.

"Grace is love at work in Redemption; love 'carrying on' in spite of sin; love reaching down to the level of the unworthy and guilty."—Champion.

The Grace of God is His unmerited and ill-merited and unmeritable favor by which deserved penalty and consequence are withheld from, and all positive blessings bestowed upon, the repentant believer.

"Grace is an English word used in the New Testament to translate the Greek word, 'Charis,' which means 'favor,' without recompense or equivalent. If there is any compensatory act or payment, however slight or inadequate, it is 'no more grace'—'charis.' When used to denote a certain attitude or act of God toward man, it is therefore of the very essence of the matter that human merit or deserving is utterly excluded. In grace God acts out from Himself, toward those who have deserved, not His favor, but His wrath. In the structure of the Epistle to the Romans grace does not enter, could not enter, till a whole race, without one single exception, stand guilty and speechless before God."—C. I. Scofield.

"Grace, then, characterizes the present age, as law characterized the age from Sinai to Calvary. 'For the law was given by Moses, but grace and truth came by Jesus Christ.' And this contrast between law as a method and grace as a method runs through the whole Biblical revelation concerning grace. It is,

66

however, of the most vital moment to observe that Scripture never, in any dispensation, mingles these two principles. Law always has a place and work distinct and wholly diverse from that of grace."—SCOFIELD.

Law and grace contrasted (C. I. SCOFIELD).

LAW	GRACE
God prohibiting, and requiring. Ex. 20:1–17.	God beseeching, and bestowing. II Cor. 5:18, 21.
A Ministry of condemnation. Rom. 3:19.	A ministry of forgiveness. Eph. 1:7.
Curses. Gal. 3:10.	Redeems from that curse. Gal. 3:13; Deut. 21:22, 23.
Kills. Rom. 7:9, 11.	Makes alive. John 10:10.
Shuts every mouth before God. Rom. 3:19.	Opens every mouth to praise Him. Rom. 10:9–10. Ps. 107:2.
Puts a great and guilty distance between man and God. Ex. 20:18, 19.	Makes guilty man nigh to God. Eph. 2:13.
Says, "An eye for an eye, and a tooth for a tooth." Ex. 21:24.	Says, "Resist not evil, but whosoever shall smite thee on thy right cheek, turn to him the other also." Matt. 5:39.
Says, "Do and live." Luke 10:28.	Says, "Believe and live." John 5:24.
Utterly condemns the best man. Phil. 3:4, 9.	Freely justifies the worst. Luke 23:34; Rom. 5:6. I Tim. 1:15; I Cor. 6:9, 11.
Is a system of probation. Gal. 3:23–25.	Is a system of favor. Eph. 2:4–5.
Stones an adulteress. Deut. 22:21.	Says, "Neither do I condemn thee." John 8:1, 11.
The sheep dies for the shepherd. I Sam. 7:9. Lev. 4:32.	The shepherd dies for the sheep. John 10:11.

"Grace always means two things, God's favor and God's gift; the attitude and the action of God; the attitude of God as expressed in His action. As some one has said, 'It is the self-moving love of God which is in constant exercise.' "—W. H. GRIFFITH THOMAS.

(b) The Scriptural fact of it.

Eph. 2:8–10—For by grace are ye saved through faith; and that not of yourselves; it is the gift of God; Not of works, lest any man should boast. For we are his workmanship, created in Christ Jesus unto good works, which God hath before ordained that we should walk in them.

S. F. II Cor. 9:14; I Peter 4:10; Acts 20:24, 32; Tit. 2:11; Rom. 11:6.

D. S. The Bible teaches that God's salvation work for us, in us, and through us is by grace, i.e., it is begun in grace, continued by grace and completed through grace.

c. The correlated manifestation of God's mercy and grace.

"The way to heaven lies, not over a toll-bridge, but over a free-bridge; even the unmerited grace of God in Christ Jesus. Grace finds us beggars, and always leaves us debtors."—Toplady.

(a) Mercy pardons; Grace justifies.

I Tim. 1:13—Who was before a blasphemer, and a persecutor, and injurious: but I obtained mercy, because I did it ignorantly in unbelief.

S. A. Ex. 34:7.

Rom. 3:24—Being justified freely by his grace through the redemption that is in Christ Jesus.

(b) Mercy removes the guilt and penalty; Grace imputes righteousness.

Prov. 28:13—He that covereth his sins shall not prosper; but whoso confesseth and forsaketh them shall have mercy.

Rom. 4:5—But to him that worketh not, but believeth on him that justifieth the ungodly, his faith is counted for righteousness.

(c) Mercy saves from peril; Grace imparts a new nature.

Ps. 6:4—Return, O Lord, deliver my soul; oh save me for thy mercies' sake.

Eph. 2:8-10—For by grace are ye saved through faith; and that not of yourselves; it is the gift of God; Not of works, lest any man should boast. For we are his workmanship, created in Christ Jesus unto good works, which God hath before ordained that we should walk in them.

(d) Mercy rescues its object; Grace transforms him.

Luke 10:33, 37—But a certain Samaritan, as he journeyed, came where he was and when he saw him, he had compassion on him, And he said, He that shewed mercy on him. Then said Jesus unto him, Go, and do thou likewise.

Tit. 2:11-12—For the grace of God that bringeth salvation hath appeared to all men, Teaching us that, denying ungodliness and worldly lusts, we should live soberly, righteously, and godly, in this present world.

S. A. Eph. 4:22-23.

D. S. Mercy and grace have their manifestation in connection with the believer's salvation, those of mercy being largely negative, while those of grace are positive.

C. The Counsel of God.

"Who worketh all things after the counsel of His own will." (Eph. 1:11, l.c.)

The counsel of God is that eternal scheme of all things adopted by the Divine Mind which embraces all His original designs, including everything in the creative and redemptive program of God, and involving or embracing the free actions of men.

As viewed by man, there are many aspects of the Divine Counsel but it is only because the counsel covers a multitude of things which are in reality but infinitesimal parts of an infinite whole, and embraces not only effects but also causes; not only the ends to be secured but also the means needful to secure them.

"Plan and purpose as we may, the plans and purposes will turn only to the final end which God has predetermined."—HENRY.

I. The Plan of God in Relation to the Universe and Men.

The Scriptures reveal a definite design on the part of God concerning the universe and men.

"Preknowledge implies fixity, and fixity implies decree . . . . . From eternity God foresaw all the events of the universe as fixed and certain. This fixity and certainty could not have had its ground either in blind fate or in the variable wills of men, since neither of these had an existence. It could have had its ground in nothing outside the Divine Mind, for in eternity nothing existed besides the Divine Mind. But for this fixity there must have been a cause; if anything in the future was fixed, something must have fixed it. This fixity could have had its ground only in the plan and purpose of God. In fine, if God foresaw the future as certain, it must have been because there was something in Himself which made it certain, or, in other words, because He had decreed it."—STRONG.

1. The Meaning of It.

By the "Plan of God" is meant that predetermined arrangement by which He renders certain all things pertaining to the universe in time and eternity. This plan comprehends all things that ever were or will be in their causes, conditions, successions and relations, and determines their certain realization. The plan of God includes both the efficacious and the permissive aspects of God's will. All things are included in God's plan, but some things He causes and others He permits. In the efficacious aspect of God's plan we include those events which He has determined to effect through secondary causes or by His own immediate agency. In the permissive aspect of God's plan we include those events which He has determined to allow independent free agents to effect.

2. The Scriptural Fact of It.

Isa. 40:13, 14—Who hath directed the Spirit of the Lord, or being his counsellor hath taught him? With whom took he counsel, and who instructed him, and taught him in the path of judgment, and taught him knowledge, and shewed to him the way of understanding?

S. F. Eph. 1:5, 9, 11.

The plan of God is based upon His sovereignty and is the expression of the good pleasure of His will. (Phil. 2:13)

3. The Scope of It.

(1) All things in general.

Eph. 1:11—In whom also we have obtained an inheritance, being predestinated according to the purpose of him who worketh all things after the counsel of His own will.

Isa. 14:26, 27—This is the purpose that is purposed upon the whole earth; and this is the hand that is stretched out upon all the nations. For the Lord of hosts hath purposed, and who shall disannul it? and his hand is stretched out, and who shall turn it back?

Isa. 46:10, 11—Declaring the end from the beginning, and from ancient times the things that are not yet done, saying, My counsel shall stand, and I will do all my pleasure; Calling a ravenous bird from the east, the man that executeth my counsel from a far country; yea, I have spoken it, I will also bring it to pass; I have purposed it, I will also do it.

Dan. 4:35—And all the inhabitants of the earth are reputed as nothing: and he doeth according to his will in the army of heaven, and among the inhabitants of the earth: and none can stay his hand, or say unto him, What doest thou?

D. S. The Scriptures declare that all things are included under the Divine plan, that He worketh all things after the counsel of his own will.

(2) Things in particular.

    a. Natural.

    (a) The permanence of the material universe.

Ps. 119:89-91—For ever, O Lord, thy word is settled in heaven. Thy faithfulness is unto all generations: thou hast established the earth, and it abideth. They continue this day according to thine ordinances: for all are thy servants.

    (b) The affairs of nations.

Acts 17:26—And hath made of one blood all nations of men for to dwell on all the face of the earth, and hath determined the times before appointed, and the bounds of their habitation.

    (c) The period of human life.

Job 14:5—Seeing his days are determined, the number of his months are with thee, thou hast appointed his bounds that he cannot pass.

Job 14:14—If a man die, shall he live again? all the days of my appointed time will I wait, till my change come.

    (d) The manner of death.

John 21:19—This spake he, signifying by what death he should glorify God.

    (e) Human actions, good and evil.

Eph. 2:10—For we are his workmanship, created in Christ Jesus unto good works, which God hath before ordained that we should walk in them.

Gen. 50:20—But as for you, ye thought evil against me; but God meant it unto good, to bring to pass, as it is this day, to save much people alive.

    b. Spiritual.

    (a) Man's salvation.

I Cor. 2:7—But we speak the wisdom of God in a mystery, even the hidden wisdom, which God ordained before the world unto our glory.

Eph. 3:10—To the intent that now unto the principalities and powers in heavenly places might be known by the church the manifold wisdom of God.

S. F. I Peter 1:1, 2; II Tim. 1:9; Acts 13:48; Eph. 1:4, 5.

    (b) The Kingdom of Christ.

Ps. 2:6-8—Yet have I set my king upon my holy hill of Zion. I will declare the decree: the Lord hath said unto me, Thou art my Son; this day have I begotten thee. Ask of me, and I shall give thee the heathen for thine inheritance, and the uttermost parts of the earth for thy possession.

Matt. 25:34—Then shall the King say unto them on his right hand, Come, ye blessed of my Father, inherit the kingdom prepared for you from the foundation of the world.

(c) The work of God in and through believers.

Phil. 2:12, 13—Wherefore, my beloved, as ye have always obeyed, not as in my presence only, but now much more in my absence, work out your own salvation with fear and trembling. For it is God which worketh in you both to will and to do of his good pleasure.

S. F. Eph. 2:10.

"The Apostle here tells that it is God who works in us even to will: that there is not a holy desire, not a good counsel, any more than there can be a just work, which does not proceed from Him, which does not originate in Him. Go back as far as we may into the origination of our acts, we can never find the point at which God was not present, at which God was not engaged, in the production of any one action which was at all right and good. As it is with the salvation of a soul, that in all true doctrine the final result is referred back to God's fore-knowledge and God's predestination and God's calling, while the fullest scope is given to man's free agency and to man's free will, so it is with the separate acts of such as shall be saved: whatever is good in them, if it be but in wish, in desire, in will, is entirely of God: left to themselves, they could no more purpose right than do it: it is God who worketh in them both to will and to do of His good pleasure."—VAUGHAN.

D. S. According to the teaching of the Scripture all things in particular are included in the Divine plan; not one thing is omitted.

This Divine plan is in harmony with God's knowledge, wisdom and benevolence. A universe with no fixed plan would be irrational and appalling. Dr. A. J. Gordon compares such a supposed situation to that of an express train plunging on in the darkness without headlights or engineer, and with no certainty that the next moment it might not plunge into the abyss.

> "Have faith! where'er thy bark is driven—
> The calms disport, the tempest's mirth,
> Know this! God rules the host of heaven,
> The inhabitants of earth."
>
> —SCHILLER.

II. The Purpose of God in Relation to Redemption.

The purpose of God in redemption is one aspect of God's counsel. It is that phase of it which relates to the salvation of men. "Having predestinated us unto the adoption of children by Jesus Christ to Himself, according to the good pleasure of His will," Eph. 1:5. God's purpose in relation to men seems to be in the following order: (1) to create; (2) to permit his fall; (3) to provide salvation in Christ sufficient for the needs of all; (4) to secure the actual acceptance of this salvation on the part of some, i.e., to make them subjects of elective grace.

1. The Meaning of It.

By the purpose of God in redemption is meant that Divine determination from eternity to select certain individuals from among the sinful race of men, upon whom to bestow the special grace of His Holy Spirit, which would effectually bring them to repentance and faith in Christ.

2. The Scriptural Fact of It.

The Scriptures forbid us to find the ground of this purpose concerning man's redemption in the moral actions of men either before or after regeneration and confine us merely to the sovereign will and mercy of God. In fact, they teach the doctrine of personal choice or election on the part of God. Rom. 9:9-13.

"If men are chosen by God upon the foresight of faith, or not chosen till they have faith, they are not so much God's elect, as God their elect; they choose God by faith, before God chooses them by love: it would not be the faith of those already chosen, but the faith of those chosen after their faith. But this is a reversal of the truth: Election is the cause of faith, and not faith of election; fire is the cause of heat, and not heat the cause of the fire; the sun is the cause of the day, and not the day the cause of the rising of the sun. If the foresight of what works might be done by His creatures was the motive of His choosing them, why did He not choose the demons to redemption, who could have done Him better service, by the strength of their nature, than the whole mass of Adam's posterity?"—CHARNOCK.

This fact is established by the teaching of the following passages of Scriptures:

Acts 13:48—And when the Gentiles heard this, they were glad, and glorified the word of the Lord: and as many as were ordained to eternal life believed.

Rom. 8:28-30—And we know that all things work together for good to them that love God, to them who are the called according to His purpose. For whom he did foreknow, he also did predestinate to be conformed to the image of His Son, that He might be the firstborn among many brethren. Moreover whom he did predestinate, them he also called: and whom he called, them he also justified: and whom he justified, them he also glorified.

John 6:37—All that the Father giveth me shall come to me; and him that cometh to me I will in no wise cast out.

S. F. John 6:44, 65; Rom. 9:22-24.

D. S. The Scriptures teach that God has from eternity purposed to save certain individuals, making them objects of his favor, giving them to His Son in a Divinely effected union by the regenerating grace of His Holy Spirit.

3. The Application of It.

The purpose of God in redemption or His elective grace has a two-fold application.

(1) In a general invitation or call.

a. The proof of it.

Isa. 45:22—Look unto me, and be ye saved, all the ends of the earth: for I am God, and there is none else.

72

Isa. 55:6—Seek ye the Lord while he may be found, call ye upon him while he is near.

S. F. Matt. 11:28; John 12:32.

b. The content of it.

The general invitation or call includes:

(a) The declaration of the plan of salvation: I Cor. 15:3, 4; Rom. 1:16.

(b) The declaration of the sinner's obligation to repent and believe: Acts 17:30, 31; John 3:16–18.

(c) The declaration of impelling motives such as fear or hope, remorse or gratitude: Jude 23; II Cor. 5:11, 14; Rom. 2:4; II Cor. 7:10; Rom. 8:24.

(d) The declaration of conditional acceptance promised: John 1:12; II Cor. 4:3, 4.

c. The medium of it—the Word of God.

"The Law of God, as impressed upon the moral constitution of man, is natural, and is inseparable from man as a moral, responsible agent (Rom. 1:19, 20; 2:14–15). But the Gospel is no part of that natural law. It is of grace, not of nature, and it can be made known to us only by a special and supernatural revelation. This is further evident, first, because the Scriptures declare that a knowledge of the Word is essential to salvation; (II Tim. 3:15; Rom. 10:14–17), and, second, because they also declare that those who neglect the Word, either written or preached, are guilty of the eminent sin of rejecting all possibility of salvation (Matt. 11:21–22; Heb. 2:3)."—A. A. Hodge.

d. The objects of it—all men indiscriminately.

(a) The express declaration of Scripture.

Matt. 22:14—For many are called, but few are chosen.

(b) The command to preach the gospel to every creature.

Mark 16:15—And he said unto them, go ye into all the world, and preach the gospel to every creature.

(c) The promise to every one who accepts it.

Rev. 22:17—And the Spirit and the bride say, Come. And let him that is athirst come. And whosoever will, let him take the water of life freely.

(d) The judgment pronounced upon those who reject it.

John 3:17, 18, 19—For God sent not his Son into the world to condemn the world; but that the world through him might be saved. He that believeth on him is not condemned; but he that believeth not is condemned already, because he hath not believed in the name of the only begotten Son of God. And this is the condemnation, that light is come into the world, and men loved darkness rather than light because their deeds were evil.

"It (the general invitation) is addressed to the non-elect equally with the elect, because it is equally their duty and interest to accept the gospel, because the provisions of salvation are equally suited to their case, and abundantly sufficient for all, and because God intends that its benefits shall actually accrue to every one who accepts it."—A. A. Hodge.

(2) In the effectual invitation or call.

a. The meaning of it.

By the effectual invitation or call is meant that exercise of divine power

73

upon the soul, immediate, spiritual and supernatural, which communicates a new spiritual life and nature, and thus makes a new mode of spiritual activity possible and desirable. Repentance, faith, trust, hope, love, are purely and simply the sinner's own acts; but as such are possible and desirable only in virtue of the change wrought in the moral condition of his faculties by the recreative power of God. At this place three erroneous views are noted:

The Pelagians deny original sin, and maintain that right and wrong are qualities attaching only to executive acts of the will. They therefore assert: 1st, that man has full ability as much to cease from sin at any time as to continue in its practice; 2nd, that the Holy Spirit produces no inward change in the heart of the subject, except as He is the author of the Scriptures, and as the Scriptures present moral truths and motives, which of their own nature exert a moral influence upon the soul.

The Semi-Pelagian view holds that grace is necessary to enable a man successfully to return to God and live. Yet from the very nature of the human will man must first of himself desire to be free from sin, and to choose God as his chief good, when he may expect God's aid in carrying his desire into effect.

The Arminians admit the doctrine of man's total depravity; in consequence of which man is utterly unable to do anything aright in the unaided exercises of his natural faculties. Nevertheless, as Christ died equally for every man, sufficient grace, enabling its subject to do all that is required of him, is granted to all. This sufficient grace becomes efficient only when the co-operation and appropriation of the sinner is secured.

b. The proof of the effectual invitation.

(a) There are passages which distinguish the Spirit's special influence from the general invitation contained in the Word.

John 6:45, 64, 65—It is written in the prophets, And they shall be all taught of God. Every man therefore that hath heard, and hath learned of the Father, cometh unto me. But there are some of you that believe not. For Jesus knew from the beginning who they were that believed not, and who should betray Him. And He said, Therefore said I unto you, that no man can come unto me, except it were given unto him of my Father.

I Thes. 1:5, 6—For our gospel came not unto you in word only, but also in power, and in the Holy Ghost, and in much assurance; as ye know what manner of men we were among you for your sake. And ye became followers of us, and of the Lord, having received the word in much affliction, with joy of the Holy Ghost.

S. F. John 3:5, 6.

(b) Those passages which teach that the Spirit's influence is necessary to the reception of the truth.

Eph. 1:17—That the God of our Lord Jesus Christ, the Father of Glory, may give unto you the spirit of wisdom and revelation in the knowledge of him.

S. F. I Cor. 2:11, 12; Phil. 1:29.

"The sun may shine in the firmament, and shine in vain, when a man is blind, but when his eyes are opened, then he discerns the light that shines around him,—so it is exactly with us,—though th' Sun of Righteousness shines be-

74

fore us, though Jesus Christ is evidently set forth, crucified among us,—yet, our natural understandings are blinded, and we require the illumination of the Holy Spirit to open our eyes, that we may discern Christ at first as our salvation, and then we need increasing light, to behold more and more clearly the character of our Lord and Saviour."—M'GHEE.

(c) Those passages which ascribe the credit to God for man's repentance and faith.

Eph. 2:8—For by grace are ye saved through faith; and that not of yourselves; it is the gift of God.

S. F. Phil. 2:13; II Tim. 2:25; Acts 11:18.

(d) Those passages which make distinctions between the subjects of the two calls.

aa. Of the subjects of the general invitation it is said, "Many be called but few chosen" (Matt. 20:16).

Of the subjects of the effectual invitation it is said, "Whom he called them he also justified" (Rom. 8:30).

bb. Of the subjects of the first it is said, "Because I have called, and ye have refused" (Prov. 1:24).

Of the subjects of the second it is said, "Every man therefore who hath learned of the Father cometh unto me" (John 6:45).

(e) There is an absolute necessity for such an effectual, spiritual call, for man by nature is "blind" and "dead in trespasses and sins" (I Cor. 2:14; II Cor. 4:4; Eph. 2:1).

D. S. The Scriptures teach that to certain individuals there is given an inward experience through the power of the Holy Spirit, imparting to them a sense of personal sin, inclining and enabling them to turn in repentance from sin and in faith to Christ, i.e., they teach an effectual invitation or call.

4. The Objections to It.

(1) It seems unjust to those not included in God's redemptive purpose.

Reply: God discriminates not merely between men as God's creatures, but between them as sinners and rebels against Himself. The inclusion of some in His redemptive purpose means nothing more or less than that pure justice is meted out to the others, while these are the recipients of mercy. God's sovereignty permits Him to emphasize either His justice or His mercy. It is not a case of a father showing partiality toward some of His children but of a sovereign showing leniency to some among condemned criminals. The pardoning of one convict by the governor does not necessitate the pardoning of all (Matt. 20:13, 15; Rom. 9:20). This action is not to be regarded as partiality, for there is nothing in any unredeemed man to call forth God's favor. The reason for our being chosen is not in us, but in Him. The principle of selection is operative in every realm of life, but is not to be explained in the spiritual realm by ascribing it to partiality any more than it is in the natural (Ps. 44:3; Isa. 45:1, 4, 5; Luke 4:25–27; I Cor. 4:7).

(2) It seems to make God arbitrary and non-rational.

Reply: This is not true. It rather represents God as exercising His sovereignty according to infinite wisdom in ways we do not understand. To deny to God the possibility of such a choice is to deny Him the exercise of His sovereign personality. And to deny that God has reason in His choice would be to impugn His wisdom. A possible reason for His choice is suggested in the following passages: I Tim. 1:16; I Tim. 1:13; Acts 9:15, 16; Eph. 2:4–8; Rom. 9:22–24.

(3) It seems to encourage men to be immoral by representing salvation as not dependent upon character or conduct.

Reply: God's redemptive purpose is always accomplished in connection with character and conduct and is represented as effecting holiness in both (I Peter 1:2; Eph. 1:4–6; Titus 2:11–14).

(4) It would discourage effort on the part of the unsaved to obtain salvation.

Reply: The fact that the objects of this redemptive purpose are known only to God refutes this argument. On the contrary, it furnishes reason for encouragement, and therefore stimulates effort. Without this purpose and its effectual accomplishment all would be lost. While it humbles the sinner by revealing to him his helpless dependence upon the sovereign mercy of God, it should encourage him to know that some will be saved and that he certainly may be saved through meeting the simple conditions of repentance and faith. This aspect of the truth should also give encouragement to Christian workers; for it gives them the assurance that God is going to save some in spite of all the adverse conditions and circumstances, and in spite of all the opposition of men and demons. Acts 18:9, 10; Rom. 3:11.

(5) It seems to imply that the sentence of eternal death and damnation is pronounced upon those not included in the redemptive purpose.

Reply: God's purpose in relation to the sinner's punishment is not a positive one like His redemption. It is rather permissive, i.e., God purposes to permit the sinner to go his own self-chosen way to his merited doom (Hosea 11:8 and 4:17; Rom. 9:22, 23; I Peter 2:8; Matt. 25:34, 41; II Pet. 3:9).

Study Questions on the Doctrine of God

1. Show from Whitelaw's note what is involved in the question of God's existence.
2. Name the various classes for whom the Bible is not intended and explain the positions taken by each.
3. Give the gist of the argument for the existence of God based upon universal belief, using quotation given.
4. Show in general how the argument from cause and effect supports belief in the existence of God, giving illustrations as quoted.
5. Give proofs offered by the application of the principle of cause and effect to the material universe: (a) Intelligence in nature (b) Personality in man (c) Man's mental and moral nature.
6. Show how the evident harmony of belief in God with known facts substantiates that belief.
7. Discuss the argument for the existence of God based upon the content of the Scriptures.
8. Give the definition of the term "attribute" with illustration.
9. Define the attributes of God in general and His natural and moral attributes in particular.
10. Give the definition of life showing two elements involved therein.
11. Give D. S. showing life to be a divine attribute and quote one passage of Scripture.
12. Give D. S. under the demonstration of the fact of life as a Divine attribute, quoting one passage of Scripture.
13. Discuss the false teaching refuted by the truth of God's spirituality, showing contrast between matter and spirit.
14. Define God's spirituality and show how He is to be apprehended, quoting one passage of Scripture.
15. Give D. S. showing the Scriptural fact of God's spirituality and quote one passage.
16. Show how the Scriptural fact of God's spirituality is illuminated by the teaching, both of the Old and New Testaments, giving D. S. with each.
17. Give the three-fold answer to the question concerning the image and likeness of God, quoting Scripture where given.
18. What is meant by the physical terms which are applied to God as though He were a man? Discuss note.
19. How are the passages which state that man saw God to be reconciled with those which declare that God has not been and cannot be seen? Give general answer with illustration. Further consideration: (a) Quote one passage of Scripture showing that spirit may be manifested in visible form. (b) In what form did God manifest Himself in the Old Testament and what clear distinction is made in connection therewith? Give one Scriptural illustration where "The Angel of the Lord" is clearly identified with God.
20. Which person of the Trinity was manifested in "The Angel of the Lord"?
21. Name and explain the error which the truth of the personality of God opposes.

22. Define and discuss the meaning of personality.

23. Give the meaning of the Jehovah titles and show the personal elements revealed by each and give D. S.

24. Give one personal pronoun which teaches the personality of God, and quote a passage of Scripture containing it.

25. Give the characteristics of personality ascribed to God with D. S.

26. Give five D. S. showing the relations which God sustains to the universe and to men, quoting passages with each of them.

27. Give the discussion from the notes of the various relationships which God sustains to the universe and to men under the following headings: (a) as Creator of all things, (b) as Preserver of all things, (c) as Benefactor of all life, (d) as the Ruler and Over-Ruler in the affairs of men, (e) as the Father of His children.

28. Give the derivation and meaning of the term Tri-unity and discuss the erroneous views refuted by the truth of the Tri-unity of God.

29. Name and define the false teaching opposed by the truth of the Divine Unity.

30. Define the Unity of God making the distinction concerning that Unity as found in note.

31. Show how the fact of the Divine Unity is established from reason and revelation, quoting one passage from the latter.

32. Discuss, from the introductory note under the trinity of personality, the meaning of person as used in connection with the persons of the Godhead.

33. Define the Trinity of God.

34. Give the six-fold manner in which the doctrine of the Trinity is intimated and implied in the Old Testament with D. S.

35. Give the five-fold manner in which the doctrine of the Trinity is taught in the New Testament, with D. S.

36. Give the summary of New Testament teaching and quote a passage with each phase.

37. Give the analogies illustrating the doctrine of the Trinity and showing their limitations.

38. Discuss the error of God originating or causing Himself to be.

39. Define and discuss the meaning of the self-existence of God.

40. Quote one passage of Scripture and give D. S. under the fact of the self-existence of God.

41. Define the term "eternity."

42. Give the three-fold usage of the word "eternal," and illustrate.

43. Quote one passage of Scripture proving the fact of God's eternity and give one illustration either in prose or poetry.

44. Discuss, from the introductory note, the immutability of God in relation to the possibility of change and in relation to His natural and moral attributes.

45. Define the Immutability of God.

46. Give the negative and positive discussion of the meaning of the Divine Immutability.

47. Quote one passage of Scripture which establishes the fact of God's Immutability and give D. S.

48. How is the statement in Jonah 3:10 that God repented, to be reconciled with His Immutability? Give discussion in notes.

49. Give the two-fold answer to Objection 2 concerning God's repentance and grief, with reference to man, in Gen. 6:6.

50. Give the definition and discussion of the meaning of God's Omniscience.

51. Quote one passage of Scripture and give the D. S. showing the fact of God's Omniscience.

52. Tell what God's knowledge in general includes and quote one passage with each division.

53. Tell what God's knowledge in particular includes and quote one passage with each division.

54. Give the D. S. under the "Application" of God's Omniscience, and discuss the problem involved.

55. Give the definition and discussion of the meaning of God's Omnipotence.

56. Quote one passage of Scripture and give D. S. showing the fact of God's Omnipotence.

57. Quote one passage of Scripture and give D. S. showing the application of God's Omnipotence in the realm of nature and give gist of the discussion in notes.

58. Give the D. S. showing the application of God's Omnipotence in the realm of human experience, giving one Scriptural illustration in connection with one Bible character.

59. Quote one passage of Scripture showing the application of God's Omnipotence in relation to men in general.

60. Quote one passage of Scripture and give the D. S. showing the application of God's Omnipotence in the heavenly realms.

61. Quote one passage of Scripture and give the D. S. showing the application of God's Omnipotence in the realm of evil spirits.

62. Discuss from the introductory notes the character and manner of God's presence in all parts of the universe, i.e., of His Omnipresence.

63. Give the definition and discussion of the meaning of God's Omnipresence.

64. Quote Psa. 139:7–10 and give D. S. showing the fact of God's Omnipresence.

65. How is the teaching concerning the Omnipresence of God to be qualified?

66. Give the two-fold application of the doctrine of God's Omnipresence.

67. Give the general discussion of the importance of God's Holiness.

68. Discuss the four-fold manner in which the importance of God's Holiness is shown.

69. Give the meaning of God's Holiness, negatively and positively considered.

70. Quote a passage of Scripture and give D. S. showing the fact of God's Holiness.

71. Give the D. S. showing the four-fold manifestation of God's Holiness and quote one passage with each phase.

72. Give the four-fold application of God's Holiness.

73. Discuss, from the introductory note under the Righteousness and Justice of God, their relation to His Holiness.

74. Define the Righteousness of God.

75. Quote a passage of Scripture and give the D. S. showing the fact of God's Righteousness.

76. Define the Justice of God.

77. Quote a passage of Scripture and give the D. S. showing the fact of God's Justice.

78. Discuss the manifestations of God's Righteousness and Justice and give D. S.

79. Define the Love of God and quote one passage supporting the definition.

80. Quote one passage of Scripture establishing the fact of God's Love.

81. Give the D. S. under the objects of God's Love and quote one passage with each.

82. Give the five-fold manifestation of God's Love and quote one passage of Scripture under each.

83. Give the various aspects of God's Love.

84. Discuss the meaning of Mercy.

85. Quote one passage of Scripture and give the D. S. establishing the fact of God's Mercy.

86. Define Grace and give a brief discussion of other meanings given to the term as found in notes.

87. Give the contrasts between Law and Grace.

88. Quote one passage of Scripture and give the D. S. establishing the fact of God's Grace.

89. Give the contrastive manifestations of Mercy and Grace, quoting one passage of Scripture with each.

90. Define the Counsel of God.

91. State that which is revealed in the Scriptures concerning the Plan of God in relation to the universe and men and give the discussion from note.

92. Define and discuss the meaning of the Plan of God in relation to the universe and men.

93. Quote one passage establishing the fact of the Plan of God in relation to the universe and men; upon what is the Plan of God based and of what is it the expression?

94. Give D. S. showing that God's Plan includes all things in general and quote one passage of Scripture.

95. Give the things in particular which are included in the Plan of God under the division "Natural" and quote one passage with each.

96. Give the things in particular which are included in the Plan of God under the division "Spiritual" and quote one passage with each.

97. Give the apparent order and the meaning of the Purpose of God in relation to redemption.

98. Quote one passage of Scripture and give the D. S. establishing the Purpose of God in relation to redemption.

99. Discuss the general invitation or call under the following: (a) proof of it with one passage of Scripture, (b) content of it (four-fold), (c) medium of it, (d) objects of it (four-fold presentation).

100. Give the meaning of the effectual invitation or call and discuss the erroneous views in note.

101. Give the five-fold classification of the passages of Scripture proving the effectual invitation or call and quote one passage with each.

102. Give the contrasts found under the distinctions between the subjects of the two calls.

103. Give the D. S. under the effectual invitation or call.

104. Give the objections raised to the teaching concerning the purpose of God in redemption, with replies.

CHAPTER THREE

THE DOCTRINE OF JESUS CHRIST

(CHRISTOLOGY)

Jesus Christ is the central figure of the world's history. It cannot forget Him while it remembers history, for history is His story. To leave Him out, would be like astronomy without the stars, or like botany with the flowers forgotten. Says Bushnell: "It would be easier to untwist all the beams of light in the sky and to separate and erase one of the primary colors, than to get the character of Jesus out of the world."

The history of the race since its inception has been the history of the preparation for His coming. The Old Testament foretells His coming in type, symbol, and direct prophecy. The history of His people Israel is a story of expectation, of yearning, of preparation.

The fact of Jesus Christ is not only firmly imbedded in human history and written upon the open page of Scripture, but it is also experimentally embodied in the lives of millions of believers and interwoven in the fabric of all civilization worthy of the name.

A. The Person of Christ.

The study of the person of Christ is most important because of the vital relation which He sustains to Christianity: a relation such as is sustained by the founders of no other religions to the religions which they have founded. You may have Confucianism without Confucius; Buddhism without Buddha; Mohammedanism without Mohammet; Mormonism without Joseph Smith; Christian Science without Mary Baker Eddy; Millennial Dawnism without Russell; but you cannot have Christianity without Christ; for, strictly speaking, Christianity is Christ and Christ is Christianity. It is not primarily a religion, it is a life and the life is His life made living in men. Christ in you "the hope of glory."

"Christianity can no more be compared with other cults than Jesus Christ can be compared with other persons. Christ is the incomparable One; He stands as far above men as the heavens are above the earth. So also is Christianity incomparable. It stands on a plane as far removed from the plane of human religions as the East is removed from the West.

"The Word of God is the basis of Christianity. That Word is Christ. From

83

Genesis through Revelation, the Scriptures present the Lord Jesus. On the Emmaus road Christ began with Moses and in the prophets and in the Psalms He opened up the things concerning Himself.

"Thus in Christianity, whether in salvation from sin's curse or in salvation from sin's power or in salvation from sin's presence, it is all made possible in and through Christ.

"Even in the line of Ethics, the ethics of Christianity are incomparably higher than the ethics of other religions. Their ethics are possible of attainment; the ethics of Christ are impossible, i.e., the latter are impossible apart from the Christ who gave them. No one can, for instance, live the life outlined in the Beatitudes or the life outlined in the Book of Philippians, apart from the indwelling and the empowering Christ."— NEIGHBOR.

The Scriptures set forth the person of Christ as the central theme of the message given to men down through the ages to the present time.

It was the theme of the message of the prophets of old.
(Acts 3:20—Comp. Acts 10:43.)

It was the theme of the message of the Apostles.
(Acts 5:41–42. See also Acts 9:19–20).

It was the theme of the message for the Jew.
(Acts 17:1–3.)

It was the theme of the message preached to the Samaritans.
(Acts 8:5.)

It was the theme of the message preached to the Gentiles.
(Gal. 1:15–16.)

It is the theme of the Gospel we are commanded to preach today.
(Mark 16:15; Rom. 1:1–3; I Cor. 15:1–4.)

God's anathema is upon those who preach any other gospel.
(Gal. 1:6–9; I Cor. 16:22.)

The statement "Our message is Jesus Christ" is the united testimony of Christian leaders from all parts of the world for nineteen centuries. In the providence of God, other men might have communicated the message, replacing Moses, and Aaron, David and Isaiah, Peter and Paul, without intrinsically changing it. But not so concerning Christ, the theme of the message. Without Him, Christianity would not be what it is. Any such change in the prominence given the person of Christ would rob it of its divine realities.

I. The Humanity of Jesus Christ.

Jesus Christ was the son of man, as he proclaimed Himself to be. As such He is the representative of all humanity. In Him all the lines of our common humanity converge.

"He was 'Son of Man,' as alone realizing all which was contained in the idea of men, as the second Adam, the head and representative of the race —the one true and perfect flower, which ever unfolded itself of the root and stock of humanity. Claiming this title as His own, He witnessed against opposite poles of error concerning His person, the Ebionite, to

84

which the exclusive title 'Son of David' might have led; and the Gnostic, which denied the reality of the human nature that bore it."—TRENCH.

"Christ is in and of the race, born of a woman, living in the line of humanity, subject to human conditions, an integral part . . . . . of the world's history."—BUSHNELL.

His humanity is shown:

1. By His human parentage.

In his birth, Jesus Christ submitted to the conditions of a human life and a human body; He became humanity's seed by a human birth.

(1) Made of a woman.

Gal. 4:4—But when the fulness of the time was come, God sent forth his Son, made of a woman, made under the law.

Matt. 1:18—Now the birth of Jesus Christ was on this wise. When as his mother Mary was espoused to Joseph, before they came together, she was found with Child of the Holy Ghost.

S. F. Matt. 2:11; Matt. 12:47; John 2:1; Heb. 10:5.

At this place it is apropos to deal with the Virgin Birth of Jesus Christ. Let us attend to some current objections.

Objection 1. The accounts of the Virgin Birth in Matthew and Luke were added centuries after the Gospels had been written.

Reply—"The chapters in Matthew and Luke, in which the record of the Virgin Birth appears, are found in all unmutilated manuscripts of the New Testament—there are many manuscripts—but from none are these chapters omitted—and they are found in all versions and translations of the manuscripts known to be genuine."—SUTTON.

"It is true that the Ebionites, as they were commonly called, possessed a gospel based upon Matthew from which the chapters on the nativity were absent. But this was not the real Gospel of Matthew: it was at best a mutilated and corrupted formula. The genuine Gospel, as the manuscripts attest, always had these chapters."—ORR.

"No copy of the Gospel of Matthew and no copy of the Gospel of Luke has ever omitted it. There are thousands upon thousand of manuscripts, and also many versions of the New Testament, carrying us back to the middle of the second century of the Christian era, but every one of them contains, and always has contained, these records of the Virgin Birth just as we have them in our English Bible today."—GRAY.

The Apostles' Creed is known to have been in existence in the early part of the second century and we quote, "Born of the Holy Spirit and the Virgin Mary."

Within sixty years after the death of Christ, His followers were talking and writing about his Virgin Birth. Ignatius of Antioch, a disciple of the Apostles, said: "Hidden from the prince of this world were the virginity of Mary, and her child-bearing . . . . . I give glory to Jesus Christ, the God who bestowed such wisdom upon you; for I have perceived that you are established in faith immovable, firmly persuaded as touching our Lord, that He is truly of the race of David according to the flesh, but Son of God by divine will and power, truly born of a virgin and baptized by John."

Objection 2. There are contradictions between the stories of Matthew and Luke of the Virgin Birth in relation to the genealogical record.

Reply—Matthew tells the story from Joseph's point of view and Luke tells it from Mary's point of view, and what one omits the other supplies, one being supplementary to the other. Luke goes more into detail than Matthew, for Mary knew more about the sacred mystery than Joseph. Both, however, agree that Jesus was born of a Virgin.

Many have said that there was a contradiction in the genealogy of Luke 3:23. The objection to this passage is that, while Matthew says that Joseph was the son of Jacob, Luke says that he was the son of Heli, and in what sense could he be both of Jacob and Heli? "He could not be by natural generation the son of both Jacob and Heli? But in Luke it is not said that Heli begat Joseph, so that the natural explanation is that Joseph was the son-in-law of Heli, who was, like himself, a descendent of David. That, in that case, he should be called son of Heli, would be in accord with Jewish usage."—Scofield.

Both Luke and Matthew were careful not to say that Jesus was the natural son of Joseph. Matthew has a periphrasis to avoid this very idea. Jacob begat Joseph, the husband of Mary, of whom was born Jesus who is called Christ, while Luke inserts the clause: "Being as was supposed the son of Joseph." Thus, it is seen that the common objection to the name of Joseph appearing in the genealogy as his father, if he were not the father of Jesus, is invalidated.

Objection 3. The Virgin Birth of Christ is so momentous that it would have been a subject of revelation on His part if it had been a historic fact.

Reply—Regarding our Lord's silence in respect to His Virgin Birth, it is presumptive to speculate on what He should or should not have said. John said his book contains only a mere fragment of our Lord's words and actions. Christ also assured His disciples that He had many things to say unto them but they could not bear them then. If this argument from the silence of Jesus is admissible, we must take into account the fact that our Lord who was doubtless an ideal member of Joseph's household, never referred to Joseph as His father, so far as the records show, though He did refer to Mary as His mother (John 19:26).

If the story of His Virgin Birth had been untrue, Christ would likely have denied it, as such a story would have cast serious reflection upon the good name of His mother. This argument from silence should carry no weight. Suffice to say that the sacred story had become current in our Lord's day. Elizabeth, the mother of John the Baptist, knew it (Luke 1:39-45), and gradually it became the common possession of all the disciples. So stupendous and glorious a fact could not long be concealed.

Objection 4. The silence of John, Mark and Paul concerning the Virgin Birth cannot be accounted for.

Reply—A deadly heresy had arisen in John's day—"a denial that Jesus Christ had come in the flesh," and John wrote his gospel to refute that heresy. With one stroke of his pen, John begins to trace the divine descent of our Lord back beyond Adam, back before the morning stars sang together, before worlds were made and systems framed, back into eternity, and says: "In the beginning was the Word," the Logos, the active Agent of Almighty God. John predicates in the first verse, His eternity, His unity with God, and His Deity, and proceeds to show throughout his gospel the glory, authority, and power of the eternal Son of God. The whole book assumes a miraculous birth.

"The objection on which much stress is laid is the silence on the Virgin Birth in the remaining Gospels, and other parts of the New Testament. This, it is held, conclusively proves that the Virgin Birth was not known in the earliest Christian circles, and was a legend of later origin. As respects the Gospels—Mark and John—the objection would only apply if it were the design of these Gospels to narrate, as the others do, the circumstances of the nativity. But this was evidently not their design. Both Mark and John knew that Jesus had a human birth—an infancy and early life—and that His mother was called Mary, but of deliberate purpose they tell us nothing about it. Mark begins his Gospel with Christ's entrance in His public ministry, and says nothing of the period before, especially of how Jesus came to be called 'the Son of God' (Mark 1:1). John traces the divine descent of Jesus and tells us that the 'Word became flesh' (John 1:14); but how this miracle of becoming flesh was wrought he does not say. It did not lie within his plan. He knew the church tradition on the subject: he had the Gospels narrating the birth of Jesus from the Virgin in his hands: and he takes the knowledge of their teaching for granted. To speak of contradiction in a case like this is out of the question."—ORR.

Paul's purpose in writing was particularly to make clear the fact of the atonement, resurrection, and second advent, consequently he passes over all the incidents in Christ's life. It would be as reasonable to argue that Paul did not believe in our Lord's miracles as to state that he placed no credence in His Virgin Birth for he was silent as to both. Paul knew that the greatest support of the Virgin Birth was found in the resurrection, therefore he built his argument on the matchless character, mediation, risen life, intercession, and spiritual presence and power of Christ, as seen in His ever-expanding church. All these facts pre-supposed the Incarnation. That Paul clearly assumed the Virgin Birth is shown by the following passages: Phil. 2:7; Rom. 8:3 and Gal. 4:4-5.

Objection 5. The disciples were divided in their belief concerning the Virgin Birth of Christ, some holding Him to be the Son of Joseph, others believing Him to be the Son of God. As they were not agreed among themselves, why should it be considered a subject of great concern today?

Reply—This objection is based upon the following passages of Scripture: Matt. 13:55—"Is not this the carpenter's son?" These words were spoken by the Jews who, when they saw the wonderful works of our Lord, were unable to account for Him on natural grounds, therefore they asked this question. There is no evidence here to show that the disciples held to any such tradition. John 1:45—"We have found Him of whom Moses in the law and the prophets did write, Jesus of Nazareth, the son of Joseph." These words are a quotation, from Philip, who had just decided to become a disciple of our Lord, and who, up to this time, had not heard of the Incarnation, hence they cannot lend support to the claim that there was held by our Lord's disciples a tradition that He was the son of Joseph. John 6:42—"And they said: 'Is not this Jesus, the son of Joseph, whose father and mother we know?'" These words were spoken by the Jews who were not disciples, and were occasioned by our Lord's remarkable discourse on the bread of life. It was at this that the unbelieving Jews murmured: "Because, as He said, 'I am the bread which came down from heaven,' and they said, 'Is not this the son of Joseph?'" Our Lord said that unbelief can never accept the fact of the Incarnation, for this truth is morally exclusive from all, except those who are the children of faith. Judging from these passages, there is no ground for the view that there existed a tradition among the disciples that our Lord was the natural son of Joseph.

Objection 6. The Virgin Birth, a suggestion from the pagan myths of incarnate gods, was adopted by the disciples to magnify Jesus.

Reply—The old pagan myths held that gods could come to earth and become incarnate in men. Their conception as to this is perhaps the most base and revolting thing we find in literature, ancient or modern. A pagan god comes to a pure family and takes the wife, or daughter, the one which best suits his depravity, and the offspring is a super-man, a god-man, a hero. Yet, no pagan writer claimed virgin birth for any one of their heroes. They did claim that their heroes such as Alexander, Caesar and others, were sons of the gods.

Tertullian, a minister in the early church, showed the pagans of his day that their myths were only subjects of public ridicule, and that there was no basis of comparison between their revolting fables and the Gospel records of the Virgin Birth of Christ. Our opponents reply that Buddha and Zoroaster, as well as others, were claimed by their followers to have been Virgin born. To this Dr. Orr replies: "No pagan writer of note for at least two hundred years after Buddha's time claimed that he was virgin born. Every student of history knows that there had never been found anything in the lives of those ancient leaders to convince any sane person that they had been supernaturally born and the intelligent people of those times did not accept those stories as true. Moreover, the Messianic predictions found in the Old Testament and fulfilled in the life of Christ, constitute further evidence. Nothing like this can be said of Buddha, or Mohammet, or any founder of a pagan religion. Prophets, centuries before Christ, predicted the place of His birth, His sufferings and atonement for sin. Therefore, the argument from pagan myths advanced to disprove His miraculous birth falls to the ground.

Further arguments are here inserted supporting the Virgin Birth of Jesus Christ, based upon statements in "The Virgin Son" by John Champion.

The Inspiration of the Scriptures is at stake if they lose out in this vital matter of setting forth the nature and person of Christ.

In short, it is not the loss of the doctrine of the Virgin Birth which is at stake, but the loss of all doctrines based on the revelation of Holy Writ. The issue here is the reliability of the revelation of the Word of God. It is well that the authority of the Scriptures has been established for centuries. Religion can no more do without authority than can the state. We cannot reject the Holy Spirit's authoritative revelation of the infinitely important matter of who Jesus Christ is, how He came, the nature of His person and place, without undermining faith in the reliability of the Scriptures on our personal relation to God. If inspiration had not sufficient influence or control to prevent Matthew and Luke from relating untruth as truth in such an important and vital matter, it loses the very element that makes inspiration inspiration. This would mean that faith in the reliability of the Bible on vital matters is shattered, and the battle of naturalism is won. Our Lord said: "The Scriptures cannot be broken." Archeologists say that few ancient writings approach the Bible in reliability, and they, of course, refer to matters which have little or nothing to do with the reliability of the Bible as an authority on God's relation to man and of man's to God. The New Testament is not less inspired than the Old. This, even enemies must assent to. Then the New Testament cannot be broken without smashing the stronghold of Christ's authority which is really like Himself, the same yesterday; today, yea and forever.

The argument from congruity offers support to faith in these narratives.

A supernatural conception is congruous with the birth of a supernatural person. Jesus Christ is the unique manifestation of the supernatural in the realm of the natural. The miracle of the Virgin Birth is in keeping with the miraculous nature of His person. Only supernatural means of incarnation seem sufficient for the entrance of a divine, pre-existent person as Moffat translates Luke's account. "How can this be?" said Mary to the angel. "I have no husband." The angel answered her: "The Holy Spirit shall come upon you, the power of the Most High will overshadow you; thus what is born will be called holy, Son of God." The Virgin Birth story is in perfect harmony with the whole chain of natural and supernatural happenings and circumstances connected with the Advent. It fits in beautifully with the Annunciation, the psalm of Elizabeth, the hymn of Mary, the song of angels, the visit of the shepherds, the appearance of the wise men from the East, and the morning star they followed, the adoration of Simeon and Anna in the temple, Herod's attempt to kill the prophetic Babe by a general massacre of children, the flight into Egypt and so on. All this commotion, notwithstanding all that happened prior and after Pentecost, is far more congruous with the Virgin Birth than with an ordinary birth.

The psychological and biological argument supports the truth of the Virgin Birth.

The fact is well known that our souls as well as our bodies come from our parents. The psychical nature of a child shows quite as many marks of being begotten by its parents as its body shows. The inheritance does not stop there. Personality is begotten, part of which is body and soul; the rest is spirit. According to biological law, each type of life produces after its own kind. When it is possible for two types to unite in offspring, in the latter the natures of both unite. The Virgin Birth unites in offspring the divine and the human, the natural and the super-natural. How impossible are both the incarnation of a pre-existent person and at the same time the begetting in this incarnation by a human father, may be seen when we remember that never have a human father and mother begotten that a new personality was not originated. The Miraculous Conception was true to the law of inheritance from both its natural and supernatural factors. The incarnation of a divine person in a human person begotten by human parents means two personalities for one being. Biologically, it is impossible to hold that the son of Mary and a human father was one and the same as the Eternal Son of God. We are compelled to take the position; either there was no pre-existent Son of God, or there was no son of a human father when Jesus was born. If God, the Son, had always existed before the incarnation, who is this second person, the son of Mary and a human father? Once we disbelieve the Biblical account there is no logical, biological or psychological stopping place short of the error of a dual personality in Christ Jesus.

89

The argument drawn from the Deity of Christ and the Trinity supports the truth of the Virgin Birth.

We have seen that the natures of the two parent lives, which united by conception in the embryo, determine the nature or natures of that begotten by them. Only that begotten by the divine and the human can be accounted generically divine and human.

Mary and Joseph had several children after the birth of Jesus. If the Virgin Birth were not true, James, Joses, Judas, Simon and their sisters were generically the same in personality as Jesus. It is the combined human and divine parentage of our Lord which settles forever the status of His person. With a human father, He would be generically the same as all of us, and leaving us with no more reason to hold to His personal Deity than to the personal deity of us all.

S. F. Psa. 69:8; Matt. 13:55, 56; Mark 6:3; Gal. 1:19.

The trinity is a doctrine which chooses Christians to believe in it, rather than that they choose it. Its acceptance is compelled by the superhuman powers, work and person of Jesus Christ. So, we conclude naturally that He and His Birth correspond with each other, and that the means of His entrance upon human life of necessity differed from ours by as much as He differs in person, work, place and power from us. If Christ is not a supernatural person, then there is no second person in the Trinity and if there is no second person in it, there is no Trinity. If the chain is here broken, the rest of its several links are of no value.

The argument from Redemption supports the truth of the Virgin Birth.

In order to a right view of the atoning work of Christ we must have a right view of His Birth. The less we see of Christ's Deity in His supernatural Birth, the less of it must we see in His atoning death. When we lose the historic Christ of the Gospels and His Virgin Birth, as therein recorded, not a ghost of the divine remains for our redemption.

To this the experience of millions who have been regenerated through faith in Christ testifies. The denials of the Virgin Birth are usually advanced by those who have not experienced regeneration by the Spirit of God, who do not believe in it. To be oneself born of the Spirit of God puts one in position to accept the supernatural of the Word of God, because he is in himself and his own experience, a witness to it. To have had a supernatural experience by which one becomes spiritually related to God prepares one for the rest of the divine revelation which is above and beyond the natural mind.

We believe in the Virgin Birth because no objection yet raised against it is either sufficient, satisfactory, or conclusive. In fact, no positive or evidential objections have been or can be made. The burden of proof rests with those who deny a commonly accepted fact. Nineteen centuries of history affirm it as true.

(2) Made of the seed of David.

Rom. 1:3—Concerning his Son Jesus Christ our Lord, which was made of the seed of David according to the flesh.

S. F. Acts 13:22–23; Luke 1:31–33.

Matt. 1:1—The book of the generation of Jesus Christ, the son of David, the son of Abraham.

Acts 13:22-23—And when he had removed him he raised up unto them David to be their king; to whom also he gave testimony, and said, I have found David the son of Jesse, a man after mine own heart, which shall fulfill all my will. Of this man's seed hath God according to his promise raised unto Israel a Saviour, Jesus.

This aspect of the human parentage of Jesus Christ never has been subjected to the attack which has centered about the doctrine of the Virgin Birth, an attack which has been increasing in intensity during this modern age. However, the Word of God declares that the Messiah must be of the seed of David just as definitely as it declares that He must be born of a virgin. As believers, we should be familiar with this body of truth which relates to the line of Christ in the Davidic Covenant. I Pet. 3:5, "But sanctify the Lord God in your hearts: and be ready always to give an answer to every man that asketh you a reason of the hope that is in you with meekness and fear."

The Messianic line may be traced with interest through the Scriptures from Shem (Genesis 9:27) through Abraham (Genesis 12:1-3), Isaac (Genesis 26:2-5), Jacob (Genesis 28:13-15), and Judah (Genesis 49:10). At this point a careful look at the Messianic line reveals specific evidences of the exercise of the grace of God. The line of Judah was carried on by the illegitimate son, Pharez, who was born to Judah's daughter-in-law. (Genesis 38). According to the Mosaic law, as it is given in Deuteronomy 23:2, illegitimacy carried a curse until the tenth generation. An examination of the genealogy, as it is given in the Gospel of Matthew, shows that David was the tenth generation from Judah and thus free of any taint so far as the sin of Judah was concerned. Moreover, within these ten generations there are other outstanding expressions of God's abundant grace. He, in redeeming love, saw fit to include Rahab, the harlot of Jericho, in the line of the Messiah. She evidently became the wife of Salmon. To this couple Boaz was born. In the book of Ruth we have the beautiful story of the marriage of Ruth, the Moabitess, to Boaz, a man of the kingly line. Ruth was the great-grandmother and Rahab the great-great-grandmother of David, the King of God's choice. These two Gentile women, the one a harlot, the other an idol-worshipper, were redeemed and given a place in the lineage of Jesus Christ, son of David and King of Kings.

The Davidic Covenant (II Samuel 7:5-16) was given to King David through God's prophet, Nathan. It was reaffirmed to Mary by the angel Gabriel in the annunciation which is recorded in Luke 1:26-37, "He shall be great, and shall be called the Son of the Highest: and the Lord God shall give unto him the throne of his father David: and he shall reign over the house of Jacob for ever: and of his kingdom there shall be no end." (vv. 32-33) In this passage the two lines of prophetic truth concerning the Messiah are perfectly blended. Christ was to be born of the Virgin (Isaiah 7:14) and of the seed of David. (II Samuel 7).

Different views have been advanced concerning the genealogies which are recorded in the Gospel of Matthew and the Gospel of Luke. Whatever may have been the purpose of the Holy Spirit in inspiring these two genealogies the fact remains that no one, especially the Jew, may raise a question concerning the right of Jesus to sit upon the throne of David. Both Joseph, the humble carpenter, and Mary, the young woman who found favor in God's sight, were of the seed of David. In the Gospel of Matthew the genealogy of Joseph is given. In the Gospel of Luke the genealogy is apparently that of Mary. It is evident that both were of royal blood. To this couple, of humble station in life but of royal blood, God entrusted His Son.

91

2. By His natural growth and development.

Luke 2:40, 46, 52—And the child grew, and waxed strong in spirit, filled with wisdom: and the grace of God was upon him. And it came to pass that after three days they found him in the temple, sitting in the midst of the doctors, both hearing them, and asking them questions. And Jesus increased in wisdom and stature, and in favor with God and man.

Jesus' humanity passed through the various stages of growth like any other member of the race. From infancy to youth, from youth to manhood, there was a steady increase both of His bodily powers and mental faculties. Just to what extent His sinless nature influenced His growth we may not be able to say. It seems clear, however, from the Scriptures, that we are to attribute Jesus' growth and development to the observance of the laws of nature; to the training He received in a godly home. It is also attributed to the instructions given at the temple, from His own personal study of the Scriptures and from His fellowship and communion with His Father. Both the human and the divine element entered into His training and development, which were as real in the experience of Jesus as in that of any other human being.

D. S. Jesus Christ was subject to the ordinary laws of human development and gradual growth in wisdom, and stature.

3. By His personal appearance.

John 4:9—Then saith the woman of Samaria unto Him, How is it that thou, being a Jew, askest drink of me, which am a woman of Samaria? For the Jews have no dealings with the Samaritans.

S. F. John 21:4–5; Mark 7:33, 34; Mark 15:34; John 20:15; John 19:5.

S. A. Acts 7:56; I Tim. 2:5.

The personal appearance of Jesus is not made a matter of particular mention in Scripture. There are few allusions to it. Evidently the person of the earthly Jesus is not to be the subject of contemplation or picture.

"We have this, however, about Him: 'He hath no form nor comeliness and when we see Him, there is no beauty that we should desire Him.' 'His visage was so marred more than any man, and His form more than the sons of men.' The conventional pictures are probably very far from his actual appearance. They are all Grecian, and Jesus was a Jew."—PATTERSON.

"The woman of Samaria evidently recognized Jesus as a Jew by His features or speech. To her He was just an ordinary Jew, at least to begin with. There is no Biblical warrant for surrounding the head of Christ with a halo, as the artists do. His pure life, no doubt, gave Him a distinguished look, just as good character similarly distinguishes men today. Of course, we know nothing definite as to the appearance of Jesus, for no picture or photograph of Him do we possess."—EVANS.

D. S. Jesus Christ had the appearance of a man, and was occasionally mistaken for other men.

4. By His possession of a complete human nature including spirit, soul and body.

When Jesus Christ became incarnate, He came into possession of a real human, physical nature, and was "made in the likeness of men." This human nature, however, was not a carnal nature. It was sinless.

(1) He possessed a physical body.

Matt. 26:12—For in that she hath poured this ointment on my body, she did it for my burial.

(2) He possessed a rational soul.

Matt. 26:38—Then saith He unto them, My soul is exceeding sorrowful, even unto death; tarry ye here, and watch with me.

(3) He possessed a human spirit.

Luke 23:46—And when Jesus had cried with a loud voice, He said: Father, into thy hands I commend my spirit; and having said thus, He gave up the ghost. (Matt. 27:50).

Jesus Christ was possessed of two natures: Divine and human.

"A union of divinity and humanity was essential to the constitution of the person of Christ. It follows, therefore, that the Christ is God-man. Divinity and humanity are united in Him, but they are not blended. Humanity is not deified, and divinity is not humanized. This is plainly impossible. Divinity cannot take into its essence anything finite, and the human is finite. Humanity cannot be so absorbed in Deity as to become part of it. The two natures must ever remain distinct, while the person of Christ formed by their union will ever be one and indivisible. That He has two natures in one person is true, and must ever be true, of the Messiah. It is confessedly mysterious, but the doctrine is not, on this account, to be rejected."—PENDLETON.

S. F. Heb. 2:14–16; Heb. 4:15; John 1:14.

There were many early attempts to explain the doctrine of the two natures of Christ. We mention these briefly.

Ebionism denied the divine nature of Christ and held Him to be only man.

Cerinthianism held that there was no union of the two natures until after the baptism, thus establishing Christ's Deity upon His baptism rather than upon His birth.

Docetism denied the reality of Christ's body, because His purity could not be linked with matter, which they held to be inherently evil.

Arianism regarded Christ as the highest of created beings, thus denying His deity and misinterpreting His temporary humiliation.

Appollinarianism made Christ only two parts human, denying to Him a human soul, which they claim to be sinful.

Nestorianism denied the union of the human and divine natures, making Christ two persons.

Eutychianism held that the two natures of Christ were mingled into one, which was predominately divine, though not the same as the original divine nature.

The denial of Christ's true physical nature is a mark of the spirit of anti-christ (1 John, 4:2, 3).

D. S. By His incarnation, Jesus Christ came into possession of a real, human, physical nature consisting of spirit, soul and body, which gave to Him a true humanity.

5. By the human and sinless limitations.

"There is not a note in the great organ of our humanity which, when touched, does not find a sympathetic vibration in the mighty range and scope of our Lord's being, saving, of course, the jarring discord of sin."—EVANS.

(1) Physical limitations.

a. Jesus Christ was subject to bodily fatigue.

John 4:6—Now Jacob's well was there. Jesus, therefore, being wearied with His journey, sat thus on the well: and it was about the sixth hour.

Comp. Isa. 40:28—Hast thou not known? hast thou not heard, that the everlasting God, the Lord, the Creator of the ends of the earth, fainteth not, neither is weary? there is no searching of his understanding.

b. Jesus Christ was subject to the necessity of sleep.

Matt. 8:24—And, behold, there arose a great tempest in the sea, insomuch that the ship was covered with the waves: but he was asleep.

Comp. Psa. 121:4-5—Behold, he that keepeth Israel shall neither slumber nor sleep. The Lord is thy keeper; the Lord is thy shade upon thy right hand.

c. Jesus Christ was subject to hunger.

Matt. 21:18—Now in the morning as he returned into the city, he hungered. Compare Psa. 50:10-12.

d. Jesus Christ was subject to thirst.

John 19:28—After this, Jesus knowing that all things were now accomplished, that the Scripture might be fulfilled, saith, I thirst.

e. Jesus Christ was subject to physical suffering and pain.

Luke 22:44—And being in an agony he prayed more earnestly: and his sweat was as it were great drops of blood falling down to the ground.

f. Jesus Christ in His bodily life was capable of death.

1 Cor. 15:3—For I delivered unto you first of all that which I also received, how that Christ died for our sins according to the Scriptures.

D. S. Jesus Christ was subject to the ordinary physical limitations of human nature, such as hunger, thirst, weariness, pain and death.

(2) Intellectual limitations.

In His humiliation, the Son of God laid aside the independent exercise of His omniscience, as well as the other attributes of Deity, making use of His infinite intelligence only under the guidance of the Holy Spirit.

a. Jesus Christ was capable of increasing in knowledge.

Luke 2:52—And Jesus increased in wisdom and stature, and in favour with God and man.

94

b. Jesus Christ was capable of obtaining knowledge by observation.

Mark 11:13—And seeing a fig tree afar off having leaves, He came, if haply he might find anything thereon: and when he came to it, he found nothing but leaves; for the time of figs was not yet.

c. Jesus Christ was capable of being restricted in knowledge.

Mark 13:32—But of that day and that hour knoweth no man, no, not the angels which are in heaven, neither the Son, but the Father.

D. S. The knowledge of Jesus Christ was subject to limitations.

(3) Moral limitations.

Heb. 2:18—For in that he himself hath suffered being tempted, he is able to succour them that are tempted.

Heb. 4:15—For we have not an high priest which cannot be touched with the feeling of our infirmities; but was in all points tempted like as we are, yet without sin.

Christ possessed no moral limitations which were due to sin or which involved the possibility of sinning.

"This must be true, otherwise it would be setting up redemption on a basis of possible overthrow. The whole scheme of redemption predetermined in the counsel of God was, according to this theory, unsettled till after the temptation; during the temptation it was in the balance.

"Our Lord Jesus Christ, on the side of His mother by birth and on the side of Joseph by law, was the Heir of David's throne, and the Messiah ordained of God. His sin and fall would in no degree have changed His essential or legal relation to the throne, nor denied His title as Messiah. Thus, had he sinned, we should have had the spectacle of an ordained but sinful Messiah.

"Our Lord was the Lamb 'foreordained before the foundation of the world!' A Lamb to be accepted for sacrifice must be 'without a spot or blemish. As the antitype, the Christ must be sinless from an essential point, and without sin because of victory over it. Had he yielded to temptation and sinned, His fall could not have changed the fact that He had been ordained as the lamb of God. If that ordination remained, we should have the fixed, ordained Lamb of God guilty of sin and denying the very demand of both type and principle that He should be without sin.

"If our Lord as Messiah of Israel and Lamb of God could have sinned, He would, as the only begotten Son of God, have failed to be the Redeemer of men.

"The Scriptures give no warrant for the teaching that our Lord might have sinned. The illustrations from Satan and Adam cannot come into court. Satan was a created angel. Adam was not the begotten Son of God, but a creation of God. Our Lord Jesus Christ was not a created angel. He was not a created man. He was begotten of God, from the seed of the woman, by and through the Holy Ghost. That which was begotten was not a person but a nature, a human nature. This human nature was holy. Scripture calls it 'that Holy thing.' It was in its quality the holiness of God. Since its quality was the holiness of God, there was no sin in it, and no possible tendency to sin. This holy, sinless, human nature was indissolubly joined to the Personality of the Son. His human nature could not have sinned without the consent of His unique Personality; that Personality would have to say: 'I will' to sin.

Since the Personality of our Lord Jesus Christ is the Personality of God, it was impossible for that Personality to consent to sin. Since His personality could not consent to sin, it was impossible for Him in His human nature (seeing that human nature was inseparably joined to His personality) to have sinned."—HALDEMAN.

D. S. Jesus Christ was tempted, and thus subject to the essential moral limitations of human nature apart from sin.

(4) Spiritual limitations.

In the incarnation Jesus Christ exchanged His independent life for the dependent life; His sovereignty for subordination; living His life as a man. He limited Himself to the means and methods by which divine power is obtained and exercised by man.

a. Jesus Christ was dependent for power upon prayer.

Mark 1:35—And in the morning, rising up a great while before day, he went out, and departed into a solitary place, and there prayed.

S. F. John 6:15; Luke 22:41–45; Heb. 5:7.

In the Scriptures, we have mention of twenty-five times that Jesus Christ prayed. He obtained power for work and for moral victory as other men do, by prayer. He was subject to human conditions for obtaining what He desired.

b. Christ was dependent for power upon the anointing Spirit.

Acts 10:38—How God anointed Jesus of Nazareth with the Holy Ghost and with power: who went about doing good, and healing all that were oppressed of the devil; for God was with Him.

The period of Christ's dependency was the period of His humiliation. It extended from Bethlehem to Olivet, or during the period of His incarnate life upon the earth. He then resumed the glory which He had with the Father before the world was, and all the prerogatives of His Godhood.

D. S. Jesus Christ was subject to human conditions for the obtaining of power and to human limitations in its exercise.

6. By the human names given to Him by Himself and others.

(1) Jesus.

Matt. 1:21—And she shall bring forth a son, and thou shalt call His name Jesus; for He shall save His people from their sins.

This name means saviour or salvation. It is a human name, in use among Israelites of the past and present.

(2) The son of man.

Luke 19:10—For the Son of man is come to seek and to save that which was lost.

Jesus Christ calls Himself "Son of man" at least eighty times in the Gospels. In doing so, He assuredly identifies Himself with the sons of man.

(3) Jesus of Nazareth.

Acts 2:22—Ye men of Israel, hear these words; Jesus of Nazareth, a man approved of God among you by miracles and wonders and signs, which God did by Him in the midst of you, as ye yourselves also know.

96

People recognized Jesus as an inhabitant of Nazareth for there He grew to manhood. This was in fulfillment of the prophecy "He shall be called the Nazarene."

(4) The prophet.

Matt. 21:11—And the multitude said, This is Jesus the prophet of Nazareth of Galilee.

This is a human term and thus clearly argues for His humanity.

(5) The carpenter.

Mark 6:3—Is not this the carpenter, the son of Mary, the brother of James, and Joses, and of Juda, and Simon? and are not his sisters here with us? And they were offended at him.

Tradition has it that Joseph died while Jesus was yet a youth, and that He undertook the responsibilities of His father's carpenter shop.

(6) The man Christ Jesus.

I Tim. 2:5—For there is one God, and one mediator between God and men, the man Christ Jesus.

By the use of the term "man" we have a positive assertion of the true humanity which Christ possessed during His earth life and still possesses in His heavenly life of intercession at the right hand of God.

D. S. Human names and titles are used with reference to Jesus Christ, which establish the truth of His humanity.

7. By the human relation which He sustained to God.

Mark 15:34—And at the ninth hour Jesus cried with a loud voice, saying, Eloi, Eloi, la-ma-sa-bach-thani? which is being interpreted, My God, my God, why hast thou forsaken me?

S. F. John 20:17.

In these passages, Jesus speaks, as a man, of and to God thus setting forth the human relationship which existed between Himself as man's representative and the new racial Head, and God.

D. S. Jesus Christ called the Father "my God," thus taking the place and assuming the character of man.

The Self-emptying of Christ.

Phil. 2:5-8—Let this mind be in you, which was also in Christ Jesus: Who, being in the form of God, thought it not robbery to be equal with God; but made Himself of no reputation, and took upon him the form of a servant, and was made in the likeness of men: And being found in fashion as a man, he humbled himself, and became obedient unto death, even the death of the cross.

The self-emptying (*kenosis*) of Christ which was a voluntary act, consisted in the surrender of the independent exercise of the divine attributes. To illustrate—Finite beings have the power to a certain degree to restrict the limits of consciousness. By acts of the will, we may exclude many things from our minds. We make an effort to forget and in a measure we succeed. When Mary Reed went to the leper community to live and die, did she not put a kind of kenosis upon her consciousness? Did she not voluntarily renounce much of the knowledge of the stirring outside world? Is not the same true of David Livingstone and Dan Crawford who went to darkest Africa to labor among the negroes? These are feeble illustrations, but they give us a faint clue of the possibilities of self-renunciation on the part of the Son of God. How the independent exercise of the divine attributes could be surrendered, even for a time, would be inconceivable, if we were regarding the Logos or Word as He is in Himself, seated upon the throne of the universe. The matter is somewhat easier when we remember that it was not the Logos as such, but rather the God-man, Jesus Christ, in whom the Logos submitted to · this humiliation, and thus made self-limitation possible. South says: "Be the fountain never so full, yet if it communicate itself by a little pipe, the stream can be but small and inconsiderable, and equal to the measure of its conveyance."

It was the union of the human and the divine that limited the Logos. The general sense is that He divested himself of that peculiar mode of existence which was proper and peculiar to Him as one with God. He laid aside the form of God. But, in so doing, He did not divest Himself of His divine nature. The change was a change of state: the form of a servant for the form of God. His personality continued the same. His self-emptying was not self-extinction, nor was the Divine Being changed into a mere man. In His humanity He retained the consciousness of Deity, and in His incarnate state carried out the mind which animated Him before His incarnation. He was not unable to assert equality, but He was able not to assert it. Thus, without trying to explain away its force, we may accept the inspired declaration that Christ truly emptied Himself.

In the above quoted passage we read: "Thought it not robbery"; that is, He viewed His possession of the fulness of the Eternal Nature as securely and inalienably His own. And so "emptied Himself," or so made Himself void of His own account. So sure was Christ of His claim of Deity that without hesitation He could empty Himself of the manifestation and limit the exercise thereof.

In Homer's "Iliad," when Andromache brings her infant son to part with Hector, the boy is terrified by the war-like plumes of his father's helmet and Hector puts them off to embrace him. So God the Son lays aside "that glorious form, that light insufferable and that far-bearing blaze of majesty." Christ emptied Himself not of His deity nor of His attributes, but simply of the outward manifestation of His deity and the independent exercise of His attributes.

The purpose of the self-emptying and incarnation was redemptive. Deity in the distinctive sense could become incarnate in human form because human personality contains the essential elements of all personality, which are: self-consciousness, intelligence, feeling, moral nature, and will. Personality is the point at which creation in the ascent returns to God. Man bears the divine image. The self-emptying of Christ in the incarnation was the voluntary suspension of the full exercise of divine attributes, though potentially all divine resources were present. We cannot fully grasp the process by which this self-emptying took place. Dr. Mullins gives certain analogies which may help:

Take the case of a mathematician, a genius, and think of him at the beginning and then at the end of his training. As a boy, he has merely the elements of mathematical knowledge. Years afterwards he is master of all mathematical learning. Now conceive of him as teaching a beginner. Again he empties his mind of the riches of acquired knowledge and becomes a beginner. Yet the acquired knowledge while out of consciousness is at his command. Again consider the case of a father whose little son has been hurt in an accident and lies at the point of death. The father drops out of his consciousness entirely the knowledge of a great system of department stores of which he is owner. He now devotes himself day and night to the task of seeing that his child is saved from death. Money, time and comfort are all surrendered for love's sake. These again are imperfect analogies, but are suggestive. In the first we have the oblivion of the teacher for the sake of the pupil and, in the last, the oblivion of affection in the interest of the beloved. So it was, Christ freely and willingly surrendered the independent exercise of His attributes for the sake of and in the interest of His beloved.

II. The Deity of Jesus Christ.

"The dimensions of Christianity are best measured by the dimensions of the Person who founded it and bounds its horizon. On the reality of His Deity hangs all other reality in Christianity and that for all eternity."— CHAMPION.

While Jesus Christ was really man, He was also truly God. "I think I understand somewhat of human nature, and I tell you all these (heroes of antiquity) were men, and I am a man, but not like Him; Jesus Christ was more than Man."—NAPOLEON to Count Montholon in Bertrand's *Memoirs*. It is not sufficient to speak of the divinity of Christ. Men claim to be divine, to be of God; we should assert His Deity—He was God.

This preliminary consideration should be made, that both the Old and the New Testaments represent Christ as acting the part of a substitute for those He came to save. (Isa. 53:5–6; Matt. 20:28; John 10:11; Gal. 3:13). If Christ is not Deity, He could not have taken the place of sinners so as to make atonement for their sins. One creature cannot, in the government of God, take the place of another. An angel cannot act in the place of a man, because all that an angel can do is, on his personal account, due to God. This is the universal law of creatureship. Or, if allowed to do so, one perfect creature could only take the place of one sinful creature. It took the Deity of Christ to give universal value to His death for the race, and to enable Him "to taste death for every man."

"A man who can read the New Testament and not see that Christ claims to be more than mere man can look all over the sky at high noon on a cloudless day and not see the sun."—BEIDERWOLF.

To those who accept the doctrine of the Trinity, no argument for the Deity of Christ, of course, is necessary. Belief in the one of necessity involves belief in the other. For if Christ be the second Person of the Trinity, He is of the same essence with the Father and with the Holy Spirit, to whom He is by a blessed necessity equal in power and glory.

In God the Father we have the source of Deity; in Jesus Christ Deity in its outflow. But in the stream is all the perfection of the fountain. The Father is the source of glory; Jesus Christ the Son is the effulgence (shining forth or off-flash) of His glory. Heb. 1:3 (R. V.): "Who being the effulgence of His glory and the very image (impress) of His substance." Image (impress) signifies the impression made by the die or graver on a coin, indicating the nature or value. Thus here it refers to the exact impress of the nature or character of God.

The subordination of the Person of the Son to the Person of the Father is an order of personality, office, and operation, which permits the Father to be officially first, the Son second, and the Spirit, third, in perfect consistency with equality. Priority is not necessarily superiority. The possibility of an order, which yet involves no inequality may be illustrated between man and woman. In office man is first and woman second, but a woman's soul is worth as much as a man's (I Cor. 11:3).

Eternally Jesus Christ is positionally subordinate to God the Father. For purposes of redemption, in the incarnation, He assumed a distinctive subordination in that He exchanged His sovereignty for servanthood (Phil. 2:5–8). Substantially and essentially this is seen in the Scriptures in the following ways:

Christ made reference to the Father's superior greatness.

John 14:28—Ye have heard how I said unto you, I go away, and come again unto you. If ye loved me, ye would rejoice, because I said, I go unto the Father: for my Father is greater than I.

Christ was begotten of the Father.

John 3:16—For God so loved the world, that he gave his only begotten Son, that whosoever believeth in Him should not perish, but have everlasting life.

Christ was dependent upon the Father.

John 5:19—Then answered Jesus and said unto them, Verily, verily, I say unto you, The Son can do nothing of Himself, but what he seeth the Father do: for what things soever he doeth, these also doeth the Son likewise.

S. F. John 5:36; John 6:57.

Christ was sent by the Father.

John 8:29—And he that sent me is with me: the Father hath not left me alone; for I do always those things that please him.

S. F. John 6:29; John 8:42.

Christ was under the Father's authority.

John 10:18—No man taketh it from me, but I lay it down of myself. I have power to lay it down, and I have power to take it again. This commandment have I received of my Father.

Christ received delegated authority from the Father.

John 13:3—Jesus knowing that the Father had given all things into his hands, and that he was come from God, and went to God.

Christ received His message from the Father.

John 17:8—For I have given unto them the words which thou gavest me; and they have received them, and have known surely that I came out from thee, and they have believed that thou didst send me.

S. F. John 8:26, 40

Christ's Kingdom was appointed by the Father.

Luke 22:29—And I appoint unto you a kingdom, as my Father hath appointed unto me.

Christ will ultimately deliver His Kingdom up to the Father.

I Cor. 15:24—Then cometh the end, when he shall have delivered up the kingdom to God, even the Father; when he shall have put down all rule and all authority and power.

Christ is and shall be subject to the Father.

I Cor. 11:3—But I would have you know, that the head of every man is Christ; and the head of the woman is the man; and the head of Christ is God.

S. F. I Cor. 15:27–28, R. V.

Though there is an eternal subordination of Christ to the Father, yet it is only subordination of order, office and operation, not of essence.

The Deity of Jesus Christ as Shown:

1. By the divine names given to Him in the Scriptures.

(1) God.

Heb: 1:8—But unto the Son he saith, Thy throne, O God, is forever and ever: a sceptre of righteousness is the sceptre of thy kingdom.

S. F. John 20:28; John 1:18; John 5:20; Rom. 9:5; Tit. 2:13.

The term is here used in the absolute sense referring to Deity. Some have argued that the term is also used in referring to human judges (John 10:34–36), but this is only a secondary usage of the term.

(2) The Son of God.

Matt. 16:16–17—And Simon Peter answered and said, Thou art the Christ, the Son of the living God, and Jesus answered and said unto him, Blessed art thou, Simon Barjona: for flesh and blood hath not revealed it unto thee, but my Father which is in heaven.

S. F. Matt. 27:40; Matt. 27:43; Mark 14:61–62; Luke 22:70; John 5:25; John 10:36; John 11:4; Matt. 8:29.

This name is used of Christ forty times in the Scriptures. Besides this, there are frequent references to "His Son" and "My Son." (John 5:18). Jesus did not claim this title for Himself, but accepted it when used of Him, or when He was so addressed by others.

(3) First and the Last; and the Alpha and Omega.

Rev. 1:17—And when I saw him, I fell at His feet as dead. And he laid his right hand upon me, saying unto me, Fear not; I am the first and the last.

Comp. Isa. 41:4—Who hath wrought and done it, calling the generations from the beginning? I, the Lord the first, and with the last; I am he.

S. F. Isa. 44:6; Rev. 22:12, 13, 15; Rev. 1:8, R. V.

Dr. Pierson tells us that this title described Christ as the subject matter of all Scripture, the Creator of all worlds and creatures, the Controller of all history, and the eternal, unchangeable Jehovah.

(4) The Holy One.

Acts 3:14—But ye denied the Holy One and the Just, and desired a murderer to be granted unto you.

Hosea 11·9—I will not execute the fierceness of mine anger, I will not return to destroy Ephraim: For I am God and not man; the Holy one in the midst of thee: and I will not enter into the city.

On the monument of Oliver Goldsmith in Westminster Abbey are the words: "He touched nothing which he did not adorn." This can be truly said of the Lord Jesus Christ.

(5) The Lord.

Acts 9:17—And Ananias went his way, and entered into the house; and putting his hands on him, said, Brother Saul, the Lord, even Jesus, that appeared unto thee in the way as thou camest, hath sent me, that thou mightest receive thy sight, and be filled with the Holy Ghost.

S. F. Acts 16:31; Luke 2:11; Acts 4:33.

This title means "master." It is the Jehovah name. Wood tells us that the "Ptolemies and Roman Emperors would allow this name to be applied to them only when they permitted themselves to be deified. The archaeological discoveries at Oxyrhyncus put this fact beyond a doubt. So when the New Testament writers speak of Jesus as Lord, there can be no question as to what they mean."

(6) Lord of All and Lord of Glory.

Acts 10:36—The word which God sent unto the children of Israel, preaching peace by Jesus Christ (He is Lord of all).

I Cor. 2:8—Which none of the princes of this world knew: for had they known it, they would not have crucified the Lord of Glory.

S. F. Psa. 24:8–10.

S. A. Isa. 9:6; Heb. 1:8.

These two titles respectively set forth Christ in His divine sovereignty and in His divine majesty.

D. S. Names and titles clearly implying Deity are used of Jesus Christ; His Godhood being thus as firmly established as that of God the Father.

2. By the divine worship which is ascribed to Him.

Worship such as Christ received was ordinarily given only to Deity. Christ, therefore in receiving such worship made a practical acknowledgment or claim of deity. When our translation was made, the term worship was used in two senses. In the lower sense of the word it meant civil respect and deference, as in Luke 14:10—"Then shalt thou have worship in the presence of them that sit at meat with thee." The term in this sense is now obsolete, but it is used in its highest Scriptural sense to denote adoration paid to God because He is God.

(1) The Scriptures recognize worship as being due to Deity alone.

Matt. 4:10—Then saith Jesus unto him, Get thee hence, Satan: for it is written, Thou shalt worship the Lord thy God, and him only shalt thou serve.

S. F. Acts 10:25, 26; Rev. 22:8–9; Acts 12:20–25; Acts 14:14, 15.

The homage therefore given to Christ in the New Testament Scriptures would be nothing short of sacrilegious idolatry if Christ were not God.

Instances are cited in the Scriptures of those who encouraged and acccepted worship due only to God, and of the swift and awful punishment which was meted out to them: Herod (Acts 12:20–25), Nebuchadnezzar (Dan. 4:29–33). Instances are also given of those who refused with abhorrence to accept worship which did not belong to them: Peter (Acts 10:25, 26), angels (Rev. 22:8–9).

(2) Jesus Christ unhesitatingly accepted worship and seemed to invite it.

John 13:13—Ye call me Master and Lord: and ye say well; for so I am.

S. F. Matt. 14:33; Luke 24:52; John 4:10; Luke 5:8; John 20:27–29.

There seems to be not the slightest reluctance on the part of Christ in the acceptance of worship. Therefore, either Christ was God or He was an imposter. But His whole life refutes the idea of imposture.

(3) It is God's revealed will that Christ should be worshipped.

Heb. 1:6—And again, when he bringeth in the first begotten into the world, he saith, And let all the angels of God worship Him.

S. F. Phil. 2:10, 11; Comp. Isa. 45:21–23; John 5:22, 23, R. V.

(4) It was the practice of the early church to address prayer and worship to Christ.

I Cor. 1:2—Unto the church of God which is at Corinth, to them that are sanctified in Christ Jesus, called to be saints, with all that in every place call upon the name of Jesus Christ our Lord, both theirs and ours.

S. F. II Cor. 12:8–10; Acts 7:59.

D. S. Jesus Christ in harmony with the revealed will of God accepted without hesitation, the worship which belongs only to Deity, which good men and angels declined with horror.

3. By the divine offices which the Scriptures assign to Jesus Christ.

(1) Creator of the universe.

John 1:3—All things were made by him, and without him was not anything made that was made.

S. F. Heb. 1:10; Rev. 3:14; Col. 1:16.

Christ is seen to be excluded from the "created things" and to be the origin of them all.

"He is above all in creation; he is the Creator. He cuts the lovely crystal of the snowflake. He hangs the glorious arch of the rainbow. He dyes the purple of the pansy. He planted the mountain crag. He sunk the azure tides of the ocean. He gives to every creature life and breath. Our ancestral history backs up into a blaze of glory, the person of the creative Christ."—DOUGLAS.

Jesus Christ is the Creator and not a creature, and as such He is infinite and not finite, Divine, not human, God and not man.

(2) Preserver of all things.

Heb. 1:3—Who being the brightness of his glory and the express image of his person, and upholding all things by the word of his power, when he had by himself purged our sins, sat down on the right hand of the majesty on high.

S. F. Col. 1:17.

"The universe is neither self-sustaining nor is it forsaken by God as the

103

Deists would have us believe. By Christ all things consist or hold together. His word is the socket in which the wheel of the universe is set and upon which it turns, 'Upholding all things by the word of His power.' The pulses of universal life are regulated and controlled by the throbbing of the mighty heart of Christ."—EVANS.

What we call the laws of nature are the volitional actions of the Son of God. The preservation of all things which is a Divine function is ascribed to Christ, thus proving His Deity.

(3) Forgiver of sins.

Mark 2:5, 10, 11—When Jesus saw their faith he said unto the sick of the palsy, Son, thy sins be forgiven thee. But that ye may know that the Son of man hath power on earth to forgive sins (he saith to the sick of the palsy), I say unto thee, Arise, and take up thy bed, and go thy way into thine house.

S. F. Mark 2:5-11; Comp. Psa. 51:4; Luke 7:48-50.

The forgiving of sins is a divine prerogative. Even the Pharisees noticed that Christ unhesitatingly assumed this right. He not only declared sins forgiven; He actually forgave them. The Jews recognized in Jesus' claim to be able to forgive sins, a claim of deity, for they said, "Who can forgive sins but God only?" The forgiveness of sins is the prerogative of God alone. In assuming it, Jesus Christ made a practical assertion of His Deity.

(4) Bestower of immortal and resurrection life.

Phil. 3:21, R. V. Who shall fashion anew the body of our humiliation that it may be conformed to the body of his glory, according to the working whereby he is able to subject all things unto himself.

S. F. John 5:28, 29; John 6:39, 44.

Many may ask did not Elijah and Elisha raise the dead? We reply that God raised the dead in answer to their prayer by delegated power, but Jesus Christ raised the dead, and will raise them, by His own Word and power. The impartation of life belongs to God alone. When the King of Syria sent Naaman to Jehoram to be healed of his leprosy he cried, "Am I God, to kill and to make alive?" Jesus Christ's ability and authority to raise the dead firmly establishes His Deity.

(5) Judge of the quick and dead.

II Tim. 4:1—I charge thee therefore before God and the Lord Jesus Christ, who shall judge the quick and the dead at his appearing and his kingdom.

S. F. Acts 17:31; Matt. 25:31-33; John 5:22, 23.

Future judgment in the New Testament is assigned to God. It is also assigned to Christ. The logical conclusion is that Christ is the God who will execute all future judgment.

The man of the Cross is to be the Man of the throne. He who is man's present Saviour will be His future judge. The issues of the judgment are all in His hands. The execution of judgment, a divine function, being assigned to Christ, furnishes ample proof of His Deity.

(6) Giver of eternal life.

John 17:2—As thou hast given him power over all flesh, that he should give eternal life to as many as thou hast given him.

S. F. John 10:28.

Only a Being who inherently possesses eternal life can bestow it, and God alone possesses eternal life in the absolute sense; therefore Jesus Christ as the bestower of eternal life must of necessity be God.

D. S. Offices and functions which distinctly belong to Deity are predicated of Jesus Christ.

4. By the New Testament fulfillments in Christ of Old Testament statements concerning Jehovah.

The statements made in the Old Testament concerning Jehovah are interpreted by the New Testament as distinctly referring to Jesus Christ.

Psa. 102:24-27—I said, O my God, take me not away in the midst of my days; thy years are throughout all generations. Of old hast thou laid the foundation of the earth: and the heavens are the work of thy hands. They shall perish, but thou shalt endure: yea, all of them shall wax old like a garment; as a vesture shalt thou change them, and they shall be changed: But thou art the same, and thy years shall have no end.

Heb. 1:10-12—And, Thou, Lord, in the beginning hast laid the foundation of the earth; and the heavens are the works of thine hands: They shall perish; but thou remainest; and they shall wax old as doth a garment; And as a vesture shalt thou fold them up, and they shall be changed; but thou art the same, and thy years shall not fail.

The unchanging Lord in Hebrews is the Jehovah spoken of by the Psalmist.

Isa. 40:3-4 compared with Luke 1:68, 69, 76.
Jesus is the Lord before whose face the messenger goes.

Jer. 17:10; Comp. Rev. 2:23.
It is Jesus who does what is distinctly said of Jehovah in the Old Testament passage.

Isa. 60:19; Comp. Luke 2:32.
Jesus is seen to be the light and glory promised in the Old Testament passages.

Isa. 6:10; Comp. John 12:37-41.
The glory of Jesus Christ which John says Isaiah saw, is referred to in the Old Testament as the glory of Jehovah of Hosts.

Isa. 8:13, 14; Comp. I Peter 2:7-8.
In the Old Testament, Jehovah is the Stone of Stumbling. In the New Testament it is Jesus Christ.

Isa. 8:12-13; Comp. I Peter 3:14-15, R. V.
Christ the Lord, whom Peter urges us to sanctify, is the Lord of hosts whom Israel was commanded to sanctify.

Num. 21:6-7; Comp. I Cor. 10:9.

Paul identifies Jehovah whom Israel tempted to put to trial, with Christ whom he says they tempted in the wilderness.

Psa. 23:1; Comp. John 10:11; I Pet. 5:4; Heb. 13:20, 21.
Jesus identifies Himself as the Lord, the Shepherd.

Ezek. 34:11, 12; Comp. Luke 19:10.
In the Old Testament Jehovah, in the New Testament Jesus, seeks and saves the lost.

The term "Lord" always refers, in the Old Testament to God, and in the New Testament to Christ, unless expressly stated otherwise.

D. S. In the thought and teaching of the New Testament, Jesus Christ occupies the place that Jehovah occupies in the thought and teaching of the Old Testament.

5. By the association of the name of Jesus Christ the Son, with that of God the Father.

II Cor. 13:14—The grace of the Lord Jesus Christ, and the love of God, and the communion of the Holy Ghost, be with you all.

S. F. I Thes. 3:11; I Cor. 12:4–6; John 14:23; Rom. 1:7; James 1:1; II Peter 1:1, R. V.; Col. 2:2, R. V.; Matt. 28:19; John 17:3; John 14:1; Rev. 7:10; Rev. 5:13.

D. S. The name of Jesus Christ is coupled with that of God the Father in numerous passages in a way in which it would be impossible to couple the name of any finite being with that of Deity by which equality with the Father is plainly implied.

III. The Character of Jesus Christ.

Jesus Christ, in His character, has received the approval and commendation of God, men, angels and demons. The following are tributes of some of the men of post-Biblical times.

"The character of Jesus tremendously reinforces His beliefs. . . . . His life was all that a life should be, when judged by the highest standards."— BISHOP McDOWELL.

"Though something of Christ's character unfolded in one age, something in another, yet eternity itself cannot fully unfold Him."—FLAVEL.

"His character has passed the test of the malicious assaults of two thousand years, and stands today before the world as faultless in every part . . . . . He was a revelation of grand and rugged manhood. His name stands as a synonym of God on earth."—BISHOP FOSTER.

1. The Holiness of Jesus Christ.
(1) The meaning of it.
a. It means that He was free from all defilement.

I John 3:5—And ye know that He was manifested to take away our sins and in Him is no sin.

S. F. Heb. 9:14, R. V.; I Peter 1:19; II Cor. 5:21; Heb. 4:15.

S. A. Lev. 11:43–45; Deut. 23:14; Heb. 7:26, R. V.

In the Old Testament it is Jehovah God who is called the Holy One. He is called the Holy One of Israel about thirty times in Isaiah. In the New Testament it is Jesus Christ who is called the Holy One, therefore, the Holiness of Christ means the same as the Holiness of God; and on the negative side it means the separation from all defilement, or freedom from all sin.

b. It means that He was absolutely and immaculately pure.

I John 3:3—And every man that hath this hope in him purifieth himself, even as he is pure.

S. F. I John 1:5; John 8:12; John 1:4.

Jesus Christ took His standard of Holiness not from the law or the customs of men, but from God. The Bible multiplies expressions and figures to produce an adequate conception of the absolute Holiness or moral purity of Christ. There is nothing in nature with which to compare it except light.

I John 1:5—This then is the message which we have heard of Him, and declare unto you, that God is light, and in Him is no darkness at all.

Comp. John 8:12—Then spake Jesus again unto them, saying, I am the light of the world; he that followeth me shall not walk in darkness, but shall have the light of life.

"The dazzling white light that glorified the face and garments of Jesus on the Mount of Transfiguration (Matt. 17:2; Luke 9:29) was the outshining of the moral purity as well as Deity within."—HALDEMAN.

"Jesus Christ set for Himself, reached, and placed before others a perfect standard. Who accuses Him of shortcomings? Mr. Huxley's attempt was pathetic. 'The highest thing we have to say of Jesus,' says Wendt, 'is that with Him teaching and life were perfectly blended. His teaching rested on His own inner experience; His works and sufferings, on the other hand, were a vivid representation and grand attestation of His teaching. Thus He was more than a mere teacher of a new religion; He was at the same time the representative of the religious relationship to God which He taught. In this inward harmony of holy teaching and living, He moved in the presence of His disciples, and we can well comprehend that, from the short space of time during which they were with Him, although they were able to understand and hold fast only a little of the contents of the teaching which struck them at first as something so new and strange, yet they retained the indelible impression of having seen and experienced in their midst in human appearance the perfect revelation of God.' This impression John records (John 1:14–17)."—SPEER.

D. S. By the Holiness of Jesus Christ is meant that He was absolutely free from all the elements of impurity and that He possessed all the elements of positive purity and perfect sanctity.

(2) The attestations to the fact of it.

a. The testimony of the unclean spirit.

Mark 1:23–24—And there was in their synagogue a man with an unclean spirit; and he cried out, saying, Let us alone; what have we to do with thee, thou Jesus of Nazareth? art thou come to destroy us? I know thee who thou art, the Holy One of God.

b. The testimony of Judas Iscariot.

Matt. 27:3–4—Then Judas, which had betrayed Him, when He saw that he was condemned, repented himself, and brought again the thirty pieces of silver to the chief priest and elders, saying, I have sinned in that I have betrayed the innocent blood. And they said, What is that to us? see thou to that.

c. The testimony of Pilate.

John 18:38—Pilate saith unto him, What is truth? And when he had said this, he went out again unto the Jews, and saith unto them, I find in him no fault at all.

S. F. John 19:4–6.

d. The testimony of Pilate's wife.

Matt. 27:19—When he was set down on the judgment seat, his wife sent unto him, saying, Have thou nothing to do with that just man: for I have suffered many things this day in a dream because of Him.

e. The testimony of the dying thief.

Luke 23:41—And we indeed justly; for we receive the due reward of our deeds: but this man hath done nothing amiss.

f. The testimony of the Roman centurion.

Luke 23:47—Now when the centurion saw what was done, he glorified God, saying, Certainly this was a righteous man.

g. The testimony of the Apostle Peter.

Acts 3:14—But ye denied the Holy One and the Just, and desired a murderer to be granted unto you.

h. The testimony of the Apostle John.

I John 3:5—And ye know that he was manifested to take away our sins; and in him is no sin.

i. The testimony of Ananias.

Acts 22:14—And he said, The God of our fathers hath chosen thee, that thou shouldest know his will, and see that Just One, and shouldest hear the voice of his mouth.

j. The testimony of the whole Apostolic company.

Acts 4:27—For of a truth against thy holy child Jesus, whom thou hast anointed, both Herod, and Pontius Pilate, with the Gentiles and the people of Israel, were gathered together.

k. The testimony of the Apostle Paul.

II Cor. 5:21—For he hath made him to be sin for us, who knew no sin; that we might be made the righteousness of God in him.

l. The testimony of Jesus Himself.

John 8:46—Which of you convinceth me of sin? and if I say the truth, why do ye not believe me?

S. F. John 14:30.

m. The testimony of God the Father.

Heb. 1:8–9—But unto the Son he saith, Thy throne, O God, is forever and ever; a sceptre of righteousness is the sceptre of thy kingdom. Thou hast loved righteousness, and hated iniquity; therefore God, even thy God, hath anointed thee with the oil of gladness above thy fellows.

S. F. Matt. 17:5.

D. S. In the mouth of many witnesses, divine, human and diabolical, the absolute holiness of Jesus Christ is firmly established.

(3) The manifestation of it.

a. By His attitude toward sin and righteousness.

Heb. 1:9—Thou hast loved righteousness, and hated iniquity; therefore God, even thy God hath anointed thee with the oil of gladness above thy fellows.

As sin in its very nature is in opposition to righteousness so Jesus Christ the Holy One must of necessity be hostile against sin and openly opposed to it. But His holiness is also seen in a real affection for and devotion to that which is right.

b. By His actions with reference to sin and God's will.

I Peter 2:22—Who did no sin, neither was guile found in his mouth.

John 8:29—And he that sent me is with me: the Father hath not left me alone; for I do always those things that please him.

S. F. Matt. 17:5; John 12:49.

"All men admit that He was a holy and pious man and wrought good among men. But He Himself claimed that He made no mistakes or errors in this effort to help men, that He came to do God's will, and that He unfailingly did it, never doing one thing that did not please God (John 6:38; 8:29)."—Speer.

No man has successfully answered the challenge which He issued in the days of His flesh. "Which of you convinceth me of sin?" (John 8:46)

c. By demanding holiness in others.

Matt. 5:48—Be ye therefore perfect, even as your Father which is in heaven is perfect.

S. F. John 5:14; John 8:11.

The holiness of Christ was manifested in demanding absolute perfection of men and refusing any compromise with evil. The whole sermon on the Mount (Matt. 5–7) is the expression of that demand.

d. By rebuking sin and sinners.

Matt. 16:23—But he turned, and said unto Peter, Get thee behind me, Satan; thou art an offense unto me; for thou savourest not the things that be of God, but those that be of men.

"He turned round to the disciples (Mark 8:33). And said unto Peter, publicly before them all, Get thee behind me, Satan. Satan means adversary, the great enemy of all good, used in the Saviour's time as a proper name. He did not call his apostle Satan, a devil, but he looked for the moment through Peter, and saw behind him His old enemy, cunningly making use of the prejudices and impulsive honesty of the undeveloped apostle. Thou art an offense, a stumbling-block instead of a foundation stone; a hindrance, by placing before him the very temptation which Satan had presented to him in the wilderness. For thou savourest (mindest, partakest of the quality of) not the things that be of God—God's wise plan for His kingdom—but those that be of men."—Peloubet.

Matt. 23:13, 33—But woe unto you, scribes and Pharisees, hypocrites! for ye shut up the kingdom of heaven against men: for ye neither go in yourselves, neither suffer ye them that are entering to go in. Ye serpents, ye generation of vipers, how can ye escape the damnation of hell?

S. A. John 4:17–18.

e. By His sacrifice to save men from sin.

I Peter 2:24—Who his own self bare our sins in his own body on the tree, that we, being dead to sins, should live unto righteousness, by whose stripes ye were healed.

S. F. I Peter 3:18; Gal. 3:13; II Cor. 5:21.

S. A. John 10:17–18.

Some make the mistake of looking upon the cross as a mere fire escape by which the burnings of hell may be avoided and the blessings of heaven enjoyed, and, while this is true of those who are really saved by the Cross, this is far from being the motive which prompted its sacrifice. It was to redeem the objects of His love from a condition that was loathsome and abhorrent, because of His hatred of sin, to a condition that was pleasing and delightful because of His love of righteousness.

f. By the punishment meted out to the impenitent.

II Thes. 1:7–9—And to you who are troubled rest with us, when the Lord Jesus shall be revealed from heaven with his mighty angels, in flaming fire taking vengeance on them that know not God, and that obey not the gospel of our Lord Jesus Christ: who shall be punished with everlasting destruction from the presence of the Lord, and from the glory of his power.

S. F. Matt. 25:31, 32, 41.

The holiness of Jesus Christ demands and defends the punishment of the finally impenitent, the permanently wicked. His holiness could not be maintained by any other mode of dealing with them.

"He died to separate men whom He loves from sin which He hates. If men refuse this separation, He leaves them to their self-chosen partnership and the doom which it involves."—TORREY.

D. S. There are multiplied manifestations of the holiness of Jesus Christ, but no record of the presence of the least taint of personal sin in Him.

2. The Love of Jesus Christ.

(1) The meaning of it.

By the love of Christ is meant His desire for and devotion to the well-being of the objects of His affection.

The above may serve as a finite definition of that which is infinite, but in the final analysis that which is infinite is incapable of being adequately or completely defined, for the simple reason that the infinite goes beyond the reach of finite experience or observation. This is obviously true of Christ's love of which Paul makes the following statement: "That ye may be able to comprehend with all saints what is the breadth, and length, and depth, and height; and to know the love of Christ which passeth knowledge."

110

(2) The objects of it.

a. God the Father.

John 14:31—But that the world may know that I love the Father; and as the Father gave me commandment, even so I do. Arise, let us go hence.

Christ's love to the Father constituted the most conspicuous motive and emotion apparent in His life. This love was like Himself without beginning of days or end of life. The Father was the eternal object of His affection. That which was so manifest in time had an existence in the unending reaches of an eternity past.

b. The Church.

Eph. 5:25—Husbands love your wives, even as Christ also loved the church, and gave himself for it.

The conjugal love of a husband for his wife is exalted into a type of Christ's love for the Church, but the truest affection which man is capable of possessing and expressing for his bride is only a faint picture of the love of Christ toward the Church for which and to which He has given Himself.

c. Individual believers.

Gal. 2:20—I am crucified with Christ; nevertheless I live, yet not I but Christ liveth in me, and the life which I now live in the flesh, I live by the faith of the Son of God, who loved me, and gave Himself for me.

Christ does not love men "en masse," but as individuals. He is a person and loves each of us as such with a personal affection.

> "Wonderful things in the Bible I see,
> But this is the dearest, that Jesus loves me."

d. His own.

John 13:1—Now before the feast of the passover, when Jesus knew that his hour was come that he should depart out of this world unto the Father, having loved his own which were in the world, he loved them unto the end.

S. F. John 17:2, 9, 12.

By "His own" Jesus doubtless meant those whose redemption He had secured (I Peter 1:18–19); those who were given to Him by God the Father; the elect believers of that and every age (John 17:2, 9, 12).

e. Obedient disciples.

John 14:21—He that hath my commandments, and keepeth them, he it is that loveth me; and he that loveth me shall be loved of my Father, and I will love him, and will manifest myself to him.

Obedience on the part of disciples does not produce Christ's love for them, for that antedates all discipleship, but it brings forth the manifestation of His love to them. Obedience furnishes Him an opportunity for special exhibitions of His love.

f. His enemies.

Luke 23:34—Then said Jesus, Father, forgive them, for they know not what they do. And they parted his raiment and cast lots.

That which would call forth animosity on the part of ordinary men called forth compassionate love on the part of Christ. Instead of cursing His enemies, He prays for them.

> "When the Jewish rulers, who had sworn the life of Jesus away before the tribunal of the Roman governor, heard first of His resurrection, they remonstrated with the witness: 'Ye intend to bring this man's blood upon us.' But to these very men the apostles preached pardon. They proclaimed that Jesus is exalted for the purpose of showing mercy to His murderers. Now that He is exalted, and His enemies are in His power, instead of taking vengeance, He gives remission of sins."—ARNOT.

g. His own kindred.

John 19:25–27—Now there stood by the cross of Jesus his mother, and his mother's sister, Mary, the wife of Cleophas, and Mary Magdalene. When Jesus therefore saw his mother, and the disciple standing by, whom he loved, he saith unto his mother, Woman, behold thy son! Then said he to the disciple, Behold thy Mother! And from that hour that disciple took her unto his own home.

S. F. I Cor. 15:7.

Jesus was natural as well as supernatural. He had a natural affection for those who were bound to Him by the ties of nature and friendship.

h. Children.

Mark 10:13–16—And they brought young children to him, that he should touch them: and his disciples rebuked those that brought them. But when Jesus saw it, he was much displeased, and said unto them, Suffer the little Children to come unto me, and forbid them not; for of such is the kingdom of God. Verily I say unto you, whosoever shall not receive the kingdom of God as a little child, he shall not enter therein. And he took them up in His arms, put His hands upon them, and blessed them.

Jesus Christ by His love for children showed the place they should hold in every normal affection. He also revealed the attitude of God's heart toward the little ones, for in all of His deeds and actions He was declaring or telling forth God.

i. Lost sinners.

Rom. 5:6–8—For when we were yet without strength, in due time Christ died for the ungodly. For scarcely for a righteous man will one die; yet peradventure for a good man some would even dare to die; But God commendeth his love toward us, in that, while we were yet sinners, Christ died for us.

S. F. Matt. 9:13.

Jesus Christ had a passion for the lost as well as a compassion. He loved them not in the capacity of sinners, but as creatures—creatures who had been made in the image and likeness of God.

> "Jesus Christ loves him who is the vilest sinner as truly as He loves the purest saint, but He does not love Him who is the vilest sinner in the same way that He loves the purest saint. His love to the sinner is one thing; His love to the obedient disciple quite another. Toward the one He has pity; in the other He takes pleasure."—TORREY.

D. S. The objects of the love of Jesus Christ have a two-fold classification,

112

Divine and human. God the Father is the pre-eminent object of Christ's love, but He also has a real love for various groups among men.

(3) The manifestation of it.

a. To the Father, as shown:

(a) By perfect obedience.

John 15:10—If ye keep my commandments, ye shall abide in my love; even as I have kept my Father's commandments and abide in His love.

S. F. John 6:38; John 10:15–18; Phil. 2:8; Matt. 26:39, 42; Psa. 40:8; John 4:34, R. V.; Luke 2:49.

Jesus gave obedience as a test of the love of His disciples, saying: "He that hath my commandments and keepeth them, he it is that loveth me," that therefore which serves as the test of their love will suffice to test His own love to the Father, and His love stands the test.

(b) By doing His pleasure.

John 8:29—And he that sent me is with me; the Father hath not left me alone; for I do always those things which please Him.

S. F. John 5:30.

Jesus' love for the Father caused Him to go beyond His express command, and do those things which He knew were pleasing to the Father, though they had never found expression in decree or law.

(c) By seeking His glory.

John 17:1 and 4—These words spake Jesus, and lifted up his eyes to heaven, and said, Father, the hour is come; glorify thy Son, that thy Son also may glorify thee. I have glorified thee on the earth, I have finished the work which thou gavest me to do.

S. F. John 7:18; John 8:50.

Very few men, if any, dedicate themselves to the glory of another. They usually seek their own name, fame and gain but Jesus dedicated Himself to seek His Father's glory. All these other things He sacrificed to attain that one great end.

D. S. Jesus Christ loved the Father and manifested that love in every possible way.

b. For men, as shown:

(a) By coming to seek and to save them.

Luke 19:10—For the Son of man is come to seek and to save that which was lost.

When the Prince of Wales came to this country some years ago, there was considerable speculation as to the purpose of his coming, but there need be no conjecture or speculation as to why Jesus Christ left the glory which He had with the Father and came to this world which had become alienated from God through sin. His purpose is made known to all. It is "to seek and to save that which was lost."

(b) By being ever on the watch for them.

John 9:35—Jesus heard that they had cast him out, and when he had found him he said unto him, Dost thou believe on the Son of God?

113

S. F. John 4:3, 4, 6, 7, 10; Mark 2:4–5.

Never for a moment did Jesus Christ lose sight of the purpose of His great mission. As geologists are ever on the watch for new mineral findings, and botanists for new floral specimens, and ornithologists for rare species of birds, so Jesus was ever alert for opportunities to reach men.

(c) By going after them.

Luke 15:4—What man of you, having a hundred sheep, if he lose one of them, doth not leave the ninety and nine in the wilderness and go after that which is lost, until he find it?

S. F. John 4:1, 4, 7.

Jesus' interest in the lost was not passive but active. There was dust upon the feet of His love and perspiration upon its brow. He took long journeys to find the objects of His redemptive passion.

(d) By finding His chief satisfaction in winning them.

John 4:32–34—But he said unto them, I have meat to eat that ye know not of. Therefore said the disciples one to another, Hath any man brought him ought to eat? Jesus saith unto them, My meat is to do the will of him that sent me, and to finish his work.

Men may be judged as to their character by that in which they find their greatest joy. In applying this test to Jesus Christ we discover that His greatest satisfaction was found in winning the lost to Himself. This distinguishes Him from all other men which shows Him to be possessed of a character which is unique.

(e) By rejoicing greatly over those found.

Luke 15:4–7—What man of you, having an hundred sheep, if he lose one of them doth not leave the ninety and nine in the wilderness, and go after that which is lost, until he find it? And when he hath found it, he layeth it on his shoulders, rejoicing. And when he cometh home, he calleth together his friends and neighbours, saying unto them, Rejoice with me; for I have found my sheep which was lost. I say unto you, that likewise joy shall be in heaven over one sinner that repenteth, more than over ninety and nine just persons, which need no repentance.

"As a shepherd rejoices over the sheep that had gone astray when he finds it, as the woman rejoices over the coin lost from her marriage necklace when it is found again; as the gold hunter rejoices over the great nugget of gold that he digs from the rock; as the merchant man seeking goodly pearls rejoices over the one pearl of great price—so, and infinitely more, does Jesus rejoice over a lost soul found."—Selected.

(f) By grieving sorely over those who refused to be saved.

Matt. 23:37—O Jerusalem, Jerusalem, thou that killest the prophets, and stonest them which are sent unto thee, how often would I have gathered thy children together, even as a hen gathereth her chickens under her wings, and ye would not.

S. F. John 5:40; Luke 19:41, 42.

Men suffer grief from various causes such as disappointment, failure, hard-

114

ship, etc. This was not true of Jesus, however. His one source of grief seemed to be in the refusal of men to be saved from sin. No woman ever grieved over her stolen jewels, no mother over a lost child, as Jesus over lost men who refused to be saved. No words can picture the agony that shot through the heart of Jesus Christ when men refused to come to Him that they might have life.

(g) By gladly laying down His life to save them.

Matt. 20:28—Even as the Son of man came not to be ministered unto, but to minister, and to give his life a ransom for many.

S. F. John 10:11.

The supreme expression of love is not in gifts or service but in sacrifice and especially in the sacrifice of life.

D. S. Jesus Christ loves men and has proved it in most practical ways, above the peradventure of a doubt.

3. The Meekness of Jesus Christ.

(1). The meaning of it.

By meekness we mean that attitude of mind that is opposed to harshness and contentiousness, and that shows itself in gentleness and tenderness in dealing with others.

II Tim. 2:24-25—And the servant of the Lord must not strive; but be gentle unto all men, apt to teach, patient; in meekness instructing those that oppose themselves; if God peradventure will give them repentance to the acknowledging of the truth.

S. F. I Cor. 4:21; Titus 3:2; II Cor. 10:1; Gal. 6:1.

The word "meekness," though never used in an evil sense, has been lifted by Christianity to a higher plane, and made the symbol of a higher good than that with which it was vested in heathen usage. Its primary meaning is "mild," "gentle." It was applied to inanimate things, as light, wind, sound, sickness. It was used of a horse, meaning "gentle."

As a human attribute, Aristotle defines it as the mean between stubborn anger and that negativeness of character which is incapable of even righteous indignation. According to this it is tantamount to equanimity. Plato opposed it to fierceness or cruelty, and uses it of humaneness to the condemned; but also of a conciliatory demeanor of a demagogue seeking popularity or power. Finder applies it to a king, mild or kind to the citizens, and Herodotus used it as opposed to anger.

These pre-Christian meanings of the word exhibit two general characteristics. 1. They express outward conduct merely. 2. They contemplate relations to men only.

The Christian word, on the contrary, describes an inward quality, and that as related primarily to God. The equanimity, mildness, kindness, represented by the classical word are founded in self-control or natural disposition. The Christian meekness is based on humility, which is not a natural quality but an outgrowth of a renewed nature, except in the case of Christ where it is the expression and manifestation of His holy nature.

(2) The fact of it.

II Cor. 10:1—Now I Paul myself beseech you by the meekness and gentleness of Christ, who in presence am base among you, but being absent am bold toward you.

S. F. Matt. 21:5; Matt. 11:29.

D. S. Jesus Christ was a pattern of meekness for us, gentle and forbearing in His relation to men.

(3) The manifestation of it as seen:
a. In longsuffering and forbearance with the weak and failing.

Matt. 12:20—A bruised reed shall he not break, and smoking flax shall he not quench (the dimly burning wick shall he not extinguish—Heb.), till he send forth judgment unto victory. Isa. 42:3.

"He cares for the poorest, the weakest, the sorely crushed with His gentle hand. He encourages, 'the slightest spark of repentant feeling,' the weakest longing to return to God."—PELOUBET.

b. In bestowing forgiveness and peace upon one who merited censure and condemnation.

Luke 7:38, 48, 50—And stood at his feet behind him weeping, and began to wash his feet with tears and did wipe them with the hairs of her head, and kissed his feet, and anointed them with the ointment. And he said unto her, Thy sins are forgiven. And he said to the woman, Thy faith hath saved thee, go in peace.

The loadstone will not draw gold nor pearl, but draws the iron which is considered an inferior metal, so Christ left the angels, those noble unfallen spirits, the gold and the pearl, and He comes to poor sinful man, and draws him into His fellowship.

In an English Cathedral, there is an exquisite stained window, which was made by an apprentice out of the pieces of glass which had been rejected by his master; so Christ is including in the building of His temple the refuse of society.

c. In imparting healing to one who sought to obtain it in an unworthy manner.

Mark 5:33-34—But the woman fearing and trembling, knowing what was done in her, came and fell down before him, and told him all the truth. And he said unto her, Daughter, thy faith hath made thee whole; go in peace, and be whole of thy plague.

Jesus looked at the motives which prompted the woman rather than her method of action. These were motives of faith and hope and found a response in the great heart of Christ.

d. In gently rebuking stubborn unbelief.

John 20:24, 25, 29—But Thomas, one of the twelve, called Didymus, was not with them when Jesus came. The other disciples therefore said unto him, we have seen the Lord. But he said unto them, Except I shall see in his hands the print of the nails, and put my finger into the print of the nails, and thrust my hand into his side, I will not believe. Jesus saith unto him, Thomas, because thou hast seen me, thou hast believed: blessed are they that have not seen, and yet have believed.

Jesus' rebuke was not the kind that caused disheartening despair, but rather the kind which encouraged right motives. It was positive rather than negative, constructive rather than destructive.

e. In tenderly correcting Peter's self-confidence, unfaithfulness, and the thrice repeated and flagrant denial of his Lord.

John 21:15-17—So when they had dined, Jesus saith to Simon Peter, Simon, Son of Jonas, lovest thou me more than these? He saith unto him, Yea, Lord; thou knowest that I love thee. He saith unto Him, Feed my lambs. He saith to him again the second time, Simon, son of Jonas, lovest thou me? He saith unto him, Yea, Lord; thou knowest that I love thee. He saith unto him, Feed my sheep. He saith unto him the third time, Simon, son of Jonas, lovest thou me? Peter was grieved because he said unto him the third time, Lovest thou me? And he said unto him, Lord, thou knowest all things; thou knowest that I love thee. Jesus saith unto him, Feed my sheep.

In Jesus' dealings with Peter we see the great shepherd restoring His wandering sheep. His discipline was always corrective.

f. In mildly reproving His betrayer.

Matt. 26:48-50—Now he that betrayed him gave them a sign, saying, Whomsoever I shall kiss, that same is he; hold him fast. And forthwith he came to Jesus, and said, Hail, master; and kissed him. And Jesus said unto him, Friend, wherefore art thou come? Then came they and laid hands on Jesus, and took him.

S. F. John 13:21, 27.

Judas had perhaps committed the greatest wrong that is possible in one's relation to a friend that of perfidy or treason, and yet Jesus exercised a forbearance with him which was marvelous.

g. In compassionately praying for His murderers.

Luke 23:34—Then said Jesus, Father, forgive them; for they know not what they do. And they parted His raiment and cast lots.

In the Sermon on the Mount, Jesus had said, Bless them that curse you, pray for them that despitefully use you and persecute you. There upon the cross, in the hour of His greatest suffering, He practiced what He preached.

D. S. The meekness of Jesus Christ was shown in the gentle manner in which He dealt with the sinful and erring.

4. The Humility of Jesus Christ.

(1) The meaning of it.

Zech. 9:9—Rejoice greatly, O daughter of Zion; shout, O daughter of Jerusalem: behold, thy King cometh unto thee; he is just, and having salvation; lowly, and riding upon an ass, and upon a colt the foal of an ass.

By humility we mean that attitude of mind and heart which is opposed to pride, self-assertion and self-reliance and that shows itself in subjugation to and dependence upon God.

The Greek word "tapeinos," translated lowly, has a history. In the classics it is used commonly in a bad and degrading sense, of meanness of condition, lowness of rank, and cringing abjectness and baseness of character. Still, even in classical Greek, this is not its universal usage. It is occasionally employed in a way which foreshadows its higher sense. Plato, for instance, says, "To that law (of God) he would be happy who holds fast, and follows it in all humility and order; but he who is lifted up with pride or money or honor or beauty, who has a soul hot with folly, and youth and insolence, and thinks that he has no

117

need of a guide or ruler, but is able himself to be the guide of others, he, I say, is left deserted of God." And Aristotle says, "He who is worthy of small things, and deems himself so, is wise." At best, however, the classical conception is only modesty, absence of assumption. It is an element of wisdom and in no way opposed to self righteousness. The word for the Christian virtue of humility was not used before the Christian era, and is distinctly an outgrowth of the Gospel.

To possess humility is to have a spirit and demeanor that is without pretention or pride and that is characterized by modesty and submission.

(2) The fact of it.

Matt. 11:29—Take my yoke upon you, and learn of me; for I am meek and lowly in heart, and ye shall find rest unto your souls.

"I believe," says Mr. Ruskin in *Modern Painter,* "the first test of a truly great man is his humility. I do not mean by humility doubt of his own power, or hesitation of speaking his opinions; but a right understanding of the relation between what he can do and say, and the rest of the world's doings and sayings. All great men not only know their business, but usually know that they know it, and are not only right in their main opinions, but they usually know that they are right in them, only they do not think much of themselves on that account. Arnolfo knows that he can build a good dome at Florence; Albert Durer writes calmly to one who has found fault with his work, "It cannot be done better"; Sir Isaac Newton knows that he has worked out a problem or two that would have puzzled anybody else; only they do not expect their fellowmen therefore to fall down and worship them. They have a curious undersense of powerlessness, feeling that the power is not in them, but through them, that they could not do or be anything else than God made them.

D. S. Jesus Christ was lowly in heart, humble in life.

(3) The manifestation of it as shown:

a. By taking the part and place of a servant.

John 13:4–5—He riseth from supper, and laid aside his garments; and took a towel, and girded himself. After that he poureth water into a basin and began to wash the disciples' feet, and to wipe them with the towel wherewith he was girded.

S. F. Phil. 2:5–8; Matt. 20:28.

"Christ shows us by example the only road to true greatness. It is the majority vote of the race that no one can be truly great without this disinterested love, and that, however great a man may seem, selfishness always diminishes or removes his crown and his throne."—PELOUBET.

b. By not seeking His own glory.

John 8:50—And I seek not mine own glory; there is one that seeketh and judgeth.

"It was the supreme passion of his being to glorify the Father. As He descended into the dark valley, this was his one cry, 'Father, glorify thy name!' Deeper and deeper still He went; and this same entreaty, breaking from His agonized heart, comes back to us yet fainter, and even fainter. 'Now is my soul troubled; and what shall I say? Father, glorify thy name!' Perhaps even the love of the race and the desire to redeem had failed to support his faint-

118

ing soul, unless his resolution had been empowered and maintained by this all-masterful desire. He was greedy, therefore, of every vestige of glory that He could win by suffering, even though it were unto death; that He might be able, though it were with but a featherweight additional, to augment the revenue of glory which, through Him, should accrue to God."—MEYER.

So filled was He with the desire for the Father's glory that no room was left for a disposition to honor or exalt Himself.

c. By avoiding notoriety and praise.

Isa. 42:2—He shall not cry, nor lift up, nor cause his voice to be heard in the street.

Many professed followers of Jesus Christ court notoriety. He shunned it. He strictly charged those whom He had benefited not to make it known. He kept no advertising bureau.

d. By associating with the despised and outcast.

Luke 15:1, 2—Then drew near unto him all the publicans and sinners for to hear him. And the Pharisees and scribes murmured, saying, This man receiveth sinners, and eateth with them.

S. F. Matt. 9:10.

"One reason why Jesus chose a publican for one of the twelve was probably to give an object lesson of hope to the most disreputable of sinners, those bound with the strongest fetters of sin. None were too far away for his gospel to reach and save them, none too deep in the mire of sin to be lifted from his depths even to the heights of glory."—PELOUBET.

e. By patient submission and silence under outrageous injury and injustice.

I Peter 2:23—Who, when he was reviled, reviled not again; when he suffered, he threatened not; but committed himself to him that judgeth righteously.

S. F. Heb. 12:3; Isa. 50:5–6; Matt. 26:60–63; Luke 23:8–10; Isa. 53:7.

Jesus, being conscious that all of the resources of God and heaven were at His disposal by which He might have vanquished every opponent and conquered every foe, submitted to the most shameful and cruel treatment because it was the fulfillment of the plan of Him whose will He came to do.

D. S. Jesus Christ displayed humility by seeking the glory of God and the good of men, rather than His own glory or good, and at the cost of great sacrifice, suffering and shame.

B. The Work of Jesus Christ.

By the work of Jesus Christ, we here refer to His work in relation to our redemption rather than to His personal ministry of teaching, preaching and healing.

I. The Death of Jesus Christ.

Christianity is distinctively a religion of atonement. It gives the death of Christ the first place in its gospel message. Thus Christianity is given a unique position among all the religions of the world. It is a redemptive religion.

Some years ago a Parliament of Religions was held in Chicago, in connection with the World's Fair. At that Parliament the great ethnic faiths of the world were represented. One by one leading men arose and spoke for Buddhism, Confucianism, Hinduism, and Mohammedanism. Then Dr. Joseph Cook, of Boston, who had been chosen to represent Christianity, arose to speak. "Here is Lady Macbeth's hand," he said, "stained with the foul murder of King Duncan. See her as she perambulates through the halls and corridors of her palatial home, stopping to cry, 'Out, damned spot! Out, I say! Will these hands ne'er be clean?'" Then turning to those seated on the platform, he said, "Can any of you who are so anxious to propagate your religious systems offer any cleansing efficacy for the sin and guilt of Lady Macbeth's crime?" An oppressive silence was maintained by them all and well they might, for none of the religions there represented, nor any other religion of earth, can offer any cleansing efficacy for the guilt of sin. Only the blood of Christ who, through the Eternal Spirit offered Himself without spot to God, can purge the conscience from dead works to serve the living God.

1. The Importance of It, as Shown:

(1) By the vital relation which it sustains to the person of Christ.

Other great men have been valued for their lives and work; and, though Jesus is valued for His work as a religious teacher, philanthropist, and as reformer, yet He is valued above all else because of His death, through which God and man are reconciled. He was first and foremost, the world's Redeemer and Saviour.

(2) By its vital connection with the Incarnation.

Heb. 2:14—Forasmuch then as the children are partakers of flesh and blood, he also himself likewise took part of the same; that through death he might destroy him that had the power of death, that is, the devil.

S. F. I John 3:5.

The Incarnation was for the purpose of the Atonement. Christ became incarnate in order that He might expiate and propitiate. He was born that He might die. He was manifested to take away sins. He became incarnate in order that, in assuming a nature like unto our own, He might offer up His life as a sacrifice for the sins of men. The Incarnation is a declaration on the part of God of His purpose to provide salvation for the world. That salvation is only to be provided through the atoning blood of Christ.

(3) By the prominent place given to it in the Scriptures.

Luke 24:27, 44—And beginning at Moses and all the prophets, he expounded unto them in all the scriptures the things concerning himself . . . . . And he said unto them, These are the words which I spake unto you, while I was yet with you, that all things must be fulfilled, which were written in the law of Moses, and in the prophets, and in the psalms, concerning me.

Besides the many prophetic and typical references to it in the Old Testament, the death of Christ is mentioned more than 175 times in the New Testament. Jesus Himself claimed, in His conversation on the way to Emmaus, that Moses, the prophets, in fact, all the Old Testament Scriptures, dealt with the subject of His death.

"The atonement is the scarlet cord running through every page in the entire Bible. Cut the Bible anywhere and it bleeds; it is red with redemption truth."
—EVANS.

120

a. It was a subject of earnest inquiry to the Old Testament prophets.

I Peter 1:11—Searching what, or what manner of time the Spirit of Christ which was in them did signify, when it testified beforehand the sufferings of Christ, and the glory that should follow.

"The central event in all human history is the death of Christ. Not only does the cross tower o'er the wrecks of time, it towers over everything else that interests man. All the centuries that came before the death of Christ on Calvary, either unconsciously, or with dim hope, were expecting it and all the centuries since get their true interpretation from it. Since this is so, it would have been beyond comprehension if some light had not been given beforehand on this great purpose of God to send a Saviour to die for men—light, not only for the encouragement of those who without it would have groped in darkness, but also to furnish such information that the person and work of the Messiah could rightly be understood when He came."—TAYLOR.

b. It was a matter of deep interest to the angels.

I Peter 1:12—Unto whom it was revealed, that not unto themselves, but unto us they did minister the things which are now reported unto you by them that have preached the gospel unto you with the Holy Ghost sent down from heaven; which things the angels desire to look into.

Here we go a step higher than the "prophets." The angels possess no intuitive knowledge of redemption. Because of their ministry to the heirs of salvation, they are naturally disposed to wish to penetrate this mystery as reflecting such glory on the love and power of their and our God. They seek to fathom "the great mystery of Godliness, God manifest in the flesh, justified in the Spirit, seen of angels."

c. It is one of the cardinal truths of the Gospel.

I Cor. 15:1, 3, 4—Moreover, brethren, I declare unto you the gospel which I preached unto you, which also ye have received, and wherein ye stand . . . . . For I delivered unto you first of all that which I also received, how that Christ died for our sins according to the Scriptures; and that he was buried, and that he rose again the third day according to the Scriptures.

d. It was the sole topic of conversation at the Transfiguration.

Luke 9:30, 31—And behold, there talked with him two men, which were Moses and Elias: Who appeared in glory, and spake of the decease which he should accomplish at Jerusalem.

Here we have that jewel, His death, raked out of the rubbish heap of Jewish traditions, and by the true representatives of the Law and the Prophets, made the one subject of talk with Christ himself.

e. It will be the central theme of heaven's song.

Rev. 5:8–12—And when he had taken the book, the four beasts and four and twenty elders fell down before the Lamb, having every one of them harps, and golden vials full of odours, which are the prayers of saints. And they sung a new song, saying, Thou art worthy to take the book, and to open the seals thereof: for thou wast slain, and hast redeemed us to God by thy blood out of every kindred, and tongue, and people, and nation; and hast made us unto our God kings and priests: and we shall reign on the earth. And I beheld, and I heard the voice of many angels round about the throne and the beasts and the elders: and the number of them was ten thousand times ten thousand, and thousands of thousands; saying with a loud voice, Worthy is the Lamb that was slain to receive power, and riches, and wisdom, and strength, and honour, and glory, and blessing.

D. S. The importance of the death of Jesus Christ is seen by the emphasis that God has given to it in the Scriptures.

2. The Necessity of It.

It is reasonable to believe that the death of Christ was necessary, else God the Father would never have subjected His dearly beloved Son to the awful punishment of the Cross. For while the Son came in response to a compassionate redeeming, love, yet he also came in filial obedience, sent forth by the Father, who prepared for Him a body for his priestly sacrifice (Heb. 10:5–9).

Jesus Christ Himself speaks of His death as a necessity. He says, And as Moses lifted up the serpent in the wilderness, even so must the Son of man be lifted up: that whosoever believeth in him should not perish, but have eternal life (John 3:14, 15).

(1) The holiness of God made it necessary.

Hab. 1:13—Thou art of purer eyes than to behold evil, and canst not look on iniquity; wherefore lookest thou upon them that deal treacherously, and holdest thy tongue when the wicked devoureth the man that is more righteous than he?

The holiness of God which is an ethical principle of the divine nature, demanded that sin be punished. "Infinite purity is a consuming fire to all iniquity."

All the Mosaic system of ceremonial cleansing, sacrifices, and offerings emphasizes the moral distance between sinful man and a Holy God, and makes forcible the later truth that "without shedding of blood there is no remission nor admission."

"When God chose that costliest means of our deliverance, sending His own Son in the likeness of sinful flesh, and for sin, we may be quite sure that at no lower price would our redemption have been possible, that nothing short of this could have satisfied that righteousness of His, which He was bound to maintain."—TRENCH.

(2) The love of God made it necessary.

John 3:16.

I John 4:10—Herein is love, not that we loved God, but that he loved us, and sent His son to be the propitiation for our sins.

S. F. I John 2:1, 2.

Jesus said that "God so loved the world that He gave His only begotten Son." The word "so" indicates intensity His love was so intense, its pressure was so great, that it burst the bounds of the Godhead of necessity, and poured itself in lavish fulness upon a lost and ruined race.

"Here is no fortuitous concourse (chance merging of circumstances), but the long-laid plan of God. Behold its procuring cause, magnificent, tender, Divine, human, spiritual, historic. It is the Beloved Son of the Father; no antagonistic power from a region alien to the blessed law and its Giver. The Law-giver is the Christ-giver; He has set Him forth. He has provided in Him an expiation which does not persuade Him to have mercy . . . . . but liberates His love along the line of a wonderfully satisfied holiness."—MOULE.

(3) The sin of man made it necessary.

I Peter 2:25—For ye were as sheep going astray; but are now returned unto the Shepherd and Bishop of your souls.

S. F. Isa. 59:1, 2; Eph. 2:13.

It was the lost, strayed condition of humanity that made necessary the death of Christ. This was the magnet that drew the Son of God from the skies. He could not be satisfied with the glory which He had with the Father before the world was, with all the adoration and admiration of all the unfallen hosts of heaven, while man remained estranged and lost from God.

Superficial views of the atonement are produced by superficial views of sin. If sin is regarded as only an offense against man, a weakness of human nature, a slight moral ailment, rather than as rebellious lawlessness and enmity against God, and therefore condemning and punishable, we shall not, of course, see any necessity for the atonement. We must see sin as the Bible describes it, as something that brings wrath and punishment in its train; as guilt that needs expiation; as crime that deserves punishment. When we see sin as God sees it, we shall also see the dire need of a Saviour—an atoning, redeeming Saviour—and the blood of His cross.

(4) The fulfillment of the Scriptures made it necessary.

Luke 24:25–27—Then he said unto them, O fools, and slow of heart to believe all that the prophets have spoken: Ought not Christ to have suffered these things and to enter into his glory? And beginning at Moses and all the prophets, he expounded unto them in all the Scriptures the things concerning himself.

Comp. with Psa. 69, Psa. 22, Isa. 53.

Said Jesus, "The Scripture of redemption and of a redeemer must be fulfilled." Again, he said, "Ought not Christ to have suffered," and then showed that the ethical necessity was based upon the Old Testament promise of redemption.

God's veracity made necessary the death of Christ. If Jesus were the true Messiah, then these predictions of His sufferings and death must be fulfilled in Him.

(5) The purpose of God made it necessary.

Acts 2:23—Him, being delivered by the determinate counsel and foreknowledge of God, ye have taken, and by wicked hands have crucified and slain.

S. F. I Pet. 1:18–20; Gal. 4:4, 5.

God's eternal purposes include the redemption of His chosen ones among men from their lost estate unto Himself. Since "There was none other good enough to pay the price of sin," God's very plan of redemption foreordained that Christ should be the Substitute for sinners.

D. S. The holiness and love of God and the sinfulness of man, together with God's promise and purpose of redemption made Christ's death necessary.

3. The Nature of It.

(1) Negatively considered.

There are a number of erroneous views concerning the nature of the death of Christ which require some attention.

a. The accident theory.

This theory views the cross of Calvary as something unforeseen in the life of Christ, as something not contained in the divine plan. It holds Christ's death to be an unexpected accident, which made Him a victim of circumstances.

This is to be refuted by saying that Jesus gave evidence during His earth-life of knowing about His forthcoming death, by foretelling it again and again.

"As astronomers know, when none others think of it, that travelling through the heavens the vast shadow is progressing towards the sun which ere long shall clothe it and hide it, so Christ knew that the great darkness which was to overwhelm Him was approaching."—BEECHER.

He was perfectly familiar with the Old Testament Scriptures, which contain countless references to the death of the Messiah (Isa. 53, Psa. 22, and Psa. 69 compared with Luke 24:26–44).

Matt. 16:21—From that time forth began Jesus to shew unto his disciples, how that he must go into Jerusalem, and suffer many things of the elders and chief priests and scribes, and be killed, and be raised again the third day.

S. F. Matt. 26:2 and Matt. 20:28; Mark 9:30–32; Isa. 53:5, 6, 11.

b. The martyr theory.

.This theory holds that Christ died a martyr's death for the cause that He had espoused; that He sealed His testimony to the truth with His blood. It places His death on a plane with that of Polycarp, John Rogers, Bishop Latimer and Bishop Ridley.

This is to be refuted thus: If this were true, then, according to the principle which Christ Himself established, "if it were not so I would have told you," He should have refuted the belief which He had planted in the minds of His disciples, that His death was redemptive (Luke 22:39–46).

Had Christ died as a martyr, the Apostle Paul should have told us so. The word was used by the other New Testament writers to describe the death of Christians, why did not Paul use it of Christ to describe His death? If this theory is true, then there is no mystery about the Atonement, as Paul declared (Eph. 5:25, 27, 32).

"Again, Christ might at least have had the same comforting presence of God, afforded other martyrs, had this been the nature of His death. But He was forsaken of God. Would it be right to make Him, who was the holiest man in all the ages, the greatest sufferer, if that man were but a martyr? Then, too, why should Christ shrink from death as He did, if it were only the death of a martyr, for other martyrs have faced it without shrinking? Christ's soul was filled with anguish at the thought of His approaching death (Luke 22:39–42), while Paul faced a martyr's fate with joy. No, Christ was not a martyr. Stephen was, but Paul never preached salvation through his death. 'Such a view of Christ's death may beget martyrs, but it can never save sinners.' "—EVANS.

124

c. The moral influence theory.

This theory views Christ's death as an example which should exert a moral influence upon mankind in order to secure its moral improvement.

"The moral theory regards the redemptive work of Christ as accomplished through His example and lessons of religious truth, operative as a practical influence with men."—MILEY.

"The example of His suffering, it is said, ought to soften human hearts and help a man to reform, repent, and better his condition. So they teach that God grants pardon and forgiveness on the basis of simple repentance and reformation."—EVANS.

This is to be refuted by the fact that the knowledge of Christ's suffering alone does not so affect men. It did not in the days of that suffering and it does not today.

"In the same way a drunkard might call a man his saviour by whose influence he was induced to become sober and industrious."—EVANS.

d. The governmental theory.

Those who hold this theory believe that God's government of the world makes necessary a manifestation of His wrath against sin. They see in Christ's death an example of suffering exhibiting the fact of God's governmental displeasure at sin.

Miley, who holds this view, says: "The substitution of Christ must be of a nature agreeing with the provisory character of the atonement. It could not, therefore, be a substitution in penalty as the merited punishment of sin, for such an atonement is absolute. The substitution, therefore, is in suffering, without the penal element. This agrees with the nature of the atonement as a moral support of justice in its office, rendering forgiveness consistent with the interest of moral government.

"Nor could the sufferings of Christ have been, in any strict or proper sense, a punishment. Demerit, the only ground of punishment, is personal to the actual sinner, and without possible interference. It is futile to attempt the transference of guilt without sin . . . . . and imputation carried over no sin to Christ."

"Christ was at no time the object of His Father's personal displeasure, but suffered only the signs—the effects, not the affectation—of divine anger."— BRUCE.

This view is to be refuted by saying that any guilty man might have been used as an example of God's displeasure and wrath at sin. An innocent man was not necessary for this; in fact it seems scarcely just to use such a one. Certainly a new being was not necessary for the purpose. There could have been no exhibition of God's displeasure at sin in the sufferings of Christ unless these sufferings were endured in connection with the meting out of justice, the infliction of penalty, the punishment of guilt. Otherwise the cross would be a mere scenic display without any reality, a mere pretended administration of government without any just or judicial action. The execution of justice is necessary in order to the true expression of justice. The former is that which the Scriptures teach took place at the cross (See Gal. 3:13; I Peter 2:24; 3:18).

e. The Love-of-God theory.

This theory teaches that Christ died to show men how much God loved them.

so that, ever after, they would know the feeling of the heart of God toward them.

This is to be refuted by the fact that men did not need such a manifestation to know of God's love for them, for the Old Testament Scriptures were full of the love of God. We grant, however, that the death of Christ did reveal God's love. But it is more, it is the provision which God's love has made for men— for their salvation from sin's guilt and penalty. According to this theory God is represented as suffering in Christ with man the consequences and results of his sin. Thus a fatal omission is made, for God not only suffered with man in the sufferings of Christ, but for man. "Christ died for us" (Rom. 5:8).

D. S. Jesus Christ did not die accidentally, nor as a martyr; neither did He die merely to exercise a moral influence upon men, nor to display God's governmental displeasure at sin; nor merely to express God's love to men.

(2) Positively considered.

It is doubtless true that no one can give a perfect or complete answer to the question, "What is the nature of the death of Christ?" The general statement, however, can be made, with the full assurance of its Scriptural soundness, that it was of a saving nature. It was God's saving work on behalf of man. There are some definite Biblical statements made and teaching given upon which the following are based:

a. It was predetermined (planned or purposed before).

Acts 2:23—Him, being delivered by the determinate counsel and foreknowledge of God, ye have taken, and by wicked hands have crucified and slain.

S. F. I Peter 1:18–20; Rev. 13:8.

The atonement had its origin in eternity. Its source was in God. The atonement was an implicit fact in the heart of God before it became an explicit fact in the history of man—a fact of eternity before it became a fact of time.

b. It was voluntary (by free choice, not by compulsion).

John 10:17–18—Therefore does my Father love me, because I lay down my life, that I might take it again. No man taketh it from me, but I lay it down of myself. I have power to lay it down, and I have power to take it again. This commandment have I received of my Father.

S. F. Gal. 2:20.

We sometimes attribute the death of Christ to the Jews and sometimes to the Roman soldiers, but in the final analysis Jesus Christ died under the contract of His own will.

"There was no compulsion laid upon Him, other than the impulsion of His own heart of love. Love compels by its impelling. There is no power which moved so mightily as love in the force of its intensity. . . . . His willingness to act for us brings out the intrinsic worth of His action."— MARSH.

c. It was vicarious (on behalf of others).

I Peter 3:18—For Christ also hath once suffered for sins, the just for the unjust that he might bring us to God, being put to death in the flesh, but quickened by the Spirit.

S. F. I Cor. 15:3; Rom. 4:25.

It has been shown that Christ's death was not an accident nor that of a

126

martyr, not on his own account; it was for the sake of others, not for Himself, that He died. The Apostle Paul says, "Christ died for our sins, according to the Scriptures."

d. It was sacrificial (as an offering for sin).

I Cor. 5:7—Purge out therefore the old leaven, that ye may be a new lump, as ye are unleavened. For even Christ our passover is sacrificed for us.

S. F. Ex. 12:13, 23 and Isa. 53:10; Heb. 9:14.

The death of Christ was effectually sacrificial on behalf of the world's sin. Therefore every member of the human race is born under the protecting shadow of the cross. As the guilt of Adam's sin is reckoned to Adam's posterity without their personal ratification or repudiation, so are his posterity made sharers of the merit of Christ's obedient action in redemption with reference to the guilt of Adam's sin, regardless of their personal approval or appropriation.

The death of Jesus Christ is potentially and provisionally sacrificial on behalf of the world's sins. In this sense, He tasted death for every man, and "gave Himself a ransom for all," and is the Saviour of all men.

e. It was expiatory (appeasing or rendering satisfactory).

Gal. 3:13—Christ hath redeemed us from the curse of the law, being made a curse for us: for it is written, Cursed is every one that hangeth on a tree.

S. F. Isa. 53:4–6.

Expiation is the annulling of guilt or taking away of sin by some meritorious interposition. Though not found in the Scriptures, no word is of more frequent use in connection with our subject. See as illustration Gen. 32:20.

f. It was propitiatory (covering or making favorable).

I John 4:10—Herein is love, not that we loved God, but that he loved us, and sent His son to be the propitiation for our sins.

S. F. Isa. 53:8, 10–12; Rom. 3:25.

"In the three cases in which this term occurs in the New Testament (which are the only cases in the Scriptures), it is applied to Him by whom atonement is affected . . . . . It supposes an offence and the turning away of the offence—two ideas which are involved in the doctrine of the atonement; and the use made of it in Scripture connects it inseparably with sacrifice as the means by which the offence is taken away."—SYMINGTON.

"Rom. 3:25 might literally be rendered 'a propitiation through faith by his blood' (Gr., *hilasterion*, 'place of propitiation'). The word occurs in I John 2:2 as the translation of *hilasmos*, 'that which propitiates,' 'a propitiatory sacrifice.' *Hilasterion* is used by the Septuagint and in Heb. 9:5 for 'mercy-seat.' The mercy-seat was sprinkled with atoning blood on the day of atonement in token that the righteous sentence of the law had been (typically) carried out, so that what must else have been a judgment-seat could righteously be a mercy-seat. In fulfillment of the type, Christ is Himself the hilasmos, 'that which propitiates,' and the hilasterion, 'the place of propitiation'—the mercy-seat sprinkled with His own blood—the token that in our stead He so honoured the law by enduring its righteous sentence that God, who ever foresaw the cross, is vindicated in having 'passed over' sins from Adam to Moses (Rom. 5:13) and the sins of be-

127

lievers under the old covenant and just in justifying sinners under the new covenant. There is no thought in propitiation of placating a vengeful God, but of doing right by His Holy law and so making it possible for Him righteously to show mercy."—SCOFIELD.

g. It was redemptive (ransoming by payment).

Gal. 4:4, 5—But when the fulness of the time was come, God sent forth his Son, made of a woman, made under the law, to redeem them that were under the law, that we might receive the adoption of sons.

S. F. Gal. 3:13; Matt. 20:28.

The term is borrowed from transactions among men, such as the release of a captive upon payment of a ransom, or the release of an imprisoned debtor by liquidating his debt.

The term supposes deliverance by a substitute, of a captive or debtor who is unable to effect his own escape. Of course it follows that emancipation and restoration result from the paying of the ransom. Christ redeemed us from the curse of a broken law by being Himself made a curse for us. His death was the ransom price paid.

"To whom this ransom is paid is a debated question: whether to Satan for His captives, or to eternal and necessary holiness, to the divine law, to the claim of God who is by nature the holy Lawgiver. The latter, referring to God and His holiness, is preferable."—EVANS.

"The completed truth is set forth in the three words which are translated redemption: *agorazo*, 'to purchase in the market.' The subjects of redemption are 'sold under sin' (Rom. 7:14), but are, moreover, under sentence of death (Ezek. 18:4; John 3:18, 19), and the purchase price is the blood of the Redeemer who dies in their stead (Matt. 20:28).

"The second word is *exagorazo*, 'To buy out the market' (Gal. 3:13). The redeemed are never again to be exposed to sale. The third is *lutroo* (Eph. 1:7; I Peter 1:18; Rom. 3:24), 'to loose,' 'to set free by paying a price.' Redemption is by sacrifice and by power (Ex. 14:30). Christ paid the price, the Holy Spirit makes deliverance actual in experience."—SCOFIELD.

h. It was substitutionary (in the place of others).

I Peter 2:24—Who his own self bare our sins in his own body on the tree, that we, being dead to sins, should live unto righteousness: by whose stripes ye were healed.

S. A. Lev. 1:2–4; II Cor.. 5:21; Rom. 4:25; Matt. 1:21; Mark 10:45.

This term does not occur in the Bible, but the principle which it represents is found throughout, in connection with the teachings concerning Christ's death, whether it be by type or plain statement. It has in it the thought of Christ taking the place of offending sinners, bearing their guilt, and suffering their punishment.

As surety for men, He voluntarily places Himself in their situation, as violators of God's holy, just, and good law: He holds Himself responsible for all their guilt; and bares His bosom to the full reward of the threatened penalty due to them for sin. He substitutes Himself in their stead, not merely in regard to punishment, but in respect of obligation to punishment. Christ submitted not only to be treated as a sin-offering, but to be made sin for us. While His holy soul was free from all the moral contaminations connected with a

128

state of moral guilt; while personal guilt never could be charged upon Him, nevertheless, it. was necessary to have imputed to Him the guilt for which He was to make atonement. This was necessary that His sufferings might partake of the nature of a punishment. Suffering, disconnected from guilt, is calamity, not punishment; to punishment, guilt is indispensably requisite. Christ had not guilt of His own; He was incapable, indeed, of contracting it; but "the Lord laid on Him the iniquity of us all."

D. S. The death of Jesus Christ was pre-determined, voluntary, vicarious, sacrificial, expiatory, propitiatory, redemptive, and substitutionary.

4. The Scope of It.

"Christ's death in its scope has a two-fold aspect, universal and restricted. It is universal in its sufficiency and restricted in its efficiency. It is sufficient for all; it is efficient for those who believe. The Scriptures represent the atonement as having been made for all men, and as sufficient for the salvation of all. Not the atonement, therefore, is limited, but the application of the atonement through the work of the Holy Spirit."—STRONG.

1. The atonement is sufficient for all. John 1:29; I Tim. 2:6; 4:10; Heb. 2:9; I John 2:2.
2. It is efficient in salvation for all who believe. John 1:12.
3. It is efficient in judgment for all who continue in unbelief. John 3:18; 16:9.

(1) For the whole world.

I John 2:2—And he is the propitiation for our sins; and not for ours only, but also for the sins of the whole world.

It is not said in the Gospel that Christ died with the intention that all should be saved, but that His atonement is a sufficient ground of salvation to all, and that all who rest on this ground by faith shall be saved.

(2) For each individual member of the race.

Heb. 2:9—But we see Jesus, who was made a little lower than the angels for the suffering of death, crowned with glory and honor: that he by the grace of God should taste death for every man.

This is only another form of the statement that Christ died for the whole world. No man, woman, or child is excluded from the blessing of the atonement. Each one is included, provisionally.

(3) For the sinful, the unjust, and the ungodly.

Rom. 5:6-8—For when we were yet without strength, in due time Christ died for the ungodly. For scarcely for a righteous man will one die: yet peradventure for a good man some would even dare to die. But God commendeth his love toward us, in that, while we were yet sinners, Christ died for us.

S. F. I Tim. 1:15; I Peter 3:18.

"The atonement has come to all men and upon all men. Its coextensiveness with the effects of Adam's sin is seen in that all the creatures, such as infants and other irresponsible persons, incapable of refusing it, are saved without their consent, just as they are involved in the sin of Adam without their consent . . . . . If they are born under the curse, so likewise they are born under the atonement which is intended to remove that curse; they remain under its shelter till they are old enough to repudiate it;

129

they shut out its influences as a man closes his window-blind to shut out the beams of the sun; they ward them off by direct opposition, as a man builds dykes around his field to keep out the streams which would otherwise flow in and fertilize the soil."—ASHMORE.

(4) For the Church and all believers.

Eph. 5:25–27—Husbands, love your wives, even as Christ also loved the church, and gave himself for it; that he might sanctify and cleanse it with the washing of water by the word, that he might present it to himself a glorious church, not having spot, or wrinkle, or any such thing; but that it should be holy and without blemish.

S. F. I Tim. 4:10.

Christ is especially the Saviour of those that believe. There is a sense in which we may say that Christ died particularly for the church. "Christ loved the church and gave Himself for it."

D. S. The whole world was included in the provision of Christ's death and in a degree shares its benefits, but it is fully effectual and redemptive for those who believe.

5. The Results of It.

(1) In relation to men in general, an age of grace is provided. Titus 2:11.

The Apostle Paul calls Jesus Christ the "Saviour of all men," showing that in His redemptive work Christ sustains a relationship to the whole race.

"Unconscious participation in the atonement of Christ, by virtue of our common humanity in Him, makes us the heirs of much temporal blessing." —STRONG.

a. A new probation is secured.

Rom. 3:25—Whom God hath set forth to be a propitiation through faith in his blood, to declare his righteousness for the remission of sins that are past, through the forbearance of God.

S. F. Acts 17:30, 31 and II Peter 3:9; John 3:16–18.

Man failed and fell under the first probation in Adam resulting in death and depravity. Through the death of Christ a new probation has been provided. Under the old, man was tested under law, with reference to the tree of the knowledge of good and evil, under the new, he is tested under grace with reference to Jesus Christ and His salvation.

"The atonement of Christ secures for all men a delay in the execution of the sentence against sin, and a space for repentance, together with a continuance of the common blessings of life which have been forfeited by transgression. It has made objective provision for the salvation of all, by removing from the divine mind every obstacle to the pardon and restoration of sinners, except their willful opposition to God and refusal to turn to Him. The atonement of Christ has also procured for all men three powerful incentives to repentance presented in the Cross, and the combined agency of the Christian church and of the Holy Spirit, by which these incentives are brought to bear upon them."—STRONG.

"It may be admitted that there are certain advantages or privileges, not of a saving nature, resulting from the death of Christ, the participation of which, by those who live under the Gospel, may be held to be strictly universal. The preservation of the human race itself may be traced to this source; and certainly we are indebted to it for the means of moral and religious improvement, for much valuable and useful knowledge, for a more full and clear exhibition of duty, for greater restraints on wickedness, and stronger incentives to righteousness, and benevolence, and purity; with many other things contributing to the prosperity of society and the welfare of individuals, which unassisted reason or civil legislation could not have secured. The system of grace, established on earth and resting as its basis on the atonement of Christ, surrounds, so to speak, 'our guilty world with an atmosphere of natural and moral good, and scatters endless variety of personal and social enjoyments.' These advantages are strictly universal; and if the sentiment that Christ died for all men were understood to have no higher reference than these, we might not feel ourselves called upon to dispute it."—SYMINGTON.

b. Men are drawn unto Him.

John 12:32-33—And I, if I be lifted up from the earth, will draw all men unto me. This he said signifying what death he should die.

Comp. with John 5:40—And ye will not come unto me that ye might have life.

S. A. Jer. 31:3.

It is true that God in the expression of His love for men through the sufferings and death of Christ is seeking to allure and attract all men from the ways of sin unto the ways of truth and righteousness, but it is apparent that all do not respond. All men are drawn, but all are not constrained. "The grace of God hath appeared to all men" (Titus 2:11), but all have not received it.

A magnet may be held in the same relationshp to a number of metals so that its drawing power is exercised with respect to them all, but the drawing power is not effectual for all. Its effectuality is dependent upon the metal and not the magnet. All men have not faith (II Thess. 3:2), therefore, all do not respond to the attraction of the cross.

c. A propitiation is provided.

I John 4:10—Herein is love, not that we loved God, but that he loved us, and sent His son to be the propitiation for our sins.

S. F. I John 2:2.

A provisional covering for the unsightliness and repugnance of man's sin and sinfulness has been procured by the death of Christ, but this potential covering which is thus made available to man must be appropriated by him if he is to realize its benefits. Just as in the garden of Eden after Adam and Eve had sinned, God provided raiment for them by means of beasts slain for that purpose, but the raiment had to be appropriated and put on by Adam and Eve before they were presentable to God.

d. The sin of the world is removed.

John 1:29—The next day John seeth Jesus coming unto him, and saith, Behold the Lamb of God which taketh away the sin of the world.

The sin of the world is that guilt which attaches itself to the world or human race through the sin of Adam. Adam, during the period of his probation and temptation, acted not only as an individual man, but as the race-man. He was the federal and biological head of the human race and therefore his action was racial as well as individual. The Apostle Paul declares that we all sinned in Adam. We acted in him and through him; thus we sinned in his sin and fell in his fall and became guilty with his guilt. But while this is true no·member of the human race is lost because of the guilt of Adam's sin, for that guilt was completely and perfectly removed by the death of Christ, as the "Lamb of God which taketh away the sin of the world." Hence the only guilt which attaches itself to that irresponsible part of humanity which includes infancy, imbecility, and idiocy is the guilt of the Adamic sin for which Christ has atoned. All, therefore, who pass out of life in this irresponsible state of mind, never having had the capacity of a rational choice, are:

> "Safe in the arms of Jesus, Safe on His gentle breast;
> There by His love o'ershaded, Sweetly their souls do rest."

The reputed teaching of the old theologians that there are infants in hell not a span long is absolutely unwarranted, having no foundation in the Scriptures, nor in the character of God. David said, at the death of his own infant child, which was born of an adulterous relationship, "I shall go to him, but he shall not return to me" (II Sam. 12:23).

D. S. Many benefits and blessings, potential and actual, are bestowed upon men in general through the death of Christ.

(2) In relation to the believer, a new creation is effected. II Cor. 5:17.

The result of the death of Christ to the believer in general is that he is "returned to the Shepherd and Bishop of your souls." The potential salvation provided in the Cross becomes actual and experimental when He places his trust in the Saviour.

a. The power of sin is potentially nullified.

Heb. 9:26—For then must he often have suffered since the foundation of the world: but now once in the end of the world hath he appeared to put away sin by the sacrifice of himself.

The Apostle says "sin" not "sins." There is a special force in the abstract. It was not this nor that sin of which Christ destroyed the power; it was sin itself which He put away by His death. He potentially destroyed the power of sin as well as atoned for actual sins.

"The atonement of Christ was not only an expiation for sin, but a triumph over it. Christ answered for sin that we should cease to answer to it. His death for sin is the death of sin. His passion for us quenches the passion of sin. The outward crucifixion of Christ which procures the benefit of pardon is the inward power which enables us to experience the inward crucifixion of self."—MARSH.

b. Redemption from the curse of the law is secured.

Gal. 3:13—Christ hath redeemed us from the curse of the law, being made a curse for us: for it is written, Cursed is every one that hangeth on a tree.

S. F. Gal. 3:10; James 2:10; Isa. 42:21.

The believer is redeemed or ransomed and thus released from the curse under which all lie who trust to the law and the works of the law for justification.

Every legal obstruction to the salvation of man is taken away. Guilt is atoned for, redemption from condemnation is procured; and every charge which the law can prefer against the sinner is completely met.

"In Him, the law is magnified and made honorable. Christ appeared to be the end of the law for righteousness. He came not to destroy the law but to fulfill it. And God hath set forth a propitiation through faith in His blood, to declare His righteousness."—SYMINGTON.

c. Deliverance from bondage to the law is provided.

Col. 2:14, R. V.—Having blotted out the bond written in ordinances that was against us, which was contrary to us; and he hath taken it out of the way, nailing it to the cross.

S. F. Rom. 7:1-4, 6, R. V.

The believer is "crucified with Christ" and this death dissolves his marriage obligation to the law, his subjection to it, leaving him free to be joined to the Risen One, for service and fruitfulness.

"Redemption from bondage to the law includes not only deliverance from its penalty, but also from the obligation to satisfy its demands. The law demands perfect obedience. It says, 'Do this and live' and 'Cursed is every one that continueth not in all things which are written in the book of the law to do them.'"—HODGE.

Subjection to the law was a state of bondage, and from it men are redeemed by the Cross and introduced into the liberty of the Gospel.

d. The barrier between Jew and Gentile is provisionally removed.

Eph. 2:14-16—For he is our peace, who hath made both one, and hath broken down the middle wall of partition between us; having abolished in his flesh the enmity, even the law of commandments contained in ordinances; for to make in himself of twain one new man, so making peace; and that he might reconcile both unto God in one body by the cross, having slain the enmity thereby.

S. F. Gal. 3:28, R. V.

"The parties here, which are made one, are not a holy God and an unholy sinner. The Jews and the Gentiles are the two, who are made one in Christ. Between these two there stood a middle wall of partition, separating them. This middle wall of partition is the law. God himself had put up this wall, separating His people Israel from the Gentiles . . . . . The law of commandments in ordinances demanded from the Jews an entire separation from the Gentiles. For a Jew to eat with a Gentile was sin. Even Peter, when he had eaten with the Gentiles in Antioch, separated himself and withdrew; this shows how deeply rooted was this prejudice. The enmity and the hatred between the Jews and Gentiles was great and can easily be traced in history. And now in the Cross of Christ, God has broken down this middle wall of partition and made an end of this enmity, the law of commandments in ordinances. It has found its end in the cross. The Jews having rejected their Messiah had filled up the measure of their guilt as a nation and had become more guilty on account of it than the Gentiles. The middle wall ceased existing . . . . . Jews and Gentiles, believing, trusting in Christ, made nigh by His blood, are made both one and constitute one new man."—GAEBELEIN.

e. The ground of sonship is furnished.

Gal. 4:3–5—Even so we, when we were children, were in bondage under the elements of the world; but when the fulness of the time was come, God sent forth his Son, made of a woman, made under the law, to redeem them that were under the law, that we might receive the adoption of sons.

If Christ is our substitute and takes our place, then, by blessed transfer and exchange, we forever have His place and are no longer seen in ourselves but in Him—sons in the Eternal Son. "That perfect **Man,** Who came, the Eternal Son, to earn salvation for the sons of men."

f. The moral distance between him and God is annihilated.

Eph. 2:13—But now in Christ Jesus ye who sometimes were far off are made nigh by the blood of Christ.

The distance between God and man is not physical for there is no such distance between them, for God is omnipresent. He filleth all and is in all. There is no spot where God is not. The distance is rather moral. It is sin that separates. (See Isa. 59:1–2.) That distance, however, is potentially exterminated by the sacrifice of the cross.

> *"By nature and by practice far—*
> *How very far! from God;*
> *Yet now by grace brought nigh to Him*
> *Thru faith in Jesus' blood.*
>
> *So nigh, so very nigh to God,*
> *Nearer, I cannot be*
> *For in the Person of His Son*
> *I am as near as He."*

g. Reconciliation with God is provided.

Rom. 5:10—For if, when we were enemies, we were reconciled to God by the death of his son, much more, being reconciled, we shall be saved by his life.

S. F. Col. 1:20, 22.

The death of Christ has brought into a state of agreement the parties who were at variance—God and His sinful creature, man.

h. The forgiveness of sins is secured.

Eph. 1:7—In whom we have redemption through his blood, the forgiveness of sins, according to the riches of his grace.

That which is practically impossible to obtain in every other realm of human experience, such as nature, society, and courts of human justice, is gloriously possible in Christ, by reason of His atoning death.

i. Cleansing from all sin is provided.

I John 1:7, 9—But if we walk in the light as he is in the light, we have fellowship one with another, and the blood of Jesus Christ, his Son, cleanseth us from all sin.

If we confess our sins, he is faithful and just to forgive us our sins and to cleanse us from all unrighteousness.

Christ's blood is the cleansing means, whereby gradually, being already justified and in fellowship with God, the believer becomes clean from all sin which would mar his fellowship with God. Faith applies the purifying blood.

Dr. Torrey asks the question, "Does this mean cleansing from the guilt of sin or does it mean cleansing from the very presence of sin itself?"

Psa. 51:7—Purge me with hyssop, and I shall be clean: wash me, and I shall be whiter than snow.

S. F. Lev. 14:19; Lev. 14:31; Jer. 33:8; Rev. 7:14; Heb. 9:22, 23; Eph. 1:7; Rom. 3:25; Rom. 5:9; Matt. 26:28; Lev. 16:30; Lev. 17:11.

Answer—From these passages it is evident that in Bible usage cleansing by blood is cleansing from guilt. Through the shed blood of Christ, all who walk in the light are cleansed continuously every hour and minute, from all the guilt of sin. There is absolutely no sin upon them; there may be sin in them. It is not the blood, but the living Christ and the Holy Spirit who deal with that.

j. The ground of his justification or acquittal from guilt is provided.

Rom. 5:9—Much more then, being now justified by his blood, we shall be saved from wrath through him.

"That righteousness covers us. It shields us. 'It is a robe which our best deeds cannot mend and which our worst deeds cannot mar.' Christ for us and in our stead is the simple answer to all things."—BISHOP.

k. Condemnation is forever removed.

Rom. 8:33, 34, R. V.—Who shall lay anything to the charge of God's elect? It is God that justifieth; who is he that condemneth? It is Christ. Jesus that died, yea rather, that was raised from the dead, who is at the right hand of God, who also maketh intercession for us.

S. F. Rom. 8:1–3, R. V.; Acts 13:38, 39.

"The sinner, who formerly crouched and trembled in every nerve at the sanctions of the law, may now lift his head in humble confidence, and bidding defiance to a whole universe of accusation say, 'Who shall lay anything to the charge of God's elect? Who is he that condemneth? It is Christ that died.' "—SYMINGTON.

Man by nature is identified with Adam through his sin and fall in the realm of condemnation, but by faith in Jesus Christ he is transferred from that realm to one which is known by the term "in Christ Jesus," where there is no condemnation, no death, no judgment.

John 5:24—Verily, verily, I say unto you, he that heareth my word, and believeth on him that sent me, hath everlasting life, and shall not come into condemnation; but is passed from death unto life.

l. Purchase of him for God is made.

I Cor. 6:20—For ye are bought with a price: therefore glorify God in your body, and in your spirit, which are God's.

S. F. Rev. 5:9, 10 R. V.; Acts 20:28; Eph. 1:13, 14; I Pet. 1:18, 19.

The price which redeemed man from sin, its guilt and penalty redeemed him to God. The believer therefore is God's purchased possession. hence Paul said to the Corinthians, "Ye are not your own? For ye are bought with a price: therefore glorify God in your body." (I Cor. 6:19, 20).

m. His death to sin is provisionally accomplished.

Gal. 6:14—But God forbid that I should glory, save in the cross of our Lord Jesus Christ, by whom the world is crucified unto me, and I unto the world.

S. F. Gal. 2:20; Rom. 6:1-3, 6, 8; II Cor. 5:14-15; I Peter 2:24.

"The cross is the secret of life (Gal. 2:20). It is the secret of one's own personal life. The 'I' is the representative of the self life, which has been the cause of all the enmity in the human heart towards God, and the source of all the weakness of human service for God ever since the fall, and that 'I' has to be dealt with by the cross.

"When the priests of the Coptic church in Egypt are ordaining a man to the priesthood they recite over him the prayer that they recite over the dead, inferring that he is dead to everything of the world and alive only to God.

"The cross is the source of all victory, and there is a five-fold victory for the Christian to win. First, victory over death (I Cor. 15:56, 57). Second, victory over self (Gal. 2:20). Third, victory over the flesh (Gal. 5:24). Fourth, victory over the world (Gal. 6:14). Fifth, victory over Satan (Col. 2:15)."—WATT.

n. The giving of all things is pledged.

Rom. 8:32—He that spared not his own Son, but delivered him up for us all, how shall he not with him also freely give us all things?

The unspeakable gift includes all other gifts. The "not sparing of his own Son" is an absolute guarantee that He will not spare any other blessing temporal or spiritual which is for our well-being.

o. Potential deliverance from the fear of death is secured.

Heb. 2:14, 15, R. V.—Since then the children are sharers in flesh and blood, he also himself in like manner partook of the same; that through death he might bring to nought him that had the power of death, that is the devil; and might deliver all them who through fear of death were all their life-time subject to bondage.

"The cross on the green hill links the today of time with the tomorrow of eternity. The cross proves that to be partaker of the sufferings of Christ insures partnership with Him in the glory."—WATT.

D. S. The benefits which belong to the believer through the death of Christ are innumerable; it is the fountain-head of all his blessings, for time and eternity.

(3) In relation to Satan and the powers of darkness, their defeat is secured. Col. 2:14, 15.

It is evident from a number of passages of Scripture that Jesus Christ had a mission in relation to the devil in connection with His Incarnation and death. This is shown by the following:

a. Satan was cast out.

John 12:31-33—Now is the judgment of this world: now shall the prince of this world be cast out. And I, if I be lifted up from the earth, will draw all men unto me. This he said, signifying what death he should die.

S. F. Rev. 12:7-9.

Jesus is here speaking anticipatively of the cross and that which would be secured by it. He is looking forward not to defeat, but to great victory—victory over the forces of evil; hence He speaks as though it had already taken place, and in the thought and reckoning of God it was just as certain as though it had.

136

b. Satan is brought to nought (provisionally rendered ineffective). Heb. 2:14 (R. V.)

The power of death is here ascribed to the devil, and Christ is represented as taking Satan's own weapon to conquer him. This finds an illustration in David who seized the sword of Goliath with which to slay him. That power which Satan has used as usurper in an unholy way, Christ in awful justice has used to bring him to nought and to secure his destruction.

c. Principalities and powers are defeated.

Col. 2:14, 15 (Weymouth)—The bond, with its requirements which was in force against us and was hostile to us, He cancelled, and cleared it out of the way, nailing it to His Cross. And the hostile princes and rulers He shook off from Himself, and boldly displayed them as His conquests, when by the Cross He triumphed over them.

S. F. Eph. 6:12, R. V.

"Christ gets such a victory for us over all our spiritual enemies as is here expressed in verse 15. The principalities and powers of darkness seized upon the human nature of Christ our substitute, as if to prevent Him from going to the cross and dying for our redemption. But He overcame them, made a show of them openly by rising from the dead, and in His triumph we triumph."— GRAY'S COMMENTARY.

"Christ came to destroy the works of the devil. He was predicted of old as he who should bruise the serpent's head: and for this purpose was he manifested in due time (I John 3:8). By His death, did He destroy him that had the power of death, that is the devil. The same work he still carries on in glory in the character of Intercessor, answering the accusations brought against his people, and protecting them from the assaults of the adversary. Satan is the accuser of the brethren; he prefers heavy charges against the disciples of Christ. Some of them are true, others false; but Christ, as the advocate with the Father, answers them all. He refutes such as are false by showing their groundlessness; and for the forgiveness of such as are true he pleads the merit of his blood. (I John 2:1, 2; Zech. 3:1–5)."—SYMINGTON.

D. S. The death of Jesus Christ, has provided for the nullification of Satan's power over believers' lives and has secured his final doom and destruction.

(4) In relation to the material universe, deliverance from the curse is assured. Rom. 8:21.

Col. 1:19, 20—For it pleased the Father that in him should all fulness dwell; and, having made peace through the blood of his cross, by him to reconcile all things unto himself; by him, I say, whether they be things in earth, or things in heaven.

S. F. Rom. 8:20–23.

"The creation of the world, there is every reason to believe, was with the view of its being a theatre on which to exhibit the work of man's redemption by the eternal Son. It is the workmanship of His hand. This is the purpose which it serves; and that it was framed with a view to its serving its purpose is surely no disputable assertion. The apostle, in express terms, not only claims for Christ the honor of the world's creation, but asserts the purpose of its creation to terminate in Him—'All things were created by Him and for Him.' He is the final as well as the efficient cause of this world's creation. Our earth was selected as the chosen spot on which the mystery of redemption was to be displayed; and all the scenes of the mediatorial economy were here exhibited. The advent of the promised Messiah took place here; here was led his instructive life; here were wrought his wondrous miracles; here were spoken his still more wondrous words; here were borne his mysterious sufferings; here was accomplished his awful decease; and here were achieved his glorious victories over men and devils, over sin and death."—SYMINGTON.

Just as the material universe was in some mysterious manner affected by the fall of man (Rom. 8:19-23, R. V.), so also is it affected by the death of Jesus Christ, which is intended to neutralize the effect of sin upon the creation. There is a cosmical effect in the atonement. The Christ of Paul is larger than the second Adam—the Head of a new humanity; He is also the center of a universe which revolves around Him, which is in some mysterious way reconciled by His death. Just how this takes place we may not be able definitely to explain.

Col. 1:20—And, having made peace through the blood of his cross, by him to reconcile all things unto himself; by him, I say, whether they be things in earth, or things in heaven.

Some day there shall be "new heavens, and a new earth, wherein dwelleth righteousness' (II Peter 3:13).

S. A. Heb. 9:23, 24; Isa. 11 and 35.

"A great fundamental doctrine runs all through Scripture—creation unto New Creation. By this we simply mean, that, in the first or present creation, which began at that point in the remote past called 'the beginning' (Gen. 1:1) God is having the tremendous issues between sin and holiness, light and darkness, Himself and all opposed to Him, once and forever wrought out. When this has been accomplished, He will bring in a New Creation, wherein shall dwell perfect righteousness; and which, being founded upon the work of Christ, and not upon the faithfulness of mere creatures, shall never pass away (see Rev. 21, II Peter 3)."—NEWELL.

D. S. Through the death of Christ the whole material universe—"all things in earth and things in heaven"—is reconciled to God.

II. The Resurrection of Jesus Christ.

"His resurrection was necessary to His being believed in as a Saviour. A dying, crucified God, a Saviour of the world, who could not save Himself would have been exploded by the universal consent of reason as a horrible paradox and absurdity. Had not the resurrection followed the crucifixion, that scoff of the Jews had stood as an unanswerable argument against Him. 'Himself He cannot save; let Him come down from the cross, and we will believe in Him.' Otherwise, surely that which was the lowest instance of human weakness and mortality could be no competent demonstration of a Deity. To save is the effect of power, and of such a power as prevails to a complete victory. But it is expressly affirmed, 'that Christ was crucified through weakness.' Death was too hard for His humanity, and bore away the spoils of it for a time. So that, while Christ was in the grave, men might as well have expected that a person hung in chains should come down and head an army, as imagine that a dead body, continuing such, should be able to triumph over sin and death, which so potently triumphs over the living. The discourse of the two disciples going to Emmaus, and expecting no such thing as a resurrection, was, upon that supposition, hugely rational and significant. 'We trusted,' said they, 'that this had been He which should have redeemed Israel''; thereby clearly implying, that upon his death they had let that confidence fall to the ground together with Him. For they could not imagine that a breathless carcass could chase away the Roman eagles, and so recover the Jews from under their subjection; which was the redemption that even the disciples (till they were further enlightened) promised themselves from their Messiah. But the argument would equally, nay, more strongly, hold against a spiritual redemption, supposing His continuance under a state of death, as being a thing in itself much more difficult. For how could such an one break the kingdom of darkness, and set His foot upon 'principalities and powers, and spiritual wickedness in high places,' who Himself fell a sacrifice to the wickedness of mortal men, and remained a captive in the lower parts of the earth, reduced to a condition, not only below men's envy, but below their very feet?—South, 1633–1716."—LAWSON.

1. The Fact of It.

II Tim. 2:8—Remember that Jesus Christ of the seed of David was raised from the dead according to my gospel.

S. F. Matt. 28:6; Mark 16:6; Luke 24:6; I Cor. 15:4–8.

It is one of the best authenticated facts of human history. It is buttressed and supported by corroborative proof, such as is found in connection with comparatively few other historical facts.

D. S. The fact of Christ's resurrection is firmly established by the Scripture.

2. The Evidences of It as seen by:

(1) The empty tomb.

Luke 24:3—And they entered in, and found not the body of the Lord Jesus.
S. F. John 20:1–8.

". . . . . Two things of interest are here involved in the question of the resurrection. First, the resurrection body left the tomb before the stone was rolled away. It was not necessary that the door be opened before the Lord of Life could come forth from the grave . . . . . The stone was rolled away not to let the Saviour out, but rather to let the women and the disciples in. Why enter? For evidence therein of the fact of the resurrection. The angel bade them enter, calling especial attention to the place where the Lord lay. What was on that stone shelf to observe? The grave wrappings were there, in such form, as we have learned, as to indicate the departure of the body therefrom without disturbing them . . . . .

"There was thus no period of time, not even the shortest, after the tomb was opened, when witnesses representing both enemies and friends were not present to verify the facts. The guards on the one hand and the women on the other, both witnessed the opening of the grave. No room is left for controversy about what happened or concerning the contents of the tomb. The body was there when the tomb was sealed. It was not there when the seal was broken. The linen cloths were there and spoke their own message, confirming the word of the angel.

"There was certainly continuous provision during those stirring exciting hours against misrepresentation of the truth . . . . .

"Then note the empty tomb in the gospels of Mark and Luke. Both of these accounts refer to the inside of the tomb and particularly to the place where

139

the body had been laid. In Mark the angel specifically directs attention to the place where they laid Him. In the Luke account, we read: 'They entered in and found not the body . . . . . But Peter arose, and ran unto the tomb, and stooping and looking in, he seeth the linen cloths by themselves.' The women were perplexed and Peter wondered at what they had seen. Thus all four of our evangelists recognize the significance of the evidence of resurrection presented within the tomb . . . . . The women of Galilee saw clearly evidences of His resurrection. It is confidently believed that as they approached the tomb they saw it open; as they entered the tomb they witnessed evidence which the grave cloths afforded, that the body had not been violently removed. On the contrary, they were face to face with proof that the body had supernaturally left the winding sheets intact. Even the head roll remained in its original shape. It had only fallen back in a place by itself when released by the body of Jesus at the instant of its change from a dead body to the resurrection body . . . . ."—WHITE.

(2) Appearances of the Risen Lord.

Acts 1:1-3—To whom also he shewed himself alive after His passion by many infallible proofs, being seen of them forty days, and speaking of the things pertaining to the kingdom of God.

a. To Mary (as consoler).

John 20:16—Jesus saith unto her, Mary. She turned and saith unto Him Rabboni, which is to say, Master.

> "Not she with traitorous kiss her Master stung,
> Not she denied him with unfaithful tongue,
> She, when disciples fled, could danger brave,
> Last at his cross and earliest at his grave."
> —SELECTED.

b. To the women (as the embodiment of restored joy).

Matt. 28:5, 8, 9—And the angel answered and said unto the women, Fear not ye: for I know that ye seek Jesus, which was crucified. And they departed quickly from the sepulchre with fear and great joy; and did run to bring His disciples word. And as they went to tell His disciples, behold, Jesus met them, saying, All hail. And they came and held Him by the feet, and worshipped Him.

c. To Simon Peter (as the restorer of souls).

Luke 24:34—Saying, The Lord is risen indeed, and hath appeared unto Peter. Comp. Psa. 23:3, and Mark 16:7.

"Why 'and Peter?' Was not Peter one of the disciples? Surely he was, the very head of the apostolic company. Why then, 'and Peter?' No explanation is given in the text, but reflection shows it was the utterance of love toward the despondent, despairing disciple who had thrice denied his Lord."—THE FUNDAMENTALS, Vol. II.

d. To the two on the way to Emmaus (as sympathetic Instructor).

Luke 24:13, 14, 25-27, 30-32—And behold, two of them went that same day to a village called Emmaus, which was from Jerusalem about three score furlongs. And they talked together of all these things which had happened. Then he said unto them, O fools and slow of heart to believe

140

all that the prophets have spoken: Ought not Christ to have suffered these things, and to enter into his glory? And beginning at Moses and the prophets, he expounded unto them in all the Scriptures the things concerning himself.

And it came to pass, as he sat at meat with them, he took bread, and blessed it and brake, and gave it to them.

And their eyes were opened, and they knew him and he vanished out of their sight. And they said unto one another, Did not our heart burn within us, while he talked with us by the way, and while he opened to us the Scriptures?

Doubtless Jesus wished to comfort them, and doubtless he did comfort them. But he had a deeper, more essential thing to do. These men were sad, not like Mary Magdalene in a personal way as having lost their Lord, but in a faithless way, as having lost their Messiah. "We trusted that it had been He which should have redeemed Israel." The cure for them was not in personal tenderness as with Mary, but a better understanding of the Scriptures.

e. To the disciples in the upper room (as Bestower of Peace).

John 20:19—Then the same day at evening, being the first day of the week, when the doors were shut where the disciples were assembled for fear of the Jews, came Jesus and stood in the midst and saith unto them, Peace be unto you.

Jesus made a will just a little while before He went to the cross. He left a legacy to His disciples—a legacy of peace. He said, "Peace I leave with you. My peace I give unto you." But they could not come into their inheritance until after the death of the Testator, and then, lo and behold! He arose to be His own administrator, and so the first thing He does is to make over to them for their possession that which He has bequeathed to them—His peace.

f. To Thomas (as Confirmer of faith).

John 20:26–29—And after eight days again his disciples were within. And Thomas with them; then came Jesus, the doors being shut, and stood in the midst, and said, Peace be unto you.

Then saith he to Thomas, Reach hither thy finger, and behold my hands, and reach thy hand and thrust it into my side; and be not faithless, but believing. And Thomas answered, My Lord and my God. Jesus saith unto him, Thomas, because thou hast seen me, thou hast believed; blessed are they that have not seen, and yet have believed.

S. F. Luke 24:10, 11.

Thomas was the unbelieving one, and yet in grace the risen Lord would satisfy even Thomas. That disciple well knew that it was our Lord's deity which was in issue in His death, so when convinced of his resurrection, he instantly gave Him divine worship.

When Jesus died upon the cross, the faith of the disciples also apparently expired. Their love and devotion still lived, but it was love for One whom they had lost and their devotion was to His memory, and expressed itself in loving ministry to His earthly remains. Joseph of Arimathea and Nicodemus buried in the new tomb, not only the body of Jesus of Nazareth, but also the faith of His followers, and the faith which they afterwards manifested is strong evidence of the reality of the resurrection of Jesus. There is no other way to account for it.

How did their faith get out of the tomb if Jesus did not bring it out? They could not have stolen that away while the soldiers slept. They had to get that by honest evidence, and get it they did.

g. To John and Peter (as One concerned with the daily affairs of life).

John 21:5-7—And Jesus saith unto them, Children, have ye any meat? They answered him, No. And he said unto them, Cast the net on the right side of the ship and ye shall find. They cast therefore, and now they were not able to draw it for the multitude of fishes. Therefore that disciple whom Jesus loved said unto Peter, it is the Lord.

The resurrection of Christ gives Him to us for the ordinary activities of life, for the hum-drum of wage-earning and the obtaining of the necessities of life. He is risen to be our daily companion in the most prosaic duties of our earthly experience.

h. To the whole company of disciples (as the embodiment of headship and authority).

I Cor. 15:4-7—And that he was buried and that he rose again the third day according to the Scriptures, and that he was seen of Cephas, then of the twelve. After that he was seen of about five hundred brethren at once, of whom the greater part remain unto this present, but some are fallen asleep. After that he was seen of James, then of all the apostles.

S. F. Matt. 28:18-20.

As the risen Christ, He takes His place at the head of the church to which He has given life and being possessed of all authority for its direction and control. His resurrection furnishes full proof of this authorization—"God raised Him from the dead."

(3) Change wrought in the disciples.

John 7:3-5—His brethren therefore said unto him. Depart hence, and go into Judea, that thy disciples also may see the works that thou doest.

For there is no man that doeth anything in secret, and he himself seeketh to be known openly. If thou do these things, shew thyself to the world. For neither did his brethren believe in him.

compared with

I Cor. 15:7—After that, he was seen of James; then of all the apostles.

Mark. 14:69-70.

compared with

Acts 2:14, 22, 23.

S. F. Gal. 1:19; Acts 3:14.

"At the time of the crucifixion of Christ, we find the whole apostolic company filled with blank and utter despair. We see Peter, the leader of the apostolic company, denying his Lord three times with oaths and cursing, but a few days later we see this same man, filled with a courage that nothing could shake. We see him standing before the council that had condemned Jesus to death and saying to them, 'Be it known unto you all, and to all the people of Israel, that by the name of Jesus Christ of Nazareth, whom ye crucified, whom God raised from the dead, even by Him doth this man stand before you whole.' " (Acts 4:10.)

142

"Later we hear Peter and the Apostles answering their demand that they should be silent regarding Jesus, with the words, 'We ought to obey God rather than man. The God of our fathers raised up Jesus whom ye slew and hanged on a tree. Him hath God exalted with His right hand to be a Prince and a Saviour, for to give repentance to Israel, and forgiveness of sins. And we are His witnesses of these things.' (Acts 5:29-32). Something tremendous must have occurred to account for such a radical and astounding moral transformation as this. Nothing short of the fact of the resurrection and of their having seen the risen Lord will explain it."—TORREY.

(4) The change in the day of rest and worship.

Acts 20:7—And upon the first day of the week, when the disciples came together to break bread, Paul preached unto them, ready to depart on the morrow; and continued his speech until midnight.

I Cor. 16:2—Upon the first day of the week let every one of you lay by him in store, as God hath prospered him, that there be no gatherings when I come.

Dr. Brooks in his "Did Jesus Rise?" says: "First, we have the Lord's day which is traced by an unbroken line of witnesses and writers back to the period of the crucifixion, and not a step beyond that. The heathen did not recognize the day, nor do they now. But it is admitted that all of the apostles and early Christians were Jews. How did it come to pass, then, without precedent, without command, without example even, in the face of all their associations, religious instructors, and established habits they began to observe the first day of the week instead of the seventh, as the special time for public and united worship? That they did so observe it does not admit of a shadow of a doubt. It is fully proved by the testimony of heathen and Christian writers. Pliny, in his letter to the emperor Trajan, says: 'The Christians affirm the whole of their guilt or error to be that they were accustomed to meet together on a stated day, and to sing hymns to Christ as to God, and to bind themselves by a sacramentum, not for any wicked purpose, but never to commit fraud, theft or adultery; never to break their word, or to refuse, when called upon, to deliver up any trust; after which it was their custom to separate and to assemble again to partake of a harmless meal.' "

"What is meant by the 'stated day' is clearly shown by Justyn Martyr, who wrote not long afterwards as follows: 'On the day called Sunday is the assembly of all who live either in the cities or in the rural districts, and the memoirs of the apostles and the writings of the apostles are read.' Among other reasons he assigns for its observance, he says it was because Jesus Christ, our Saviour, rose from the dead upon it. Barsadanes, a heretical writer of the same period, in his letter to the emperor Marcus Aurelius Antonius, says: 'Lo, wherever we be all of us are called by the one name of the Messiah, Christians, and upon one day which is the first day of the week, we assemble ourselves together.' Dionysius, Bishop of Corinth, Melito, Bishop of Sardis, Irenaeus, Bishop of Lyons, and other writers, speak to the same effect, that the weekly celebration of Christ's resurrection is one upon which no diversity exists.

"The Christian first day perpetuates in the dispensation of grace the principle that one-seventh of the time is especially sacred, but in all other respects is in contrast with the Sabbath. One is the seventh day and the other is the first. The Sabbath commemorates God's creation day, the first Christ's resurrection. On the seventh day God rested. On the first day Christ was ceaselessly active. The Sabbath commemorates a finished creation, the first day a finished redemption. The Sabbath was a day of legal obligation. The first day one of voluntary worship and service. The Sabbath is mentioned in the Acts only in connection with the Jews, and in the rest of the New Testament but twice. In these passages the seventh-day Sabbath is explained to be to the Christian not a day to be observed, but a type of the present rest into which he enters."—SCOFIELD, REFERENCE BIBLE.

(5) Positive testimony of the early disciples.

Peter at Pentecost:

Acts 2:14, 22–24—But Peter, standing up with the eleven, lifted up his voice. and said unto them, Ye men of Judea, be this known unto you, and hearken to my words: Ye men of Israel, hear these words; Jesus of Nazareth, a man approved of God among you by miracles and wonders and signs, which God did by him in the midst of you, as ye yourselves also know; Him, being delivered by the determinate counsel and fore-knowledge of God, ye have taken, and by wicked hands have crucified and slain:

Whom God hath raised up having loosed the pains of death: Because it was not possible that he should be holden of it.

Paul on Mars Hill:

Acts 17:31—Because he hath appointed a day, in the which he will judge the world in righteousness by that man whom he hath ordained; whereof he hath given assurance unto all men, in that he hath raised him from the dead.

Apostolic skepticism was the first step toward apostolic faith. It demanded proof ere it would yield to the hope. These were hard headed, matter-of-fact men, not given to nervous excitements, keen to detect frauds, quick to reject cunningly devised fables, even when they gathered about a dearly beloved Master. They had all of our modern demand for reality. They would not believe until the evidence, in all of its overwhelming force was before them. Then only did skepticism give place to faith.

Such skepticism is worth while. It brought a faith that was clear, fixed, resolute, revolutionary.

(6) Christ's own witness.

Rev. 1:18—I am he that liveth, and was dead, and behold, I am alive for ever-more, Amen; and have the keys of hell and death.

D. S. Jesus Christ arose from the dead according to the Scriptures, as attested by many infallible proofs.

3. The Results of It.

(1) It is the fulfillment of God's promise to the fathers.

Acts 13:32–33—And we declare unto you glad tidings, how that the promise which was made unto the fathers, God hath fulfilled the same unto us their children, in that he hath raised up Jesus again; as it is also written in the second psalm, Thou art my son, this day have I begotten thee.

Question: What was the promise made to the fathers of which the resurrection of Christ is the fulfillment?

Answer:

Acts 3:25—Ye are the children of the prophets and of the covenant which God made with our fathers, saying unto Abraham, And in thy seed shall all kindreds of the earth be blessed.

Comp. Gen. 22:18—And in thy seed shall all the nations of the earth be blessed because thou hast obeyed my voice.

S. F. Gen. 26:4; Gen. 12:3; Gal. 3:16; Gen. 3:15.

The risen Jesus Christ is the seed in which all nations shall be blessed in His turning them away from their iniquities. Furthermore, the resurrection is the substance of the promise made to the fathers.

Acts 26:6-8.

Comp. with Acts 23:6.

Jesus, the resurrected One, the first fruits of them that slept, is the fulfillment of this promise made to the fathers. His resurrection is indeed the guarantee of the fulfillment of all the promises of God.

It declares Him to be the Son of God with power, and thus that the promises of the Bible, all of which He endorses (Luke 24:44) are the sure Word of God.

It reveals God's ability to keep His Word, and also His mighty power to usward. He that keepeth His word in raising the dead can surely fulfill all His promises. Comp. Acts 13:38, 39: "Be it known unto you therefore, men and brethren, that through this man is preached unto you the forgiveness of sins, and by him all that believe are justified from all things, from which ye could not be justified by the law of Moses."

If we wish to know that all the promises of God are yea and amen in Christ Jesus, we have only to look to that marvelous fulfillment of God's word and promise that has already taken place—the resurrection—and see in that the guarantee of the fulfillment of all.

(2) It establishes the Deity of Jesus Christ beyond a doubt.

Rom. 1:4—And declared to be the Son of God with power, according to the spirit of holiness, by the resurrection from the dead.

S. F. Luke 24:3; Acts 2:36.

"This title, 'The Lord Jesus,' is very pertinent and suitable to His Resurrection, for, however this glorious name was due to Him, even from His birth, yet, it is observed, it is never completely and fully given to Him until after His resurrection. Lord, He is called, and Jesus, He is called before; but in all the Gospel you never meet with these, all in one appellation, till His Resurrection. The first place that names Him the 'Lord Jesus' is here in Luke 24. After His rising again, it is said, they found not the body of the Lord Jesus. There it begins; never afore; but, then, after, frequently. By His Resurrection, He was declared to be the Son of God with power; then made known to be the Lord and Christ. Then this beautiful wreath was put upon His head and He was publicly proclaimed—The Lord Jesus Christ."—BROWNING.

Torrey says: "If Jesus rose from the dead He is beyond per-adventure the Son of God. That is what He claimed to be. He was put to death for making that claim. Before His death he said that God would set His seal to that claim by raising Him from the dead, and this very thing God did. It is more clearly

145

demonstrated by the resurrection that Jesus is the Son of God, than if God should shout it every night from the heavens. Faith in the deity of Christ does not rest upon theological or philosophical speculations, but upon an established fact. The one who denies the deity of Christ is unscientific. He shuts his eyes to facts and their evident meaning. Once settle it that Jesus rose from the dead, and Christianity is all settled upon a foundation that is impregnable. And it is settled that 'now is Christ risen from the dead.' "

(3) It is a proof of the provisional justification of believers.

Rom. 4:23, 25—Now it was not written for his sake alone, that it was imputed to him; But for us also, to whom it shall be imputed, if we believe on him that raised up Jesus our Lord from the dead, who was delivered for our offences, and was raised again for our justification.

(4) Through it believers are begotten unto a living hope.

I Peter 1:3, 4—Blessed be the God and Father of our Lord Jesus Christ, which according to his abundant mercy hath begotten us again unto a lively hope by the resurrection of Jesus Christ from the dead, to an inheritance, incorruptible, and undefiled, and that fadeth not away, reserved in heaven for you.

The resurrection of Jesus Christ is the truth which, made living in our hearts by the Holy Spirit, results in the new birth unto a living hope, and an incorruptible and untarnishable inheritance (Comp. Rom. 10:9). Through our believing in a risen Christ, Christ "which is our Hope" (I Tim. 1:1) begins to live in us. The resurrection of Christ also forms the firm foundation of fact upon which to build our hope for the future.

(5) It makes the unchanging priesthood of Christ available to the believer.

Heb. 7:22-25—By so much was Jesus made a surety of a better testament. Wherefore he is able also to save them to the uttermost that come unto God by him, seeing he ever liveth to make intercession for them.

S. F. I John 2:1; John 11:42; Rom. 8:34.

(6) It gives an illustration of the measure of God's power which is placed at the believer's disposal.

Eph. 1:19-20—And what is the exceeding greatness of his power to usward who believe, according to the working of his mighty power, which he wrought in Christ, when he raised him from the dead and set him at his own right hand in the heavenly places.

(7) It makes possible the believer's fruitage unto God.

Rom. 7:4—Wherefore my brethren, ye also are become dead to the law by the body of Christ; that ye should be married to another, even to him who is raised from the dead, that we should bring forth fruit unto God.

(8) It is God's pledge of future judgment.

Acts 17:31—Because he hath appointed a day, in the which he will judge the world in righteousness by that man whom he hath ordained; whereof he hath given assurance unto all men, in that he hath raised him from the dead.

Jesus Christ claimed that God would judge the world by Him (John 5:22, 27-29). "For the Father judgeth no man, but hath committed all judgment unto the son. And hath given him authority to execute judgment also, because he is the son of man. Marvel not at this; for the hour cometh in the which all that are in the graves shall hear his voice, and shall come forth; they that have done good, unto the resurrection of life, and they that have done evil, unto the resurrection of damnation (Judgment)."

By raising Christ from the dead God has set His seal to that claim. If men ask how it may be known that a judgment day is coming, in which Christ shall judge the world in righteousness, it may be replied "because Jesus Christ has arisen from the dead." The sure fact of the resurrection of Christ in the past points unerringly forward to the sure coming of judgment in the future. Belief in a judgment day is no guess of theologians, but is a positive fact and faith founded in a proved fact.

(9) It furnishes us an impregnable ground of assurance of our own future resurrection. II Cor. 4:14—Knowing that he which raised up the Lord Jesus shall raise up us also by Jesus, and shall present us with you.

S. F. I Thes. 4:14.

"Just as the first ripe ears of corn which grew on the plains and the mountain sides of Palestine were immediately brought into the temple, and waved before the Lord, as a pledge that every ear of corn standing on and growing in Palestine should be safely reaped and gathered in; so the resurrection of Christ is a demonstration that we his people shall be raised again . . . . . As surely as the sepulchre of Christ became an empty sepulchre, so surely the sepulchres of his people shall become empty sepulchres also; as surely as he got up, and sang a jubilee of life and immortality, so surely shall his people come out of the grave. How beautifully has the prophet Isaiah expressed it! 'Awake and sing, ye that dwell in dust; for thy dew is as the dew of herbs, and the earth shall cast out the dead. Thy dead men shall live; together with my dead body shall they arise.' "—BEAUMONT.

D. S. The results of the Resurrection of Jesus Christ are many and far-reaching, constituting an essential part of the believer's faith and salvation.

Study Questions on the Doctrine of Jesus Christ

1. In general, why is the study of the person of Christ important? How does the Scriptural record reveal this importance?
2. Give six objections which are raised to the virgin birth of Christ and refute each.
3. Briefly state five arguments for the virgin birth and show how each supports it.
4. Distinguish between the genealogies of Matthew and Luke and give proofs showing that Jesus was legal heir to the throne of David.
5. Give D. S. showing Jesus' natural growth and development as a proof of His humanity.
6. Quote one passage of Scripture which proves Christ's humanity from His appearance as a man.
7. Give the three elements of Christ's human physical nature and quote one passage with one.
8. Describe the relation which the two natures of Christ sustain to each other and to His person.
9. Define briefly the false theories concerning the two natures of Christ.

147

10. Describe the human limitations of Jesus Christ, under the following heads: Physical, Intellectual, Moral, and Spiritual.

11. Give the gist of the arguments showing that Jesus Christ could not have sinned.

12. Give the human names applied to Christ which prove His humanity.

13. Quote one passage showing the human relationship which Christ sustained to God.

14. Discuss the note on the Self-emptying of Christ and show what was involved in it.

15. Of what does the subordination of the person of the Son to the person of the Father consist? How is this shown in the Scriptures?

16. Give the divine names which are used of Christ in the Scriptures, proving His deity?

17. Give the four-fold proof of the deity of Christ as shown from the worship ascribed to Him, and quote one passage with each.

18. Name the offices which belong to God alone that are assigned to Jesus Christ.

19. Cite two illustrations in which the New Testament fulfillment in Christ of an Old Testament statement concerning Jehovah is seen and quote two passages with each.

20. Quote one passage in which the name of Jesus Christ is associated with that of God the Father in such a way as to prove deity.

21. Give the negative and positive meanings of the Holiness of Christ.

22. Give the names of those by whom the holiness of Christ is attested and quote one passage with one of them.

23. Give the six-fold manifestation of Christ's holiness, quote one passage of Scripture with one, and give D. S.

24. Define the Love of Christ.

25. Give the objects of Christ's love and quote one passage with one.

26. Give the three-fold manifestation of Christ's love to the Father and its seven-fold manifestation to men. Quote one passage under each group.

27. Define the Meekness of Jesus Christ.

28. Quote one passage establishing the fact of Christ's meekness, and give D. S.

29. Give the seven-fold manifestation of the meekness of Christ and quote one passage with one.

30. Define the Humility of Jesus Christ.

31. Give the five-fold manifestation of the humility of Jesus Christ and give D. S.

32. What may Christianity be called in relation to the other religions of the world, and what place does it give to the death of Christ?

33. Give in general the three-fold importance of the death of Christ and show in particular how its importance is emphasized by the prominence given to it in the Scriptures.

34. Give the four-fold necessity of the death of Christ and quote one passage with each.

ÿ. Give five false theories held concerning the nature of the death of Christ and refute each.

ÿ6. Give the eight aspects of the nature of the death of Christ, positively considered.

37. Give the four-fold scope of Christ's death with D. S.

38. Give the results of the death of Christ in relation to the following: men in general, believers, Satan and the powers of darkness, the material universe; and quote one passage under each division.

39. Show from the introductory note that the Resurrection of Christ has a two-fold necessity.

40. Quote one passage proving the fact of Christ's resurrection.

41. Name and discuss the evidences of the resurrection of Jesus Christ.

42. Give the results of the resurrection of Jesus Christ and quote one passage with each of three.

43. What was the promise made to the fathers of which the resurrection of Christ is the fulfillment?

CHAPTER FOUR

THE HOLY SPIRIT

(PNEUMATOLOGY)

There is much confusion and error current in this day concerning the personality, operations, and manifestations of the Holy Spirit. Conscientious but misguided scholars have held wrong views concerning this doctrine. It is vital to the faith of every Christian that its Scriptural teaching be seen in its true light and held in right proportion.

In seeking for a panoramic view of the Person and work of the Holy Spirit, we may best succeed by dividing the facts concerning Him into two periods, pre-pentecostal and post-pentecostal.

1. Pre-pentecostal.

The Holy Spirit was pre-existent as the Third Person of the Godhead, and thus has always been active, but the period preceding Pentecost was not the time of His special activity. The Old Testament period was one of preparation and of waiting. The truths known were simple ones and came by way of object lessons. There was and could be very little personal contact of man with God. Occasionally a patriarch or a prophet spoke face to face with Him, but even then they did not always understand the things of which they talked.

Of course, the Spirit was active in this period, but the number of times He is mentioned in the Old Testament, as contrasted with the number of times in the New, show us the marked difference in His ministrations. He is spoken of eighty-eight times in the Old Testament and more than half as many times in the Book of Acts alone; while in the entire New Testament He is mentioned more than three times for every reference to Him in the Old.

During this period the Spirit came upon men temporarily only, to inspire them for special service, and left them when the particular task was ended. He did not usually abide with them or dwell in them.

2. Post-pentecostal.

This period, which extends from Pentecost to the present day may truly be termed the dispensation of the Spirit. As in the Old Testament God appeared to men, and during the earth-life of Christ dwelt with men, so after Pentecost, in the Spirit, God comes to dwell in men. He comes to abide.

"There is a very real sense in which the Holy Ghost is incarnate in the church even as Christ was incarnate in the human body of Jesus of Nazareth. Of course this must not be pressed too far. There is a point of the most emphatic difference. In the case of Jesus, there was Deity, united with unfallen humanity. The Holy Spirit's union with the church is the presence of God in fallen humanity."—O'REAR.

Pentecost marked the dawning of a new day in the Holy Spirit's relation to mankind. He came to inhabit the Church. All the effectual work which the Church has done has been wrought in the power of the Spirit. Unbelief, doubt, and criticism may attack it, but not overwhelm it. The Church, the true body of Christ, indwelt by the Holy Spirit of God, is as indestructible as the Throne of God.

A. The Nature of the Holy Spirit.

I. Personality of the Holy Spirit.

1. The Meaning of It.

By the Personality of the Holy Spirit is meant that He possesses or contains in Himself the elements of personal existence as contrasted with impersonal existence or animal life.

It is difficult to define Personality when used of the Divine Being. God cannot be measured by human standards. God was not made in the image of man, but man in the image of God. God is not a deified man; man is rather a limited god. Psa. 8:5, R. V. "For thou hast made him a little lower than God." Only God has perfect personality.

Personality may be said to exist when there is found united in a single combination intelligence, emotion, and volition, or self-consciousness and self-determination.

When a being possesses the attributes, properties and qualities of Personality, then personality may be unquestionably predicated.

As suggested under the doctrine of the Trinity, the term Person, when applied to the members of the Trinity, is to be used in a qualified or limited sense, referring to personal distinctions, rather than to separate organisms as when used of men.

2. The Proof of It.

(1) The necessity for proof.

It is a matter of historical record that the personality of the Holy Spirit has been disputed and denied. While the Scriptures furnish no ground for such disputation or denial, there are some possible explanations of the manner in which these errors of interpretation arose. It may have been:

> a. **Because, as contrasted with the other persons of the God-head, the Spirit seems impersonal.**

"Various manifestations of God the Father make it comparatively easy to conceive of His Fatherhood in terms of Personality; the Incarnation makes it almost, if not altogether, impossible to disbelieve in the Personality of Jesus Christ; but the acts and workings of the Holy Spirit are so secret and mystical, so much is said of His influence, grace, power and gifts, that we are prone to think of Him as an influence, a power, a manifestation or emanation of the divine nature rather than as a Person."—EVANS.

152

b. Because of the names and symbols used of the Holy Spirit, which are suggestive of the impersonal, such as: breath, wind, power, fire, oil, and water. See as illustration:

John 3:5–8—Jesus answered, verily, verily, I say unto thee, except a man be born of water and of the Spirit, he cannot enter into the Kingdom of God. That which is born of the flesh is flesh; that which is born of the Spirit is spirit. Marvel not that I said unto thee, ye must be born again. The wind bloweth where it listeth, and thou hearest the sound thereof, but canst not tell whence it cometh and whither it goeth, so is everyone that is born of the Spirit.

Acts 2:1–4—And when the day of Pentecost was fully come, they were all with one accord in one place. And suddenly there came a sound from heaven as of a rushing mighty wind, and it filled all the house where they were sitting. And there appeared unto them cloven tongues like as of fire, and it sat upon each of them. And they were all filled with the Holy Ghost and began to speak with other tongues, as the Spirit gave them utterance.

S. F. John 20:22; I John 2:20; Eph. 5:18; I Thess. 5:19; John 7:38, 39.

c. Because the Holy Spirit is not always associated with the Father and the Son in the salutations and greetings of the New Testament. See as illustration:

I Thes. 3:11—Now God himself and our Father and our Lord Jesus Christ, direct our way unto you.

d. Because the word or name "Spirit" is neuter in the Greek (Pneuma).

(2) Proof of the Holy Spirit's Personality.

a. Masculine personal pronouns applied to the Holy Spirit.

John 15:26—But when the Comforter is come, whom I will send unto you from the Father, even the Spirit of truth, which proceedeth from the Father, he shall testify of Me.

John 16:7–8, 13, 14—Nevertheless, I tell you the truth; It is expedient for you that I go away; for if I go not away, the Comforter will not come unto you; but if I depart, I will send him unto you. And when he is come, he will reprove the world of sin, and of righteousness, and of judgment. Howbeit when he, the Spirit of truth, is come, he will guide you into all truth; for he shall not speak of himself, but whatsoever he shall hear, that shall he speak; and he will shew you things to come. He shall glorify me; for he shall receive of mine, and shall shew it unto you.

We turn to grammar to establish the Personality of the Holy Spirit, because the use of neuter pronouns has been largely responsible for the idea of the impersonality of the Spirit which is prevalent today.

The Greek word for Spirit is "pneuma," a neuter noun. This argument becomes more remarkable when we see that masculine pronouns are used in connection with *pneuma*, except where the construction compels a neuter (Rom. 8:16), thus showing that the Bible idea of the Personality of the Holy Spirit dominates grammatical construction.

Christ, the supremely authoritative spokesman of God, pours into the New Testament depository of truth the many times repeated personal pronouns referring to the Holy Spirit, which show beyond all question that He recognized the Spirit as Personal in nature.

There is another grammatical testimony which must be mentioned, and that is Christ's use of the masculine noun "parakletos" in referring to the Spirit (John 14:16-17). Jesus, Himself was a Comforter (I John 2:2) to the disciples, and He offers consolation to them as He is about to depart by promising them another Comforter (*parakletos*). Everything Jesus was to the disciples, the other was to be, and more, because of Jesus' human limitations—a Person coming to take the place of a Person.

b. Associations of the Holy Spirit with the other Persons of the Godhead and with individuals.

Matt. 28:19—Go ye, therefore, and teach all nations, baptizing them in the name of the Father, and of the Son and of the Holy Ghost.

Acts 15:28—For it seemed good to the Holy Ghost, and to us, to lay upon you no greater burden than those necessary things.

S. F. II Cor. 13:14.

Such associations, which are personal, can only be understood in relation to personalities.

c. Personal characteristics ascribed to the Holy Spirit.

By characteristics we do not mean hands, feet, or eyes, for these denote corporeity, but qualities such as knowledge, feeling and will, which denote Personality.

(a) Intelligence.

I Cor. 2:10, 11—But God hath revealed them unto us by his Spirit; for the Spirit searcheth all things, yea, the deep things of God. For what man knoweth the things of a man, save the spirit of man which is in him? even so the things of God knoweth no man, but the Spirit of God.

Rom. 8:27—And he that searcheth the hearts knoweth what is the mind of the Spirit, because he maketh intercession for the saints according to the will of God.

The Holy Spirit is not merely an illuminating power or influence, but is a Person possessed of intellect, Who knows the deep things of God and reveals them to us.

(b) Will.

I Cor. 12:11—But all these worketh that one and the self-same Spirit, dividing to every man severally as he will.

An "it," that which is impersonal is not possessed of volition.

(c) Love.

Rom. 15:30—Now I beseech you, brethren, for the Lord Jesus Christ's sake, and for the love of the Spirit, that ye strive together with me in your prayers to God for me.

"We owe our salvation just as truly to the love of the Spirit as we do to the love of the Father and the love of the Son."—TORREY.

(d) Goodness.

Neh. 9:20—Thou gavest also thy good Spirit to instruct them, and withheldest

154

not thy manna from their mouth, and gavest them water for their thirst.

(e) Grief.

Eph. 4:30—And grieve not the Holy Spirit of God, whereby ye are sealed unto the day of redemption.

One cannot grieve the law of gravitation nor cause the east wind to mourn. Therefore, unless the Holy Spirit is a Person, Paul's injunction here was meaningless and superfluous.

d. Personal acts ascribed to the Holy Spirit.

Throughout the Scriptures the Holy Spirit is represented as a Personal agent, performing acts attributable only to a Person.

(a) He searcheth the deep things of God.

I Cor. 2:10—But God hath revealed them unto us by his Spirit, for the Spirit searcheth all things, yea, the deep things of God.

(b) He speaks.

Rev. 2:7—He that hath an ear let him hear what the Spirit saith unto the churches; To him that overcometh will I give to eat of the tree of life, which is in the midst of the paradise of God.

The Spirit is also spoken of as crying out (Gal. 4:6) and as bearing testimony (John 15:26).

(c) He makes intercession.

Rom. 8:26 R. V.—And in like manner the Spirit also helpeth our infirmity; for we know not how to pray as we ought but the Spirit himself maketh intercession for us with groanings which cannot be uttered.

(d) He teaches.

John 14:26—But the Comforter, which is the Holy Ghost, whom the Father will send in my name, he shall teach you all things, and bring all things to your remembrance, whatsoever I have said unto you.

S. F. John 16:12–14 and Neh. 9:20.

(e) He leads and guides.

Rom. 8:14—For as many as are led by the Spirit of God, they are the sons of God.

S. F. Acts 16:6–7.

(f) He calls and commissions men.

Acts 13:2—As they ministered to the Lord, and fasted, the Holy Ghost said, Separate me Barnabas and Saul for the work whereunto I have called them.

Acts 20:28—Take heed therefore unto yourselves, and to all the flock over the which the Holy Ghost hath made you overseers, to feed the church of God, which he hath purchased with his own blood.

e. Personal treatment received by the Holy Spirit.

(a) He is rebelled against and grieved.

Isa. 63:10. R. V.—But they rebelled and grieved his Holy Spirit; therefore he as turned to be their enemy and himself fought against them.

S. F. Eph. 4:30.

(b) He is lied to.

Acts 5:3—But Peter said Ananias, why hath Satan filled thine heart to lie to the Holy Ghost and to keep back part of the price of the land?

(c) He is blasphemed.

Matt. 12:31, 32—Wherefore I say unto you all manner of sin and blasphemy shall be forgiven unto men; but the blasphemy against the Holy Ghost shall not be forgiven unto men. And whosoever speaketh a word against the Son of man, it shall be forgiven him; but whosoever speaketh against the Holy Ghost, it shall not be forgiven him, neither in this world, neither in the world to come.

Webster says that to blaspheme means "to speak of the Supreme Being in terms of impious irreverence; to revile or speak reproachfully of God, Christ, or the Holy Spirit." To blaspheme thus is clearly impossible unless the object of irreverence be personal.

D. S. By the use of personal pronouns, by personal associations, personal characteristics possessed, personal actions performed and treatment received, the Scriptures prove the Holy Spirit to be a person.

Theoretically, we may believe this. Do we in our real thought of Him, or in our practical attitude toward Him, treat Him as a person? Do we regard Him as indeed as real a person as Jesus Christ—as loving, wise and strong, as worthy of our confidence and love and surrender as He? He came to be to the disciples, and to us, what Christ had been to them during the days of His personal companionship with them (John 14:16, 17).

Do we know "the communion and fellowship of the Holy Ghost?" (II Cor. 13:14).—TORREY.

3. The Importance of It, as Shown:

(1) In connection with worship.

If the Holy Spirit is a Divine Person and yet is unknown or ignored as such, He is being deprived and robbed of the love and adoration which are His due. If, on the other hand, however, He is only an influence, force, or power emanating from God, we are practicing idolatry or false worship.

(2) From the standpoint of service.

It is necessary to decide whether the Holy Spirit is a power or force that we are to get hold of and use, or whether He is a Person of the God-head, Who is to control and use us. The one conception leads to self-exaltation and self-assertion, the other to self-abasement and self-renunciation.

(3) By reason of its relation to Christian experience.

It is of the highest experimental value that we know whether the Holy Spirit is only a mere influence and impersonal force, or whether He is an ever-present Friend and Helper, a Divine Companion and Guide.

II. The Deity of the Holy Spirit.

The Scriptures emphatically teach the Deity of the Holy Spirit. There have been those, however, who have denied this. Arius, a presbyter of Alexandria in the fourth century, led in the teaching by holding that God is One Eternal Person, that He created Christ, Who in turn created the Holy Spirit, thus denying His Deity. This teaching gained a strong hold in the early church, but was corrected by the Nicene Creed in 325 A. D.

1. The Meaning of It.

By the deity of the Holy Spirit is meant that He is One with God, and One in the God-head, co-equal, co-eternal, and con-substantial with the Father and the Son.

2. The Proof Given.

Even more apparent than the Personality of the Holy Spirit is the truth of His Deity. The Scriptures abound with evidence of this fact.

(1) Divine names given to Him.

a. He is called "God."

Acts 5:3-4—But Peter said, Ananias, why hath Satan filled thine heart to lie to the Holy Ghost, and to keep back part of the price of the land? Whiles it remained, was it not thine own? and after it was sold, was it not in thine own power? why hast thou conceived this thing in thine heart? thou hast not lied unto men, but unto God.

b. He is called "Lord."

II Cor. 3:18, R. V.—But we all, with unveiled face, beholding as in a mirror the glory of the Lord, are transformed into the same image from glory to glory, even as from the Lord the Spirit.

The Holy Spirit is clearly identified with God in the above passages in such a way as to prove His Deity unmistakably.

(2) Divine attributes ascribed to Him.

Attributes which belong to God alone are freely used of the Holy Spirit.

a. Eternity.

Heb. 9:14—How much more shall the blood of Christ, who through the eternal Spirit offered himself without spot to God, purge your conscience from dead works to serve the living God.

b. Omnipresence.

Psa. 139:7-10—Whither shall I go from thy spirit? Or whither shall I flee from thy presence? If I ascend up into heaven, thou art there, if I make my bed in hell, behold, thou art there. If I take the wings of the morning and dwell in the uttermost parts of the sea; Even there shall thy hand lead me, and thy right hand shall hold me.

c. Omnipotence.

Luke 1:35—And the angel answered and said unto her, The Holy Ghost shall come upon thee, and the power of the Highest shall overshadow thee; therefore also that holy thing which shall be born of thee shall be called the Son of God.

d. Omniscience.

I Cor. 2:10-11—But God hath revealed them unto us by his Spirit: for the Spirit searcheth all things, yea the deep things of God. For what man knoweth the things of a man, save the spirit of man which is in him? even so the things of God knoweth no man, but the Spirit of God.

S. F. John 14:26; John 16:12-13.

(3) Divine works performed by Him.

    a. Creation.

Job 33:4—The Spirit of God hath made me and the breath of the Almighty hath given me life.

S. F. Psa. 104:30.

    b. Impartation of life.

Rom. 8:11—But if the Spirit of him that raised up Jesus from the dead dwell in you, he that raised up Christ from the dead shall also quicken your mortal bodies by his Spirit that dwelleth in you.

S. F. John 6:63; Gen. 2:7.

S. A. John 3:5–8; Titus 3:5; James 1:18.

The Holy Spirit is the author of both physical and Spiritual life.

    c. Authorship of divine prophecy.

II Peter 1:21—For the prophecy came not in old time by the will of man; but holy men of God spake as they were moved by the Holy Ghost.

S. F. II Sam. 23:2–3.

(4) The application of Old Testament statements concerning Jehovah to the Holy Spirit by the New Testament writers.

Isa. 6:8–10—Also I heard the voice of the Lord, saying Whom shall I send and who will go for us? Then said I, here am I; send me. And he said, Go, and tell this people, Hear ye indeed, but understand not; and see ye indeed, but perceive not. Make the heart of this people fat, and make their ears heavy, and shut their eyes, lest they see with their eyes, and hear with their ears and understand with their hearts and convert, and be healed.

Comp. with Acts 28:25–27—And when they agreed not among themselves, they departed, after that Paul had spoken one word, Well spake the Holy Ghost by Esaias the prophet unto our fathers, Saying, go unto this people and say, hearing ye shall hear, and shall not understand; and seeing ye shall see, and not perceive; For the heart of this people is waxed gross, and their ears are dull of hearing, and their eyes have they closed; lest they should see with their eyes, and hear with their ears, and understand with their heart, and should be converted, and I should heal them.

S. F. Ex. 16:7, Comp. with Heb. 3:7–10.

"The prophets were the messengers of God; they uttered His words, delivered His commands, pronounced His threatenings and announced His promises, because they spake as they were moved by the Holy Ghost. They were the organs of God because they were the organs of the Spirit. The Spirit, therefore, must be God."—HODGE.

(5) The way in which the name of the Holy Spirit is coupled in equality with that of God and of Christ.

    a. In the Apostolic Commission.

Matt. 28:19—Go ye, therefore, and teach all nations, baptizing them in the name of the Father and of the Son and of the Holy Ghost.

b. In the administration of the Church.

I Cor. 12:4–6—Now there are diversities of gifts but the same Spirit. And there are differences of administrations, but the same Lord. And there are diversities of operations, but it is the same God which worketh all in all.

c. In the Apostolic Benediction.

II Cor. 13:14—The grace of the Lord Jesus Christ, and the love of God and the communion of the Holy Ghost be with you all. Amen.

D. S. In many unmistakable ways, God, in His word, distinctly proclaims that the Holy Spirit is not only a Person, but a Divine Person.

B. The Names of the Holy Spirit.

Many names are given to the Holy Spirit in the Scriptures which reveal to us various aspects of His Person and work. The numerousness of these titles seems to warrant a special study of them.

I. Names of the Holy Spirit Which Are Descriptive of His Own Person.

1. The Spirit.

I Cor. 2:10, R. V.—But unto us God revealed them through the Spirit; for the Spirit searcheth all things, yea the deep things of God.

The Greek word "pneuma" as applied to the Holy Spirit, involves both the thought of "breath" and that of "wind."

(1) As "breath."

John 20:22—And when he had said this, he breathed on them, and saith unto them, receive ye the Holy Ghost.

Gen. 2:7—And the Lord God formed man of the dust of the ground, and breathed into his nostrils the breath of life; and man became a living soul.

S. F. Psa. 104:30; Job 33:4.

S. A. Ezek. 37:1–10.

The Spirit is the outbreathing of God—the life of God going forth to quicken.

(2) As "wind."

John 3:6–8—That which is born of the flesh is flesh; and that which is born of the Spirit is spirit. Marvel not that I said unto thee, Ye must be born again. The wind bloweth where it listeth, and thou hearest the sound thereof, but canst not tell whence it cometh, and whither it goeth; so is every one that is born of the Spirit.

S. F. Acts 2:1–4.

2. The Holy Spirit.

Luke 11:13—If ye then, being evil, know how to give good gifts unto your children; how much more shall your heavenly Father give the Holy Spirit to them that ask him?

S. F. Rom. 1:4.

The essential moral character of the Spirit is emphasized by this name. He is Holy in Person and character and is also the direct author of holiness in men.

The Spirit is not called Holy with more frequency than the other Persons of the Trinity because He is more holy, for infinite holiness does not admit of degrees. He is thus officially designated because it is His work to make holy.

3. The Eternal Spirit.

Heb. 9:14—How much more shall the blood of Christ, who through the eternal Spirit offered himself without spot to God, purge your conscience from dead works to serve the living God?

Just as eternity is an attribute or characteristic of the nature of God, so also it may be and is ascribed to the Holy Spirit as one of the personal distinctions in the Being of God.

II. Names of the Holy Spirit Which Set Forth His Relationship to God.

1. The Spirit of God.

I Cor. 3:16—Know ye not that ye are the temple of God, and that the Spirit of God dwelleth in you?

This name portrays the Holy Spirit as proceeding from God. He is sent by the Father and by the Son. He is the personal power and energy of the Godhead.

2. The Spirit of Jehovah.

Isa. 11:2, R. V.—And the Spirit of Jehovah shall rest upon him, the Spirit of wisdom and understanding, the Spirit of counsel and might, the Spirit of knowledge and of the fear of Jehovah.

This name refers to Him as the One by Whom the prophets spoke.

3. The Spirit of the Lord Jehovah.

Isa. 61:1, R. V.—The Spirit of the Lord Jehovah is upon me; because Jehovah hath anointed me to preach good tidings unto the meek; he hath sent me to bind up the broken-hearted, to proclaim liberty to the captives, and the opening of the prison to them that are bound.

This title shows Him to be the agent through whom the Lordship of Jehovah is exercised.

4. The Spirit of the Living God.

II Cor. 3:3—Forasmuch as ye are manifestly declared to be the epistle of Christ ministered by us, written not with ink, but with the Spirit of the living God; not in tables of stone, but in fleshy tables of the heart.

The Spirit is here portrayed as the One Who writes the image of Christ upon the "fleshy tables of the hearts," and by whom the believer becomes a living epistle.

D. S. Names are given to the Holy Spirit which show His identity with Deity and emphasize His divine nature, authority and power.

III. Names of the Holy Spirit Which Set Forth His Relationship to the Son of God.

1. The Spirit of Christ.

Rom. 8:9—But ye are not in the flesh, but in the Spirit, if so be that the Spirit of God dwell in you. Now if any man have not the Spirit of Christ, he is none of his.

S. F. Acts 2:36, R. V.

This name shows the Spirit's relation to the anointed Messiah. The Spirit Himself is the anointing as well as the Anointer.

2. The Spirit of His Son.

Gal. 4:6—And because ye are sons, God hath sent forth the spirit of his Son into your hearts, crying, Abba, Father.

The Spirit of His Son produces in the heart of the believer the Spirit of sonship and gives him the assurance thereof.

3. The Spirit of Jesus.

Acts 16:6-7, R. V.—And they went through the region of Phrygia and Galatia, having been forbidden of the Holy Spirit to speak the word in Asia: and when they were come over against Mysia, they assayed to go into Bithynia; and the Spirit of Jesus suffered them not.

S. F. Matt. 28:19, Comp. with Acts 1:1-2.

This name merely emphasizes the Spirit's relation to the human Jesus.

4. The Spirit of Jesus Christ.

Phil. 1:19—For I know that this shall turn to my salvation through your prayer, and the supply of the Spirit of Jesus Christ.

Comp. with

Acts 2:32-33, R. V.—This Jesus did God raise up, whereof we all are witnesses. Being therefore by the right hand of God exalted and having received of the Father the promise of the Holy Spirit, he hath poured forth this, which ye see and hear.

S. F. Isa. 11:2, R. V., Comp. with Heb. 1:9.

This name identifies the divine Messiah with the human Jesus and shows the relation which the Holy Spirit sustains to Him as so identified.

D. S. Names are given to the Holy Spirit which reveal His relation to the Son of God in His pre-existent state, during His life upon earth, and after His Resurrection.

IV. Names of the Holy Spirit Which Set Forth His Relation to Men.

1. Spirit of Burning.

Isa. 4:4—When the Lord shall have washed away the filth of the daughters of Zion, and shall have purged the blood of Jerusalem from the midst thereof by the spirit of judgment and by the spirit of burning.

Comp. with

Matt. 3:11 l.c.—He shall baptize you with the Holy Ghost and with fire.

This name represents the Spirit as the One who searches, illuminates, refines, and purifies from dross.

2. Holy Spirit of Promise.

Eph.1:13 R.V.-In whom ye also, having heard the word of the truth, the gospel of your salvation, in whom having also believed, ye were sealed with the Holy Spirit of promise.

Comp. with

Acts 1:4-5—And being assembled together with them commanded them that they should not depart from Jerusalem, but wait for the promise of the Father, which saith he, ye have heard of me. For John truly baptized with water; but ye shall be baptized with the Holy Ghost not many days hence.

Acts 2:33—Therefore, being by the right hand of God exalted, and having received of the Father the promise of the Holy Ghost, he hath shed forth this, which ye now see and hear.

This name refers to the Holy Spirit as the fulfillment of the promise of the Father to the Son. The Spirit also gives the believer the assurance that the promises of God made to Him are sure.

3. Spirit of Truth.

John 15:26—But when the Comforter is come, whom I will send unto you from the Father, even the Spirit of truth, which proceedeth from the Father, he shall testify of me.

S. F. John 14:17; John 16:13.

S. A. I John 4:6 and I John 5:6.

As God is Love, so the Spirit is Truth. He possesses, reveals, imparts, leads into, testifies of, and defends the Truth. In this way He is opposed to the "Spirit of error." (I John 4:6)

4. Spirit of Life.

Rom. 8:2, R. V.—For the law of the Spirit of life in Christ Jesus made me free from the law of sin and of death.

He is not only the Living but also the Life giving spirit.

5. Spirit of Grace.

Heb. 10:29—Of how much sorer punishment, suppose ye, shall he be thought worthy, who hath trodden under foot the Son of God, and hath counted the blood of the covenant, wherewith he was sanctified, an unholy thing, and hath done despite unto the Spirit of grace?

It is through the Spirit that we know of the grace of God. As the Person of the God-head Who brings to completion any act of God begun, the Spirit carries on the work of Grace begun in the life of a believer.

6. Spirit of Glory.

I Peter 4:13-14—But rejoice, inasmuch as ye are partakers of Christ's sufferings; that, when his glory shall be revealed, ye may be glad also with exceeding joy. If ye be reproached for the name of Christ, happy are ye; for the Spirit of glory and of God resteth upon you.

S. F. Eph. 3:16–19, Comp. with Rom. 8:16–17.

The Spirit not only is a glorious person but, also, is the revealer of the riches of the glory of God to us.

7. Comforter.

John 14:26—But the Comforter, which is the Holy Ghost, whom the Father will send in my name, he shall teach you all things, and bring all things to your remembrance, whatsoever I have said unto you.

S. F. John 15:26.

S. A. John 16:7.

The same Greek word here translated "Comforter" is translated "Advocate" when used of Christ in I John 2:2. It means "called to one's aid," "appearing on behalf of," as a lawyer in a court of law. The thought of "Strengthener" is also involved, one Who invigorates and makes strong. A very personal relation is here set forth. In ordinary speech it might be rendered "Part-taker," "one standing by our side to aid." We may fitly say of Him:

> "Ever present, truest Friend,
> Ever near Thine aid to lend."

D. S. Names are given to the Holy Spirit which are descriptive of Him in His relation to men, either actually or potentially.

C. The Work of the Holy Spirit.

In taking up the work of the Holy Spirit we need to bear in mind the truth that all the Persons of the Trinity are active in the work of each individual Person. Some would tell us that God the Father worked in Creation, God the Son in Redemption, and God the Holy Spirit in Salvation. This is not true, however, for in each manifestation of the works of God, the whole Trinity is active; the Father is the Author, the Son is the Executor, and the Spirit is the Energizer of each act. Hence, the Spirit is the One who energizes and brings to completion the acts begun.

I. In Relation to the Material Universe.

1. With Regard to Its Creation.

Psa. 33:6—By the word of the Lord were the heavens made; and all the host of them by the breath of his mouth.

Job. 33:4—The Spirit of God hath made me, and the breath of the Almighty hath given me life.

2. With Regard to Its Restoration and Preservation.

Gen. 1:2 —And the earth was without form, and void; and darkness was upon the face of the deep. And the Spirit of God moved upon the face of the waters.

Psa. 104:29–30—Thou hidest thy face, they are troubled; thou takest away their breath, they die, and return to their dust. Thou sendest forth thy Spirit; they are created; and thou renewest the face of the earth.

S. F. Isa. 40:7.

The present order of development in nature and in man from the early chaotic, undeveloped state and its maintenance is effected through the agency of the Holy Spirit.

D. S. The Holy Spirit is seen to be an Active Agent in the creation and maintenance of the material universe.

II. In Relation to Unregenerate Men.

The principal work of the Holy Spirit in relation to the unsaved is that of conviction. Distinction must be made between the conviction of conscience and that of the Holy Spirit. Conscience convicts of wrong doing—The Spirit of wrong being. Conscience must be likened to a court—judge, jury and witnesses—all dealing with the wrong done, from which there is no escape. The Spirit convicts and, at the same time, brings a ray of light by revealing a solution and way of escape. This is sometimes called "Evangelical conviction."

1. He Strives with Them.

Gen. 6:3—And the Lord said, My spirit shall not always strive with man for that he also is flesh; yet his days shall be an hundred and twenty years.

The Spirit strives with men; seeking to restrain them from a course of lawlessness and godlessness.

This striving is done through the medium of human instrumentalities, such as Enoch, Noah, and all believers. Jesus said, "Ye are the salt of the earth." It is the function of light to hold back or restrain darkness, and that of salt to preserve from corruption. So the Holy Spirit, through the Church and individual believers, by influence, example and testimony, strives with men against courses of sin and iniquity.

2. He Witnesses to Them.

John 15:26—But when the Comforter is come, whom I will send unto you from the Father, even the Spirit of truth, which proceedeth from the Father, he shall testify of me.

S. F. Acts 5:30–32.

The Spirit witnesses to the unsaved by means of the truth concerning Jesus Christ.

3. He Convicts or Convinces Them.

John 16:8–11—And when he is come, he will reprove the world of sin, and of righteousness, and of judgment. Of sin, because they believe not on me. Of righteousness, because I go to my Father, and ye see me no more. Of judgment, because the prince of this world is judged.

The Spirit here convicts or reproves the world of sin, righteousness, and judgment.

He convicts, not primarily of the sin of lawbreaking, but of the sin of unbelief, "of sin, because they believe not on me." Acts 2:36–37. As all sin has its root in unbelief, so the most aggravated form of unbelief is the rejection of Christ. The Spirit, however, in fastening this truth upon the conscience, does not extinguish, but, on the contrary, consummates and intensifies the sense of all other sins.

He convicts the world of Christ's Personal righteousness, involving the veracity of His claims, as attested by His going to the Father (Acts 2:33). This righteousness is a fulfillment and manifestation of all other righteousness. Its conviction brings about a self-condemnation.

He also convicts of a provided righteousness, which Christ received to bestow on all such as should believe on Him.

He convicts the world of judgment made certain by reason of the judgment of Satan already accomplished. In it all other judgments were decided and are grounded. This judgment of Satan was secured at the cross and he was potentially rendered powerless. This, together with the judgment of those who choose to remain allied to Satan, will be consummated at the great day.

In this three-fold work, the Spirit is glorifying Christ. He shows us that it is sin not to believe in Christ, reveals to us the righteousness of Christ, and the victorious work of Christ in relation to Satan. Our task is only to preach the word of truth, looking to the Holy Spirit to produce the conviction. (Acts 2:4, 37).

D. S. The Holy Spirit by the truth strives with men and brings them under conviction.

III. In Relation to Believers.

1. He Regenerates.

John 3:3-6—Jesus answered and said unto him Verily, Verily, I say unto thee, except a man be born again, he cannot see the kingdom of God. Nicodemus saith unto him, How can a man be born when he is old? Can he enter the second time into his mother's womb, and be born? Jesus answered, verily, verily, I say unto thee, except a man be born of water and of the Spirit, he cannot enter into the kingdom of God. That which is born of the flesh is flesh; and that which is born of the Spirit is spirit.

S. F. Tit. 3:5; John 6:63; I Pet. 1:23; Eph. 5:25, 26.

S. A. I Cor. 2:4, Comp. with I Cor. 3:6.

As Jesus was begotten of the Holy Spirit, so every man who becomes a child of God, must be begotten of the Spirit of God.

Jesus Christ, in His Resurrection and Ascension, assumed His full prerogative as Life-giver to His mystical body, the Church. The new birth or the regenerative act, therefore, is the imparting of the divine nature to man, (II Pet. 1:4), rather than a change of nature, the Holy Spirit being the medium of the transmitting of the new nature.

2. He Baptizes Into the Body of Christ.

John 1:32-34—And John bare record, saying I saw the Spirit descending from heaven like a dove, and it abode upon him. And I knew him not; but he that sent me to baptize with water, the same said unto me, upon whom thou shalt see the Spirit descending and remaining on him, the same is he which baptizeth with the Holy Ghost. And I saw, and bare record that this is the Son of God.

I Cor. 12:12, 13—For as the body is one, and hath many members, and all the members of that one body, being many are one body; so also is Christ. For by one Spirit are we all baptized into one body, whether we be

165

Jews or Gentiles, whether we be bond or free; and have been all made to drink into one Spirit.

S. F. Acts 1:5.

The baptism of the Holy Spirit is that act which takes place at conversion, by which the individual is made a member of the body of Christ. This work has been accomplished in the life of every believer, though it is not always recognized.

It is not something to be attained by the believer after regeneration. It is something that has been obtained for him at regeneration. The baptism of the Spirit began at Pentecost, but reaches down across the centuries until the last member has been added to the church. "By one Spirit," says Paul, "are we all baptized into one body."

3. He Indwells.

I Cor. 6:15-19—Know ye not that your bodies are the members of Christ? shall I then take the members of Christ and make them the members of an harlot? God forbid. What! know ye not that he which is joined to an harlot is one body? for two, saith he, shall be one flesh. But he that is joined unto the Lord is one spirit. Flee fornication. Every sin that a man doeth is without the body; but he that committeth fornication sinneth against his own body. What? know ye not that your body is the temple of the Holy Ghost which is in you, which ye have of God and ye are not your own? For ye are bought with a price, therefore glorify God in your body, and in your spirit, which are God's.

S. F. I Cor. 3:16; Rom. 8:9.

The Spirit comes to indwell or take up His abode in the life of the believer at regeneration and abides there, no matter how imperfect or immature that life may be. The indwelling of the Spirit is an advance upon the work of regeneration. He thus enables growth, in the new life begun. We need to realize and recognize His abiding presence in the temple of our bodies. This recognition should make them hallowed and lead us to keep them undefiled and free from sin. Recognition of His presence is also the secret of the realization of His Power.

(1) He seals.

Eph. 1:13-14—In whom ye also trusted, after that ye heard the word of truth, the gospel of your salvation; in whom also after that ye believed ye were sealed with that Holy Spirit of promise. Which is the earnest of our inheritance until the redemption of the purchased possession, unto the praise of his glory.

S. F. Eph. 4:30.

He seals—making the believer His own. The Ephesians well understood the figure of the seal, for Ephesus was a seaport, carrying on an extensive lumber business. The lumber merchant came to Ephesus, selected and purchased his timber and stamped it with the acknowledged sign of ownership, the signet. Oftentimes he left his purchase in the harbor with other floats and sometime later sent a trusted agent, who compared the impress with the signet and took away the lumber belonging to his master. The Spirit is the signet seal of ownership which God places upon the life. He is the divine imprint and the pledge of the everlasting inheritance.

166

(2) He gives assurance.

Rom. 8:14, 16—For as many as are led by the Spirit of God, they are the sons of God. The Spirit itself beareth witness with our spirits that we are the children of God.

The Spirit gives the assurance and confidence which are necessary to the peace and quiet rest promised to the child of God. He witnesses to the fact of the Sonship of the believer (II Cor. 1:12, 22).

(3) He strengthens.

Eph. 3:16, R. V.—That he would grant you, according to the riches of his glory, to be strengthened with might by his Spirit in the inner man.

The results of this strengthening are seen in verses 17-19. The Spirit's power becomes operative in our lives in the actual embodiment and enthronement of Christ, described as His dwelling (permanently settling) in our hearts, being rooted and grounded in love, made strong to apprehend with all the saints what is the breadth and length and heighth and depth and to know the love of Christ which passeth knowledge, resulting in our being filled with all the fulness of God.

4. He Infills.

Eph. 5:18-20—And be not drunk with wine, wherein is excess; but be filled with the Spirit; Speaking to yourselves in psalms and hymns and spiritual songs, singing and making melody in your heart to the Lord; Giving thanks always for all things unto God and the Father in the name of our Lord Jesus Christ.

S. F. Acts 4:8, 31; Acts 2:4; Acts 6:3; Acts 7:54, 55; Acts 9:17, 20; Acts 13:9, 10; Acts 13:52.

S. A. Luke 1:15; Luke 1:41; Luke 1:67, 68; Luke 4:1; John 7:38, 39.

The Scriptures make mention of only one baptism of the Holy Spirit, while the infilling of the Spirit is not confined to a single experience, but may be repeated times without number. There need be no long searching before receiving this. It may occur at conversion, and is to be sought afresh in each new emergency or act of service.

There are two things essential to its realization; first, complete yieldedness of life, and, second, a definite appropriation by faith.

5. He Liberates.

Rom. 8:2—For the law of the Spirit of life in Christ Jesus hath made me free from the law of sin and death.

The preceding chapter (Rom. 7:9-24) defines the law of sin and death. Paul says "when I would do good evil was present" (7:21). "To will is present with me, but to do that which is good is not" (7:18, R. V.). Paul had been well educated in the law of God, given to Moses, and knew that he was commanded to observe its precepts, but he found another law within himself which strove against this law—the law of sin and death. In his distress, with his mind approving God's law, and his actions approving the law of sin and death, Paul discovered in Christ Jesus a third law, the law of the Spirit of life, which set him free from the law of sin and death. It is the work of the Spirit to set us free from the control of the lower law and to enable us to walk in harmony with the higher law.

167

6. He Directs.

Rom. 8:14—For as many as are led by the Spirit of God, they are the sons of God.

(1) He calls to special service.

Acts 13:2, 4—As they ministered to the Lord, and fasted the Holy Ghost said, Separate me Barnabas and Saul for the work whereunto I have called them. So they, being sent forth by the Holy Ghost, departed unto Seleucia; and from thence they sailed to Cyprus.

The Holy Spirit not only directs the general tenor of the Christian life but calls out men for special work, such as missions, the ministry, teaching, etc.

This passage does not tell us how the Spirit calls men, presumably because He does not always call men in the same way. It is for us to be willing to be called, to desire it, to seek it, and then wait for the Holy Spirit to call us. He does not call all to foreign missionary work, though every Christian should be willing to answer that call. He does, however, call every Christian to some field of service, and will lead him, if yielded, to that specific field.

(2) He guides in service.

Acts 8:27–29—And he arose and went: and behold, a man of Ethiopia, an eunuch of great authority under Candace, queen of the Ethiopians, who had the charge of all her treasure, and had come to Jerusalem for to worship, Was returning and sitting in his chariot read Esaias the prophet. Then the Spirit said unto Philip, Go near, and join thyself to this chariot.

Upon our surrender to God, the Spirit not only directs our personal lives but also guides us in leading others into the light and life and love of God in Jesus Christ our Lord.

7. He Equips for Service.

(1) He illumines.

I Cor. 2:12, 14—Now we have received, not the spirit of the world, but the spirit which is of God; that we might know the things that are freely given to us of God. But the natural man receiveth not the things of the Spirit of God; for they are foolishness unto him; neither can he know them, because they are spiritually discerned.

There is no darkness in the Scripture—"the entrance of Thy word giveth light." There is, however, darkness in man. Therefore, "in thy light shall we see light" (Psa. 36:9). Man's mind must first be illumined by the Spirit of God before it can rightly interpret or understand the Word of God.

(2) He instructs.

John 16:13, 14, R. V.—Howbeit when he, the Spirit of truth, is come, he shall guide you into all the truth; for he shall not speak from himself; but what things soever he shall hear, these shall he speak and he shall declare unto you the things that are to come. He shall glorify me; for he shall take of mine, and shall declare it unto you.

We may be taught of God by receiving instruction from others who have been illumined by the Spirit. John believed this, else he would never have written his epistle to teach others. However, the Holy Spirit is the Divine teacher, and we will never be truly taught until we are taught of Him.

The truth concerning which He is to teach seems to be along two lines; first, concerning the things of Christ, which glorify him, and, second, concerning the things of the future.

(3) He empowers.

I Thes. 1:5 For our gospel came not unto you in word only, but also in power, and in the Holy Ghost, and in much assurance, as ye know what manner of men we were among you for your sake.

S. F. Acts 1:8; I Cor. 2:1-5.

" 'More power' is the universal cry, and it is the purpose and provision of God that His children should be adequately and permanently empowered. On the day of Pentecost the mighty gift was brought in fulfillment so that men who were weak and timid before, became strong and bold for Christ. No limit is known to that power. It is still 'The exceeding abundantly, above all that we ask or think' that God would have us to expect and receive."— Soltau.

8. He produces the Fruit of Christlike Graces.

Gal. 5:22, 23—But the fruit of the Spirit is love. joy, peace, long suffering, gentleness, goodness, faith, Meekness, temperance: against such there is no law.

Comp. with Rom. 14:17; Rom. 15:13; Rom. 5:5.

All real beauty of character, all real Christlikeness in us, is the Holy Spirit's work. He is to the Christian what the sap is to the tree,—the source of productive life and power.

The fruit spoken of is not service or soul winning, though this needs to be emphasized, but the fruit of Christian character.

"Fruit does not consist in some strenuous exercise. It is not a laborious performance to bring forth some excellence. It is a natural normal result of a healthy condition. If the soul is in health, and the Spirit fills it, there will be fruit."—O'Rear.

The fruit of the Spirit as here described is really a portrayal of the character of Jesus Christ. We have here in substance that which Paul states in Gal. 2:20, "Christ liveth in me."

9. He Makes Possible All Forms of Communion with God.

(1) Prayer.

Jude 20—But ye, beloved, building up yourselves on your most holy faith, praying in the Holy Ghost.

S. F. Eph. 6:18; Rom. 8:26, 27, R. V.

"The Holy Spirit is the great Director of prayer, and only prayer in the Spirit is accepted and answered. He examines and tests the motives for our asking. He suggests the subjects for our petitions. He undertakes all the wonderful mystery of prayer from within expressed in words, or in groanings that are unutterable. He understands the will of God for us, the plans designed for us by God; the service we can acceptably render to God. To us the next day or hour is veiled but not to Him, therefore, He loves and longs to have such control of our thoughts and desires, as to be able, unhindered, to indite prayer, and such prayer as He knows is according to the will of God, and so must be answered. '—SOLTAU.

"It is Christ's mediatorship with the Father, and the Holy Ghost's mediatorship with us that gives us this high privilege of praying in the name of Jesus, as it is written 'For through Him we both have access in one Spirit unto the Father.' "—GORDON.

(2) Worship and praise.

Phil. 3:3, R. V.—For we are the circumcision, who worship by the Spirit of God and glory in Christ Jesus, and have no confidence in the flesh.

S. F. Acts 2:11.

Worship is the creature adoring and contemplating His Maker, God. This must be carried on in complete reliance upon the guidance of the Spirit, counting self as a thing to be distrusted and renounced.

Someone has said, "In our prayers we are taken up with our needs, in our thanksgiving we are taken up with our blessings, but in our worship we are taken up with Himself."

(3) Thanksgiving.

Eph. 5:18–20, R. V.—And be not drunken with wine, wherein is riot, but be filled with the Spirit, speaking one to another in psalms and hymns and spiritual songs, singing and making melody with your heart to the Lord; Giving thanks always for all things in the name of our Lord Jesus Christ to God even the Father.

The Spirit-filled life is a life of thanksgiving, accompanied by a life of thanks-living.

10. Shall Quicken the Believer's Body.

Rom. 8:11, 23—But if the Spirit of him that raised up Jesus from the dead dwell in you, he that raised up Christ from the dead shall also quicken your mortal bodies by his Spirit that dwelleth in you. And not only they, but ourselves also, which have the first-fruits of the Spirit, even we ourselves groan within ourselves, waiting for the adoption, to wit, the redemption of our body.

Resurrection is attributed to the Holy Spirit, as it is, also, to the other members of the Trinity. He shall make alive our bodies after death.

IV. In Relation to Jesus Christ.

1. Conceived by the Holy Spirit.

Luke 1:35—And the angel answered and said unto her. The Holy Ghost shall come upon thee, and the power of the Highest shall overshadow thee; therefore also that holy thing which shall be born of thee shall be called the Son of God.

"The Holy Spirit produced the human body for the Son of God by a creative act. Of that body, the Son of God spoke as a prepared body (Heb. 10:4, 5). It was impossible for One who is absolutely holy to clothe Himself with a body, coming into existence by the natural generation. If that had been the case, He would have had a body to which the taint of sin was attached. While it is true that Mary had a body which was sinful, yet the power of holiness in the Son of God, repulsed every particle of that, and the Holy Spirit in preparing the body could not permit anything unholy to enter the physical body of our Lord."—GAEBELEIN.

A life so unique as that of Christ, in its character and achievement demands a beginning and an ending so wonderful that nothing short of the virgin birth and miraculous resurrection would be appropriate.

2. Anointed with the Holy Spirit.

Acts 10:38—How God anointed Jesus of Nazareth with the Holy Spirit and with power; who went about doing good, and healing all that were oppressed of the devil; for God was with him.

S. F. Isa. 61:1; Lk. 4:14, 18, Comp. with Isa. 11:2.

S. A. Matt. 12:17–18.

All the anointings in the Old Testament of prophets, priests and kings, find their antitypical fulfillment in this anointing of Jesus by the Holy Spirit, who, too, in due time, would fulfill the office of prophet, priest, and king.

3. Led by the Spirit.

Matt. 4:1—Then was Jesus led up of the spirit into the wilderness to be tempted of the devil.

Jesus, as the servant of Jehovah, for which position He had emptied Himself of His sovereignty, took His own initiative in nothing, but always acted under orders, being directed in His movement by the Holy Spirit, to whom He was subject.

4. Filled with the Holy Spirit.

Luke 4:1—And Jesus being full of the Holy Ghost returned from Jordan, and was led by the Spirit into the wilderness.

S. A. John 3:34, R. V.

There was nothing in the life of Jesus which opposed itself to the Holy Spirit, therefore, He filled every department and avenue of His being with His presence and power.

5. Accomplished His Ministry in the Power of the Spirit.

Luke 4:18, 19—The Spirit of the Lord is upon me, because he hath anointed me to preach the gospel to the poor; he hath sent me to heal the brokenhearted, to preach deliverance to the captives, and recovering of sight to the blind, to set at liberty them that are bruised, To preach the acceptable year of the Lord.

S. F. Isa. 61:1; Luke 4:14.

6. Sacrificially Offered Himself Through the Spirit.

Heb. 9:14—How much more shall the blood of Christ, who through the eternal Spirit offered himself without spot to God, purge your conscience from dead works to serve the living God?

171

In the sacrifice of Himself, as in all else, Jesus Christ was directed by and dependent upon the Holy Spirit.

7. Resurrected by the Power of the Spirit.

Rom. 8:11—But if the Spirit of him that raised up Jesus from the dead dwell in you, he that raised up Christ from the dead shall also quicken your mortal bodies by his Spirit that dwelleth in you.

S. F. Rom. 1:4.

Jesus Christ was raised from the dead by the coordinate power of the Triune God. The Holy Spirit, therefore, had a prominent part in His resurrection.

8. Commandment to the Apostles After His Resurrection, Given Through the Holy Spirit.

Acts 1:1, 2—The former treatise have I made O Theophilus, of all that Jesus began both to do and teach, Until the day in which he was taken up, after that he through the Holy Ghost had given commandments, unto the apostles whom he had chosen.

Jesus Christ seemed to have continued under the direction of the Spirit in the work given to Him by the Father until He had again taken his place at the right hand of God, in complete exaltation.

9. Bestower of the Holy Spirit.

Acts 2:33—Therefore being by the right hand of God exalted, and having received of the Father the promise of the Holy Ghost, he hath shed forth this, which ye now see and hear.

The Holy Spirit came on the day of Pentecost as the result of Christ's ascension and session at the right hand of God as our great High Priest.

D. S. Jesus Christ lived His life in absolute dependence upon, and subjection to, the Holy Spirit.

V. In Relation to the Scriptures.

1. The Author of Them.

II Peter 1:20, 21—Knowing this first, that no prophecy of the scripture is of any private interpretation. For the prophecy came not in old time by the will of man; but holy men of God spake as they were moved by the Holy Ghost.

S. F. II Tim. 3:16; II Pet. 3:15, 16.

S. A. John 16:13.

The Scriptures represent the Holy Spirit as being the Divine Agent for the communication of the truth of God to men. This is definitely declared concerning the Old Testament scriptures, and is clearly implied and stated concerning the New.

2. The Interpreter of Them.

Eph. 1:17—That the God of our Lord Jesus Christ, the Father of glory, may give unto you the spirit of wisdom and revelation in the knowledge of him.

S. F. I Cor. 2:9–14; John 16:14–16.

Man's impotency to interpret truth already revealed is just as marked as is his inability to communicate the revelation apart from the aid of the Holy Spirit.

D. S. The Scriptures were given by the inspiration of the Holy Spirit, and their true interpretation is only possible through His illumination.

Study Questions on the Doctrine of the Holy Spirit

1. In viewing the Person and work of the Holy Spirit, into what two periods do we divide the facts? Discuss each.
2. Define the Personality of the Holy Spirit.
3. Give four possible explanations of the errors of interpretation which arose concerning the Personality of the Holy Spirit.
4. Give the five-fold proof of Personality as contained in the D. S.
5. Quote one passage (a) in which a personal pronoun is used of the Holy Spirit, (b) in which He is associated with the other Persons of the Godhead.
6. Give the Personal characteristics ascribed to the Holy Spirit and quote one passage with one of them.
7. Give (a) the personal acts ascribed to the Holy Spirit and (b) the personal treatment received by the Holy Spirit.
8. How is the importance of the doctrine of the personality of the Holy Spirit seen?
9. Define the Deity of the Holy Spirit and give the five-fold proof of it.
10. Give the divine names, divine attributes and divine works ascribed to the Holy Spirit quoting one passage under each group.
11. Quote one passage from the Old Testament and one from the New Testament showing that statements concerning Jehovah refer to the Holy Spirit.
12. Mention three instances in which the name of the Holy Spirit is coupled in equality with that of God and of Christ and quote a passage to support one.
13. Give the names of the Holy Spirit which are descriptive of His own Person and quote one passage with each.
14. Quote one passage in which the Spirit is likened to "breath."
15. Give the names of the Holy Spirit which set forth His relationship to God and give D. S.
16. Give the names of the Holy Spirit which set forth His relation to the Son of God.
17. Give the names of the Holy Spirit which show His relation to men and quote one passage with one.
18. Give D. S. showing the relation of the work of the Holy Spirit to the material universe.
19. Give the three-fold work of the Holy Spirit in relation to the unregenerate and quote and discuss John 16:8–11.
20. Give the ten-fold work of the Holy Spirit in relation to the believer, discuss

the third, seventh and ninth phases, and quote a passage with one other phase.

21. Discuss the nine-fold work of the Holy Spirit in relation to Jesus Christ.
22. Give the two-fold work of the Holy Spirit in relation to the Scriptures, and quote one passage with each.

CHAPTER FIVE

THE DOCTRINE OF MAN

(ANTHROPOLOGY)

In every normal individual, there is an innate desire to know something of one's ancestry and ancestral history. And what is true of us as individual men and women concerning our origin is also true of us as racial representatives of the human species or order of beings. What is man and whence came he?

A. Creation.

There is no trustworthy evidence that man came from beneath as a product of the life forces or potencies of the material universe. There is, however, strong evidence that his origin was from above, through the power of God put forth in creation. The occurrence of the Hebrew word for create, "bara," in this connection, shows the absolute separation of mankind from the animal kingdom.

I. The Fact of It.

1. Man's Creation Decreed.

Gen. 1:26—And God said, Let us make man in our image, after our likeness; and let them have dominion over the fish of the sea, and over the fowl of the air, and over the cattle, and over all the earth, and over every creeping thing that creepeth upon the earth.

2. Man's Creation Declared.

Gen. 1:27—So God created man in his own image, in the image of God created he him: male and female created he them.

II. The Method of It.

1. Negatively Considered: It Was Not by Evolution or Natural Development by Reason of Forces Within Matter, Organic or Inorganic.

Only the works of man himself proceed on the principle of evolution or development. He starts from nothing, beginning in ignorance, helplessness, and inexperience. This is true only in human affairs; man has gone from the ploughshare to the steamshovel; from the raft to the ocean liner; from the cave to the skyscraper. But the birds build their nests today as at the beginning. For, the moment we pass the boundary and enter the Divine sphere, no trace or signs of evolution is found.

175

(1) **The evolutionary theory represents man as rising from a lower order of being, while the Scriptures declare his origin to be due to the direct creative action of God.**

(2) **The evolutionary theory represents man as being the result of successive changes in the material forms due to resident forces within, while the Scriptures declare that man's physical being is the result of God's action upon it from without.**

(3) **The evolutionary theory represents man as the climax of development, ascending through the lower forms of animal life, while the Bible declares him to belong to the distinctive human order, whose entrance into being was immediate and direct.**

"As a result of careful investigation, the following statement is made: The failure of evolutionists to establish the claim that original life-germs came into existence by natural processes; their inability to show that, in the world of living things, there exists a law of development and improvement; the complete breakdown of their claim that, by natural processes, lower species of plants and animals may be transmuted into higher; the fact that in all early and late excavations and researches not one connecting link between any of the millions of different species has been found; the fact that mental science and all the physical sciences have not yet discovered a particle of evidence showing, or even suggesting, that any animal ever has reached or ever can reach a point where, slowly or suddenly, it can come into possession of a human soul, a human mind, or a human body; the fact that biologists, geologists and archaeologists have overwhelmingly silenced the assertion that the human race began low down and through countless ages has worked itself up to its present civilized state; the downfall of the assertion that scholarly men are all evolutionists; the recent abandonment of Darwinian evolution by those who once held the theory, and who at the present moment are making vigorous assaults upon it; the absolute incompetence of evolutionists to formulate any system of ethics or religion that at all approaches that of the Bible —in view, therefore, of this array of facts, it is shown that the hypothesis of Darwinian evolution has collapsed beyond any hope of restoration."—TOWN-SEND.

2. Positively Considered.

(1) Called into being by an act of creation.

Gen. 1:27—So God created man in his own image, in the image of God created he him; male and female created he them.

(2) Given a physical organism by an act of Formation.

Gen. 2:7, f.c.—And the Lord God formed man of the dust of the ground.

S. F. Ecc. 12:7.

(3) Made a complete living personal being by final action.

Gen. 2:7, l.c.—And man became a living soul.

S. F. Zech. 12:1.

S. A. Isa. 43:7.

In harmony with this threefold preparation of man for his life and work upon the earth, we find three Hebrew words describing it. A passage in Isaiah 43:7 illustrates the meaning of these three verbs: "I have created (*bara*) him for my glory [that is, produced him out of nothing]; I have formed (*asah*) him [that is, caused him to exist in a shape or form appointed]; yea, I have made (*yatzar*) him [that is, made the final dispositions and arrangements respecting him]."

D. S. The Scriptures clearly and emphatically show that man is the result of the immediate, special, creative, and formative acts of God.

B. Original Condition.

"Those who believe in the ascent of man teach that he began life on a far lower scale than that upon which he now lives. The only fall they recognize is upward. They teach that man has attained higher heights than any upon which he may have been placed at his inception. This cannot be true, because the Scriptures teach the very opposite. Indeed, there is abundant evidence to show that man has been degraded from a very much higher stage. Both the Bible and science agree in making man the crowning work of God. We must not forget that while man, from one side of his nature, is linked to the animal creation, he is yet supra-natural—a being of a higher order and more splendid nature; he is in the image and likeness of God."—EVANS.

I. Possessed the Image of God.

Gen. 1:27—So God created man in his own image, in the image of God created he him, male and female created he them.

S. F. Gen. 5:1; Gen. 9:6.

1. The Image of God Does Not Denote Physical Likeness.

Col. 1:15—Who is the image of the invisible God, the firstborn of every creature.

S. F. John 4:24; John 1:18; Luke 24:39; I Sam. 15:29.

According to the teachings of these passages, God is not a man. He is, rather, a Spirit, and as such He has no physical parts or substance, but is invisible.

2. It May Mean a Formal Image and Likeness, a Likeness in Form.

Phil. 2:6—Who being in the form of God, thought it not robbery to be equal with God.

S. F. Psa. 17:15, R.V.; Num. 12:7–8; Heb. 1:3; Isa. 6:1; Acts 7:56; I John 3:2.

Just what this form is we do not know: it doubtless includes the intellectual, moral, volitional, and emotional natures, though in substance it is spirit. Some think, however, that it refers to man's creation, according to the model and pattern set forth in Christ, Who is said to be the image of God.

3. It Could Refer to a Triune Likeness, Man a Tripartite Being, God a Triune Being.

I Thes. 5:23—And the very God of peace sanctify you wholly; and I pray God your whole spirit and soul and body be preserved blameless unto the coming of our Lord Jesus Christ.

S. F. Matt. 26:12—Christ's body—Greek, soma
Matt. 26:38—Christ's soul—Greek, psuche
Matt. 27:50; Luke 23:46—Christ's spirit—Greek, pneuma

4. It Doubtless Includes the Personal Image—Both God and Man Possess Personality.

Ex. 3:13, 14—And Moses said unto God, Behold, when I come unto the children of Israel, and shall say unto them, The God of your fathers hath sent me unto you; and they shall say to me, What is his name? what shall I say unto them? And God said unto Moses, I AM THAT I AM: and he said, Thus shalt thou say unto the Children of Israel, I AM hath sent me unto you.

This aspect of God's image in man remains undestroyed by sin, though it has been marred and made defective.

5. It Must Involve Endless Being, with Which God Has Endowed Man.

Matt. 25:46—And these shall go away into everlasting punishment: but the righteous into life eternal.

Unending existence is an inseparable part of man's heritage as a creature made after the image and likeness of God. He is indestructible. He cannot be annihilated.

6. It Certainly Means Intellectual and Moral Likeness.

Col. 3:10—And have put on the new man, which is renewed in knowledge after the image of him that created him.

S. F. Eph. 4:23, 24.

II. Possessed Intellectual Faculties.

Gen. 2:19, 20—And out of the ground the Lord God formed every beast of the field, and every fowl of the air; and brought them unto Adam to see what he would call them; and whatsoever Adam called every living creature, that was the name thereof. And Adam gave names to all cattle, and to the fowl of the air, and to every beast of the field; but for Adam there was not found an help meet for him.

S. F. Gen. 1:28.

"Man resembles God in his possession of a rational nature. Man's capacity in this regard is the source of all scientific knowledge. He reads the meaning of nature and discovers that it is stamped with the marks of reason. Man understands God by reason of the marks of intelligence in the world about him. Reason in man answers to reason in God."– MULLINS.

He had sufficient intelligence when created to think, reason, and speak; to draw conclusions and make decisions. He had a language and apparently was the master of it. He could select suitable names from his divinely given vocabulary for the beasts presented before him, and was capable of having dominion over them.

Man was a rational being. In this he differed from all inferior animals. Of many of them it may be said that they excel man in sagacious instinct. What is instinct? Dr. Paley said: "An instinct is a propensity prior to experience and independent of instruction." It is a blind, unreasoning impulse that prompts animals to do certain things without knowing why or caring to improve the manner of doing them. Hence, the instincts of animals act with unchangeable uniformity, and there is no improvement. Migratory birds perform their migrations just as birds did a thousand years ago; the beaver constructs its habitation as it was made in other centuries; and the bee builds its cell as in the days of antiquity. Of all inferior animals it has to be said that they are irrational. The difference between them and man is as wide as the poles.

"This is evident, because men are proper subjects of moral government, and without a rational nature they could not be accountable. Human governments recognize this view of the matter, for they do not hold idiots and lunatics responsible. The reason is that in idiots the rational powers have never been sufficiently unfolded to furnish a basis for moral accountability; and in the case of lunatics the intellect, though once developed, has been so impaired as to nullify moral obligation."—PENDLETON.

III. Possessed a Holy Moral Nature.

Ecc. 7:29—Lo, this only have I found, that God hath made man upright; but they have sought out many inventions.

S. F. Gen. 2:15–17; Rom. 5:12, 14.

"This means that he was created a holy being, and this was the chief glory with which he was crowned. It was great glory to be made like God in his intellectual excellencies, but it was the greatest glory to be made like him in his moral perfections."—PENDLETON.

D. S. Man was created in the image of God, possessing intellectual faculties and a holy nature with the responsibility of developing a holy character.

C. Probation.

Man's probation was absolutely essential in order to the complete expression and exercise of his intellectual and moral freedom.

"Suppose there had been no prohibition in the garden, what would have become of our first parents' free moral agency? Had they been created with such an endowment, they would have had no opportunity to exercise it, and that would have virtually made them slaves to the will of God. The same would have been true if God had created them without the power of choice. In either case they would have been different beings from men as we know them today, and therefore could not have been the progenitors of the human race. To have created man sinful would have made God the Author of sin— a thought that is intolerable, and would have partly destroyed his free agency, because it would have given him a bias toward evil."—KEYSER.

Man was not created in a neutral moral condition, but was given a holy nature, which, if allowed full exercise without external incitement to sin and inward response to the same, would have expressed itself in character and conduct which were also holy. This unhindered exercise of the moral nature apart from a testing would have been an infringement on the exercise of his moral freedom. It was necessary for him to have the right and freedom to choose the right, and freedom to choose evil as well as good.

I. The Meaning of It.

By the probation of man we mean that time during which he was subjected to a particular test, consisting of a positive command concerning the tree of the knowledge of good and evil. The results were to be either the continued favor of God for obedience, or the imposing of the penalty of death for disobedience.

II. The Fact of It.

Gen. 2:15–17—And the Lord God took the man, and put him into the garden of Eden to dress it and to keep it. And the Lord God commanded the

179

man, saying, Of every tree of the garden thou mayest freely eat: But of the tree of the knowledge of good and evil, thou shalt not eat of it: for in the day that thou eatest thereof thou shalt surely die.

III. The Period of It.

The period covered by the probation extended from the creation of Adam and Eve to the time of their failure and disobedience.

D. S. Man's probation which was for the purpose of his testing is clearly shown to have covered the period of his innocence.

D. Fall.

Man was not created a sinner, but sin entered into the world of men through his own conscious and voluntary choice. The doctrine of the Fall is not limited to the Christian religion, for all religions contain either an account of the fall or an intimation of it, and recognize the fact that there is something radically wrong with the race, but they are all vague concerning the cause or origin of this depravity of attitude and action; to the revelation of God alone must we look for this.

How long our first parents remained in a sinless state, retaining the moral image of God in which they were made, it is impossible to say. The matter comes not within the horizon of human knowledge. Some suppose that man's state of innocence continued about a century, and others have thought that it was only a few days in duration. Conjecture is useless and vain. It is enough for us to know that it continued until the fact was proved that man was capable of obedience. This fact being proved, it follows that his obedience might have been permanent. That is to say, as there was nothing to make his obedience impracticable while he rendered it, so there was no reason why that obedience might not have been perpetual. What was done for a day or a year might have been done for an indefinite number of days or years, and would have been done, but for man's voluntary decision to disobey.

I. The Fact of It.

Rom. 5:12—Wherefore, as by one man sin entered into the world, and death by sin; and so death passed upon all men, for that all have sinned.

S. F. Gen. 3:1-6; Rom. 5:13-19; I Tim. 2:14.

Adam and Eve, the first of the human race, sinned against God, and thus fell from the standing of favor and the state of innocence in which they were created.

II. The Manner of It.

1. The Tempter—Satan Through the Serpent.

Gen. 3:1—Now the serpent was more subtil than any beast of the field which the Lord God had made. And he said unto the woman, Yea, hath God said, Ye shall not eat of every tree of the garden? (Rev. 12:9; 20:2)

"Why was Satan the tempter? It was well it was so; for thus the enticement came to man from without; it did not have its initiative from within the sphere of his own being. That in a measure mitigates man's sin, and leaves him redeemable, though a fallen creature. The fact that Satan took upon himself the guise of the serpent also extenuates man's transgression, for man

180

was thereby deceived, enticed into the act of disobedience. This will be made clear by supposing that our first parents had eaten of the forbidden fruit without a tempter and without deception. Then their sin would have been so heinous, coming from the very depths of their own being, that they would scarcely have been savable, and therefore a Saviour would perhaps never have been provided. So far as we can understand the teaching of the divine Word, the angels who fell cannot be redeemed. It may have been so because their temptation came from within, through no outward allurement and deception."—KEYSER.

2. The Temptation.

(1) First step (taken by the woman).

The woman listening apparently alone, unprotected and near the forbidden spot.

(2) Second step (taken by the serpent).

The serpent's insinuating question which was apparently innocent, but which contained an insinuated doubt of God's Word, "Hath God said?" It also insinuated a doubt as to the love and justice of God, magnifying the one prohibition, and minimizing the extensive permissions.

(3) Third step (taken by the woman).

The woman replying to, and parleying with the slanderer. She showed that she understood the words of Genesis 2:16–17.

(4) Fourth step (taken by the woman).

Tampering with the Word of God. She left out "every" and "freely," and put in "neither shalt thou touch it," and softened "in the day that thou eatest thereof, thou shalt surely die" to "lest ye die."

Gen. 3:2–3—And the woman said unto the serpent, We may eat of the fruit of the trees of the garden: But of the fruit of the tree which is in the midst of the garden, God hath said, Ye shall not eat of it, neither shall ye touch it, lest ye die.

Comp. with

Gen. 2:17—But of the tree of the knowledge of good and evil, thou shalt no eat of it: for in the day that thou eatest thereof thou shalt surely die.

(5) Fifth step (taken by the serpent).

This consisted of an open denial of punishment for sin, and of the accusing of God of lying. It also contained another bold accusation. He accused God of selfishness, jealousy, and a determination to degrade and lord it over His creatures.

(6) Sixth step (taken by the woman).

Believing the Tempter. She saw that the tree was (see I John 2:16) good for food (lust of the flesh), pleasant to the eyes (lust of the eye), and desirable to make one wise (pride of life).

(7) Seventh step (taken by the woman).

Obeying the Tempter, she took of the fruit and ate (woman yielded, being deceived).

(8) Eighth step (taken by the woman).

Becoming a tempter. She gave to her husband and he did eat (man yielded but was not deceived) (I Tim. 2:14). Adam disobeyed with open eyes, deliberately, instead of trying to help his wife, and asking pardon for her, and protection for himself. To him were the prohibition and the warning given (Gen. 2:16–17). He was the head of the race and he brought sin upon the race (Rom. 5:12, 16–19).

III. The Results of It.

1. To Adam and Eve in Particular.

(1) An apparent loss of a suitable personal appearance accompanied by consciousness of nakedness and a sense of shame.

Gen. 3:7—And the eyes of them were opened and they knew that they were naked; and they sewed fig leaves together, and made themselves aprons.

S. A. Ps. 104:2; Matt. 13:43; Dan. 12:3.

It would seem that the unfallen spirits of Adam and Eve possessed an encircling halo of light which saved them from the appearance and consciousness of nakedness. This was apparently lost through their disobedience and sin, causing them a sense of unfitness of appearance in the presence of God and perhaps in the presence of each other.

(2) A craven fear of God.

Gen. 3:8–10—And they heard the voice of the Lord God walking in the garden in the cool of the day; and Adam and his wife hid themselves from the presence of the Lord God amongst the trees of the garden. And the Lord God called unto Adam, and said unto him, Where art thou? And he said, I heard thy voice in the garden, and I was afraid, because I was naked; and I hid myself.

They doubtless had a holy fear of God, in the sense of reverential awe, but this gave them joy and pleasure in God's presence. This was replaced however, as a result of the fall, by a cowardly attitude of mind and heart which inclined them to flee from God's presence and hide themselves.

(3) Expulsion from the garden.

Gen. 3:23, 24—Therefore the Lord God sent him forth from the garden of Eden, to till the ground from whence he was taken. So he drove out the man and he placed at the east of the garden of Eden Cherubims, and a flaming sword which turned every way, to keep the way of the tree of life.

Immortality in a fallen depraved sin cursed body was a deeper, darker penalty than even God Himself desired for man, hence he was shut off from the tree of life.

2. To the Race in General.

Since the federal headship of the race was vested in Adam, his action was representative. The sin, therefore, was racial as well as individual. Hence there were results which came to the entire human species as a consequence of Adam's sin.

(1) Ground cursed so that it would not yield good alone, necessitating laborious toil on man's part.

Gen. 3:17–19—And unto Adam he said, Because thou hast hearkened unto the voice of thy wife, and hast eaten of the tree, of which I commanded thee, saying, Thou shalt not eat of it; Cursed is the ground for thy sake; in sorrow shalt thou eat of it all the days of thy life. Thorns also and thistles shall it bring forth to thee; and thou shalt eat the herb of the field; In the sweat of thy face shalt thou eat bread till thou return unto the ground; for out of it wast thou taken; for dust thou art, and unto dust shalt thou return.

This action showed that God's justice was mingled with mercy, for work was and is a real blessing to man in his fallen state.

(2) It resulted in sorrow and pain to woman in child-bearing, and her subjection to man.

Gen. 3:16—Unto the woman he said, I will greatly multiply thy sorrow and thy conception; in sorrow shalt thou bring forth children, and thy desire shall be to thy husband, and he shall rule over thee.

Childbearing seems to have been a part of God's creative plan, although apparently it was not fulfilled until after the fall. Suffering and sorrow however, in connection therewith were added as a consequence of man's sin.

(3) All men are sinners and resting under condemnation.

Rom. 5:12—Wherefore as by one man sin entered into the world, and death by sin; and so death passed upon all men, for that all have sinned.

S. F. Rom. 3:19; Rom. 3:9, 10; Rom. 3:22, 23; Isa. 53:6; Gal. 3:10; Eph. 2:3; John 3:36.

(4) It has resulted in physical and spiritual death in time and the threatened penalty of eternal death.

Gen. 2:17—But of the tree of the knowledge of good and evil, thou shalt not eat of it; for in the day that thou eatest thereof thou shalt surely die.

S. F. Rom. 6:23; Ezek. 18:4; Gen. 3:19.

S. A. Gen. 5:5; Rom. 5:12.

"The threatened penalty claims attention. It is in these words: 'in the day that thou eatest thereof, thou shalt surely die.' Most persons, perhaps, in reading this language receive the impression that natural death is referred to, and no doubt it is, but the death of the body by no means exhausts the reference. The bodies of Adam and Eve did not die actually on the day of transgression, but they died virtually. They were at once placed under the law of mortality—sin put them there—and the seeds of death were planted in them. There was, in consequence of sin, subjection to disease, infirmity, and dissolution; and the physical death of the guilty pair became just as certain when they sinned as if it had occurred while yet they were eating of the fatal fruit. Not only did the natural death of Adam result from his sin, but the natural death of all his posterity results from the same cause. Spiritual death, however, is also evidently referred to; and this is a far more fearful result than bodily death. The latter takes place when the spirit leaves the body, the former takes place when God leaves the spirit. The cessation of union, communion, and fellowship with God is so great a calamity that death is its most fitting designation. The spirit cut off from God, as the source of its blessedness feels a wretchedness which language is powerless to define. It may wander to the outermost limits of space in quest of something to satisfy its large desires, but that something is not found. It has never been found, and it never will be found. The life of the soul is in its union with the blessed God; the death of the soul, not its annihilation, consists in its separation from God. The consummation of spiritual death is death eternal. This consummation is sure to come, unless spiritual death is abolished by the impartation of spiritual life."—PENDLETON.

(5) Unredeemed men are in helpless captivity to sin and Satan and are regarded children of the devil.

Rom. 7:14, 15, 23, 24—For we know that the law is spiritual: but I am carnal, sold under sin. For that which I do I allow not: for what I would, that do I not; but what I hate, that do I. But I see another law in my members, warring against the law of my mind, and bringing me into captivity to the law of sin which is in my members. O wretched man that I am! who shall deliver me from the body of this death?

S. F. I John 3:8–10; John 8:33–35; Eph. 2:3; John 8:44; I John 5:19, R. V.

"Man's transgression was a crime of the greatest enormity. As to its nature, it was not merely disobedience to divine law on the part of the offender. It was gross infidelity, in believing the devil rather than God; discontent and envy, in thinking that God had denied him what was essential to his happiness; prodigious pride, in desiring to be like God; sacrilegious theft, in purloining what God had reserved to Himself as a token of His sovereignty; suicide and murder, in bringing death upon himself and upon all his posterity.

"It was in full view of the benevolence of the great Creator, who had bestowed upon him everything that was necessary for the perfection and perpetuation of his happiness. It was against the clearest convictions of conscience and with a mind fully illuminated by the Divine Spirit. The act was committed in the very presence of God, with a will sufficiently fortified to resist temptation, and without any compulsion whatever."—WAKEFIELD.

D. S. By an act of disobedience man fell from his state of innocence, thus bringing upon himself and his posterity sorrow, pain and death.

Study Questions on the Doctrine of Man

1. Show how the fact of man's creation by God is established in the Scriptures and quote one passage.
2. Describe the method of man's creation, negatively considered, contrasting the Evolutionary Hypothesis with the Biblical account.
3. Discuss the method of man's creation, positively considered; quote one passage with each point involved and give D. S.
4. Quote one passage which shows that man was created in God's image.
5. Give the detailed meaning both negative and positive of the image of God and quote one passage under each point.
6. Discuss the Scriptural teaching of man's intellectual faculties and moral nature. Give D. S.
7. Discuss necessity of the Probation of man from introductory note and give definition.
8. Quote a passage of Scripture proving the fact of man's probation; state period of its duration and give D. S.
9. Quote one passage of Scripture proving man's fall.
10. Describe the manner of the fall under following heads: the tempter, the temptation.
11. Give the results of the fall (a) to Adam and Eve in particular; (b) to the race in general.
12. Give D. S. under the fall of man.

CHAPTER SIX

THE DOCTRINE OF SIN

(HAMARTIOLOGY)

There are two great moral qualities or principles which receive emphasis in the Scripture. These two are: holiness and its antagonist, sin. The former might be said to be moral right and the latter moral wrong All other moral principles and qualities may be put into classifications capable of being identified with one of these two. Sin, therefore, like its opponent, is given ample and adequate treatment.

A. The Meaning of It.

I. Negatively Considered.

1. Not a fortuitous or chance happening, carrying with it no guilt for those concerned—not an accident.

Rom. 5:12—Wherefore, as by one man sin entered into the world, and death by sin; and so death passed upon all men, for that all have sinned:

There are those who teach that sin is accidental; but as we have seen, the teaching of the Bible is, that sin resulted from an act of responsible disobedience on the part of Adam.

2. Not a mere creature weakness for which man is not blameworthy or guilty.

Jer. 17:9—The heart is deceitful above all things, and desperately wicked: who can know it?

There are those who hold that sin is only a kind of infirmity or weakness, because of which we are very unfortunate, but in no wise culpable or guilty. But this, like the former view, is contrary to the truth of the Scriptures.

3. Not the mere absence of good nor a lack of positive righteousness— not a negation.

Rom. 7:14—For we know that the law is spiritual: but I am carnal, sold under sin.

S. F. Context.

That sin is a negation is the teaching of Christian science—that evil is the absence of good, and sin is the absence of righteousness. This is not so, for there are forms of sin which are very malignant and aggressive. The Word of

God declares sin and evil to have a positive existence, and to be an offense against the Lord.

4. Not outgrown good—not a step backward.

I John 3:4, R. V.—Every one that doeth sin doeth also lawlessness; and sin is lawlessness.

Sin cannot be defined as immaturity, lack of development, or the remnant of primitive characteristics.

II. Positively considered.

"In the Old and New Testaments alike sin is thought of chiefly as a breach or rupture of relations between the sinner and the personal God. We look briefly at the Old Testament teaching. Sin manifests itself in many ways, but the ruling thought in them all is the departure of the sinner from Jehovah's will. There was indeed transgression of law, but it was Jehovah's law. There were forms of selfishness, but these were in their essence the exaltation of self against Jehovah. There was the sinful disposition, the wrong motive, but it consisted chiefly in alienation of heart from Jehovah.

"In the New Testament, Jesus portrayed the ideal human life as a life of fellowship with God. Sin is the want of this fellowship. Jesus traces sin to the inner motive of men. The sinful thought is in quality the same as the outward act. Thus Jesus greatly deepened the sense of guilt. The exalted standard of His own life became the measure of human obligation and at the same time the criterion for judging sin and guilt."—MULLINS.

1. Failure to Meet One's Obligation to God.

(1) Coming short of the glory of God.
Rom. 3:23—For all have sinned and come short of the glory of God.

Weakness is ascribed to the flesh or carnal nature of man (Rom. 8:3, 4), which simply means its inability to measure up to the divine standard.

(2) Omission of duty.
James 4:17—Therefore to him that knoweth to do good, and doeth it not, to him it is sin.

"Here we pass from the negative to the positive side of the Christian life, and we learn that to leave undone what we know we should do, is to sin. Suppose that from the present moment we never do any more evil or harm, or injury of any kind to any man, would we be sinless? No. But our sinfulness would be seen in our not doing all the good we should do."—FROST.

(3) Backsliding.
Jer. 14:7—O Lord, though our iniquities testify against us, do thou it for thy name's sake; for our backslidings are many; we have sinned against thee.

Backsliding is the allowance of distance between the soul and God, which distance is identified with sin and iniquity. (Isa. 59:1, 2.)

2. Wrong Attitude toward the Person of God.

(1) The thought of foolishness.
Prov. 24:9—The thought of foolishness is sin: and the scorner is an abomination to men.

This doubtless refers to thoughts which are derogatory and dishonoring to the being of God

(2) Practice of pride and arrogance.

Prov. 21:4—An high look and a proud heart, and the plowing of the wicked is sin.

This practice involves self-exaltation and self-assertion which denote a wrong attitude of mind and heart toward God Himself.

(3) Murmurings against God.

Num. 21:7—Therefore the people came to Moses, and said, We have sinned for we have spoken against the Lord, and against thee; pray unto the Lord, that he take away the serpents from us. And Moses prayed for the people.

S. F. Lev. 24:15, 16; I Cor. 10:10, 11; Jude 16.

These express dissatisfaction with the divine plan and providence.

(4) Blasphemy against the Holy Ghost.

Mark 3:29, R. V.—But whosoever shall blaspheme against the Holy Spirit hath never forgiveness, but is guilty of an eternal sin.

The word "blasphemy" properly signifies detraction or slander. In the New Testament it is applied to vituperation directed against God as well as against men; and in this sense it is to be understood as an aggravated form of sin.

3. Wrong Action in Relation to the Will of God.

(1) Doubtful indulgence.

Rom. 14:23, R. V.—But he that doubteth is condemned if he eat, because he eateth not of faith; and whatsoever is not of faith is sin.

S. F. Rom. 14:19–22; I John 3:18–22.

The believer must give God the benefit of the doubt. Indulgence in questionable things will inevitably bring condemnation.

(2) Rebellion and stubbornness.

I Sam. 15:23, R. V.—For rebellion is as the sin of witchcraft, and stubbornness is as idolatry and teraphim. Because thou hast rejected the word of Jehovah, he hath also rejected thee from being king.

Strong wills are sources of great good when arrayed on the side of righteousness and the will of God, otherwise they are productive of great evil.

(3) Disobedience.

Jer. 3:25—We lie down in our shame, and our confusion covereth us: for we have sinned against the Lord our God, we and our fathers, from our youth even unto this day, and have not obeyed the voice of the Lord our God.

This represents open defiance of and insubordination to the sovereignty of God.

(4) Lawlessness.

I John 3:4, R. V.—Every one that doeth sin doeth also lawlessness; and sin is lawlessness.

"This is perhaps the most common definition of sin. The law fixes the line between good and evil, and any step across its boundary is sin. The law of which God speaks can be no other than His own, laid down in His own Word. Any breaking over the boundary of God's law is sin."—Cogswell.

4. Wrong Action in Relation to Men.

(1) Favoritism.

James 2:9—But if ye have respect to persons, ye commit sin, and are convinced of the law as transgressors.

S. F. James 2:1–4.

This places our dealings with men not upon the basis of either merit or mercy but upon that of personal satisfaction or gain, which is obviously wrong.

(2) All unrighteousness.

I John 5:17—All unrighteousness is sin: and there is a sin not unto death.

This views human relationships and actions from the Godward point of view, for sin is always against God. All wrongs therefore committed against our fellow-men are thus recognized as such.

(3) Despising one's neighbour.

Prov. 14:21—He that despiseth his neighbour sinneth: but he that hath mercy on the poor, happy is he.

This is direct disobedience to the command "Thou shalt love thy neighbour as thyself," and is also inconsistent with a life lived in harmony with God.

5. Wrong attitude toward Jesus Christ—unbelief.

John 16:8, 9—And when he is come, he will reprove the world of sin, and of righteousness, and of judgment: of sin, because they believe not on me;

Unbelief is the root sin from which all others have sprung. It was after unbelief was allowed to enter the heart of Eve, that there was found a response to the three-fold appeal of the temptation. Unbelief is still a root sin which produces a multifold harvest, especially unbelief in Christ. This is the sin that shuts God away from the soul and which, if persisted in, will shut the soul away from God.

6. Wrong Tendency of Nature.

Rom. 7:15–17—For that which I do I allow not: for what I would, that do I not; but what I hate, that do I. If then I do that which I would not, I consent unto the law that it is good. Now then it is no more I that do it. but sin that dwelleth in me.

S. A. Rom. 8:7; I John 1:8; Jer. 13:23.

The Scriptures recognize an evil principle within the nature of man which is called sin. It is this which gives the natural man a bent or bias toward disobedience and wickedness.

D. S. Sin is any transgression of, or want of conformity to, the revealed will of God, either in condition or conduct.

B. The Fact of It.

I. A fact of revelation.

Rom. 3:23—For all have sinned, and come short of the glory of God.

188

Rom. 5:12—Wherefore, as by one man sin entered into the world, and death by sin; and so death passed upon all men, for that all have sinned:

S. F. Gal. 3:22; Ecc. 7:20.

II. A fact of observation.

Sin is everywhere manifest to those who have eyes to see. The eye must be blind indeed that does not see the blighting, blasting, brutalizing and bestial workings of sin in the world of human life. A single issue of a daily newspaper, a single visit to the public institutions of a great city, a single trip through its crowded thoroughfares, ought to be sufficient to reveal the hideous forms which sin assumes, and convince anyone of its reality.

III. A fact of human experience.

Isa. 6:5—Then said I, Woe is me! for I am undone; because I am a man of unclean lips, and I dwell in the midst of a people of unclean lips: for mine eyes have seen the King, the Lord of hosts.

S. F. I Tim. 1:15; Josh. 7:20; Jer. 17:1.

S. A. Luke 5:8; Job 40:4.

Consciousness gives no uncertain witness to the reality of sin. Everyone knows he is a sinner. No one of responsible years has lived free from the sense of personal guilt and moral defilement. Remorse of conscience for wrongdoing hounds all the sons and daughters of Adam, while the sad and terrible consequences of sin are seen in the physical, mental and moral deterioration and degeneration of the race.

D. S. The Scriptures declare, observation discovers and human experience teaches the fact of sin.

C. The Extent of It.

The Scriptures teach that sin has affected the heavens and the earth and their inhabitants.

I. The Heavens.

Eph. 6:11, 12, R. V.—Put on the whole armor of God, that ye may be able to stand against the wiles of the devil. For our wrestling is not against flesh and blood, but against the principalities, against the powers, against the world-rulers of this darkness, against the spiritual hosts of wickedness in the heavenly places.

S. F. Isa. 14:12–15; Job 1:6; Zech. 3:1; Luke 10:18.

S. A. Rev. 12:7–9.

The sin and fall of Satan have affected the heavens, infesting the heavenly realms with fallen beings. He himself seemingly has access to heaven and his emissaries infest the heavenly places where they make warfare with the believer.

II. The Earth.

1. The vegetable kingdom.

Gen. 3:17, 18—And unto Adam he said, Because thou hast hearkened unto the voice of thy wife, and hast eaten of the tree, of which I commanded thee, saying, Thou shalt not eat of it; cursed is the ground for thy sake;

in sorrow shalt thou eat of it all the days of thy life; Thorns also and thistles shall it bring forth to thee; and thou shalt eat the herb of the field;

Isa. 55:13—Instead of the thorn shall come up the fir tree, and instead of the brier shall come up the myrtle tree: and it shall be to the Lord for a name, for an everlasting sign that shall not be cut off.

The vegetable kingdom has been cursed because of man's sin, but will be redeemed from the curse at Christ's return to reign.

2. The animal kingdom.

Gen. 9:1–3—And God blessed Noah and his sons, and said unto them, Be fruitful, and multiply, and replenish the earth. And the fear of you and the dread of you shall be upon every beast of the earth, and upon every fowl of the air, upon all that moveth upon the earth, and upon all the fishes of the sea; into your hand are they delivered. Every moving thing that liveth shall be meat for you; even as the green herb have I given you all things.

Isa. 11:6–9—The wolf also shall dwell with the lamb, and the leopard shall lie down with the kid; and the calf and the young lion and the fatling together; and a little child shall lead them. And the cow and the bear shall feed; their young ones shall lie down together; and the lion shall eat straw like the ox. And the suckling child shall play on the hole of the asp, and the weaned child shall put his hand on the cockatrice' den. They shall not hurt nor destroy in all my holy mountain: for the earth shall be full of the knowledge of the Lord, as the waters cover the sea.

The animal kingdom has suffered in consequence of man's sin, the nature of animals as well as of men being affected, but this realm also will share in the peace and glory of the millennium.

3. The race of mankind.

Ecc. 7:20—For there is not a just man upon earth, that doeth good, and sinneth not.

(1) All have sinned.

Rom. 3:10, 23—As it is written, There is none righteous, no, not one: For all have sinned, and come short of the glory of God.

S. F. Psa. 14:2–3; Isa. 53:6; I John 1:8–10.

(2) All guilty before God.

Rom. 3:19, R. V.—Now we know that what things soever the law saith, it speaketh to them that are under the law; that every mouth may be stopped, and all the world may be brought under the judgment of God:

S. F. Psa. 130:3; Psa. 143:2; Gal. 3:10.

(3) Children of wrath.

Eph. 2:3—Among whom also we all had our conversation in times past in the lusts of our flesh, fulfilling the desires of the flesh and of the mind; and were by nature the children of wrath, even as others.

S. F. John 8:44; I John 3:8–10.

We are "children of wrath" by nature and remain children of wrath as long as we are outside of Christ. The only nature which the unbeliever possesses is that which is in open antagonism to and at enmity with God and which therefore justly merits His abiding wrath.

(4) Estranged from God.

Eph. 4:18—Having the understanding darkened, being alienated from the life
   of God through the ignorance that is in them, because of the blindness
   of their heart:

S. F. I Cor. 2:14.

This means that man has become alienated from God, so that God is no longer the object of his affection.

(5) Corrupt and deceitful in nature.

Jer. 17:9—The heart is deceitful above all things, and desperately wicked: who
   can know it?

S. F. Gen. 6:5, 12; Gen. 8:21; Psa. 94:11; Rom. 1:19–31.

This reveals the abnormal relation which man sustains toward himself and his fellowmen because of sin.

(6) Enslaved by sin and dead in sin.

Rom. 6:17—But God be thanked, that ye were the servants of sin, but ye have
   obeyed from the heart that form of doctrine which was delivered you.

Eph. 2:1—And you hath he quickened, who were dead in trespasses and sins;

S. F. Rom. 7:5; Rom. 7:7–8, 14–15, 19, 23, 24.

Sin has robbed man of his truest life and liberty and makes him an abject slave with the silence of death upon his spiritual faculties and powers.

(7) Antagonistic to God and identified with His adversary.

Rom. 8:7–8—Because the carnal mind is enmity against God: for it is not subject
   to the law of God, neither indeed can be. So then they that are in the
   flesh cannot please God.

Eph. 2:2—Wherein in time past ye walked according to the course of this world,
   according to the prince of the power of the air, the spirit that now
   worketh in the children of disobedience.

(8) Body weakened and death doomed.

II Cor. 4:7—But we have this treasure in earthen vessels, that the excellency
   of the power may be of God, and not of us.

S. F. Rom. 8:11.

The execution of the sentence of physical death began with the inception of human sin and will continue until Christ's redemptive work is completed.

(9) Debased in character and conduct.

Tit. 3:3—For we ourselves also were sometimes foolish, disobedient, deceived,
   serving divers lusts and pleasures, living in malice and envy, hateful,
   and hating one another.

S. F. Eph. 2:3; Col. 3:5, 7.

Through sin, man has become the recipient of a depraved nature, of which depravity of character and conduct is the inevitable expression.

D. S. Sin seems to have permeated the whole universe, including every realm and affecting every race and species among creatures with baneful results.

Study Questions on the Doctrine of Sin

1. Give the four-fold negative definition of sin.
2. Discuss in a general way the Old and New Testament conceptions of sin.
3. Outline in full the definition of sin, positively considered.
4. Quote one passage showing that sin is a fact of revelation.
5. What other witnesses testify to the fact of sin? Give a gist of their testimony.
6. What realms have been affected by sin? Quote one passage with each.
7. What are the resultant effects of sin in the race of man?
8. Give D. S. under the extent of sin.

CHAPTER SEVEN

THE DOCTRINES OF SALVATION

(SOTERIOLOGY)

Salvation is a comprehensive term, including within its scope many aspects. For instance, there is salvation from the past, in the present, and for the future, or from the penalty, the power and the presence of sin. There is salvation of the spirit in regeneration, of the soul in sanctification, and of the body in glorification. Included in these various aspects are the doctrines which together constitute that which theologians call soteriology. We speak of them as the doctrines of salvation.

A. Regeneration.

It is evident that the Scriptures refer to a great change in all who become Christians. This is inseparable from repentance toward God and faith toward our Lord Jesus Christ. This is the reason for Regeneration being presented in such close connection with Repentance and Faith.

"Since God is a Trinity, and the Father and the Son have so prominent a share in man's redemption, it would be only rational to infer that the Holy Spirit would also have some part in this beneficent work. After the atonement was made by the incarnate Logos, and He had ascended to God's right hand, justice was satisfied, the government of God was upheld in righteousness, and therefore all obstructions were removed, so that the grace of God could be poured forth freely upon man for his recovery. Right at that juncture something was necessary before our Redeemer in His glorified theanthropic person could come into vital contact with sinful man. Since man's spirit is the center of his ethical being, and since salvation is preeminently an ethical transaction, it stands to reason that he must be spiritually awakened and enlightened in order to receive and apprehend the things of Christ and accept Him by faith. Right there is the juncture where the work of the Holy Spirit is needed—to create the new life. Thus it will be seen that God, in devising a plan for man's moral and physical recovery, has established vital contact at every successive point. There are no gaps, no cleavages, in the work of redeeming grace from beginning to end. All is vitalized; all organic."—KEYSER.

I. The importance of it.

1. Strategic relation sustained to the family of God.

John 1:12—But as many as received him to them gave he power to become the sons of God, even to them that believe on his name.

Access into the family of God is the same as that by which entrance is obtained into the families of men, namely, by generation or birth. A life and nature must be imparted in the one instance as in the other. In the case of the child of God it is an impartation of eternal life and the divine nature.

2. Strategic relation sustained to the kingdom of God.

John 3:3–5—Jesus answered and said unto him, Verily, verily, I say unto thee, Except a man be born again, he cannot see the kingdom of God. Nicodemus saith unto him, How can a man be born when he is old? Can he enter the second time into his mother's womb and be born? Jesus answered, Verily, verily, I say unto thee, except a man be born of water and of the Spirit, he cannot enter into the kingdom of God.

Regeneration, or the new birth, is the door into the kingdom of God, and apart from it, that door must remain inevitably closed, and God and man remain forever separate.

Christ emphasized the importance of this doctrine by the words he used in this remarkable interview with Nicodemus. Each time he stated the condition, it was with the emphatic expression, "Verily, verily." Jesus thus showed that the new birth was not merely optional but absolutely obligatory.

D. S. Regeneration is most important. It marks the line of cleavage between eternal life and eternal death, between eternal sonship and eternal alienation.

II. *The meaning of it.*

1. Negatively considered.

(1) Not baptism—not identified with it nor resulting from it.

I Cor. 4:15—For though ye have ten thousand instructors in Christ, yet have ye not many fathers: for in Christ Jesus I have begotten you by the Gospel.

Comp. I Cor. 1:14.

S. F. Acts 8:13–14, 18–23; Acts 11:12–14; Acts 10:44–48.

Those who teach baptismal regeneration interpret John 3:5 and Titus 3:5 as furnishing ground for believing that regeneration takes place only in connection with baptism. But whatever interpretation may be put upon these passages, it is certain that they do not support this doctrine. Some interpret them figuratively, in the light of Eph. 5:26, "That he might sanctify . . . it with the washing of water by the Word." If baptism and regeneration were identical, then Paul's language in the passage quoted above is inconsistent and contradictory.

"One important conclusion follows from the Spirit's use of truth in regeneration. It is that regeneration is not effected through the act of baptism. In a number of New Testament passages baptism is clearly associated with conversion, and nearly always with the beginnings of the Christian life (see Acts 2:38; Rom. 6:3, 4; I Peter 3:21). But there is no conclusive evidence that in any of these passages baptism is regarded in the Catholic sense as an act which of itself regenerates without reference to the mind of the recipient. Nor do they sustain the view of others that baptism completes the act of regeneration. The error in both views is in regarding baptism as a means to a given end, when it is only the symbolic outward expression of the end when it has been otherwise accomplished. Baptism symbolizes regeneration but it does not produce it. The true significance of baptism is moral and spiritual. It is the answer of a good conscience toward God. Here truth is clearly distinguished from symbol. And the symbol only has value as a mirror for truth."—MULLINS.

(2) Not reformation—not a natural forward step nor a mere reversal of mental and moral attitude.

John 3:3–6—Jesus answered and said unto him, Verily, verily, I say unto thee, Except a man be born again, he cannot see the kingdom of God. Nicodemus saith unto Him, How can a man be born when he is old? can he enter the second time into his mother's womb, and be born? Jesus answered, Verily, verily, I say unto thee, Except a man be born of water and of the Spirit, he cannot enter into the kingdom of God. That which is born of the flesh is flesh; and that which is born of the Spirit is spirit.

See John 1:13; James 1:18.

Nicodemus was an exponent of the Pharisaic belief and teaching which lay great emphasis upon outward conformity to the law, but Jesus said in substance, "Outward conformity to either ceremonial or moral requirement is insufficient. Regeneration alone can meet the need of man and the requirement of God." The former is of the flesh, the latter of the Spirit; outward conformity is of the will of men, but the new birth is by the will of God.

"The Pharisees were the best people of their day; and yet they were the greatest failures. Against no others did Jesus hurl so fierce denunciations. Why? Because they put reformation in the place of repentance and faith; because they were employing human means for accomplishing what only the Holy Spirit could accomplish. And so, today, every device for the betterment of society which does not strike at the root of the disease and apply the remedy to the seat of life, the human soul, is Pharisaical and is doing a Pharisee's work."—LASHER.

2. Positively considered, it is

(1) A spiritual generation.

II Peter 1:4, R. V.—Whereby He hath granted unto us his precious and exceeding great promises; that through these ye may become partakers of the divine nature, having escaped from the corruption, that is in the world by lust.

S. F. I John 3:9; I John 4:7; John 1:13; James 1:18; I Peter 1:23.

Regeneration is represented as a divine begetting or procreation.

"Birth is always the condition of life, whether in the physical or spiritual realm. There is no life without birth. It is just as true in the spiritual realm as in the physical. Birth is the root idea of regeneration, and hence it is that the word regeneration means an act and not a process, an act of God not of man, an act of God through the Holy Spirit by which the divine nature of the living God is implanted in man.

"Every child has a parent. If I am a child of God, God is my parent. We have links between the son and the father back to Adam. So in regeneration, there is a life communicated—even the very life of God. We are as certainly partakers of the Divine nature by our second birth as we were of the human nature by our first birth."

(2) A spiritual quickening or resurrection.

Eph. 2:1, 5, 6—And you hath he quickened, who were dead in trespasses and
sins; Even when we were dead in sins, hath quickened us together with
Christ (by grace are ye saved). And hath raised us up together, and
made us sit together in heavenly places in Christ Jesus.

S. F. John 5:21; John 5:25.

Resurrection is the restoration to life of that in which life has become
extinct. Through sin man's spirit came into a condition of spiritual death. A
severance between God and himself was effected through disobedience. Death
is disunion. In regeneration man is reunited with God. Regeneration is reunion.
Man is quickened out of his spiritual death and disunion into a spiritual life of
union and communion with God.

(3) A spiritual translation.

Col. 1:13—Who hath delivered us from the power of darkness, and hath translated us into the kingdom of his dear son.

S. F. I John 3:14; John 5:24, R. V.

This designation views regeneration in the resultant change of sphere which
it effects. It is a transfer from one kingdom to another, from the kingdom of
darkness, in which sin and Satan rule, into the kingdom of His dear Son. As
man transfers his allegiance from self and sin and Satan to God, he finds himself
in a new sphere of life and action.

(4) A spiritual creation.

Eph. 2:10—For we are His workmanship, created in Christ Jesus unto good
works, which God hath before ordained that we should walk in them.

S. F. Gal. 6:15; II Cor. 5:17.

S. A. Ezek. 36:26, 27; Eph. 4:24; Col. 3:10. R. V.

In Paul's statement in II Corinthians, we have set forth a new unit, "A new
creature," in a new sphere, "In Christ Jesus," with a new order, "old things are
passed away and behold all things are become new."

"Regeneration is a supernatural act of God. It is not evolution, but involu-
tion—the communication of a new life. It is a revolution—a change of
direction resulting from that life. It is a crisis with a view to a process.
A new governing power comes into the regenerate man's life by which he is
enabled to become holy in experience."—Evans.

D. S. Regeneration is the Holy Spirit's gracious, sovereign quickening act,
in which the divine life and nature is imparted to the soul of man, causing a
reversal of his attitude toward God and sin,—the expression of which, in repentance and faith, is secured through the instrumentality of the Word of God.

III. The necessity of it.

The necessity for regeneration is as extensive as the boundaries of the
human race and as intensive as the depravity and wickedness of the human
heart. The need exists wherever man is found for "he who is accustomed to do
evil, cannot do that which is good." It is shown by:

1. The inability of that which belongs to one Kingdom or order to enter another by itself unaided.

John 3:3–7—Jesus answered and said unto him, Verily, verily, I say unto thee,

Except a man be born again, he cannot see the kingdom of God. Nicodemus saith unto him, How can a man be born when he is old? can he enter the second time into his mother's womb, and be born? Jesus answered, Verily, verily, I say unto thee, Except a man be born of water and of the Spirit, he cannot enter into the kingdom of God. That which is born of the flesh is flesh: and that which is born of the Spirit is spirit. Marvel not that I said unto thee, Ye must be born again.

S. F. Gal. 6:15.

That which is in the mineral kingdom cannot of itself unaided gain entrance into the kingdom just above it, the vegetable kingdom. Vegetable life must reach down into the mineral kingdom and impart itself to that which is in that domain and thus lift it from the one to the other. The same is true of that which is in the vegetable kingdom in relation to the animal kingdom. The same principle also obtains with reference to man in the kingdom of God. Man is now in the kingdom of nature which has become the kingdom of darkness, even Satan's kingdom, and unless he is born from above, he must there forever remain. The life of God in the Holy Spirit must reach down into that kingdom and impart itself to those who are its subjects and thus translate them into the kingdom of God.

2. By man's condition of spiritual death.

Eph. 2:1—And you hath he quickened who were dead in trespasses and sins.

S. F. I Tim. 5:6.

S. A. I Cor. 2:14.

The necessity of man's regeneration grows out of his utter lack of spiritual life—his death in trespasses and sin.

3. By man's lack of a holy spiritual nature and the perversity of his Adamic nature.

Jer. 13:23—Can the Ethiopian change his skin, or the leopard his spots? then may ye also do good, that are accustomed to do evil.

S. F. John 3:6; Rom. 7:18; Rom. 8:7, 8; Jer. 17:9, 10.

"In his natural estate man is darkened in understanding, corrupted in affection, and alienated from God."—TIFFANY.

To live a life pre-supposes a nature from which that life is to proceed. "Men do not gather grapes of thorns or figs of thistles." To live the natural life pre-supposes a natural birth; to live the spiritual life pre-supposes a spiritual birth. Depravity has sundered man from God, so that, in the expressive language of Scripture, he is "alienated from the life of God." How is a reunion to be brought about? As two parties, God and man, are at variance, a subjective change must take place in one or both of the parties before there can be a reconciliation. But God is unchangeable, therefore the change, if it takes place at all, must be effected in man. We therefore see the necessity of regeneration. It is as necessary as the salvation of the soul is desirable, for there can be no salvation without reconciliation to God.

D. S. The necessity of regeneration lies in man's lack of a spiritual life and nature and in his inability to change his sphere of living.

197

IV. The Mode of It.

1. On the divine side—a sovereign act of power.

James 1:18—Of his own will begat he us with the word of truth, that we should be a kind of first-fruits of his creatures.

S. F. John 3:5; John 1:13.

S. A. Titus 3:5.

"Men are born again of God. God sovereignly interposes. Something is infused. In the salvation of every person there is an actual putting forth of divine power whereby the dead sinner is quickened—the unwilling sinner is made willing—the desperately hard sinner has his conscience made tender, and he who rejected God and despised the Gospel offer is brought to cast himself down at the feet of Jesus."—Bishop.

2. On the human side—a two-fold act of dependent faith.

(1) The written word, received and believed.

James 1:18—Of his own will begat he us with the word of truth, that we should be a kind of first-fruits of his creatures.

S. F. I Peter 1:23; Acts 2:41; I Cor. 4:15.

While the Holy Spirit is the immediate agent in regeneration, yet he uses the instrumentality of "the word of truth," the incorruptible seed of the Word of God, "which liveth and abideth forever."

Man was lost by doubting God's word; he is saved by believing it.

(2) The Living Word believed and received.

John 1:1, 12—In the beginning was the Word, and the Word was with God and the Word was God. But as many as received Him to them gave he power to become the sons of God, even to them that believe on His name.

S. F. Gal. 3:26; I John 5:1.

Belief in Christ is essential, both as an accompaniment and an evidence of regeneration. The belief, of course, is to be of the heart and identical with the act of receiving Christ.

D. S. Regeneration, a divine work, is wrought by a divine Agent; but it also has a human aspect with accompanying human requirements.

V. The results of it.

The results of regeneration constitute the fruitage of a renewed life and are expressive of the Christ life made living in men.

1. A radical change in life and experience.

II Cor. 5:17, R. V.—Wherefore if any man is in Christ, he is a new creature; the old things are passed away; behold, they are become new.

Regeneration is not gradual in its occurrence, but immediate, though it may be gradual in some of its manifestations.

2. Sonship with God.

John 1:12—But to as many as received him, to them gave he power to become the sons of God, even to them that believe on his name.

198

S. F. Gal. 3:26.

Regeneration is the doorway through which we enter the family life of our heavenly Father. Alienation is thus exchanged for filial relationship.

3. The indwelling of the Holy Spirit.

I Cor. 3:16—Know ye not that ye are the temple of God, and that the Spirit of God dwelleth in you?

S. F. I Cor. 6:19; Rom. 8:9–11.

The Holy Spirit takes up His abode within us as the Spirit of sonship, teaching us to recognize and realize the privileges which are ours through that same relationship.

4. Liberated from the sphere and slavery of the flesh.

Rom. 8:2, 9—For the law of the Spirit of life in Christ Jesus hath made me free from the law of sin and death. But ye are not in the flesh, but in the Spirit, if so be that the Spirit of God dwell in you. Now if any man have not the Spirit of Christ, he is none of his.

"While the regenerated man is not in the flesh, he still has the flesh (Gal. 5:16, 17). The new nature received in regeneration does not expell, destroy nor eradicate the old nature. The two exist side by side. The old nature is present, but its deeds are to be put to death through the Spirit (Rom. 8:13). The flesh is present but we are not under its dominion. It is said by some that Gal. 5:17 represents a lower experience. In Rom. 8 we get a higher experience when the carnal nature is eradicated. But in Rom. 8:12, 13 we see the flesh still present but triumphed over."

5. A living Faith in Christ.

I John 5:1—Whosoever believeth that Jesus is the Christ is born of God; and every one that loveth him that begat loveth him also that is begotten of him.

A man who rejects the deity of Christ lacks an essential evidence of the new birth.

6. Victory over the world.

I John 5:4—For whatsoever is born of God overcometh the world; and this is the victory that overcometh the world, even our faith.

S. A. I John 2:15–17; Rev. 3:4, 5 compared with I John 5:4, 5.

Faith is the nexus between the soul and God, the connecting link between human weakness and divine power. It thus becomes a channel through which God's omnipotence becomes available in human experience.

7. Cessation of sin as a life practice.

I John 3:4, 9, R. V.—Every one that doeth sin doeth also lawlessness, and sin is lawlessness. Whosoever is begotten of God doeth no sin, because his seed abideth in him; and he cannot sin, because he is begotten of God.

Regeneration is unto repentance, which involves the renunciation of sin.

8. Establishment of righteousness as a life practice.

I John 2:29, R. V.—If ye know that he is righteous, ye know that every one also that doeth righteousness is begotten of him.

Regeneration includes the rectifying of the ruling disposition in the life, and thus involves our being made righteous.

9. Christian love.

I John 3:14, R. V.—We know that we have passed out of death into life, because we love the brethren. He that loveth not abideth in death.

Love is an essential attribute of the divine life, whether within the being of God or man.

D. S. The results of regeneration are both real and revolutionary, effecting life and nature, character and conduct.

B. Repentance.

Repentance is the first aspect of the believer's initial experience of salvation, called conversion. True conversion is an essential part and proof of regeneration. Regeneration is God working in and conversion is man working out his salvation in repentance and faith. Repentance is largely negative and has to do with sin in its many aspects and forms, and especially with the sin of unbelief.

I. The importance, as shown in:

1. The earlier New Testament ministries.

(1) John.

Matt. 3:1–2—In those days came John the Baptist, preaching in the wilderness of Judaea, and saying Repent ye: for the kingdom of heaven is at hand.

(2) Jesus.

Matt. 4:17—From that time Jesus began to preach, and to say, Repent: for the kingdom of heaven is at hand.

(3) The Twelve.

Mark 6:12—And they went out, and preached that men should repent.

2. Christ's commission, after His resurrection.

Luke 24:47—And that repentance and remission of sins should be preached in his name among all nations, beginning at Jerusalem.

3. The later New Testament ministries.

(1) Peter.

Acts 2:38—Then Peter said unto them, Repent, and be baptized every one of you in the name of Jesus Christ for the remission of sins, and ye shall receive the gift of the Holy Spirit.

(2) Paul.

Acts 26:20—But shewed first unto them of Damascus, and at Jerusalem, and throughout all the coast of Judaea, and then to the Gentiles, that they should repent and turn to God, and do works meet for repentance.

S. F. Acts 17:30; Acts 20:21; Rom. 3:25.

4. The expression of God's desire and will for all men.

II Peter 3:9, R. V.—The Lord is not slack concerning his promise, as some count slackness, but is longsuffering to youward, not wishing that any should perish, but that all should come to repentance.

S. F. Acts 17:30.

5. The part it plays in man's salvation.

Luke 13:3—I tell you, Nay: but, except ye repent, ye shall all likewise perish.

S. F. James 5:20.

D. S. The importance of repentance is seen by the place it occupies, and the emphasis given to it, in divine revelation.

II. The meaning of it.

1. As touching the intellect:

Repentance is a change of mind or view concerning one's obligation to the will and word of God.

Matt. 21:29—He answered and said, I will not; but afterward he repented, and went.

S. F. Luke 15:18; Luke 18:13.

The word used for "repent" here means to change one's mind, thought; i.e. views regarding the matter; it is to have another mind about a thing; it is a revolution of thoughts concerning our views and attitude. Peter called upon the Jews to change their minds and their views concerning Christ, and to express that change in baptism (Acts 2:36–40).

"The word of which 'Repentance' is a translation, in the New Testament, has as its primary meaning 'after-thought,' and as its secondary meaning 'a change of mind.' It is easy to see how the secondary followed the primary signification, for in all ages after-thought has discovered reasons for a change of mind."—PENDLETON.

2. As touching the emotions:

Repentance involves two essential elements:

(1) Hatred of sin.

Psa. 97:10—Ye that love the Lord, hate evil, he preserveth the souls of his saints; he delivereth them out of the hand of the wicked.

"This is one of the essential elements involved in Repentance. It is inseparable from the change of mind already referred to, for this change of mind is in view of sin, because sin is seen to be a great evil. Regarded in this light, it becomes an object of abhorrence. At this point, Repentance and Regeneration coincide; hatred of sin is among the primary impulses of Regeneration: and it cannot be abstracted from Repentance without changing its character. The repenting sinner hates the sin and the sins of which he repents; the sin which is depravity or corruption of nature, and the sins which are actual transgressions prompted by a sinful nature. Sin is not really hated unless it is hated in all its forms—hated in its inward workings and in its outward manifestations. Sin is the abominable thing which God

201

hates, and it becomes the object of the repenting sinner's hatred."—PENDLETON.

(2) Sorrow for sin.

II Cor. 7:9—Now I rejoice, not that ye were made sorry, but that ye sorrowed to repentance: for ye were made sorry after a godly manner, that ye might receive damage by us in nothing.

S. F. Psa. 38:18.

"This accompanies hatred of sin. He, who repents, hates the sins he is sorry for, and is sorry for the sins he hates. The hatred and the sorrow are reciprocal. Indeed, each may be regarded as either the cause or the effect of the other, so close is their relation (Matt. 11:20, 21).

"Remorse is sorrow for the consequences of sin, but Repentance condemns the sin which brought the consequences. Tears are in the eyes of repentance, confession is on its lips, God's mind about sin is in its thoughts, walking from sin is its way, brokenness is in its heart, taking hold of Christ are its hands, and humbleness of manner is its attitude."

3. As touching the will:

Repentance involves the formation of a new purpose with reference to sin and God's will.

Luke 15:18-20—I will arise and go to my father, and will say unto him, Father, I have sinned against heaven, and before thee, and am no more worthy to be called thy son: make me as one of thy hired servants. And he arose, and came to his father. But when he was yet a great way off, his father saw him, and had compassion, and ran, and fell on his neck, and kissed him.

S. F. Matt. 21:29; I Thes. 1:9.

"Repentance is not only a heart broken for sin, but from sin." Man's volition, like his emotions, is closely associated with and related to his intellect, and the voluntary exercise of the one involves the exercise of the other. This is true in repentance. A real change of mind toward God and sin also necessitates a real purpose respecting them.

D. S. Repentance may be defined as a change of mind toward sin and God's will, leading to a change of feeling concerning them, and a change of purpose in relation to them.

III. *The manifestation of it.*

Repentance is an inward action of the soul, but it has its outward expression or manifestation. It is made manifest:

1. In the confession of sin.

(1) To God.

Psa. 32:3-5—When I kept silence, my bones waxed old through my roaring all the day long. For day and night thy hand was heavy upon me: my moisture is turned into the drought of summer. I acknowledged my sin unto thee, and mine iniquity have I not hid. I said, I will confess my transgressions unto the Lord; and thou forgavest the iniquity of my sin.

S. F. Psa. 38:18.

S. A. Luke 18:13; Luke 15:21.

"All sin is committed against God, against His nature, His will, His authority, His law, His justice, His goodness; and the evil of sin arises chiefly from the fact that it is opposed to God, and out of harmony with his character. The evil of sin as committed against God is the thing which gives the true penitent special anxiety and trouble. He justifies God and condemns himself."
—PENDLETON.

(2) To man.

There must also be confession to man in so far as man has been wronged in and by our sin.

James 5:16—Confess your faults one to another, and pray one for another, that ye may be healed. The effectual fervent prayer of a righteous man availeth much.

S. F. Matt. 5:23, 24; Luke 19:8, 9.

The confession to man should be as public as the wrong which was done him. If it were an open public wrong which besmirched his reputation, and robbed him of his standing with men, the confession should also be open and public. If it is possible to rectify the wrong which has been done, no means should be left unused to accomplish it. Restitution must follow repentance.

2. In the forsaking of sin.

Prov. 28:13—He that covereth his sins shall not prosper: but whoso confesseth and forsaketh them shall have mercy.

S. F. Isa. 55:7; Matt. 3:8, 10; I Thes. 1:9; Acts 26:18.

When repentance is genuine, men turn from darkness to light, and from the power of Satan unto God; they forsake that which God forgives, and renounce that which He remits.

D. S. Confession of sin and wrong, together with reparation for the same, when possible, is the outward expression of the inward act of repentance.

IV. The mode of it.

1. On the divine side—bestowed by God.

Acts 11:18—When they heard these things, they held their peace, and glorified God, saying, Then hath God also to the Gentiles granted repentance unto life.

S. F. II Tim. 2:24, 25 R. V.; Acts 5:30, 31; Acts 3:26.

Repentance is not something which one can originate within himself, or can produce by himself. It is a divine gift, the result of God's gracious work in the soul of man, by which he is inclined to this change; God grants him repentance.

2. On the human side—accomplished through means.

(1) Through the ministry of the Word.

Acts 2:37, 38, 41—Now when they heard this, they were pricked in their hearts, and said unto Peter and to the rest of the apostles, Men and brethren, what shall we do? Then Peter said unto them, Repent and be baptized every one of you in the name of Jesus Christ for the remission of sins, and ye shall receive the gift of the Holy Ghost. Then they that gladly received his word were baptized: and the same day there were added unto them about three thousand souls.

S. F. II Tim. 2:24, 25, R. V.; Acts 26:19, 20.

S. A. Gal. 6:1; I Thes. 1:5, 6, 9, 10.

"The very gospel which calls for repentance produces it. How well this is illustrated in the experience of the people of Nineveh (Jonah 3:5–10). When they heard the preaching of the Word of God by Jonah they believed the message and turned from their wickedness. Not any message, but the gospel is the instrument that God uses to bring about this desired end. Furthermore, the message must be preached in the power of the Holy Spirit (I Thes. 1:5, 9)."

(2) Through the goodness of God.

Rom. 2:4—Or despisest thou the riches of his goodness and forbearance and longsuffering; not knowing that the goodness of God leadeth thee to repentance?

S. A. Luke 6:35; Eph. 4:32; I Peter 2:3.

The purpose of all God's goodness in His dealings with men is to dissuade them from a course of sin and to lead them into righteousness of life.

(3) Through reproof and chastisement.

Rev. 3:19—As many as I love, I rebuke and chasten: be zealous therefore, and repent.

S. A. Heb. 12:6, 10, 11.

The purpose of all God's severity in His dealings with men is to produce in them the peaceable fruits of righteousness through true repentance.

(4) Through godly sorrow.

II Cor. 7:8–11—For though I made you sorry with a letter, I do not repent, though I did repent: for I perceive that the same epistle hath made you sorry though it were for but a season. Now I rejoice, not that ye were made sorry, but that ye sorrowed to repentance for ye were made sorry after a godly manner, that ye might receive damage by us in nothing. For godly sorrow worketh repentance to salvation not to be repented of: but the sorrow of the world worketh death. For behold this self-same thing, that ye sorrowed after a godly sort, what carefulness it wrought in you, yea, what clearing of yourselves, yea, what indignation, yea, what fear, yea, what vehement desire, yea, what zeal, yea, what revenge? In all things ye have approved yourselves to be clear in this matter.

God has benevolent motives in all sorrow which He permits to come into the lives of His children and others and that motive is to bring them to repentance.

(5) Through the realization of God's holiness.

Job 42:5, 6—I have heard of thee, by the hearing of the ear: but now mine eye seeth thee. Wherefore I abhor myself, and repent in dust and ashes.

An experimental sense of God's holiness is productive of a personal sense of sin, which is an essential element of repentance.

D. S. Repentance is God's gift bestowed through various instrumentalities.

V. *The results of it.*

Since repentance and faith are inseparable, their results are difficult of separate identification. Certain results, however, are attributed to repentance in the Scriptures.

1. Joy in heaven.

Luke 15:7, 10—I say unto you, that likewise joy shall be in heaven over one sinner that repenteth, more than ninety and nine just persons, which need no repentance. Likewise I say unto you, there is joy in the presence of the angels of God over one sinner that repenteth.

S. A. II Peter 3:9.

There is joy in the presence of the angels of God, as well as in the heart of God Himself, over the repentance of sinners.

2. Pardon and forgiveness.

Isa. 55:7—Let the wicked forsake his way, and the unrighteous man his thoughts: and let him return unto the Lord, and He will have mercy upon him; and to our God, for He will abundantly pardon.

S. F. Luke 24:47; Mark 1:4; Acts 2:38;.Acts 3:19.

Repentance qualifies one for the reception of forgiveness and pardon, though it does not entitle him to it. Only the blood of Christ can do this.

3. Reception of the Holy Spirit.

Acts. 2:38—Then Peter said unto them, Repent and be baptized every one of you in the name of Jesus Christ for the remission of sins, and ye shall receive the gift of the Holy Ghost.

S. F. Eph. 1:13.

Repentance is an essential part of the subjective requirement for the bestowal of the Holy Spirit. It is this which puts the soul in a receptive attitude.

D. S. The repentant sinner makes heaven glad, receives forgiveness and the seal of the Holy Spirit.

C. Faith.

Faith is the positive aspect of true conversion, the human side of regeneration. In repentance, the sinner turns away from sin, while in faith he turns to Christ. These are inseparable, the one from the other. True repentance cannot exist apart from faith, nor faith, from repentance. It has been said that repentance is faith in action, and faith is repentance at rest.

"There is the rationalistic view of faith, making it merely the ascent to truth demonstratively proved; there is the Romanist view of faith, which makes it a sort of good work of a mystical and spiritual kind. But when we turn to Scripture all such subtleties and errors vanish like mist before the sun."—ANDERSON.

Beside the initial act of saving faith, there are also other aspects of the subject which are deserving of attention.

I. *The importance of it.*

1. Essential to a right relationship with God.

Heb. 11:6—But without faith it is impossible to please him: for he that cometh to God must believe that he is and that he is a rewarder of them that diligently seek him.

S. F. John 3:36; John 3:16–18.

This relationship was lost through unbelief and through faith only can it be regained. Someone has said, "Without faith it is impossible to please God or to be pleased with God."

2. Essential to a normal Christian life.

Rom. 1:17—For therein is the righteousness of God revealed from faith to faith: as it is written, The just shall live by faith.

The Christian life is essentially a faith life. Therefore, with this principle absent or inoperative, the life can neither be truly Christian nor normal.

3. Essential as a foundation in the temple of character and as the medium to a fruitful life.

II Peter 1:5–7—And besides this, giving all diligence, add to your faith virtue, and to virtue, knowledge; And to knowledge, temperance; and to temperance, patience; and to patience, godliness; And to godliness, brotherly kindness; and to brotherly kindness, charity.

Faith is the foundational quality and mediating element which makes possible the embodiment of all other Christian graces.

4. Essential as the primal of the three cardinal graces.

I Cor. 13:13—And now abideth faith, hope, charity, these three; but the greatest of these is charity.

Though love is the greatest of the triad of Christian graces, faith is the first and makes possible the others.

5. Essential as the paramount requirement in Christ's dealings with man; as shown in the case of:

(1) The Syro-Phoenician Woman.

Matt. 15:21–28, see vs. 28—Then Jesus answered and said unto her, O woman, great is thy faith; be it unto thee even as thou wilt. And her daughter was made whole from that very hour.

This woman had perseverance but Jesus commended her faith.

(2) The Centurion.

Matt. 8:5–10, see vs. 10—When Jesus heard it, he marveled, and said to them that followed, Verily I say unto you, I have not found so great faith, no, not in Israel.

This man possessed a high degree of humility, but Jesus marveled at his faith.

(3) Bartimaeus.

Mark 10:46–52, see vs. 52—And Jesus said unto him, Go thy way; thy faith hath made thee whole. And immediately he received his sight, and followed Jesus in the way.

The blind man was fired with the white heat of an unquenchable earnestness, but Jesus healed him on the basis of his faith.

(4) The Palsied Man.

Mark 2:1-5, see vs. 5—When Jesus saw their faith, he said unto the sick of the palsy, Son, thy sins be forgiven thee.

The four who bore the palsied man showed great ingenuity and courage, but Jesus saw their faith.

6. Essential to save man from doom and secure his highest destiny.

John 3:36—He that believeth on the Son hath everlasting life; and he that believeth not the Son shall not see life, but the wrath of God abideth on him.

S. F. Rev. 21:8; John 16:8, 9.

God's salvation from an ignominious doom to a noble destiny can only be appropriated and experienced through faith.

D. S. In faith all the other graces find their source, and by it only can the individual secure the Divine approval.

II. The meaning of it.

1. Natural faith—possessed by all.

Natural faith is that confidence or belief possessed by all men in varying degrees, which rests upon material testimony and apparently trustworthy evidence. It is insufficient, however, to meet the moral and spiritual needs of man or the requirements of God.

2. Spiritual faith—possessed only by believers.

Spiritual faith is that belief or confidence possessed by regenerate believers in varying degrees which rests upon the knowledge of God and His will as obtained through revelation and personal experience.

(1) In relation to salvation.

This is faith in its initial aspect and is synonymous with belief, as contrasted with other aspects which are to be identified with trust.

a. Believing the gospel of Christ.

Rom. 1:16—For I am not ashamed of the gospel of Christ: for it is the power of God unto salvation to every one that believeth; to the Jew first, and also to the Greek.

S. F. I John 5:10-11.

" 'Faith cometh by hearing and hearing by the word of God.' 'Faith cometh by hearing,' whether it be the faith of the gospel, or of the news of some temporal calamity or good. There are no two ways of believing anything. And hearing comes—the true hearing—by the Word of God: not by reasoning founded on it.

"In its first and simplest phase in Scripture, faith is the belief of a record or testimony. He who truly hears the good news of Christ believes it just

207

as a little child believes a mother's words. And none but such shall ever enter the Kingdom."—ANDERSON.

b. Receiving the Christ of the gospel.

John 1:12—But as many as received him, to them gave he power to become the sons of God, even to them that believe on his name.

"At every pier along the new embankment of the Thames, there hangs a chain that reaches to the water's edge at its lowest ebb. But for this, some poor creature, struggling with death, might drown with his very hand upon the pier. An appeal to perishing sinners to trust in Christ is like calling on a drowning wretch to climb the embankment wall. The glad tidings, the testimony of God concerning Christ, is the chain let down for the hand of faith to grasp. Once rescued, it is not the chain, the river waif would trust for safety, but the rock immovable beneath his feet; yet, but for the chain, the rock might have only mocked his struggles. And it is not the gospel message the ransomed sinner trusts in, but the living Christ of whom the Gospel speaks; but yet it was the message that his faith at first laid hold upon, and by it he gained an eternal standing-ground upon the Rock of Ages."—ANDERSON.

(2) In relation to God.

"Trust springs from confidence in the person trusted; and that again depends on knowledge of the person confided in. In this sense faith may be great or little, weak or strong. Trust in God has as many degrees as there are saints on earth. Some believers could not trust Him for a single meal; others can look to Him, without misgivings, to feed a thousand hungry mouths, or to convert a thousand Godless sinners. Our faith, in this sense, depends entirely on our knowing God, and on communion with Him."— ANDERSON.

Trust thus has in it the element of hope. (Rom. 8:24.)

a. To believe God or trust His Word.

John 5:24, R. V.—Verily, verily, I say unto you, He that heareth my word, and believeth him that sent me, hath eternal life, and cometh not into judgment, but hath passed out of death into life.

S. F. I John 5:10, R. V.; Acts 27:22–25; Rom. 4:3.

S. A. Gen. 15:4–6; Rom. 4:19–21, R. V.

To believe God is to rely upon, or have unhesitating assurance of, the truth of God's testimony, even though it is unsupported by any other evidence; and to rely upon or have unfaltering assurance of the fulfillment of His promises, even though everything seen seems against fulfillment. It is taking God at His word. "Faith is not belief without evidence. It is belief on the very best of evidence, the Word of Him who cannot lie (Tit. 1:2). Faith is so rational that it asks no other evidence than this all-sufficient evidence. To ask other evidence than the Word of 'Him who cannot lie' is not rationalism, but consummate irrationalism."

b. To believe in God or trust Him.

II Chron. 20:20—And they rose early in the morning, and went forth into the wilderness of Tekoa: and as they went forth, Jehoshaphat stood and said, Hear me, O Judah, and ye inhabitants of Jerusalem; Believe in the Lord your God, so shall ye be established; believe his prophets, so shall ye prosper.

S. F. Psa. 37:3-5; John 14:1, R. V.

To believe in God is to rely upon, or put confidence in, God Himself. When we believe God we fix our eyes upon what He has said (Rom. 4:20); when we believe in God we fix our eyes upon what He is, upon His Person, upon Himself. There are two Hebrew words for "trust" and "faith," the first translated "believe" and "trust" means primarily "to prop," "to stay," "to support" and "to stay oneself." The second word, translated "trust," seems to mean "to cast oneself upon." When we believe God we stay ourselves upon His Word; when we believe in God we stay ourselves upon Himself.

(3) In relation to prayer.

Faith, in this relationship, is the acceptance of God's provision through the fulfillment of His promises, as expressed in both act and attitude.

"We must understand the promises on which we base our prayer; we must believe that they are worth their full face value and then claim their fulfillment by a volitional act of faith, thereby giving substance to that which, at the moment, may be unseen, and perchance non-existent, so far as our knowledge and vision are concerned, but which to faith is a splendid reality."—EVANS.

a. Assurance of God's power to fulfill His Word.

Jer. 32:17—Ah Lord God! behold, thou hast made the heaven and the earth by thy great power and stretched out arm, and there is nothing too hard for thee:

b. Assurance of God's will as revealed in his Word.

John 15:7—If ye abide in me, and my words abide in you, ye shall ask what ye will, and it shall be done unto you.

c. Assurance of God's answer as promised in His Word.

I John 5:14, 15—And this is the confidence that we have in him, that, if we ask anything according to his will, he heareth us: and if we know that he hear us, whatsoever we ask, we know that we have the petitions that we desired of him.

S. F. Mark 11:24.

S. A. Heb. 11:1.

Faith is thus seen to be "the assurance of things hoped for, the conviction of things not seen."

(4) In relation to works.

Faith is the root and tree of which works are the fruit. We are not saved by faith and works, but by a faith that works. We are saved by faith alone, but by a faith that does not remain alone.

a. Faith the cause; works the effect.

James 2:20-22, 26—But wilt thou know, O vain man, that faith without works is dead? Was not Abraham our father justified by works, when he had offered Isaac his son upon the altar? Seest thou how faith wrought with his works, and by works was faith made perfect? For as the body without the spirit is dead, so faith without works is dead also.

S. A. Rom. 4:1-12; Rom. 11:6.

209

b. Faith the claim; works the evidence.

James 2:14, 18—What doth it profit, my brethren, though a man say he hath faith, and have not works? can that faith save him? Yea, a man may say, Thou hast faith, and I have works: shew me thy faith without thy works, and I will shew thee my faith by my works.

S. A. Eph. 2:8, 9.

"Faith and works are both of divine appointment, they are both needful to the true believer. Without faith one is not a believer, and apart from works one cannot evidence his faith to others.

"They are both found in the life of the true believer. Faith is the means and condition of his salvation, while works are the fruit and evidence of it.

"Each of them has its own place, purpose, and use. Faith is the means of salvation, its tap root. Works are the product and fruit of faith and salvation. Faith begins, promotes, controls, and culminates spiritual life, while works evidence, beautify and crown it."—HOTTEL.

(5) In relation to its possessor.

Faith, in relation to the one who possesses it, must be consistent, that is, it must be the expression of his inner life. When properly analyzed, it is comprised of three elements.

a. Intellectual—involving the assent of the mind.

Rom. 10:14–17—How then shall they call on him in whom they have not believed? and how shall they believe in him of whom they have not heard? and how shall they hear without a preacher? And how shall they preach, except they be sent? as it is written, How beautiful are the feet of them that preach the gospel of peace, and bring glad tidings of good things! But they have not all obeyed the gospel. For Esaias saith, Lord, who hath believed our report? So then faith cometh by hearing, and hearing by the word of God.

S. F. Acts 11:13, 14; John 20:31; Rom. 1:16; I Cor. 15:1–4; John 3:31–34; Psa. 9:10; Acts 10:43.

The gospel is not so much a promise or a covenant as it is a message, a proclamation. It is the "good news" of God, concerning His Son, Jesus Christ our Lord. And true faith is the belief of that "good news." See John 2:23, 24.

"It needs to be emphasized that there is neither merit nor virtue in faith, nor even in the letter of the truth believed; but that to believe God is eternal life. To believe God, whether it be as with Abraham, the promise of a family (Gen. 15:5, 6), or, as with us, the testimony to a person and a fact. Faith is the opened lattice that lets in the light of heaven to the soul, bringing gladness and blessing with it."—EVANS.

b. Emotional—involving the response of the heart.

Rom. 10:9, 10—If thou shalt confess with thy mouth the Lord Jesus, and shalt believe with thine heart that God hath raised him from the dead, thou shalt be saved. For with the heart man believeth unto righteousness; and with the mouth confession is made unto salvation.

S. F. Matt. 13:20; Acts 8:5–8.

An intellectual assent to Christ as Saviour, or even as the Saviour, is insufficient. There must be a heart response to Him as my Saviour which springs from the sense of realized need and deep seated desire. The emotional element is a real essential.

c. Volitional—involving the consent of the will.

John 1:12—But as many as received him, to them gave he power to become the sons of God, even to them that believe on his name.

Faith not only receives the word of Christ, it reaches out and lays hold upon the person of Christ.

"There is a volitional element in faith. There must be a will to believe. Hence faith involves not mere passive acquiescence in the truth, but an active response to the demands of truth. Faith is stepping out on the promises of God."—DAVIS.

It is putting the intellectual belief and the emotional desire into action along the line indicated by both.

No one or two of these elements are sufficient. All are necessary to the possession and the expression of a genuine faith.

D. S. Faith in its various relationships has numerous degrees extending from an initial belief to a reliant trust. It involves the intellect, sensibilities and will, and finds expression in works which harmonize with the truth believed.

III. The manner of it.

The Scriptures represent faith as a bestowal of God's grace and also emphasize human responsibility in connection therewith, giving to it both divine and human aspects.

1. The Divine side—originates with the Triune God.

(1) God the Father—originating source.

Rom. 12:3—For I say, through the grace given unto me, to every man that is among you, not to think of himself more highly than he ought to think; but to think soberly, according as God hath dealt to every man the measure of faith.

S. F. I Cor. 2:4, 5; Phil. 1:29.

(2) God the Son—mediating source.

Heb. 12:2—Looking unto Jesus the author and finisher of our faith; who for the joy that was set before him endured the cross, despising the shame, and is set down at the right hand of the throne of God.

S. F. Luke 17:5.

S. A. Matt. 14:28–31.

(3) God the Holy Spirit—energizing source.

I Cor. 12:4, 8, 9—Now there are diversities of gifts, but the same Spirit. For to one is given by the Spirit the word of wisdom; to another the word of knowledge by the same Spirit; To another faith by the same Spirit; to another the gifts of healing by the same Spirit.

S. F. Gal. 5:22, 23.

211

Faith is obtained as the result of the enabling power and gracious work of God the Father, Son, and Holy Spirit.

2. Human side—secured by the use of means.

(1) The Word of God heard and heeded.

Rom. 10:17—So then faith cometh by hearing, and hearing by the word of God.

S. F. Acts 4:4.

S. A. Gal. 3:2–5; Rom. 4:19, 20.

(2) Yielded will.

John 5:36–40—But I have greater witness than that of John: for the works which the Father hath given me to finish, the same works that I do, bear witness of me that the Father hath sent me. And the Father himself, which hath sent me, hath borne witness of me. Ye have neither heard his voice at any time, nor seen his shape. And ye have not his word abiding in you: for whom he hath sent, him ye believe not. Search the Scriptures; for in them ye think ye have eternal life: and they are they that testify of me. And ye will not come to me, that ye might have life.

S. A. John 5:6–9.

(3) A right motive.

John 5:44—How can ye believe, which receive honour one of another; and seek not the honour that cometh from God only?

S. F. Acts 8:13; Acts 8:18–24.

S. A. John 2:23–25.

(4) Prayer.

Luke 17:5—And the apostles said unto the Lord, Increase our faith.

S. F. Matt. 17:20, 21; Mark 9:23, 24.

These human elements enter into the production of faith and for them men are responsible.

D. S. Faith, though divine in origin, is secured through the use of means.

IV. *The results of it.*

The results of faith are many and far reaching. Faith is the principle of the new life possessed by the justified one, and therefore, of necessity, every desirable result is vitally related to, and dependent upon Faith.

1. Salvation (initial).

Eph. 2:8–10—For by grace are ye saved through faith; and that not of yourselves: it is the gift of God: not of works, lest any man should boast. For we are his workmanship, created in Christ Jesus unto good works, which God hath before ordained that we should walk in them.

Salvation, in its broadest meaning, is a most comprehensive term, and may be used to include all aspects of the believer's life, from justification to glorification. Here we use it as covering only the primary aspects of that life.

(1) Forgiveness.

Acts 10:43—To him give all the prophets witness, that through his name whosoever believeth in him shall receive remission of sins.

(2) Justification.

Rom. 5:1—Therefore being justified by faith, we have peace with God through our Lord Jesus Christ.

(3) Sonship with God.

Gal. 3:26—For ye are all the children of God by faith in Christ Jesus.

S. F. John 1:12.

(4) Eternal life.

John 20:31—But these are written, that ye might believe that Jesus is the Christ, the Son of God; and that believing ye might have life through his name.

S. F. I John 5:11.

(5) Partaking of the divine nature.

II Peter 1:4—Whereby are given unto us exceeding great and precious promises; that by these ye might be partakers of the divine nature, having escaped the corruption that is in the world through lust.

(6) Indwelling of Christ.

Eph. 3:17, R. V.—That Christ may dwell in your hearts through faith; to the end that ye, being rooted and grounded in love.

2. A normal Christian experience. (Faith, the principle of the new life.)

Hab. 2:4—Behold, his soul which is lifted up is not upright in him: but the just shall live by his faith.

God has blessed us with all spiritual blessings in the heavenly places in Christ Jesus, but faith is the medium through which they enter the experience of the Christian and find expression through his life.

(1) Sanctification.

Acts 26:18—To open their eyes, and to turn them from darkness to light, and from the power of Satan to God, that they may receive forgiveness of sins, and inheritance among them which are sanctified by faith that is in me.

S. A. Acts 15:9.

(2) Keeping power of God.

I Peter 1:5—Who are kept by the power of God through faith unto salvation ready to be revealed in the last time.

(3) Victorious life.

I John 5:4–5—For whatsoever is born of God overcometh the world, and this is the victory that overcometh the world, even our faith. Who is he that overcometh the world, but he that believeth that Jesus is the Son of God?

S. F. Rev. 3:4, 5.

(4) Rest and peace.

Matt. 11:28—Come unto me, all ye that labour and are heavy laden, and I will give you rest.

S. F. Isa. 26:3; Phil. 4:6, 7; John 14:1, R. V.

213

(5) Joy and satisfaction.

I Peter 1:8—Whom having not seen, ye love; in whom, though now ye see him not, yet believing ye rejoice with joy unspeakable and full of glory.

(6) Made channel of blessing.

John 7:38–39—He that believeth on me, as the Scripture hath said, out of his belly shall flow rivers of living water. (But this spake he of the Spirit, which they that believe on him should receive: for the Holy Ghost was not yet given; because that Jesus was not yet glorified.)

S. F. Acts 2:33.

3. Holy achievements.

Heb. 11:1, 2, R. V.—Now faith is assurance of things hoped for, a conviction of things not seen. For therein the elders had witness borne to them.

Faith releases the omnipotence of God and makes it available for the doing of His will and work.

(1) Physical healing.

Matt. 9:22, 29—But Jesus turned him about, and when he saw her, he said, Daughter, be of good comfort; thy faith hath made thee whole. And the woman was made whole from that hour. Then touched he their eyes, saying, According to your faith be it unto you.

S. F. James 5:14, 15.

(2) Answer to prayer according to God's will.

Matt. 21:22—And all things, whatsoever ye shall ask in prayer, believing, ye shall receive.

S. F. James 1:5–7; Mark 11:24; I John 5:14, 15.

S. A. Heb. 6:12; Luke 1:45.

(3) Wonder working power.

Matt. 21:21—Jesus answered and said unto them, Verily I say unto you, If ye have faith, and doubt not, ye shall not only do this which is done to the fig tree, but also if ye shall say unto this mountain, Be thou removed, and be thou cast into the sea; it shall be done.

S. F. John 14:12; Heb. 11:32–34; Matt. 17:19, 20; John 11:40.

(4) All things made possible.

Mark 9:23—Jesus said unto him, If thou canst believe, all things are possible to him that believeth.

S. A. Matt. 19:26; Phil. 4:13.

D. S. By faith we lay hold of God's almightiness. Faith can do anything that God can do.

D. Justification.

When Job propounded the question, "How should a man be just with God?" (Job 9:2), he presented he problem of cen uries the problem that has puzzled the mind of man ever s nce he bec m a sinn r The sense of sin and he sense of God are universally innate in the nature of m n, and flow out into the streams of his consciousness through the medium of experience, i. e., by means

214

of observation and reflection. As a result of this a sense of need becomes his. Man naturally possesses the abstract sense of rightness and wrongness which we call conscience. He also finds himself naturally aligned with the wrongness and against the rightness, for which he has an accompanying sense of self-condemnation and of guilt in relation to God. It is from this experience that there arises this felt need of being put upon just and righteous terms with God.

"'Justification by Faith' is a phrase weighty alike with Scripture and history. In the New Testament it is the main theme of the two great dogmatic and doctrinal epistles, Romans and Galatians. It was the war-cry of the reformers in the great spiritual upheaval of the sixteenth century. Though this single truth does not exhaust the epistles referred to, by any means, yet in a broad sense it may fairly be said to constitute the message of St. Paul, as well as the truth of the great Reformation of the Western Church.

"Luther, led by his profound experience, maintained that Justification by Faith was the article of a standing or falling church, and Dr. Edward Harold Browne has added that it also is the article of a standing or falling soul."—MOULE.

I. The meaning of it.

1. Negatively considered.

(1) Not the making righteous of, nor the imparting of righteousness to its recipients.

"To Thomas Aquinas and Peter Lombard, among other middle age school men, justification was used to mean about the same thing as regeneration; and in the decree of the Council of Trent, justification is taken as equivalent to sanctification, it being there described as 'not the mere remission of sins, but also the sanctification and renovation of the inner man.' "—MOULE.

(2) Not a change in the moral state or character of its subjects.

Justification does not deal with our subjective, but rather with our objective, salvation. It has to do with our standing before God judicially rather than our state of life morally and spiritually.

2. Positively considered.

(1) Theoretical definition.

By justification we mean that act of God by which, on account of Christ, to Whom the sinner is united by faith, He declares that sinner to be no longer under condemnation, but to have a standing of righteousness before Him.

"By derivation the word 'Justification' means to make just, to make conformable to a true standard. Thus it would seem to mean a process by which wrong is corrected, bad made good, good made better, and some person or thing actually improved and thus justified. With lawyers no improvement of condition is thought of, but the establishment of a position before judge or jury, literal or figurative. They mean the winning of a favorable verdict, or the statement of the verdict, the sentence of acquittal or vindicated right as the case may be.

"In common everyday use, we speak of justification; to justify an opinion, to justify a course of conduct, to justify a statement, to justify a friend. What do we mean? Not to readjust or improve your thoughts or your words, not to educate your friend to be more wise or more able, no, but to win a verdict for thought or word or action or friend at the bar of judgment, whether the bar of judgment be public opinion, common conscience, society or what not."

(2) Scriptural definition.

The words translated "justify" and "justification" signify, not "To make righteous," but to "declare righteous," "just," or "free from guilt and exposure to punishment."

Ex. 23:7—Keep thee far from a false matter; and the innocent and righteous slay thou not; for I will not justify the wicked.

S. F. Deut. 25:1; Job 27:5; Psa. 143:2; Prov. 17:15; Isa. 5:23; Isa. 50:8; Isa. 53:11.

"The word 'justify' is used in this ordinary sense in Deut. 25:1. Here it is plain that the judges are not to devote themselves to moral improvement of the plaintiffs and to make the righteous man better, but only to vindicate his position as satisfactory to the law of Israel. They are to declare him righteous if he is legally so.

"But the application of the term changed when salvation was in question. The verdict in question became no longer a matter of Hebrew law or public opinion but of the Eternal Judge of all the earth. The word justification both in religious terminology and in common parlance is a word connected with law. It has to do with the acquittal, vindication, and acceptance before a judgment seat. It is a forensic and technical term and has to do with the standing of sinful men before a holy God."

D. S. Justification is the judicial act of God, whereby those who put faith in Christ are declared righteous in His eyes and are free from guilt and punishment.

II. The scope of it.

Justification begins with the believer's present, and extends in two directions, the past, and the future. It deals with the sin and the guilt of both, judicially, and establishes him as eternally righteous before God.

1. The remission of sins, including the removal of their guilt and penalty.

Acts 13:38, 39—Be it known unto you therefore, men and brethren, that through this man is preached unto you the forgiveness of sins. And by him all that believe are justified from all things, from which ye could not be justified by the law of Moses.

S. F. Rom. 8:1, R. V.; Rom. 8:33, 34; Num. 23:21; Mic. 7:18, 19.

In justification there is a complete vindication of the believer from all non-conformity to and transgression of the law of God.

2. The reckoning of Christ's righteousness and the restoration of God's favor.

II Cor. 5:21—For He hath made him to be sin for us, who knew no sin; that we might be made the righteousness of God in him.

S. F. Phil. 3:9, R. V.; II Chron. 20:7; James 2:23.

S. A. Rom. 3:21, 22.

"There is an arrangement in England whereby the King can of his royal clemency pardon a criminal, but he cannot reinstate the man in the position

216

of one who has never broken the law. To the end of his days the man will be a pardoned criminal. But the King of Kings not only can forgive, but can clear the offender and reinstate him by regarding him as 'right' in the eyes of the law."—THOMAS.

"From the moment of conversion to the end of earthly life, justification is absolutely the same. The believer may need to be forgiven as a child of the Father, but he can never again be as a criminal before the Judge. Justification is the act of a judge, forgiveness is the act of a parent.

"Justification covers the past, present, and future. The sin question between the soul and God is forever settled. He may be a disobedient child, and therefore need the father's chastening rod, but he can never be an alien sinner facing the condemnation of the judge."—DEAN.

D. S. In Christ Jesus all that believe are justified from all things; they are made righteous in him.

III. *The Method of it.*

The method is divine, not human. Man justifies the innocent only; God justifies the guilty; man justifies on the ground of merit; God justifies on the ground of mercy.

1. Negatively considered.

(1) Not by moral character.

I Cor. 4:4, R. V.—For I know nothing against myself; yet am I not hereby justified; but he that judgeth me is the Lord.

S. F. Luke 16:15.

In order for man to be justified on this ground, his moral character would have to be perfect, and this is true of no one. "There is no man that liveth and sinneth not." "There is no salvation by character. What men need is salvation from character."

(2) Not by works of the law.

Rom. 3:20—Therefore by the deeds of the law there shall no flesh be justified in his sight; for by the law is the knowledge of sin.

S. F. Gal. 2:16.

S. A. Tit. 3:5; Rom. 4:2–7; Gal. 5:4.

"The law was not given to save, or to justify anyone, but to stop argument and show that all are guilty (Rom. 3:19); to give knowledge of sin (Rom. 3:20; Rom. 7:7); to show the exceeding sinfulness of sin (Rom. 7:13); to lead the sinner to Jesus (Gal. 3:24). "At the Bar of God no man can be counted righteous in His sight because of his obedience to law. No man can render a perfect and perpetual obedience, therefore justification by obedience to the law is impossible (Gal. 3:10; James 2:10; Rom. 3:23). The burden of the Epistle to the Romans is to set forth this great truth. As a means of establishing right relations with God the law is totally insufficient. The only thing the law can do is to stop the mouth of every man, and declare him guilty before God. It is a question of Moses or Christ, works or faith, law or promise, doing or believing, wages or free gift."—EVANS.

2. Positively considered.

(1) Judicially by God.

Rom. 8:33—Who shall lay anything to the charge of God's elect? It is God that justifieth.

S. A. Rom. 3:24.

In regeneration we have the sovereign action of God, "Who worketh all things after the counsel of His own will;" Eph. 1:11, while in justification we have His judicial action. In the latter God is seen to be acting on just and equitable ground and in harmony with law.

(2) Causatively by grace.

Rom. 3:24—Being justified freely by His grace through the redemption that is in Christ Jesus.

Comp. John 15:25 l. c.—They hated me without a cause.

Men are justified by God as a judicial act, yet as an act of free grace through the redemption that is in Christ Jesus. "Freely" means without a cause, i. e., without a producing cause on our part. It is so translated in the second passage quoted above.

(3) Meritoriously and manifestly by Christ.

a. By His death meritoriously.

Rom. 5:9, R. V.—Much more then, being justified by (in) His blood, shall we be saved from the wrath of God through Him.

S. A. Rom. 3:24, l. c.

Men are justified or counted righteous in Christ's blood, i. e., on the ground of Christ's propitiatory death.

b. By His resurrection, manifestly.

Rom. 4:25—Who was delivered for our offenses, and was raised again for (because of) our justification.

Men are justified declaratively or manifestly by Christ's resurrection. Jesus was raised because of our justification, i. e., the resurrection of Christ shows the justifying value of His death as the grounds of our justification.

"Christ on Calvary, added up the penalty demanded, gave Himself as an equivalent, paid thus in equivalent the amount demanded; but God in raising Christ from the dead, has put to His own hand, and receipted the account so that, not only have we it paid by our security, but settled by Him who made the just demand."—MACKAY.

(4) Mediately by faith.

Rom. 5:1—Therefore being justified by faith we have peace with God through our Lord Jesus Christ.

S. F. Rom. 4:5; Rom. 3:23, 26; Acts 13:39.

Faith is not the procuring cause of justification, nor can it be regarded as its ground or basis. It has only a mediating function, through which justification is received. It constitutes a condition prerequisite to man's justification, but is not a cause of it.

"Faith is the acceptance of God's method of justification. Faith appropriates what grace provides. All was finished centuries ago. Faith now gives credence and credit to the record, and is thus counted for righteousness, as apprehending all that God's justice has demanded and grace has provided."—MACKAY.

(5) Evidentially by works.

James 2:14, 24, R. V.—What doth it profit, my brethren, if a man say he hath faith, but have not works? Can that faith save him? Ye see that by works a man is justified, and not by faith only.

We are not to slight good works, for they have their place, but they do not precede justification but rather follow it. The faith that justifies is a real faith that leads to action which is accordant with the truth believed. We are justified by faith without works. The working man is not the justified man, but the justified man is the working man. The tree shows its life by its fruits, but it was alive before the fruit or even the leaves appeared.

"There is no contradiction between Paul and James touching the matter of faith and works. Paul is looking at the matter from the God-ward side, and asserts that we are justified, in the sight of God, meritoriously, without any works on our part. James considers the matter from the man-ward side, and asserts that we are justified, in the sight of man, evidentially by works, and not by faith alone. In James it is not the ground of justification as with Paul, but the demonstration of it."—EVANS.

D. S. Man is justified not by character or conduct, but by the grace of God as a judicial act on the provided ground of Christ's redemption, as shown by His resurrection; it is appropriated by faith and manifested by works.

IV. The Results of it.

1. Freedom from incrimination.

Rom. 8:1, 33, 34—There is therefore now no condemnation to them which are in Christ Jesus, who walk not after the flesh, but after the Spirit. Who shall lay anything to the charge of God's elect? It is God that justifieth. Who is he that condemneth? It is Christ that died, yea rather, that is risen again, who is even at the right hand of God, who also maketh intercession for us.

Dr. Moule gives the following paraphrase of this latter passage: "Who will lodge a charge against God's chosen ones? Will God who justifies them? Who will condemn them if the charge is lodged? Will Christ who died, nay, rather, who rose, who is on the right hand of God who is actually interceding for us?"

2. Peace with God.

Rom. 5:1—Therefore being justified by faith, we have peace with God through our Lord Jesus Christ.

S. F. Eph. 2:14–17.

This peace is legal or judicial and is in contrast to the peace of God, which is experimental (Phil. 4:6, 7).

3. Assurance and realization of future glorification.

Titus 3:7, R. V.—That being justified by His grace, we might be made heirs according to the hope of eternal life.

S. A. Rom. 8:30.

Justification gives the believer the right and title to the future glory of which the Scriptures give us the promise.

D. S. Justification brings freedom from condemnation, judicial peace, and the hope of future glory.

E. Sanctification:

Sanctification deals with our state almost entirely, just as justification deals with our standing. In justification we are declared righteous in order that in sanctification we may become righteous. Justification is that which God does for us, while sanctification is largely that which God does in us. Justification puts us into a right relationship with God legally, while Sanctification exhibits the fruit of that relationship experimentally, in a life separated from a sinful world and dedicated unto God. Justification makes us safe, while Sanctification makes us sound.

There is, however, an aspect of Sanctification called "positional," which should not be overlooked. This aspect of it is similar to Justification. In Justification, however, the believer is viewed from the legal viewpoint, while in positional Sanctification he is viewed from the moral. In Justification he is positionally righteous while in this phase of Sanctification he is positionally holy.

I. The meaning of it.

1. The process of setting apart, or the state of being set apart for God.

Lev. 27:14–16—And when a man shall sanctify his house to be holy unto the Lord, then the Priest shall estimate it, whether it be good or bad; as the priest shall estimate it so shall it stand. And if he that sanctified it will redeem his house, then he shall add the fifth part of the money of thy estimation unto it, and so shall it be his. And if a man shall sanctify unto the Lord some part of a field of his possession, then thy estimation shall be according to the seed thereof: an homer of barley seed shall be valued at fifty shekels of silver.

S. A. Num. 8:17; II Chron. 7:16; Jer. 1:5; Matt. 23:17; John 10:36; Lev. 8:33–36.

2. The process of setting apart or the state of being set apart from ceremonial or moral defilement.

II Chron. 29:5–18, Especially 5, 18—And said unto them, hear me, ye Levites, sanctify now yourselves, and sanctify the house of the Lord God of your fathers, and carry forth the filthiness out of the holy place. Then they went in to Hezekiah the King, and said. We have cleansed all the house of the Lord, and the altar of burnt offering, with all the vessels thereof, and the shewbread table, with all the vessels thereof.

S. F. Lev. 11:44; Lev. 20:7; I Thes. 5:22–23; Heb. 9:13; I Thes. 4:3–7, R. V.

S. A. I Chron. 15:12, 14; Ex. 19:20–22.

These two meanings of the word "Sanctification" are closely connected. One cannot be truly separated to God without being separated from sin.

3. God shown to be holy by the revelation of His character.

Ezek. 36:23—And I will sanctify my great name, which was profaned among

220

the heathen, which ye have profaned in the midst of them; and the heathen shall know that I am the Lord, saith the Lord God, when I shall be sanctified in you before their eyes.

S. F. Ezek. 28:22; Ezek. 38:16; Ezek. 39:27.

The root from which this and kindred words spring is the Greek word "hagios." The nearest thought to holiness of which the profane Greek was capable was, "the sublime, the consecrated, the venerable." The moral element was utterly wanting. In adopting this word for Scripture usage, therefore, a new meaning had to be put into it. Using the word "holy" from the highest sense, as applied to God, the best lexicographers define it as "that which deserves and claims moral and religious reverence." Holiness when applied to God is defined as "that element in the Divine Nature which lies at the basis of, determines, and molds the reverence which is due from man to God." The word also has a meaning in classic Greek of "devoted to the gods"; an animal for sacrifice, a house for worship, a vessel for sacred use, a garment for priestly wear, a man for service, becomes by such designation, holy. So in Scripture, a person or thing, is termed holy by reason of being set apart from sin and possessed of absolute purity.

D. S. By sanctification is meant the process of setting apart or the state of being set apart for God and from the world. It is accompanied by a revelation of God's holiness.

II. *The period of it.*

Sanctification may be viewed as past, present, and future, or instantaneous, progressive and complete.

1. Initial stage—contemporaneous with conversion.

I Cor. 1:2, R. V.—Unto the church of God which is at Corinth, even them that are sanctified in Christ Jesus, called to be saints with all that call upon the name of our Lord Jesus Christ in every place, their Lord and ours.

S. A. I Cor. 6:11, R. V.

This stage of Sanctification is instantaneous, and has a two-fold aspect, positional and practical. It is synchronous with our acceptance of Christ as Saviour and Lord. The two aspects of Sanctification which are included in this stage are very similar to, if not almost synonymous with justification and regeneration, including conversion.

(1) Positional Sanctification as to standing morally, holy and perfect in Christ.

Heb. 10:9, 10, 14—Then said he, Lo I come to do thy will O God. He taketh away the first, that he may establish the second. By the which will we are sanctified through the offering of the body of Jesus Christ once for all. For by one offering he hath perfected for ever them that are sanctified.

S. A. I Cor. 1:30–31; Gal. 6:14; Eph. 1:6; Col. 2:10; Heb. 9:26.

There is a sense, therefore, in which every true believer is already sanctified. By the offering of the body of Jesus Christ "once for all" we are separated from sin, and separated unto God—"perfected forever" as far as our standing before God is concerned. In Christ we thus get a new standing, morally as well as judicially, in holiness as well as in righteousness.

221

(2) Practical Sanctification—as to state—a new nature received, involving changed desires and purposes.

I Peter 1:2—Elect according to the foreknowledge of God the Father, through sanctification of the Spirit, unto obedience and sprinkling of the blood of Jesus Christ; Grace be unto you, and peace, be multiplied.

S. A. I John 3:9; I Peter 1:3–5; II Thes. 2:13.

Practical sanctification has to do with the subjective aspect of our salvation, and has its beginning in regeneration, and thus in its initial stage is synonymous with it. We are set apart by the regenerating act of God from those who have a natural descent from Adam and who through sin are the children of the Devil, to the Fatherhood of God through spiritual sonship in Christ Jesus.

There is another sense in which a Christian may be already sanctified. If he has fulfilled the requirements of Rom. 12:1-2 (R. V.) in presenting himself a living sacrifice to God. Such an offering is "well-pleasing to God." As God in the Old Testament showed His pleasure in an offering by sending down fire to take it to Himself, so, when the whole body is thus offered to God, He still accepts it by fire, the fire of the Holy Spirit, and takes to Himself that which is thus presented. The believer, then, so far as the will, the governing purpose of his life, the center of his being, is concerned is sanctified, is wholly God's by dedication and consecration. He may and will daily discover, as he studies the Word of God, illumined by the Holy Spirit, acts of his, habits of life, forms of feelings, speech and action that are not in conformity with this central purpose of his life. These must be confessed to God as blameworthy, and be put away, and this department of his life and being brought by God's Spirit and the indwelling Christ, into conformity with God's will as revealed in His word.

2. Progressive stage—contemporaneous with the believer's earth life.

II Cor. 7:1—Having therefore these promises, dearly beloved, let us cleanse ourselves from all filthiness of the flesh and spirit, perfecting holiness in the fear of God.

S. F. II Peter 3:18, R. V.; II Cor. 3:18, R. V.; Eph. 4:11–15; I Thes. 3:12; I Thes. 4:1, 9–10, R. V.

Justification differs from Sanctification thus; the former is an instantaneous act with no progression: while the latter is a crisis with a view to a process—an act, which is instantaneous and which at the same time carries with it the idea of growth unto completion.

According to II Cor. 3:18 we are being transformed from one degree of character or glory to another. It is because sanctification is progressive that we are exhorted to "abound more and more" (I Thes. 3:12; 4:1, 9, 10) in the graces of the Christian life. There is such a thing as "perfecting holiness." God's gift to the church of pastors and teachers is for the purpose of the perfecting of the saints in the likeness of Christ until, at last, they attain unto that divine standard (Eph. 4:11–15; Phil. 3:10–15).

3. Final stage—contemporaneous with the coming of Christ.

I Thes. 3:12-13, R. V.—And the Lord make you to increase and abound in love one toward another, and toward all men, even as we also do toward you: To the end he may establish your hearts unblameable in holiness before our God and Father at the coming of our Lord Jesus with all his saints.

222

S. F. I Thes. 5:23, R. V.; Phil. 3:12–14, R. V.; I John 3:2, R. V.

This stage has to do with the completion and perfection of the believer's sanctification. He will then be entire, wanting nothing, like Christ in all things. He will be completely freed from sin and perfected in holiness.

D. S. Sanctification begins at the inception of the believer's salvation, is co-extensive with his life on earth, and will reach its climax and perfection when Christ returns.

III. *The manner of it.*

Like other aspects of the believer's salvation, sanctification is accomplished in a two-fold way. There is a part which God only can and does take, and there is a part assigned to man, for which he is responsible.

1. On the Divine side.

(1) The work of God the Father.

I Thes. 5:23, 24, R. V.—And the God of peace, himself, sanctify you wholly; and may your spirit and soul and body be preserved entire without blame at the coming of our Lord Jesus Christ. Faithful is he that calleth you, who will also do it.

S. F. John 17:17, R. V.; Jude 1.

(2) The work of Christ the Son.

Eph. 5:25, 26, R. V.—Husbands, love your wives, even as Christ also loves the Church, and gave himself up for it; that he might sanctify it, having cleansed it by the washing of water with the word.

S. F. Heb. 10:10, R. V.; I Cor. 1:30, R. V.; Gal. 6:14, R. V.

S. A. Ex. 11:7; Ex. 12:13.

(3) The work of the Holy Spirit.

II Thes. 2:13—But we are bound to give thanks to God always for you, brethren beloved of the Lord, for that God chose you from the beginning unto salvation in sanctification of the Spirit and belief of the truth.

S. F. I Peter 1:2.

S. A. Lev. 8:10–12.

As God in the old dispensation set the first-born apart to Himself, so God in the new dispensation sets apart the believer unto Himself and separates him from sin. It is, however, the Triune God, Father, Son and Holy Spirit, who does this, each person performing His respective part. God the Father planned it; God the Son provided it; God the Holy Spirit performs it.

2. On the human side, it is:

(1) By faith in Christ's redemptive work.

Acts 26:18—To open their eyes, and to turn them from darkness to light, and from the power of Satan unto God, that they may receive forgiveness of sins, and inheritance among them which are sanctified by faith that is in me.

S. F. I Cor. 1:30, R. V.; Heb. 13:12–13.

S. A. Gal. 6:14; Acts 15:9.

As the believer appropriates Christ and His redemptive work by faith he becomes sanctified experimentally, i. e., he is actually separated from sin, and set apart unto God.

"It is 'by faith we live' (Rom. 1:17); 'by faith we walk' (II Cor. 5:7); 'by faith we stand' (II.Cor. 1:24); 'by faith we fight' (I Tim. 6:12); 'by faith we overcome' (I John 5:4)."—MARSH.

(2) By the Word of God.

John 17:17—Sanctify them through thy truth; thy word is truth.

S. F. John 15:3; Psa. 119:11.

S. A. Eph. 5:26.

The word of God read, believed, and obeyed, is an effective means of the believer's sanctification.

(3) By a complete dedication of life.

Rom. 12:1, 2—I beseech you therefore, brethren, by the mercies of God, that ye present your bodies a living sacrifice, holy, acceptable unto God, which is your reasonable service. And be not conformed to this world; but be ye transformed by the renewing of your minds that ye may prove what is that good, and acceptable, and perfect will of God.

S. A. John 17:18, 19.

(4) By submission to Divine discipline.

Heb. 12:10–11—For they verily for a few days chastened us after their own pleasure; but he for our profit, that we might be partakers of His holiness. Now no chastening for the present seemeth to be joyous, but grievous: nevertheless afterward it yieldeth the peaceable fruit of righteousness unto them which are exercised thereby.

S. A. I Cor. 11:32.

We become partakers of God's holiness through the administration of chastisement by our Heavenly Father, and our submission to the same.

(5) By renunciation of sin and pursuit of holiness.

Rom. 6:18, 19—Being then made free from sin, ye become the servants of righteousness. I speak after the manner of men because of the infirmity of your flesh; for as ye have yielded your members servants to uncleanness and to iniquity unto iniquity; even so now yield your members servants to righteousness unto holiness.

S. A. II Cor. 7:1; Tit. 2:11, 12.

We are sanctified by self-judgment, personal renunciation of sin and pursuit of holiness.

D. S. Sanctification is effected as the believer works out his own salvation in the consciousness of the Divine inworking.

F. Prayer.

The term prayer as used in the largest sense includes all forms of communion with God. It embraces worship, praise, thanksgiving, supplication and intercession. The definite teaching, however, as found in the Scriptures on the subject of prayer deals principally with the last two aspects. The laws governing them.

however, are the same, in the main, as those which condition the other forms of communion.

The importance of prayer can be measured only by the prominence given to it in the Scriptures and in the lives of those who have been signally used of God.

I. The reason or necessity for it.

1. Because it is right.

Luke 18:1—And he spake a parable unto them to this end, that men ought always to pray and not to faint.

S. A. Gen. 18:25.

"These two Scriptures bring us into the realm of Ethics, which has to do with the rightness and oughtness of things. When a man is ethically sound, he is what he ought to be."—DIXON.

Jesus Christ declared that prayer is an ethical procedure, that the man who prays does that which is right, and by implication the man who does not pray does not do that which is right. He is unethical.

2. Because it is commanded.

Col. 4:2, R. V.—Continue steadfastly in prayer, watching therein with thanksgiving.

S. F. I Thes. 5:17; I Cor. 7:5, R. V.

It is God's revealed will for His people to pray, and obedience thereto makes it necessary.

3. Because it is sinful to neglect it.

I Sam. 12:23—Morever as for me, God forbid that I should sin against the Lord in ceasing to pray for you; but I will teach you the good and the right way.

In ceasing to pray for others we not only wrong them but sin against God.

4. Because neglect of it grieves God.

Isa. 43:21-22, R. V.—The people which I formed for myself that they might set forth my praise. Yet thou hast not called upon me, O Jacob; but thou hast been weary of me, O Israel.

S. F. Isa. 64:6-7, R. V.

Prayerlessness meets the Divine displeasure and rebuke, because of the wrong attitude toward God which it represents on the part of the man.

5. Because it is a medium through which God bestows blessing.

Matt. 7:11—If ye then, being evil, know how to give good gifts unto your children, how much more shall your Father which is in heaven give good things to them that ask him?

S. F. James 4:2; Matt. 21:22.

S. A. Dan. 9:3.

There are many things which God gives and the believer receives through the medium of prayer alone.

6. Because it is essential to victory over the forces of evil.

Eph. 6:12-18. Verse 18—Praying always with all prayer and supplication in the Spirit, and watching thereunto with all perseverance and supplication for all saints.

The demand of our day is very distinct and urgent. It is for a spiritual force, which will enable the Christian warrior effectively to oppose adverse powers as they seek, at each point of the conflict, to hinder through him the accomplishment of the Divine plan of redemption. That which can supply the demand in the greatest possible measure is prayer. To know how to use all that is implied in this is to bring on to the battlefield an irresistible power.

7. Because of the obligation imposed by Christ's example.

Heb. 5:7—Who in the days of his flesh, when he had offered up prayers and supplications with strong crying and tears unto him that was able to save him from death, and was heard in that he feared.

S. F. Mark 1:35.

There was need and reason for prayer in the life of the Son of God, making it obviously needful in the life of his followers.

8. Because of the emphasis given to it in the early church.

Acts 6:4—But we will give ourselves continually to prayer, and to the ministry of the word.

S. F. Rom. 1:9; Col. 1:9; Acts 12:5.

The Apostles regarded prayer as one of the two most important forms of employment that could engage their time or attention. They gave it a place of equality with the ministry of the Word and rightly so. For the ministry of the Word apart from prayer leads to formalism; while prayer apart from the ministry of the Word tends to fanaticism.

D. S. The necessity of prayer is shown by its ethical character, its scriptural obligation, its vital relation to all bestowed blessing and victory, and its emphasis in the life of Christ and the early church.

II. The qualifications for it.

1. Negatively considered.

(1) Regarding iniquity in the heart a disqualification for prayer.

Psa. 66:18—If I regard iniquity in my heart, the Lord will not hear me.

S. F. Hab. 1:13; Isa. 59:1, 2.

The word here translated "regard" is the same as that translated "behold" in Hab. 1:13, and means "to look upon with favor." God demands that we take the same attitude toward sin that he Himself takes, which is one of hatred and abhorrence (see Psa. 97:10). If we take a favorable attitude toward sin, God of necessity must take an unfavorable attitude toward us.

(2) Refusal to heed God's word a disqualification for prayer.

Prov. 28:9—He that turneth away his ear from hearing the law, even his prayer shall be abomination.

S. F. Zech. 7:11-13; Prov. 1:24, 25, 28, R. V.

Those who will not give heed to God's Word which He has spoken will not be heard when they speak.

(3) Disregarding the cry of the needy a disqualification for prayer.

Prov. 21:13—Whoso stoppeth his ears at the cry of the poor, he also shall cry himself, but shall not be heard.

S. A. James 2:14–16; I John 3:16–18.

Those who refuse to hear the cry of those in need will also be refused when they cry to God in the time of their need.

(4) A wrong relationship in the home. I Pet. 3:7.

2. Positively considered.

(1) True penitence.

Luke 18:13–14—And the publican, standing afar off, would not lift up so much as his eyes unto heaven, but smote upon his breast, saying, God be merciful to me a sinner. I tell you, this man went down to his house justified rather than the other; for every one that exalteth himself shall be abased; and he that humbleth himself shall be exalted.

S. F. Acts 11:13–14; Acts 10:24, 30–32.

A penitent sinner who holds himself in readiness to turn in repentance from sin and in faith to Christ, when he knows the way, can pray so that his prayer will be heard. "An impenitent sinner never prays. Impenitence involves not one of the elements of a spirit of prayer. Holy desire, holy love, holy fear, holy trust, not one of these can the sinner find within himself. He has, therefore, none of that artless spontaneity, in calling upon God, which David exhibited when he said, 'Thy servant hath found in his heart to pray this prayer unto thee.' The whole atmosphere of prayer, therefore, is foreign to his tastes. If he drives himself unto it for a time, by forcing upon his soul the forms of devotion, he cannot stay there."

(2) Faith in Christ.

I John 5:13–15, R. V.—These things have I written unto you, that ye may know that ye have eternal life, even unto you that believe on the name of the Son of God. And this is the boldness which we have toward him, that, if we ask anything according to his will, he heareth us, and if we know that he heareth us what so ever we ask we know that we have the petitions which we have asked of him.

S. F. Heb. 11:6.

"Faith is the inevitable and essential accompaniment of all true prayer. Our faith accepts the assurance that prayer will be heard and answered, and pleads the fulfillment of Divine revelation, and apart from our belief in God as the Hearer of prayer there could not be any real prayer or genuine blessing."— HASTINGS.

(3) Righteousness and Godliness.

Psa. 34:15—The eyes of the Lord are upon the righteous, and his ears are open unto their cry.

S. F. Psa. 32:6; Prov. 15:8; Psa. 145:19; Heb. 12:28–29; I Peter 3:12; II Cor. 7:1.

Those who are righteous and godly in their lives can offer effectual prayer.

(4) Obedience.

I John 3:22—And whatsoever we ask, we receive of him, because we keep his commandments and do those things that are pleasing in his sight.

Obedience does not furnish the ground upon which God answers our prayer, but it does fulfil a required condition.

5) Abiding in Christ.

ohn 15:7, R. V.—If ye abide in me, and my words abide in you, ask whatsoever ye will, and it shall be done unto you.

3. F. Psa. 91:1, 14, 15.

Those who dwell in the secret place of the most high, which is Christ, who abide in Christ and have Christ's word abiding in them, can pray acceptably to God.

(6) Humility.

Psa. 10:17—Lord thou hast heard the desire of the humble; thou wilt prepare their heart, thou wilt cause thine ear to hear.

S. F. Psa. 9:12; Zeph. 2:3.

"The figures of the 'poor' whose cry is not forgotten, of the 'meek' whose 'desire' is heard, of the 'humble' to whom grace is given, meet us constantly in psalm, and prophecy, and epistle."—HASTINGS.

True humility or lowliness of heart qualifies one for effectual prayer.

(7) Joyful trust.

Psa. 37:4-5—Delight thyself also in the Lord and he shall give thee the desires of thine heart. Commit thy way unto the Lord, trust also in him; and he shall bring it to pass.

God finds delight in those who find delight in Him; thus the desires of their hearts become the desires of His heart. He will then bring to pass the answer of their prayers.

D. S. Prevailing prayer involves certain requirements which must be met.

III. *The persons addressed in it.*

1. God.

Acts 12:5—Peter therefore was kept in prison; but prayer was made without ceasing of the church unto God for him.

S. F. Neh. 4:9.

God who is the Supreme and sovereign ruler of the Universe is the proper object of prayer. All prayer should be addressed to Him.

(1) God the Father.

Matt. 6:9—After this manner therefore pray ye: Our father which art in heaven, Hallowed be thy name.

S. F. Eph. 1:17; Eph. 3:14; John 17:1; John 17:11, 25; John 16:23; Acts 4:24.

Jesus by precept and example has taught us to pray to God the Father.

(2) God the Son.

I Cor. 1:2—Unto the church of God which is at Corinth, to them that are sanctified in Christ Jesus called to be saints, with all that in every place call upon the name of Jesus Christ our Lord, both theirs and ours.

S. F. Acts 7:59, R. V.; I Cor. 12:8–9, R. V.; I Cor. 12:3; II Tim. 2:22; Acts 9:8, 17, 20, 21; Rom. 10:9, 10, 12, 13.

By the precedent established by the practice of Spirit-filled men in the Scriptures it is shown to be proper to pray to Jesus Christ.

The question is sometimes asked, "Should we pray to the Holy Spirit?" There is nothing to forbid prayer to the Holy Spirit except the absence in Scriptures of any precedent or example of so doing. There is no recorded prayer in the Bible to Him, but the communion of the Holy Spirit is spoken of. Some may think that this implies prayer. The Scriptures intimate that prayer is to be made to the Father in the name of Jesus Christ the Son, in the power and under the guidance of the Holy Spirit (see Eph. 2:18). The relation of the Holy Spirit to prayer is set forth in such passages as Rom. 8:15–16, 26, 27, R. V.

D. S. The goal of prayer is the ear of God.

IV. *The subjects of it.*

1. Ourselves.

John 17:1—These words spake Jesus, and lifted up his eyes to heaven, and said, Father, the hour is come; glorify thy Son, that thy Son also may glorify thee.

S. F. I Chron. 4:10; Psa. 106:4–5; II Cor. 12:7–8; Heb. 5:7.

(1) As lacking wisdom.

James 1:5—If any of you lack wisdom, let him ask of God, that giveth to all men liberally, and upbraideth not; and it shall be given him.

(2) As in destitute circumstances.

Psa. 102:17—He will regard the prayer of the destitute, and not despise their prayer.

S. F. Psa. 69:33, R. V.

(3) As under oppression.

Ex. 22:22, 23—Ye shall not afflict any widow, or fatherless child. If thou afflict them in any wise, and they cry at all unto me, I will surely hear their cry.

S. F. Isa. 19:20; James 5:4.

(4) As suffering.

James 5:13, R. V.—Is any among you suffering? let him pray. Is any cheerful? let him sing praise.

Prayer should be made for ourselves, but this may be done unselfishly and for God's glory.

2. Fellow Christians.

James 5:16—Confess your faults one to another, and pray one for another, that ye may be healed. The effectual fervent prayer of a righteous man availeth much.

S. F. Rom. 1:9; Psa. 36:9–10.

We should pray for one another i. e., believers, should pray for fellow-believers.

3. Christian workers.

Eph. 6:18-20—Praying always with all prayer and supplication in the Spirit, and watching thereunto with all perseverance and supplication for all saints. and for me. that utterance may be given unto me, that I may open my mouth boldly, to make known the mystery of the Gospel. For which I am an ambassador in bonds; that therein I may speak boldly, as I ought to speak.

S. F. Col. 4:3; II Thes. 3:1, 2; Matt. 9:38

Ministers and messengers of the Gospel have a prominent place in the prayers of Christians.

4. Young converts.

I Thes. 3:9-13—For what thanks can we render to God again for you, for all the joy wherewith we joy for your sakes before our God; Night and day praying exceedingly that we might see your face, and might perfect that which is lacking in your faith? Now God himself and our Father, and our Lord Jesus Christ, direct our way unto you. And the Lord make you to increase and abound in love one toward another, and toward all men, even as we do toward you. To the end he may stablish your hearts unblameable in holiness before God, even our Father, at the coming of our Lord Jesus Christ, with all his saints.

S. F. John 17:9, 20.

Beginners in the Christian life should be included among the subjects of prayer, especially those whom we have been instrumental in leading to Christ.

5. The sick.

James 5:14-16—Is any sick among you? let him call for the elders of the church; and let them pray over him, anointing him with oil in the name of the Lord. And the prayer of faith shall save the sick, and the Lord shall raise him up, and if he have committed sins, they shall be forgiven him. Confess your faults one to another, and pray one for another, that ye may be healed. The effectual fervent prayer of a righteous man availeth much.

"Two principles may be laid down here concerning healing:

"First there are three forms of healing:

"The Supernatural.—This explains itself. It is that form of healing in which God himself, without the use of means and by the direct touch of His own omnipotence, heals the body.

"The Natural.—Where health returns through rest, sleep, nourishing food, change of scene, and cessation from violating those natural laws by the transgression of which health has been lost, and through the observance of which it again returns.

"The Remedial.—Where remedies and means, either medical or surgical, are concerned in the restoration to health.

"Second, all healing is divine healing; God alone heals. No physician will

230

claim that medicines or remedies heal. They furnish a means upon which the healing life force within lays hold and uses in the process of healing. And back of all such life is the God of life, who alone heals, for only He who is the creator of life can restore and renew it when impaired. If God is thus back of, and makes use of, all these forms of healing it is for God alone and not for us to decide which form He shall use. No Christian man dare say, 'I will not use means,' lest he may be thereby saying, 'I will not obey God.' To look to God only and refuse all means is to confine God to the supernatural and rule Him out of the natural. But God will not have it so. For what we call the natural is simply God working through the natural. The natural is God's ordinary way of working, the supernatural his extraordinary way of working. If it is wholly a matter for God to choose as to whether He will heal, it must be wholly for God to choose how he will heal."—McConkey.

6. Children.

I Chron. 29:18–19—O Lord God of Abraham, Isaac, and of Israel, our fathers, keep this for ever in the imagination of the thoughts of the heart of thy people, and prepare their heart unto thee; and give unto Solomon my son a perfect heart, to keep thy commandments, thy testimonies, and thy statutes, and to do all these things, and to build the palace for the which I have made provision.

S. A. Eph. 6:4.

Bringing up children in the nurture and admonition of the Lord makes necessary earnest prayer for them on the part of the parents.

7. Rulers.

I Tim. 2:1–3—I exhort therefore, that first of all supplications, prayers, inter-cessions, and giving of thanks, be made for all men; For Kings, and for all that are in authority; that we may lead a quiet and peaceable life in all godliness and honesty. For this is good and acceptable in the sight of God our Saviour.

S.F. II Peter 2:10–11; I Peter 2:17.

It is God's revealed will for believers to pray for government officials.

8. Israel.

Rom. 10:1—Brethren, my heart's desire and prayer to God for Israel is, that they might be saved.

S. F. Joel 2:17; Isa. 62:6–7; Psa. 122:6–7.

Israel should be a subject of unceasing prayer.

9. Those who mistreat us.

Luke 6:28—Bless them that curse you, and pray for them which despitefully use you.

S. F. Matt. 5:44; Luke 23:34; Acts 7:60.

Prayer is to be the Christian's response to unkind treatment.

10. All men.

I Tim. 2:1—I exhort therefore that, first of all, supplications, prayers, interces-sions, and giving of thanks, be made for all men.

All mankind with its many classifications and divisions is to be included in the prayer of the believer.

D. S. Prayer covers the widest possible scope including every aspect of human experience and all classes and conditions of men.

V. The method of it.

1. The time of it.

(1) At stated periods.

Psa. 55:16, 17—As for me, I will call upon God; and the Lord shall save me. Evening, and morning, and at noon will I pray, and cry aloud; and he shall hear my voice.

S. F. Dan. 6:10; Acts 10:9, 30.

According to the example of holy men of the Bible we should have stated times of prayer.

(2) At meals.

I Tim. 4:4–5—For every creature of God is good, and nothing to be refused, if it be received with thanksgiving; for it is sanctified by the word of God and prayer.

S. F. Matt. 14:19; Acts 27:35.

According to the example of Christ and Paul, prayers of thanksgiving and blessing should precede our meals.

(3) In great extremities.

Psa. 50:15—And call upon me in the day of trouble; I will deliver thee, and thou shalt glorify me.

S. F. Psa. 77:1, 2; Psa. 86:7; Psa. 60:11; Psa. 130:1.

S. A. I Chron. 5:20; II Chron. 13:13–16; II Chron. 20:1–19; Jonah 2:2, R. V.; Jonah 2:7; Psa. 30:2, 3.

Prayer should be offered to God in the day of trouble, in the day of battle; when overpowered by the enemy and sorely perplexed; when all of human help fails and our souls faint within us, we should cry unto God even from these overwhelming depths.

(4) At all seasons.

Eph. 6:18, R. V.—With all prayer and supplication praying at all seasons in the Spirit, and watching thereunto in all perseverance and supplication for all saints.

S. F. Psa. 116:1, 2; Luke 18:1; I Thes. 5:17.

"Prayer, as we have seen, is, in the highest conception of it, a state rather than an act. A full fruition of its benefits depends on a continuity of its influences. Reduce it to isolated experiments daily, and separate these by long blank hours in which the soul has no glimpse of God for its refreshment, and how can prayer be other than a toil and often a drudgery?"— PHELPS.

We should pray always and at all seasons without ceasing.

2. The place of it.

(1) In private.

Matt. 6:6, R. V.—But thou, when thou prayest, enter into thine inner chamber, and having shut the door, pray to the father who is in secret, and thy father who seeth in secret shall recompense thee.

S. F. Matt. 14:23.

In private prayer we should seek a place apart, where we can be closed in with God.

(2) In public.

Acts 27:35—And when he had thus spoken, he took bread and gave thanks to God in the presence of them all; and when he had broken it, he began to eat.

S. A. John 11:41; John 17:1.

Prayer should be offered both in the assembly of believers and unbelievers.

(3) Everywhere.

I Tim. 2:8—I will therefore that men pray everywhere, lifting up holy hands, without wrath and doubting.

Any place on earth may be a veritable Bethel, a meeting place with God, a house of prayer.

3. The manner of it.

(1) Attitude of body—Not important or commanded.

a. Standing.

Mark 11:25—And when ye stand praying, forgive, if ye have ought against any; that your Father also which is in heaven may forgive you your trespasses.

S. A. John 17:1.

b. Kneeling.

I Kings 8:54—And it was so, when Solomon had made an end of praying all this prayer and supplication unto the Lord, he arose from before the altar of the Lord, from kneeling on his knees, with his hands spread up to heaven.

S. F. Luke 22:41.

c. Prostrate.

Matt. 26:39—And he went a little farther, and fell on his face, and prayed, saying, O my father if it be possible, let this cup pass from me; nevertheless not as I will, but as thou wilt.

The Scriptures sanction no special bodily attitude in prayer; the soul may be in prayer regardless of the posture or attitude of the body.

(2) Attitude of soul—all important and obligatory.

a. Sincerity.

Psa. 145:18—The Lord is nigh unto all them that call upon him, to all that call upon him in truth.

S. F. Matt. 6:5.

b. Simplicity.

Matt. 6:7—But when ye pray, use not vain repetitions, as the heathen do; for they think that they shall be heard for their much speaking.

S. F. Matt. 26:44.

c. Earnestness.

Heb. 5:7—Who in the days of his flesh, when he had offered up prayers and supplications with strong crying and tears unto him that was able to save him from death, and was heard in that he feared.

S. F. Luke 22:44; Acts 12:5, R. V.

d. Persistence.

Col. 4:2—Continue in prayer, and watch in the same with thanksgiving.

e. Definiteness.

Psa. 27:4—One thing have I desired of the Lord, that I will seek after; that I may dwell in the house of the Lord all the days of my life, to behold the beauty of the Lord and to enquire in his temple.

S. F. Matt. 18:19; Mark 11:24.

f. Trustfulness.

Matt. 21:22—And all things, whatsoever ye shall ask in prayer, believing, ye shall receive.

S. F. James 1:6, 7; Heb. 11:6; John 14:13; Rom. 8:26; 27, R. V.

"Prayer should be made in the attitude of a needy and helpless soul whose only refuge is in God."—FROST.

D. S. Prayer should be continuous as to time, universal as to place; the one praying is to be concerned, not with bodily posture, but with attitude of soul.

VI. *The Results of it.*

1. Great achievements.

James 5:16—Confess your faults one to another, and pray one for another, that ye may be healed. The effectual fervent prayer of a righteous man availeth much.

No one can fathom the depth of meaning included in the word "much" of this passage, but there is no doubt but what it contains well nigh infinite possibilities.

2. Definite answers.

John 14:13, 14—And whatsoever ye shall ask in my name that will I do, that the Father may be glorified in the Son. If ye shall ask anything in my name, I will do it.

S. F. Mk. 11:24.

God does not send substitutes as answers to prayer; He grants the very thing for which the Holy Spirit has led us to make request.

3. Accomplishment of the Divine purpose.

I John 5:14, 15—And this is the confidence that we have in him, that, if we ask anything according to his will, he heareth us. And if we know that he hear us, whatsoever we ask, we know that we have the petitions that we desired of him.

The aim of prayer is not to overcome God's reluctance but to lay hold of his willingness, i.e., to secure the purpose and provision of His will.

4. Glorification of God.

John 14:13—And whatsoever ye shall ask in my name, that will I do, that the Father may be glorified in the Son.

S. F. I John 3:22; John 17:1.

This not only constituted a result but also a worthy aim or end of prayer. The glory of God should be the motive in all of our praying, as well as in all of our life and service.

D. S. The effectual fervent prayer of a righteous man availeth much in relation to both God and man.

Study Questions on the Doctrines of Salvation

1. How is the importance of regeneration seen? (consult notes) Give D. S.
2. With what two things is regeneration not to be confused? Discuss each.
3. Give the four-fold positive designation of regeneration, quote one passage with each, and give D. S.
4. Wherein does the necessity for regeneration lie?
5. How is regeneration accomplished?
6. What are the results of regeneration? Give D. S.
7. How is the importance of repentance shown? Give D. S.
8. Define repentance as touching the three elements of personality and give D. S.
9. Discuss the two elements involved in repentance as related to the emotions.
10. How is repentance manifested? Quote one passage with each aspect.
11. Quote one passage showing how repentance is accomplished on the divine side.
12. How is repentance accomplished on the human side?
13. What are the results of repentance?
14. What relation do faith and repentance sustain to each other?
15. Where does the importance of faith lie? Quote one passage with each aspect and give D. S.
16. Classify and define the two kinds of faith.
17. Outline in full the various relationships sustained by spiritual faith.
18. Give the three-fold manner in which faith is obtained on the divine side and quote one passage with one.
19. What means are used in the obtaining of faith on the human side? Quote one passage with one of them.
20. Outline the results of faith in full.
21. What is the experience of man which leads to the question, "How should a man be just with God?"
22. Discuss the historical setting of the phrase "Justification by Faith."

23. Give and discuss the two-fold negative definition of justification.
24. Give the theoretical and Scriptural definitions of justification, quoting a passage under the latter and giving D. S.
25. Discuss the scope of justification, quoting one passage with each aspect.
26. How does the divine method of justification differ from the human?
27. Discuss the method of justification, negatively and positively considered.
28. What are the results of justification?
29. Distinguish between sanctification and justification.
30. Give the three-fold meaning of sanctification.
31. Give the three stages of sanctification, quote one passage with each and give D. S.
32. Discuss the two-fold aspect of the initial stage of sanctification and identify each phase with an aspect of salvation. Give another sense in which the believer many be said to be already sanctified.
33. How is sanctification accomplished on the divine side? Quote a passage with each aspect?
34. How is sanctification accomplished on the human side?
35. Give D. S. under the manner of sanctification.
36. Why should men pray? Quote one passage with each reason given.
37. What things are to be regarded as disqualifications for prayer?
38. What are the qualifications for prayer?
39. To what persons is prayer to be addressed? Quote one passage with each.
40. Answer the question, "Should we pray to the Holy Spirit?"
41. For whom should we pray? Outline in full.
42. Discuss the principles laid down concerning healing.
43. When should we pray.
44. Where should we pray?
45. How should we pray? Attitude of body? Attitude of soul?
46. What are the results of true prayer?

CHAPTER EIGHT
THE DOCTRINE OF THE CHURCH
(ECCLESIOLOGY)

The teaching of the Scriptures concerning the Church is just as plain and positive as that which pertains to any other doctrine, and yet the conception of men, even professing Christians, in regard to it, seems to be very indefinite and vague. This is doubtless due to the fact that, according to human usage the term "Church" has numerous and varied meanings. It is used to distinguish the religious people from the non-religious. It is used denominationally, in discriminating between the sects, as the Presbyterian, the Methodist, the Catholic Church. It is used in relation to literature to discriminate between sacred and secular. It is used in relation to buildings, as a designation of a meeting-house where Christians assemble for worship. This terminology, and other somewhat similar usage, tends to obscure the real meaning of the word. When, however, we come to the Scriptural usage of the term we find that this vagueness disappears.

A. The Meaning of It.

The English word "Church" is the translation of the Greek word "ecclesia" which means "called out." It was used of an assembly or congregation that might be called out for various purposes. The significance of this term as used in the New Testament is twofold. It refers to those who are called out from among the nations as a people for his name who constitute the Church, the Body of Christ. In this sense it is an organism. It also refers to those who are called out of any given community to carry out the principles and precepts of Christ found in the New Testament, as a body of Christians. In this sense it is an organization.

I. As an organism.

The Church is the mystical body of Christ of which He is the living Head and regenerate believers are the members.

I Cor. 12:12-13—For as the body is one, and hath many members, and all the members of that one body, being many, are one body, so also is Christ. For by one Spirit are we all baptized into one body, whether we be Jews or Gentiles, whether we be bond or free; and have been all made to drink into one Spirit.

S. F. Eph. 1:22–23.

S. A. Eph. 3:4–6.

The Church thus viewed as an organism is "the people for His name" which God is now taking out from among the Gentiles, according to Acts 15:14. This is the age of Divine election and selection which has for its objective the formation of the Body of Christ, which is to be His bride.

II. As an organization.

A Church is a body of baptized believers gathered together by the Holy Spirit for the purpose of carrying out the principles and precepts of God's Word.

Acts 16:5—And so were the churches established in the faith, and increased in number daily.

S. F. Acts 2:41–42.

"The Church in the New Testament is a very simple organization. Everybody who is able to yield himself to Jesus Christ, and who does so, taking him as Saviour and obeying him as Lord, is entitled to membership in it. And all members stand on the same level. There is no barrier to admission in differences of race, sex, age, wealth or culture. In Jesus Christ there is neither Jew nor Gentile, Greek nor barbarian, male nor female, bond nor free. The church administers its own affairs. It bows to no authority on earth higher than itself. Jesus Christ is its only lawgiver. The New Testament is its law book, but it administers the laws which have been divinely given to it. It disciplines its members who are in any way disorderly. According to the New Testament, it has but two kinds of officers—bishops or pastors, whose duty it is to minister in spiritual things, feeding the flock of God, and deacons, who were appointed to look after the temporalities of the Church."—GOODCHILD.

The Church, whether viewed in its larger aspect as an organism, including all true believers gathered out of the nations between the first and second advents of Christ, or in the local aspect, as an organization, including believers in any given community, is not to be identified either with the Kingdom of God or the Kingdom of Heaven. The Kingdom of God is that sphere or realm in which the sovereignty of God is acknowledged and His will obeyed, including unfallen angels and redeemed men of all ages. The Church, however, includes only men who are redeemed in this age, and therefore is only a part of the Kingdom of God.

The Kingdom of Heaven has a threefold aspect as set forth in the New Testament: First, that which was true concerning it in the days of John the Baptist and Christ, when offered to Israel. Then it was "at hand" in the Person of the King. Second, "in mystery form," as presented in the parables of Matthew 13. Here the Kingdom of Heaven includes the entire sphere of Christian profession, and is synonymous with Christendom. Third, the prophetic aspect as set forth in the teaching of Jesus and the other New Testament writers. The only common ground between the church and the Kingdom of Heaven is that which is real in the profession of faith, included in its present aspect or form. The Church is thus within the Kingdom of Heaven in the present-day application of the term.

D. S. The church as an organism includes all regenerate believers gathered out of the world between the first and second advents of Christ, while as an organization it includes local believers united for the service of Christ in any given assembly.

B. The Fact of It, as Set Forth:

I. In types and symbols.

1. The body with its members.

Rom. 12:4-5—For as we have many members in one body, and all members have not the same office, so we being many, are one body in Christ, and every one members one of another.

S. F. I Cor. 12:12-27; Col. 1:18.

The Apostle Paul had received a twofold ministry, concerning the Gospel and concerning the Church. These two are inseparably joined and an intimation of both was given at his conversion. Christ in His glory was a part of the saving vision which came to Paul. The Gospel thus received identified the redeemed sinner with his Saviour Lord. The message was "Saul, Saul, why persecutest thou me?" Paul's persecution was of Christians not of Christ, but there he learned that Christians are one with Christ and He with them.

"When our Lord spoke of the mysteries of the Kingdom of Heaven in Matthew 13, He said: 'I will utter things which have been kept secret from the foundation of the world.' The Apostle Paul often speaks of the mysteries made known. He reminds the readers of Ephesians that he had mentioned the mystery before in a few words. Then, he had stated 'the mystery of the Christ,' what is it? Not merely concerning the church, as the body of Christ, but Christ Himself. This mystery of a risen Christ, who has a body composed of believing Jews and Gentiles, is the mystery, which, in other ages, was not made known unto the sons of men. The church was in the counsel of God before the foundation of the world, but He let ages go past till He was pleased to make it known."—GAEBELEIN.

The analogy of the head and the body illustrating Christ and the Church in their mutual relations is very apt. As the head functions through the body and its members, so Christ functions through the Church and its members. As there is a mutual dependence between the head and the body so is there between Christ and the church. Christ is dependent upon the church as the medium for expressing Himself and accomplishing his purposes. The church is dependent upon Christ for wisdom and direction in doing this. Christ is dependent upon the church to do His work. The church is dependent upon Christ for power to do it. As the members of a body are mutually essential to that body and its head so are the members of the church mutually essential to each other and to Christ.

2. The bride in relation to her espoused husband.

II Cor. 11:2—For I am jealous over you with godly jealousy: for I have espoused you to one husband, that I may present you as a chaste virgin to Christ.

S. F. Eph. 5:31, 32; Rev. 19:7.

      (1) Adam and Eve. Gen. 2:18, 21-24.

      (2) Isaac and Rebecca. Gen. 24:61-67.

      (3) Joseph and Asenath. Gen. 41:45.

The church is now the body of Christ in process of formation, and when completed will be presented as the bride; only the espousal as yet has taken place. The consummation of the marriage relationship awaits a future fulfillment. Its celebration will be at the "Marriage supper of the Lamb."

"If it is objected that, inasmuch as the church is, in the New Testament, called the 'body' of Christ (I Cor. 12:12-27), and therefore Scripture cannot intend that the 'bride' refers to the same group of believers, since the bride is not a part of the husband but separate from him, we must remember that the Scriptures both in Genesis 2:21-24 and in Ephesians 5:28-32 recognize husband and wife as separate persons, yet 'one flesh.' It is quite Scriptural therefore to understand the two Bible metaphors of 'body' and 'bride' as two aspects of the same relationship between Christ and His Church, the body expressing a relationship of life, and the bride a relationship of love."—S. S. TIMES.

3. The Temple with its foundation and building stones.

Eph. 2:21-22—In whom all the building fitly framed together groweth unto an holy temple in the Lord; in whom ye also are builded together for an habitation of God through the Spirit.

S. F. I Peter 2:4-6.

The symbolic and prophetic significance of the temple was fourfold. It was typical of heaven itself, or the sanctuary not made with hands (Heb. 9:24). It was typical of the believer's body, which is the shrine or temple of the Holy Ghost (I Cor. 6:19). It was typical of the church which is being built for an habitation of God in the Spirit (Eph. 2:21-22, R. V.; I Cor. 3:16). In this analogy individual believers are represented by building stones which when joined together constitute "a spiritual house," "a holy temple in the Lord." The temple is also typical of the physical body of Christ (John 2:19-21).

II. In prophetic utterance.

1. The promise of the Church.

Matt. 16:16-18—And Simon Peter answered and said, Thou art the Christ, the Son of the living God. And Jesus answered and said unto him, Blessed art thou, Simon Barjona; for flesh and blood hath not revealed it unto thee, but my Father which is in heaven. And I say also unto thee, That thou are Peter and upon this rock I will build my church and the gates of hell shall not prevail against it.

The church was not in existence while Christ was upon earth. At the time of the utterance of the above it was a thing still in the future. Jesus said, "I will build my church." It was a fact of prophecy, not of history, at the time of Christ's death.

2. The pre-instruction of the Church.

Matt. 18:15-20 (see especially verse 17): And if he shall neglect to hear them, tell it unto the church; but if he neglect to hear the church, let him be unto thee as an heathen man and a publican.

In this passage we have instructions given for the church before it came into existence, in order that when established it might have instructions to guide it in certain fundamental matters of discipline. The church referred to is doubtless the body of Christ, but the body of Christ functioning through the body of believers in any community. Further information and instruction concerning the church, which Jesus promised that the Holy Spirit would furnish, is to be found in the epistles (John 16:12-14).

III. In positive description.

Eph. 5:25-27—Husbands, love your wives, even as Christ also loved the church, and gave himself for it: that he might sanctify and cleanse it with the washing of water by the word. That he might present it to himself a glorious church, not having spot, or wrinkle, or any such thing: but that it should be holy and without blemish.

S. F. Eph. 1:22, 23.

This passage teaches that the church is the object of Christ's sacrificial love, the subject of His sanctifying truth and power, and the recipient of His sovereign grace and glory.

D. S. The church is a fact of revelation, made known through the use of figures, prophecies and plain statements.

C. The Ordinances of It.

"It is obviously a matter of great importance that we should have sound and scriptural opinions and clear convictions regarding the ordinances; for all through the Christian history, even from the earliest times until now, these sacred rites have been the occasion of great and long, and often fierce debates."—DARGAN.

The word "ordinance" comes from two Latin words which in their final meaning signify "that which is ordered or commanded." This term has been used to describe the two institutions, Baptism and the Lord's Supper, which Christ left to the churches for their observance.

There are certain erroneous views of the ordinances which need refuting. The Romanist conceives that in some way the mere performance of these acts itself brings a blessing, or confers spiritual grace. There is nothing in the acts themselves to bring grace, nothing mysterious, nothing miraculous; God blesses the performance of these acts as he blesses obedience and worship in other things.

Others have considered that these rites were an intended means of impressing the world. This possibly grew out of the saying of Paul in I Cor. 11:26: "As oft as ye eat this bread and drink this cup ye do proclaim the Lord's death till he come." But the "proclaiming" here need not be to the outside world, but rather means the exhibition to those who are taking part in the ordinance, and thus is for their special benefit.

Some have adopted the practice of a merely formal or ritualistic use of the ordinances, observing them as a custom or churchly performance, without any true conception of their intent. Such observance has no real value, for as ordinances they have an important relation to experience which they symbolize. And if there be no vital experience there can be no true symbolism.

The true view of the ordinances seems to embrace a threefold significance: They are symbolized Christian truths: they are memorials unto Christ, observed in obedience to Him, expressive of love and devotion; they are Christian rites, which designate those who properly observe them as Christ's disciples.

241

I. Baptism.

"Baptism simply sets forth in visible symbol Christ's death and burial and resurrection, and also our death to the old life of sin, our burial in the likeness of his death, and our resurrection to walk with him in a new life."— GOODCHILD.

It is obligatory in the church age because:

1. Commanded by Christ.

Mark 16:15, 16—And he said unto them, Go ye into all the world, and preach the gospel to every creature. He that believeth and is baptized shall be saved; but he that believeth not shall be damned.

S. F. Matt. 28:19, 20.

2. Practiced by the early Church.

Acts 2:41–42—Then they that gladly received his word were baptized; and the same day there were added unto them about three thousand souls. And they continued steadfastly in the apostles' doctrine and fellowship, and in breaking of bread and in prayers.

S. F. Acts 8:35–39; Rom. 6:1–5.

This passage suggests the following order: conversion, baptism, admission into church membership, orderly walk, observance of the Lord's Supper and united prayer.

II. The Lord's Supper.

"The communion of the Lord's Supper was intended to be a reminder of the Lord's suffering for us. It is a celebration of his death. The Saviour knew how short human memory is. And out of consideration of our weakness and aptness to forget he established this simple memorial supper in which we taste of broken bread symbolizing His body which was broken for us, and we sip of the crushed fruit of the vine, which is a symbol of His blood poured out for our sins. It is a reminder of the Lord's sufferings that brings Calvary and its cross very vividly before us. But the supper looks forward as well as backward. It is a commemoration and it is a prophecy. It shows forth the Lord's death 'till He come.' "—GOODCHILD.

It is obligatory in the church age because:

1. Commanded by Christ.

I Cor. 11:23–26—For I have received of the Lord that which also I delivered unto you. That the Lord Jesus the same night in which he was betrayed took bread: And when he had given thanks he brake it, and said, Take, eat; this is my body, which is broken for you; this do in remembrance of me. After the same manner also he took the cup, when he had supped, saying this cup is the new testament in my blood; this do ye, as oft as ye drink it, in remembrance of me. For as often as ye eat this bread, and drink this cup ye do shew the Lord's death till he come.

2. Observed by the early Church.

Acts 2:42—And they continued steadfastly in the apostles' doctrine and fellowship, and in breaking of bread, and in prayer.

S. F. Acts 20:11.

There are a number of questions which may be asked in relation to the two ordinances, such as these: What is the proper method of observing baptism and the Lord's supper? Who is qualified to administer them? Who are fit subjects or recipients of them? And to whom does the responsibility for their proper observance or administration belong? These questions will be answered variously according to the different interpretations of the passages upon which the answers are based. Suffice it for us to say in general that these are church ordinances and are therefore not to be administered or observed in promiscuous assemblies, or by individuals, but by the church in the regular local assembly, and according to the pattern furnished by the Lord Jesus Christ.

D. S. The church is the custodian of the two ordinances, baptism and the Lord's Supper, and is responsible for their administration.

D. The Mission of It.

I. To constitute a dwelling place for God.

Eph. 2:20-22, R. V.—Being built upon the foundation of the apostles and prophets, Christ Jesus Himself being the chief corner stone. In whom each several building, fitly framed together, groweth into a holy temple in the Lord. In whom ye also are builded together for a habitation of God in the Spirit.

II. To bear witness unto the truth.

I Tim. 3:15—But if I tarry long, that thou mayest know how thou oughtest to behave thyself in the house of God, which is the church of the living God, the pillar and ground of the truth.

III. To make known the manifold wisdom of God.

Eph. 3:10—To the intent that now unto the principalities and powers in heavenly places might be known by the church the manifold wisdom of God.

IV. To bring eternal glory to God.

Eph. 3:20-21—Now unto him that is able to do exceeding abundantly above all that we ask or think, according to the power that worketh in us, unto him be glory in the church by Christ throughout all ages, world without end. Amen.

V. To edify its members.

Eph. 4:11-13—And he gave some, apostles; and some, prophets; and some, evangelists; and some, pastors and teachers; For the perfecting of the saints, for the work of the ministry, for the edifying of the body of Christ; Till we all come in the unity of the faith, and of the knowledge of the Son of God, unto a perfect man, unto the measure of the stature of the fulness of Christ:

VI. To discipline its members.

Matt. 18:15-17—Moreover if thy brother shall trespass against thee, go and tell him his fault between thee and him alone; if he shall hear thee, thou hast gained thy brother. But if he will not hear thee, then take with thee one or two more, that in the mouth of two or three witnesses every word may be established. And if he shall neglect to hear them tell it unto the church; and if he neglect to hear the church, let him be unto thee as a heathen man and a publican.

S. F. I Cor. 5:1–5, 9–13.

VII. *To evangelize the world.*

Matt. 28:18–20—And Jesus came and spake unto them saying, All power is given unto me in heaven and in earth. Go ye therefore, and teach all nations baptizing them in the name of the Father and of the Son and of the Holy Ghost. Teaching them to observe all things whatsoever I have commanded you and lo I am with you alway, even unto the end of the world. Amen.

"The purpose for which a church exists is missions. Take out of a church the missionary idea and you have a life without an objective, a barren tree that cumbers the ground, and an empty house over whose door is written 'Ichabod.' Limit the gospel in its scope or power and you cut its heart out. Christ lived and died for all men. The business of the church is to make him known to all. Our Christian religion revolves around two foci: 'Come' and 'Go.' Everyone who accepts the invitation 'Come' must hear immediately the imperative command 'Go.' It is the driving wheel of the machinery of a church or denomination. Stop that wheel and the machinery is motionless and useless. It is the authority for Christian education. Colleges and seminaries were founded to fit men to 'Go.' When they cease to function they ought to be revitalized or buried."—McDANIEL.

D. S. The mission of the church is to glorify God by winning men to Christ, building them up in Christ and sending them out for Christ.

Study Questions on the Doctrine of the Church

1. Give the fourfold usage of the word "church."
2. What is the derivation of the word "church" and what is its twofold significance?
3. Define the Church (1) as an organism; (2) as an organization. Describe the simple organization of the New Testament Church.
4. Define the Kingdom of God and show the Church's relation to it.
5. Give the threefold aspect of the Kingdom of Heaven, and show the Church's relation to it.
6. Give and discuss three types of the church and quote one passage with each.
7. How does prophetic utterance set forth the fact of the church?
8. Discuss the word "ordinance"; name the two ordinances, and discuss the erroneous views concerning them.
9. What threefold significance does the true view of the ordinances embrace?
10. Why is baptism obligatory? Quote Acts 2:41, 42, and name the order which it suggests.
11. What is the purpose of the Lord's Supper?
12. Show why the Lord's Supper is obligatory and quote one passage with each reason.

13. What general answer may be given to the various questions and perplexities which arise concerning the Lord's Supper?
14. Give the sevenfold mission of the church; quote one passage with each of two, and give D. S.

CHAPTER NINE
THE DOCTRINE OF ANGELS
(ANGELOLOGY)

A. Angels (proper).

"The moon is 240,000 miles from our earth. Our next door neighbor in our solar system is the planet Mars. Mars is 37,000,000 miles from man's habitation. Next we reach the planet Saturn at a distance of 750,000,000 miles from us. Saturn's diameter is nine and one-half times larger than our own and this planet is surrounded by immense rings measuring nearly 200,000 miles across. 2,793,000,000 miles from the sun is the planet Neptune. There are other planets still unknown, beyond Neptune, which belong to the outermost regions of our solar system, and beyond are the almost infinite heavens. There, almost 25,000,000,000 miles from our earth every star is a shining sun. Say the astronomers, 'Whatever star we approach, we find it a sun like a blinding furnace. These innumerable centres of light, heat, electricity and gravitational attraction only appear to us as small luminous points on account of the immense spaces which separate us from them. The nearest sun, our nearest star in space, is removed 276,000 times the distance which separates from the sun, i. e., 25,000,000,000 miles from the earth. Traveling at the rate of forty miles an hour it would take us 75,000,000 years to reach it.' But even this inconceivable space dwindles in view of the fact that in a distance of 60,000 billion miles there are other wonderful suns, yes, whole galaxies of planetary systems.

"The Spiral Nebulae, which the powerful telescopes bring within human vision, are not, as once supposed, balls of gaseous matter, but agglomerations of suns, in such a distance and in such numbers that the mind of man cannot even express them. Of all this vastness, Camille Flammarion declares: 'Then I understand that all the stars which have ever been observed in the sky, the millions of luminous points which constitute the Milky Way, the innumerable celestial bodies, suns of every magnitude and of every degree of brightness, solar systems, planets and satellites, which by millions and hundreds of millions succeed each other in the void around us, that whatever human tongues have designated by the name of universe, do not in the infinite represent more than an archipelago of celestial islands and not more than a city in a grand total of population, a town of greater or lesser importance. In this city of limitless empire, in this town of a land without frontiers, our Sun and its system represent a single point, a single house among millions of other habitations. Is our solar system a palace or a hovel in this great city? Probably a hovel. And the earth? The Earth is a room in the solar mansion—a small dwelling, miserably small.' "— GAEBELEIN.

David also tells of the wonder which filled his being as he contemplated these great heavens (Psalm 8:3-4): "When I consider thy heavens, the work of thy fingers, the moon and the stars, which thou hast ordained: What is man, that thou art mindful of him? and the son of man, that thou visitest him?" He further adds in Psalm 19:1, "The heavens declare the glory of God; and the firmament sheweth his handiwork."

In the face of all this, a vital question arises: Is man the only creature of God in this vast space, amidst these millions and millions of flaming worlds, who has a mind to appreciate and contemplate this workmanship of God? Has God no other creatures of intelligence to praise Him for all His works? Are these multi-millions of stars without tenants? The question is an old one. The ancients thought of it. For centuries it has occupied some of the great minds of our race. Astronomers have been asked about other inhabited worlds and often have given an affirmative answer. Many of these answers, however, have only been speculative and conjectural.

At present, therefore, the Word of God is our only reliable source of information. Does the Bible answer our question about other beings in this immense space which we call the heavens? And if there are such beings in existence, who are they, where are they and what are they doing? The Bible is not silent on these questions. It gives us a positive answer. There is another class of beings above man. These beings are the angels of God, the heavenly hosts, the tenants of the heavens, the innumerable company of the unseen servants of God. There are also those of this same class of beings who were once His servants, but who are now in rebellion against His rule.

Angels are subjects of the Divine government, and the important part which they have taken in the history of man renders it proper to make special reference to them and a special study of them. Their existence is everywhere taken for granted in the Scriptures.

"The term 'angel' in its literal import, suggests the idea of office—the office of a messenger, rather than the nature of the messenger. Hence, we read in Luke 7:24: 'And when the messengers of John [in the original Greek 'the angels of John'] were departed.' It seems that when the Bible was written, it was so common for some superior spiritual being to be divinely sent as a messenger to men, that such a being in process of time was called 'angel,' that is 'messenger.' It is easy, too, to see that the order of beings to which the messenger belonged would likewise be called 'angels.' The term 'angel,' being used to designate a spirit bearing a message, would also be employed as descriptive of kindred spirits even though they might not be appointed to bear messages. Thus, the heavenly host are termed 'angels,' though it may be, that comparatively few of their vast numbers are engaged in the delivery of messages."—PENDLETON.

I. Their Existence.

"The mythologies of nearly all the ancient nations speak of such beings. Babylonian mythology pictured them as gods who conveyed messages from gods to men. Roman and Greek mythology had its genii, semi-gods, fauns, nymphs and naiads, who visited the earth. Hesiod, next to Homer, the earliest Greek poet, said: 'Millions of spiritual creatures walked the earth.' Egypt and Eastern nations believed in such superhuman, unseen creatures. The belief is well-nigh universal. Mythologies are the faint and distorted echoes of a common primeval knowledge possessed by the race. If such beings of a higher rank than man did not exist we would not find them in the traditional beliefs of the nations of old.

"From Genesis to Revelation the angels of God are prominently mentioned, one hundred and eight times in the Old Testament and one hundred and sixty-five times in the New Testament. They are seen throughout sacred history. Their activities in heaven and on earth in the past are recorded in both Testaments, also their future manifestations are prophetically revealed."—GAEBELEIN.

1. Established by the teaching of the Old Testament.

Ps. 68:17—The chariots of God are twenty thousand, even thousands of angels: the Lord is among them, as in Sinai, in the holy place.

S. F. Ps. 104:4.

S. A. Dan. 8:15–17.

2. Established by the teaching of the New Testament.

Mark 13:32—But of that day and that hour knoweth no man, no, not the angels which are in heaven, neither the Son, but the Father.

S. F. Matt. 13:41; Matt. 18:10; Matt. 26:53; Mk. 8:38; Lk. 22:43; John 1:51; Eph. 1:21; Col. 1:16; II Thes. 1:7; Heb. 1:13; Heb. 12:22; I Peter 3:22; II Peter 2:11; Jude 9; Rev. 12:7; Rev. 22:8, 9.

The five times in the Old Testament where we read "Sons of God," it refers to these supernatural beings (Gen. 6:2; Gen. 6:4; Job 1:6; Job 2:1; Job 38:7).

"But it must be noted that, while angels are called Sons of God, they are never called the Sons of the Lord. It is in the Hebrew always Benai Elohim (Elohim is God's name as Creator) and never Benai Jehovah. The Benai Jehovah are sinners redeemed and brought into the filial relationship by redemption. The Benai Elohim are unfallen beings, Sons of God by creation. The angels are the Sons of God in the first creation; sinners saved by grace are the Sons of God in the new creation."—GAEBELEIN.

"That the title 'sons of God' is restricted to angels in the Old Testament is the view taken by Josephus, Philo Judaeus, and the authors of 'The Book of Enoch' and 'The Testament of the Twelve Patriarchs'; indeed, it was generally accepted by learned Jews in the early centuries of the Christian era. In regard to the Septuagint, all MSS. render the Hebrew 'sons of God' by 'angels of God' in Job 1:6, and 2:1, and by 'My angels' in Job 38:7— passages in which there was no dogmatic reason for tampering with the text. In Gen. 6:2, 4, the Codex Alexandrinus and three other MSS., exhibit the same rendering, while others have 'sons of God.' Augustine, however, admits that in his time the greater number of copies read 'angels of God' in the latter passage also. It seems, therefore, extremely probable that this was the original reading; and certainly the interpretation which it involves was adopted by the majority of the earlier Christian writers.

"In Luke's genealogy of our Lord, Adam is called a son of God. And so also Christ is said to give to them that receive Him power to become the sons of God. For these are born again of the Spirit of God as to their inner man even in the present life. And at the resurrection redeemed men will be clothed with a spiritual body, a building of God; so that they will be in every respect equal to the angels, being altogether a new creation."— PEMBER.

D. S. The existence of angels is clearly shown by the teaching of both the Old and the New Testaments.

II. Their Characteristics.

1. Created Beings.

Ps. 148:2, 5—Praise ye him, all his angels; praise ye him, all his hosts. Let them praise the name of the Lord: for he commanded, And they were created.

S. F. Neh. 9:6; Col. 1:16 R. V.

Angels are not eternal, as God is, nor self-existent, but created and dependent creatures.

"When were they created? The Bible gives no definite answer to this question. But there is at least one passage from which we can learn by inference that they were created in the beginning, when God created the heavens and the earth. When that beginning was, no scientist will ever discover by research. Perhaps millions of years before man was put here the earth existed in another condition from what it is now. It must have been at the time of that original creation, when God created the class of beings whom we call angels. All was created by Him in the person of His Son, and for Him, including the invisible things, thrones, dominions, principalities and powers (Col. 1:16)."

"In the beautiful words with which Jehovah answered Job out of the whirlwind, we find this hint as to the time when the angels came into being: 'Where wast thou when I laid earth's foundation? . . . When the morning-stars sang together, And all the sons of God shouted for joy?' (Job 38:4–7). That Jehovah here refers to creation is perfectly clear. They were, therefore, in existence when God laid the foundation of the earth, when He first created. And as they beheld His wonders in creation, they shouted for joy."—GAEBELEIN.

2. Spirit Beings.

Heb. 1:13, 14—But to which of the angels said he at any time, Sit on my right hand, until I make thine enemies thy footstool? Are they not all ministering spirits, sent forth to minister for them who shall be heirs of salvation?

S. F. Eph. 6:12 R. V.

Angels in their ordinary form of being are spirits without physical bodies. This does not, however, deny the possibility of their materialization.

3. Personal Beings.

II Sam. 14:20—To fetch about this form of speech hath thy servant Joab done this thing; and my lord is wise, according to the wisdom of an angel of God, to know all things that are in the earth.

S. F. II Tim. 2:26; Rev. 22:8, 9; 12:12.

Personal characteristics are ascribed to angels; they are intelligent, voluntary, active and therefore personal agents.

4. Unmarriageable Beings.

Matt. 22:30—For in the resurrection they neither marry, nor are given in marriage, but are as the angels of God in heaven.

The unfallen angels in heaven neither marry nor are given in marriage. The Scriptures nowhere teach that angels are sexless beings. The inferential teaching of the Scriptures is rather to the opposite, that there is sex in the angelic order, and that they belong to the male sex. This inference is based upon the use of pronouns of the masculine gender in speaking of angels. See Dan. 8:16, 17; Lk. 1:12, 29, 30; Rev. 12:7; 20:1; 22:8, 9. The names of angels are few and limited in the Scriptures but those which are given seem to be masculine. Note the following: Gabriel, Michael, Satan, Abaddon, Apollyon.

The Scriptures do, however, teach that marriage is not God's order or plan for the angels.

5. Deathless Beings.

Lk. 20:35, 36—But they which shall be accounted worthy to obtain that world, and the resurrection from the dead, neither marry, nor are given in marriage: Neither can they die any more: for they are equal unto the angels; and are the children of God, being the children of the resurrection.

Angels are exempt from dissolution: they do not die. The deathlessness of angels and men is derived from God and dependent on His will. Angels are exempt from death because God made them so. They will never die or cease to be, because it is not the Divine Will that they return to their original nothingness, or cease to live their spirit life. It is clear that the equality specially referred to here is the impossibility of dying—"neither can they die any more." For this reason redeemed men in their glorified state are equal to the angels, and, like the angels, are incapable of death.

6. Swift Beings.

Matt. 26:53—Thinkest thou that I cannot now pray to my Father, and He shall presently give me more than twelve legions of angels?

S. F. Dan. 9:21.

To give us some faint idea of the rapidity of their movements, the sacred writers represent them as having wings, and as flying on their errands to execute the commands of the Almighty. These forms of expression need not be understood literally: for wings, and flight, by means of wings, pertain to material beings, and we have seen that angels are spirit beings. Of all creatures coming within the range of our vision, those which have wings and fly exemplify the highest speed. Angelic activity is, therefore, very impressively taught by the figurative language used. There must, however, be a basis and a reason for the use of this figurative language, and they are to be found in the velocity of angelic movement. Here, again, our conceptions fail; for as physical motion alone comes within the circle of our knowledge, we cannot possibly say what is the nature of the movement by which a spirit goes from one place to another. There is transition from locality to locality, but who can explain it? We only know that it must be inexpressibly rapid. The thought to be emphasized in Matt. 26:53 is that so many angels, their supposed residence being in heaven, could instantly appear in defense of their Lord. How these legions of angels could pass with more than telegraphic rapidity from heaven to sad Gethsemane is more than we know. We only know that the possibility of the thing indicates an activity and swiftness truly wonderful.

7. Powerful Beings.

(1) Of superhuman power.

Ps. 103:20—Bless the Lord, ye his angels, that excel in strength, that do his commandments, hearkening unto the voice of his word.

S. F. II Pet. 2:11.

S. A. Isa. 37:36; Matt. 28:2; Rev. 20:1-3.

"The Bible teaches that angels are a class of created beings above man. Man is made a little lower than the angels (Ps. 8:5; Heb. 2:7). This disposes of another conception. Some teach that believers who die, as well as children, become angels. Man can never be an angel, for angels are forever distinct from human beings. Man redeemed is not lifted in redemption to the dignity of an angel, but in Christ man is carried into a higher rank than angels can ever occupy."—GAEBELEIN.

(2) Of delegated power.

II Thes. 1:7, R. V.—And to you that are afflicted rest with us, at the revelation of the Lord Jesus from heaven with the angels of his power in flaming fire.

Angels are possessed of superhuman power, yet it has its fixed limits; they are mighty but not almighty. They are said to "excel in strength." We are not, however, to suppose they possess self-originated strength; they do not. They have the power that God gives them, for power in the highest sense of the word, belongs to Him alone. It has been His pleasure to endow angelic spirits with such power as has often appeared wonderful to men. As further illustrations of this, see II Sam. 24:16; Rev. 18:1, 21.

8. Beings of Superior Intelligence.

II Sam. 14:17, 20—Then thine handmaid said, The word of my lord the king shall now be comfortable: for as an angel of God, so is my lord the king to discern good and bad: therefore the Lord thy God will be with thee. To fetch about this form of speech hath thy servant Joab done this thing: and my lord is wise, according to the wisdom of an angel of God, to know all things that are in the earth.

S. F. Matt. 24:36.

In these passages it is assumed that an angel of God is wise and endowed with superior knowledge. Nor is it strange that the history of God's favored people from the days of Abraham encouraged and confirmed this view. There had been frequent angelic interpositions, the natural effect of which was to create the belief that angels excel in wisdom as well as strength. They were, no doubt, created intelligent spirits, their knowledge beginning with their existence. But we may safely conclude that it has been increasing ever since. Their opportunities of observation, and the many experiences they have had in connection, as we may suppose, with direct revelations from God, must have added greatly to the stock of their original intelligence.

9. Glorious Beings.

Lk. 9:26—For whosoever shall be ashamed of me and of my words, of him shall the Son of man be ashamed, when he shall come in his own glory, and in his Father's and of the holy angels.

Angels are beings of superhuman dignity and glory.

10. Beings of Various Ranks and Orders.

(1) A company, not a race.

Matt. 22:30—For in the resurrection they neither marry, nor are given in marriage, but are as the angels of God in heaven.

S. F. Lk. 20:36.

(2) Constitute an organization.

I Kings 22:19—And he said, Hear thou therefore the word of the Lord: I saw the Lord sitting on his throne, and all the host of heaven standing by him on his right hand and on his left.

S. F. Gen. 32:1; Deut. 4:19; 17:3; Matt. 25:41; 26:53; Eph. 2:2; Rev. 2:13, 16:10.

(3) Occupy different positions.

I Thes. 4:16—For the Lord himself shall descend from heaven with a shout, with the voice of the archangel, and with the trump of God; and the dead in Christ shall rise first.

S. F. Col. 1:16; I Peter 3:22; Jude 9.

"The angels are in no sense a race, but a company or companies, each individual being an original creation. Hence, the grounds of social affinity arising out of our own race relations are entirely wanting in them."—MILEY.

There is however no hindrance to social affinity in relation to angels.

"There is between them a mutual apprehension of all that is pure and good and lofty, and a reciprocal response of loving sympathy. In this there is ample ground for social contact."—MILEY.

Scripture indicates that in the angelic world, this vast kingdom of light and glory, there are different grades and ranks. In Eph. 1:21 and Col. 1:16 we read of principalities, thrones, dominions and powers, which exist in this unseen world. They are in the heavenlies.

We also know there is an Archangel. Christendom speaks of archangels, and follows certain traditional apocryphal views of different archangels; but in Scripture only one archangel is seen; his name is Michael, which means, "Who is like God?" His name occurs three times: In Dan. 12:1, where his special work is mentioned in behalf of the remnant of Israel, he is called the "Great Prince"; in Jude, verse 9, where we hear of his contending with the devil for the body of Moses; and in Rev. 12, where he appears as the victorious leader of the heavenly hosts warring against Satan and his angels. His voice will be heard when the Lord comes for His own (I Thes. 4:17).

Then we find Gabriel in Scripture. Gabriel means, "The Mighty One." Both

Jews and Christians have called him an archangel, but without any Scriptural foundation, for he is never called by that name. He is a very august person. He himself bears witness to his place in glory, for he said to Zechariah, the ministering priest, "I am Gabriel, that stand in the presence of God" (Luke 1:19). From the throne of God he was commissioned (besides announcing the birth of John the Baptist) to bring to earth two of the greatest messages which ever left the courts of heaven. When Daniel prayed his great prayer of humiliation, Gabriel was called upon to carry the answer to the praying prophet of God. So swiftly did he pierce the immeasurable space that it took him but a few minutes to reach Daniel and to interrupt his prayer (Dan. 9:21-23). But the greatest of all the messages any angel ever carried to earth was the message sent through Gabriel to the Virgin of Nazareth, announcing the coming incarnation of the Son of God (Lk. 1:26-38).

The Cherubim and Seraphim are angelic beings of a very high rank and are always seen in connection with the throne of God. The Seraphim appear only in Isaiah's temple vision (Isa. 6). Ezekiel (see Prophecy of Ezekiel) and John (see Revelation), saw the Cherubim as living creatures, erroneously translated, "beasts."

11. Numerous Beings.

Deut. 33:2, R. V.—And he said, Jehovah came from Sinai, and rose from Seir unto them; He shined forth from mount Paran, and he came from the ten thousands of holy ones; at his right hand was a fiery law for them.

S. F. Dan. 7:10; Rev. 5:11.

In Heb. 12:22, the angels are spoken of as an innumerable company, literally myriads. According to Lk. 2:13 multitudes of angels appeared on the night of the nativity of Christ, shouting for joy at the inception of the new creation as they did at the beginning of the old. "How large their number is only He knows whose name is Jehovah-Sabaoth, the Lord of Hosts."—GAEBELEIN.

D. S. Angels are possessed of special and superior faculties and powers which fit them for their superhuman work.

III. Their Moral Nature.

1. All created Holy, as shown by:

(1) The character of God.

Gen. 18:25—That be far from thee to do after this manner, to slay the righteous with the wicked; and that the righteous should be as the wicked, that be far from thee: Shall not the judge of all the earth do right?

(2) Character of God's creative work.

Gen. 1:31—And God saw everything that he had made, and, behold, it was very good. And the evening and the morning were the sixth day.

Comp. with Hab. 1:13.

(3) The record of their sin.

Jude 6—And the angels which kept not their first estate, but left their own habitation, he hath reserved in everlasting chains under darkness unto the judgment of the great day.

S. F. II Peter 2:4.

By the character of God which is absolutely holy, by the character of His creative works with which He, as a Holy Being, was well pleased, and by the record of the angels' fall, the fact is fully established that angels were created holy.

2. Many Obedient—Confirmed in Goodness.

Matt. 25:31—When the Son of man shall come in his glory, and all the holy angels with him, then shall he sit upon the throne of His glory.

S. F. Ps. 99:7, R. V.; Matt. 6:10; 18:10; Mk. 8:38.

S. A. Ps. 103:20; II Cor. 11:14.

The angels, who have maintained their personal integrity and loyalty to God, are confirmed in holiness; their obedience has become habitual and their goodness, a permanent quality of character. They are called "holy angels." Their holiness, like the holiness of God, is not only an exemption from all moral impurity, but an assemblage of all moral excellences. These excellences, infinite in the character of God, are of necessity finite in the character of angels, because they are creatures. Holy angels are objects of God's complacent love. They are just what He would have them to be. They shine in His moral image and reflect His glory. They therefore exclaim, with reverential awe, "Holy, holy, holy is the Lord of hosts; the whole earth is full of his glory" (Isa. 6:3). They have an appreciative sense of the holiness of the Divine Character; they feel for it an intense admiration, for they are holy beings, and out of their holiness arises love for holiness as exemplified in God.

3. Many Disobedient—Confirmed in Wickedness.

II Peter 2:4—For if God spared not the angels that sinned, but cast them down to hell, and delivered them into chains of darkness, to be reserved unto judgment.

S. F. Matt. 6:13 R. V.; Matt. 13:19; I John 5:18; Jude 6; Rev. 12:7, 9.

S. A. Matt. 25:41; John 8:34; Rev. 12:7; 22:11 R. V.

There are numerous angels who have so identified themselves with Satan in his disobedience and sin against God as to be called his angels. The term as used in the Scriptures implies and indicates continuance and confirmation in wickedness.

D. S. Originally angels were holy in nature; some became holy in character through obedience, others sinful in character through disobedience.

IV. Their Employment.

"Our English word 'angel' is from the Greek word 'angelos,' meaning, 'one sent,' 'a messenger.' This Greek word is a translation of the Hebrew word 'Mal'akh,' which also means 'messenger.' 'Holy' angels, then, are God's servants or messengers. They do His will in many ways. They are also servants of God on earth."
—MULLINS.

1. Good Angels.

(1) Engage in the direct worship of God.

Ps. 89:7 R. V.—A God very terrible in the counsel of the holy ones, and to be feared above all them that are round about him?

S. A. Ps. 99:1, 2; Isa. 6:2, 3; Matt. 18:10.

In various parts of the Scriptures the angels are represented as participating in the worship, praise and service of Jehovah. As illustrations of this see Dan. 7:10 where myriads of angels are standing in the presence of God for His worship and ministry; and in the Psalms where the Holy Spirit calls upon them for ascriptions of praise (Ps. 103:20; 148:1, 2). The ministry of good angels is varied; it has to do with the holy work and worship of God, and helpful service to and for men.

(2) Rejoice in God's work.

Job 38:4, 7—Where wast thou when I laid the foundations of the earth? declare, if thou hast understanding. When the morning stars sang together, and all the sons of God shouted for joy?

S. F. Luke 15:10.

(3) Execute God's will.

Ps. 103:20—Bless the Lord, ye his angels, that excel in strength, that do his commandments, harkening unto the voice of his word.

(4) Guide the affairs of nations.

Dan. 10:10-14, 20, 21—And behold, an hand touched me, which set me upon my knees and upon the palms of my hands. And he said unto me, Oh Daniel, a man greatly beloved, understand the words that I speak unto thee, and stand upright: for unto thee am I now sent. And when he had spoken this word unto me, I stood trembling. Then said he unto me, Fear not Daniel; for from the first day that thou didst set thine heart to understand, and to chasten thyself before thy God, thy words were heard, and I am come for thy words. But the prince of the kingdom of Persia withstood me one and twenty days: but, lo, Michael, one of the chief princes, came to help me; and I remained there with the kings of Persia. Now I am come to make thee understand what shall befall thy people in the latter days; for yet the vision is for many days. Then said he, Knowest thou wherefore I come unto thee? and now will I return to fight with the prince of Persia: and when I am gone forth, lo, the prince of Grecia shall come. But I will shew thee that which is noted in the scripture of truth: and there is none that holdeth with me in these things, but Michael your prince.

(5) Guide and guard believers.

Ps. 91:11—For he shall give his angels charge over thee, to keep thee in all thy ways.

S. F. Acts 8:26, compare with Acts 8:29 and Acts 10:13.

S. A. Heb. 1:14, Dan. 6:22.

(6) Minister to God's people.

Heb. 1:14—Are they not all ministering spirits, sent forth to minister for them who shall be heirs of salvation?

S. F. I Kings 19:5-8; Matt. 4:11; Lk. 22:43.

(7) Defend and deliver God's servants.

II Kings 6:17—And Elisha prayed, and said, Lord, I pray thee, open his eyes, that he may see. And the Lord opened the eyes of the young man; and he saw: and, behold, the mountain was full of horses and chariots of fire round about Elisha.

S. F. Gen. 19:11; Dan. 6:22; Acts 5:19, 20; 12:7-11; 27:23, 24.

(8) Guard the elect dead.

Lk. 16:22—And it came to pass, that the beggar died, and was carried by the angels into Abraham's bosom: the rich man also died and was buried.

S. F. Matt. 28:2-5; Lk. 24:22-24; John 20:11, 12; Jude 9.

(9) Will accompany Christ at His return.

Matt. 25 31—When the son of man shall come in his glory, and all the holy angels with him, then shall he sit upon the throne of his glory.

a. Will aid in the separation of the righteous from the wicked.

Matt. 13:49—So shall it be at the end of the world; the angels shall come forth, and sever the wicked from among the just.

S. F. Matt. 25:31, 32.

b. Will aid in the punishment of the wicked.

II Thes. 1:7, 8—And to you who are troubled rest with us, when the Lord Jesus shall be revealed from heaven with his mighty angels, in flaming fire taking vengeance on them that know not God, and that obey not the gospel of our Lord Jesus Christ.

2. Evil Angels.

(1) Oppose God's purposes.

Zech. 3:1—And he shewed me Joshua the high priest standing before the angel of the Lord, and Satan standing at his right hand to resist him.

S. F. Dan. 10:10-14.

(2) Afflict God's people.

II Cor. 12:7—And lest I should be exalted above measure through the abundance of the revelations, there was given to me a thorn in the flesh, the mes-· senger of Satan to buffet me, lest I should be exalted above measure

S. F. Lk. 13:16.

(3) Execute Satan's purposes.

Matt. 25:41—Then shall he say also unto them on the left hand, Depart from me, ye cursed, into everlasting fire, prepared for the devil and his angels.

S. F. Matt. 12:26, 27.

(4) Hinder God's saints and servants.

Eph. 6:11, 12—Put on the whole armour of God, that ye may be able to stand against the wiles of the devil. For we wrestle not against flesh and blood, but against principalities, against powers, against the rulers of the darkness of this world, against spiritual wickedness in high places.

S. F. 1 Thes. 2:18.

Evil angels are employed in the execution of Satan's purposes, which are diametrically opposed to those of God, and have to do with the hindrance and harm of the spiritual life and well-being of God's people.

D. S. Holy angels render assistance to God in His service to men, while evil angels assist Satan in his service against both God and man.

B. Satan.

The subject of Satan takes us into the realm of spirit or the spiritual, and thus out of the realm of matter. This makes impossible investigation or inquiry by the means and methods used in the material sciences.

Dr. George Soltau asks the question, "Is there such a Being as Satan?" and replies as follows: "Multitudes of scholars and intellectual people deny his existence, and that he ever did exist, save in the imagination of ancient and illiterate people. By so doing such are ignorant of his presence and power. How shall the question be decided? Only by reference to, and careful study of Holy Scripture, which must be the final court of appeal in all such questions. Whatever evidence can be found it must be carefully weighed, and speculation must cease before it."

I. His Existence.

John 13:2—And supper being ended, the devil having put into the heart of Judas Iscariot, Simon's son to betray him.

S. F. Matt. 13:19; Acts 5:3; I Peter 5:8; Eph. 6:11, 12; Zech. 3:1–2; Job 1:6; Rev. 12:9.

"In the Old Testament Satan is referred to in seven Books, under different names. In the New Testament he is referred to by all the writers, and will be found mentioned in nineteen Books. Would all these authors, writing during a period of 1600 years, be astray with regard to his existence? Assuredly not."—SOLTAU.

D. S. According to the Scriptures, there is a being called the devil or Satan—a real being who has a real existence.

II. His Original Estate.

It appears to be taught in the Scriptures that the devil was created perfect in his ways, a person of great beauty and brightness, and exalted in position and honor; that as a result of pride because of his own superiority, he sought to direct to himself the worship due to God alone; and that in consequence of his sin he was degraded in person, position, and power, becoming the opponent of God and the enemy of man.

An interesting question concerns Ezek. 28:1–19: Is it a description of the original state of Satan? Two personages are in view: first, the prince of Tyre, verses 1–10. The prince of Tyre seems to refer primarily to Ethbaal II, and verses 1–10 were fulfilled in the siege of Tyre by Nebuchadnezzar, which lasted thirteen years (B.C. 598–585); the king of Tyre in verses 11–19 seem to refer in part to a worthy monarch, and in part to a supernatural personage. It is generally believed by conservative and devout Bible students that the king of Tyre is to be regarded as a representative (type) or incarnation of Satan, and verses 11–19 a description of Satan's original character, position and apostasy.

"While these words were spoken to the King of Tyrus, they were intended, without doubt, for Satan, the instigator of the King of Tyrus' sin. The king of Tyrus has never been in Eden, nor has any other man since Adam was expelled. It will be noted also that the Eden referred to was one that existed prior to Adam's Eden and was noted for its mineral beauty, while Adam's Eden was noted for its vegetable beauty, where God made every tree which was beautiful to the eye and good for fruit to grow. Satan was not only in Eden, but he was there as the anointed Cherub, the one in authority, and that by divine appointment; 'I have set thee so.' Verse 15 could not be applied to any man and be in harmony with other Scripture. For, since the fall, all men have been conceived in sin and shapen in iniquity."—PRATT.

258

1. Created perfect in wisdom and beauty.

Ezek. 28:12—Son of man, take up a lamentation upon the king of Tyrus, and say
   unto him. Thus saith the Lord God; Thou sealest up the sun, full of
   wisdom, and perfect in beauty.

2. Set upon the mountain as covering cherub (as director of worship).

Ezek. 28:14—Thou art the anointed cherub that covereth; and I have set thee so;
   thou wast upon the holy mountain of God; thou hast walked up and
   down in the midst of the stones of fire.

3. Sinless in conduct.

Ezek. 28:15—Thou wast perfect in thy ways from the day that thou wast created,
   till iniquity was found in thee.

4. Heart lifted up with pride and false ambition.

Ezek. 28:17—Thine heart was lifted up because of thy beauty, thou hast corrupted thy wisdom by reason of thy brightness; I will cast thee to the
   ground, I will lay thee before kings, that they may behold thee.

S. F. Isa. 14:12–17.

S. A. I Tim. 3:6.

5. Degraded in moral character and deposed from high position.

Ezek. 28:16—By the multitude of thy merchandise they have filled the midst of
   thee with violence, and thou hast sinned; therefore I will cast thee as
   profane out of the mountain of God and I will destroy thee, O covering
   cherub, from the midst of the stones of fire.

S. F. Isa. 14:12.

S. A. Ezek. 28:17.

The 16th verse (as quoted above) speaks of Satan's sin, and the 17th verse of
the cause of the sin, which was pride, being puffed up because of his beauty. Paul
ascribes Satan's condemnation to this cause (I Tim. 3:6): "Lest he should be
puffed up with pride and fall into the condemnation of the devil."

"Lucifer, son of the morning (Isa. 14:12–14), can be none other than Satan.
This tremendous passage marks the beginning of sin in the universe. When
Lucifer said, 'I Will,' sin began."—SCOFIELD.

Milton describes the arrogant rebellion of Satan in words of poetry clear and
cutting:

> "What time his pride
> Had cast him out of heaven, with all his host,
> Of rebel angels; by whose aid, aspiring
> To get himself in glory above his peers,
> He trusted to have equaled the Most High,
> If he opposed; and, with ambitious aim,
> Against the throne and monarchy of God
> Raised impious war in heaven and battle proud,
> With vain attempt."

Shakespeare takes up this thought by causing one of his characters to say to Cromwell:

> "Cromwell, I charge thee, fling away ambition;
> By that sin fell the angels; how can man then,
> The image of His Maker, hope to win by't?"

D. S. Satan was created as an angel of God, of high rank and order, possessing great beauty and brightness of person, and being superior in power and wisdom, until iniquity was found in him, when he sought to assume the position and prerogatives of God.

III. His Nature.

1. Personality, as shown by:

(1) Personal Pronouns.

Job 1:8—And the Lord said unto Satan, Hast thou considered my servant Job, that there is none like him in the earth, a perfect and an upright man, one that feareth God, and escheweth evil?

S. F. Job 2:1, 2; Zech. 3:2.

Personal pronouns are used of Satan which unmistakably reveal personality.

(2) Personal characteristics.

I Tim. 3:6—Not a novice, lest being lifted up with pride he fall into the condemnation of the devil.

Characteristics and elements of personality are clearly ascribed to Satan.

(3) Personal actions.

John 8:44—Ye are of your father the devil, and the lusts of your father ye will do He was a murderer from the beginning, and abode not in the truth, because there is no truth in him. When he speaketh a lie, he speaketh of his own: for he is a liar, and the father of it.

S. F. I John 3:8; Heb. 2:14.

S. A. I Chron. 21:1; Psa. 109:6; Zech. 3:1.

Actions which can be performed only by a person are accredited to Satan.

2. Character.

(1) His craftiness.

a. His strategies.

II Cor. 2:11—Lest Satan should get an advantage of us; for we are not ignorant of his devices.

The devil has many and subtle devices of which we should not be ignorant.

b. His wiles.

Eph. 6:11, 12 R. V.—Put on the whole armor of God, that ye may be able to stand against the wiles of the devil. For our wrestling is not against flesh and blood, but against the principalities, against the powers, against the world-rulers of this darkness, against the spiritual hosts of wickedness in the heavenly places.

S. A. Eph. 4:14 R. V.

Satan is a great strategist, and uses so many wiles, i. e., makes so many subtle assaults that we need the whole armor of God to stand against him.

(2) His miraculous power.

II Thes. 2:9—Even him, whose coming is after the working of Satan with all power and signs and lying wonders.

S. A. Rev. 13:11, 14; Matt. 24:24.

Satan displays such power and signs and wonders of falsehood as to identify himself as being superhuman.

(3) His deceptiveness.

II Cor. 11:14—And no marvel, for Satan himself is transformed into an angel of light.

S. F. II Thes. 2:9, 10.

Satan's deceptive power is so great as to ensnare all those who receive not the love of the truth.

D. S. In personality and character Satan is the embodiment and expression of evil.

IV. His position—most exalted.

Jude 9, R. V.—Yet Michael the archangel, when contending with the devil he disputed about the body of Moses, durst not bring against him a railing judgment, but said, the Lord rebuke thee.

The position of Satan was so exalted as to make him exempt from criticism and condemnation by his fellow-creatures.

1. Prince of the power of the air.

Eph. 2:2—Wherein in time past ye walked according to the course of this world, according to the prince of the power of the air, the spirit that now worketh in the children of disobedience.

S. A. Matt. 12:26 R. V.; Acts 26:18; Col. 1:13.

Satan is given the title of the Prince of the Power of the air, and is credited with possessing a kingdom, indicating his authority and power in relation to the heavenly realms.

2. Prince of this world.

John 14:30—Hereafter I will not talk much with you; for the prince of this world cometh and hath nothing in me.

S. F. John 12:31; John 16:11.

In the above passages Jesus thrice refers to Satan as the prince of this Satanic system. He also recognized him as such in the temptation in the wilderness (Luke 4:5-7), where Satan offers him all the kingdoms of the world and the glory of them, if he would fall down and worship him. "It has sometimes been held that the claim of possession of the earth was a lie, this being asserted on the ground that Satan is exposed in Scripture as a liar. Such a conclusion is impossible for at least two reasons: It would have been no temptation had he not possessed the kingdoms he offered; and any such false claim would have been immediately branded as a lie by the Son of God."—CHAFER.

How the devil came to be prince of this world it may be impossible for us to say positively, but that he is so admits of no question, if we accept the teaching of Jesus Christ. Any one who will study the ruling principles of commercial life, of political life, of social life, and, above all, of international relations, to such a one it will become perfectly evident that the devil is the one who is the master of the present order of things. If we ever doubted before that there was a devil, and just such a devil as the Bible pictures, we can scarcely doubt it now, when we consider the action of the rulers of the earth in the recent mad World War and the events which have followed it.

3. The god of this age.

II Cor. 4:4—In whom the god of this world (age) hath blinded the minds of them which believe not, lest the light of the glorious gospel of Christ, who is the image of God, should shine unto them.

S. A. II Thes. 2:3, 4.

Satan is the god of this age: the self-constituted object of world-worship.

D. S. Satan, though deposed from the high position to which he was originally appointed, still holds a place of recognized power and authority.

V. His present habitation.

According to the Scriptures Satan does not seem to be restricted to any one place in the universe.

1. He has access to the presence of God.

Job 1:6—Now there was a day when the sons of God came to present themselves before the Lord, and Satan came also among them.

S. F. Rev. 12:10.

The Scriptures teach that for some reason, which is not revealed, Satan is permitted to have access into the presence of God. He appears there in the capacity of "the slanderer," "the accuser of our brethren . . . which accuseth them before our God day and night." Hence the necessity for the intercessory work of Christ.

2. Inhabits the heavenly realms.

Eph. 6:11, 12—Put on the whole armour of God that ye may be able to stand against the wiles of the devil. For we wrestle not against flesh and blood, but against principalities, against powers, against the rulers of the darkness of this world, against spiritual wickedness in high places.

Satan and the principalities, the powers, the world-rulers of this darkness, the spiritual hosts of wickedness have their abiding place in the heavenlies. This Satan-infested realm is to be the future heritage and home of the church. The casting out of Satan will probably be contemporaneous with the rapture (Rev. 12:7–9 with I Thes. 4:16, 17).

3. Active upon the earth.

Job 1:7—And the Lord said unto Satan, Whence comest thou? Then Satan answered the Lord, and said, from going to and fro in the earth, and from walking up and down in it.

S. F. I Peter 5:8.

The earth seems to be the special field of Satan's activity; he goes to and fro in the earth, and walks up and down in it, seeking whom he may devour.

D. S. Satan, though not omnipresent, has access to all places, making the heavenlies his abode, but the earth the especial scene of his activities.

VI. His Work.

1. Originated sin.

(1) In the universe.

Ezek. 28:15—Thou wast perfect in thy ways from the day that thou wast created, till iniquity was found in thee.

Sin was not a creation but an origination. It came into existence by the aid of that which had prior existence, namely, personality and the power of free choice. God created this being not as the Devil, but as a holy angel, who originated sin through disobedience and transformed himself into the wicked Devil which he is today.

(2) In the race.

Gen. 3:1-13—See especially verse 13—And the Lord God said unto the woman, what is this that thou hast done? And the woman said, The serpent beguiled me, and I did eat.

S. F. II Cor. 11:3.

The origin of sin in the human race may be traced, though not directly, yet indirectly to Satan. Adam and Eve were the responsible agents to whom the origin of sin should be directly accredited. Satan, however, is responsible for the external incitement to disobedience and sin, which influenced them.

2. Causes suffering.

Acts 10:38—How God anointed Jesus of Nazareth with the Holy Ghost and with power; who went about doing good, healing all that were oppressed of the devil; for God was with him.

S. F. Luke 13:16.

In the final analysis Satan is the ultimate source of all suffering, because he is the ultimate source of all sin, its primal cause. He is also immediately responsible for many individual cases of sickness and disease; of which examples are furnished us in the New Testament.

3. Causes death.

Heb. 2:14—Forasmuch then as the children are partakers of flesh and blood, he also himself likewise took part of the same; that through death he might destroy him that had the power of death, that is, the devil.

Satan seems to have the right to use the mighty weapon of death, under special permission. It is true, however, that Jesus Christ at the cross wrested this weapon of death out of Satan's hands and with it won from him a glorious victory.

Col. 2:15 (Weymouth): And the hostile princes and rulers He shook off from Himself, and boldly displayed them as His conquests when by the Cross He triumphed over them (I Sam. 17:51).

4. Allures to evil.

I Thes. 3:5—For this cause, when I could no longer forbear, I sent to know your

..ith, lest by some means the tempter have tempted you, and our labour be in vain.

S. F. I Chron. 21:1 R. V.; Matt. 4:1, 3, 4, 6, 8, 9; I Cor. 7:5.

Satan incites men to sin. He so arranges times and controls events and circumstances as to make the greatest possible appeal to the sinful tendencies of man. He is the tempter.

5. Ensnares men.

II Tim. 2:26—And that they may recover themselves out of the snare of the devil, who are taken captive by him at his will.

S. F. I Tim. 3:7.

Satan lays snares for men and takes them captive.

6. Inspires wicked thoughts and purposes.

John 13:2—And supper being ended, the devil having now put into the heart of Judas Iscariot Simon's son, to betray him.

S. F. Acts 5:3.

Satan seems to have the power of mental suggestion, which in the individual becomes auto-suggestion, and which unless halted and hindered by the Word and Spirit of God will also in him be expressed by word and action.

7. Takes possession of men.

John 13:27—And after the sop Satan entered into him. Then said Jesus unto him, What thou doest, do quickly.

S. F. Eph. 4:27.

This form of work is only in connection with rare occasions and special individuals, and only by their consent, or when they leave an opening for him. See James 4:7. The more frequent form of Satan's possession is through the medium of demons.

8. Blinds the minds of men.

II Cor. 4:4 (R. V.)—In whom the god of this age hath blinded the minds of the unbelieving, that the light of the gospel of the glory of Christ, who is the image of God, should not dawn upon them.

S. F. Weymouth translation.

Unbelief of the truth seems to be the same as a special invitation to Satan to bring in the darkness of error and falsehood. He blinds the minds of unbelieving men to prevent them from receiving the light of the gospel.

9. Dissipates the truth.

Mark 4:15—And these are they by the wayside, where the word is sown; but when they have heard, Satan cometh immediately, and taketh away the word that was sown in their hearts.

S. F. Luke 8:12 R. V.; Matt. 13:19.

Satan is the arch-thief or robber of the universe in relation to both God and man.

10. Produces a fruitage of evil doers.

Matt. 13:25, 38–39—But while men slept, his enemy came and sowed tares among the wheat, and went his way. The field is the world; the good seed are the children of the kingdom; and the tares are the children of the wicked one. The enemy that sowed them is the devil; the harvest is the end of the world; and the reapers are the angels.

Satan sows tares in God's field. He mixes his children up with God's, both in the field of the world and in the visible church.

11. Energizes his ministers.

II Cor. 11:13–15—For such are false apostles, deceitful workers, transforming themselves into the apostles of Christ. And no marvel; for Satan himself is transformed into an angel of light. Therefore it is no great thing if his ministers also be transformed as the ministers of righteousness; whose end shall be according to their works.

S. F. Rev. 3:9.

S. A. Eph. 2:2, 3.

Satan has his authorized ministers and churches to carry on his work.

12. Opposes God's servants.

(1) Hinders them.

I Thes. 2:18 R. V.—Because we would fain have come unto you. I Paul, once and again; and Satan hindered us.

(2) Resists them.

Zech. 3:1—And he shewed me Joshua the high priest standing before the angel of the Lord, and Satan standing at his right to resist him.

S. F. Dan. 10:13.

(3) Buffets them.

II Cor. 12:7—And lest I should be exalted above measure through the abundance of the revelations, there was given to me a thorn in the flesh, the messenger of Satan to buffet me, lest I should be exalted above measure.

This opposition, however, results in good to them. It keeps them humble and drives them to prayer (II Cor. 12:8–9). Satan's hindrance of Paul's going to Thessalonica gave to the saints there and to the generations since this precious epistle (Rev. 2:10). Satan buffets, resists and hinders God's servants in every possible way, but God's grace is sufficient to give them the victory.

13. Tests believers.

Luke 22:31—And the Lord said, Simon, Simon, Behold, Satan hath desired to have you, that he may sift you as wheat.

Only good comes of this in the end. Simon came out of Satan's merciless sieve purer wheat than he was before. Satan simply succeeded in removing the chaff. (Rom. 8:28).

14. Accuses believers.

Rev. 12:9, 10—And the great dragon was cast out, that old serpent, called the Devil, and Satan, which deceiveth the whole world; he was cast out into

the earth, and his angels were cast out with him. And I heard a loud'
voice saying in heaven, Now is come salvation, and strength, and the
kingdom of our God, and the power of his Christ: for the accuser of our
brethren is cast down, which accused them before our God day and night.

S. F. Job 1:6–11.

15. Will energize the Antichrist.

II Thes. 2:9–10 R. V.—Even he, whose coming is according to the working of
Satan with all power and signs and lying wonders, and with all deceit
of unrighteousness for them that perish; because they received not the
love of the truth, that they might be saved.

S. F. Rev. 12:9, 17; Rev. 13:1–2, 7.

Satan will give power to the lawless One to utterly deceive the perishing—them
who receive not the love of the truth: and to make war against the people of God.

D. S. The ministry of Satan is multifold, including in its scope the opposition
of God and the frustration of His purposes, as well as the oppression, affliction
and temptation of men.

VII. His Destiny.

1. To be perpetually cursed.

Gen. 3:14, 15—And the Lord God said unto the serpent, Because thou hast done
this, thou art cursed above all cattle, and above every beast of the field,
upon thy belly shalt thou go, and dust shalt thou eat all the days of thy
life. And I will put enmity between thee and the woman, and between
thy seed and her seed; it shall bruise thy head, and thou shalt bruise his
heel.

S. A. Isa. 65:25.

2. To be treated as a conquered enemy.

Col. 2:15 R. V.—Having despoiled the principalities and the powers he made a
show of them openly, triumphing over them in it.

S. F. John 12:31; John 16:8–11; I John 3:8, R. V.; I John 5:18, W. T.

S. A. Heb. 2:14.

3. To be cast out of the heavenlies.

Rev. 12:9—And the great dragon was cast out, that old serpent, called the Devil,
and Satan, which deceiveth the whole world; he was cast out into the
earth, and his angels were cast out with him.

4. To be confined in the abyss for a thousand years.

Rev. 20:1–3—And I saw an angel come down from heaven having the key of the
bottomless pit and a great chain in his hand. And he laid hold on the
dragon, that old serpent, which is the Devil and Satan, and bound him a
thousand years. And cast him into the bottomless pit, and shut him up,
and set a seal upon him, that he should deceive the nations no more, till
the thousand years should be fulfilled; and after that he must be loosed
a little season.

266

5. To be loosed a little season after the Millennium.

Rev. 20:3—Last clause, 7-9—And after that he must be loosed a little season. And when the thousand years are expired, Satan shall be loosed out of his prison. And shall go out to deceive the nations which are in the four quarters of the earth, Gog and Magog, to gather them together to battle; the number of whom is as the sand of the sea, And they went up on the breadth of the earth and compassed the camp of the saints about, and the beloved city; and fire came down from God out of heaven and devoured them.

6. To be cast into the lake of fire.

Rev. 20:10—And the devil that deceived them was cast into the lake of fire and brimstone, where the beast and the false prophet are, and shall be tormented day and night for ever and ever.

The career of Satan since his rebellion has been downward, ever downward. The point of his descent began with the point of his attempted ascent. When he said "I Will Ascend," then he began to descend. When he began to exalt himself God began to abase him. That abasement will continue until he has been stripped of the last vestige of authority and power, and cast in abject impotence as the arch-criminal of the universe into the eternal burnings.

> "Him the almighty Power
> Hurled headlong flaming from the ethereal sky,
> With hideous ruin and combustion, down
> To bottomless perdition: there to dwell
> In Adamantine chains and penal fire,
> Who durst defy the Omnipotent to arms."
> —MILTON.

D. S. Satan is under a perpetual curse; his conquest was secured at the cross; he is destined to be cast out of the heavenlies, confined in the abyss and finally consigned to the lake of fire.

VIII. Believer's course in relation to him.

1. Redemption rights to be claimed.

Heb. 2:14, R. V.—Since then the children are sharers in flesh and blood, he also himself in like manner partook of the same; that through death he might bring to nought him that had the power of death, that is the devil.

S. F. Col. 2:15 R. V.; Rev. 12:11 R. V.; I John 3:8 R. V.; Eph. 6:16 R. V.

The death of Jesus Christ includes in its provision not only substitution for the believer's penalty for sin, but also representation for the believer's nature of sin (Rom. 8:3-4, Gal. 2:20). He was crucified with Christ. The believer's attitude therefore is to be a death-attitude toward sin and everything sinful. He is to take the attitude of one who has been put to death to a life of sin, and has been raised from the dead to a life of righteousness. Such an attitude makes the believer invulnerable to the attacks of Satan so long as it is maintained.

2. Full equipment to be appropriated.

Eph. 6:11-18 R. V. See especially verse 11—Put on the whole armor of God, that ye may be able to stand against the wiles of the devil.

267

A complete panoply has been provided for the believer's equipment. No part should be omitted, no aspect of life left unguarded, if we are to be able to stand against the wiles of the devil.

3. Strict self-control to be maintained.

Eph. 4:27—Neither give place to the devil.

Comp. with

Gal. 5:22-23—But the fruit of the Spirit is love, joy, peace, longsuffering, gentleness, goodness, faith, meekness, temperance; against such there is no law.

No access into the life should be afforded Satan through evil passion or practice. To guard against this, self is to be kept under the control, not of self, but of Christ through the Holy Spirit. It is not that kind of self-control which is expressed by the set jaw or tense muscle but in a will, fully yielded to God. It is spiritual self-control.

4. Unceasing vigilance to be exercised.

1 Peter 5:8—Be sober, be vigilant, because your adversary the devil, as a roaring lion, walketh about, seeking whom he may devour.

S. A. II Cor. 2:11; I John 5:18.

The fact of Satan's existence, activity, power, and malignancy should make us circumspect and watchful.

5. Trustful resistance to be made.

James 4:7—Submit yourselves therefore to God. Resist the devil and he will flee from you.

S. F. I John 2:14; I Pet. 5:8, 9; I John 5:18, 19.

We are potentially and provisionally made free from Satan's power (I John 5:18, Weymouth: Col. 1:13; John 10:28–29). By meeting conditions we may always be victorious over him. See Rev. 12:11.

D. S. The believer is to take an attitude of confidence toward his adversary, the devil, relying on God's provision and power through Christ for victory over him.

C. Demons.

The meaning of the term "demons" must of necessity come first in our study of the subject.

According to classical usage, it refers to gods and demi-gods, or tutelary deities. Homer called them gods, but we must remember that Homer's gods are merely supernatural men. It was sometimes used of a sort of intermediate and inferior divinity. "The deity," says Plato, "has no intercourse with man; but all the intercourse and conversation between gods and men is carried on by the mediation of demons."

"If we inquire whence these demons, we shall be told that they are the spirits of men of the golden age acting as tutelary deities—canonized heroes, precisely similar both in their origin and functions to the Romish saints."—PEMBER.

When we come to the Scriptures, there is uncertainty on the part of some people as to whether demons are to be classed with evil angels or not, but that there is positive teaching concerning each, there can be no doubt.

Instead of the word "devils" of our English Bibles, the word "demons" should be substituted. This has been done in the American Standard Revised Version. "Devil" is the translation of the Greek "diabolos," a noun used in the singular number and applied to Satan. "Demon" is the translation of the Greek "daimon" or "daimonion" or plural "daimonia."

I. Their Existence.

1. Recognized by Jesus.

Matt. 12:27-28, R. V.—And if I by Beelzebub cast out demons, by whom do your sons cast them out, therefore shall they be your judges. But if I by the Spirit of God cast out demons, then is the kingdom of God come unto you.

S. F. Matt. 8:28-32, R. V.

S. A. Matt. 10:8, R. V.; Mark 16:17, R. V.

Jesus Christ recognized the existence of demons by speaking of them and to them.

2. Recognized by the seventy.

Luke 10:17, R. V.—And the seventy returned with joy, saying, Lord, even the demons are subject unto us in thy name.

The seventy whom Jesus appointed and sent out two by two before His face had to cope with demons, and returned with the report that the demons were subject unto them through the name of Christ.

3. Recognized by the Apostles.

(1) Paul.

I Cor. 10:20-21, R. V.—But I say, that the things which the Gentiles sacrifice, they sacrifice to demons, and not to God; and I would not that ye should have communion with demons. Ye cannot drink the cup of the Lord, and the cup of demons; ye cannot partake of the table of the Lord and of the table of demons.

S. F. I Tim. 4:1, R. V.

S. A. Acts 16:14-18, R. V.

The apostle Paul recognized the reality of demons in his day and gave warnings against them.

(2) James.

James 2:19, R. V.—Thou believest that God is one; thou doest well, the demons also believe and shudder.

James recognized the existence of demons and accredited them with shudder.ng because of their belief in God.

D. S. The existence of demons is clearly established by the combined testimony of Christ and His disciples.

II. Their Nature.

1. Essential nature.

(1) Personal intelligences.

Matt. 8:29, 31, R. V.—And behold, they cried out, saying What have we to do with thee, thou Son of God? art thou come hither to torment us before the time? And the demons besought him, saying, If thou cast us out, send us away into the herd of swine.

S. F. Luke 4:35, 41, R. V.; James 2:19, R. V.; Mark 1:23–24, R. V.; Acts 19:13, 15, R. V.

Personal characteristics and actions are ascribed to demons which show that they are possessed of personality and also of intelligence.

(2) Spirit-beings.

Luke 9:38, 39, 42, R. V.—And behold, a man from the multitude cried, saying. Teacher, I beseech thee to look upon my son; for he is mine only child; and behold, a spirit taketh him, and he suddenly crieth out; and it teareth him that he foameth, and it hardly departeth from him, bruising him sorely. And as he was yet a coming, the demon dashed him down, and tear him grievously. But Jesus rebuked the unclean spirit, and healed the boy, and gave him back to his father.

S. F. Mark 5:2, 7–9, 12, 13, 15.

Demons are spirit-beings; they are regarded as being identical with unclean spirits in the New Testament.

(3) Apparently disembodied spirits.

Matt. 12:43–44, R. V.—But the unclean spirit when he is gone out of the man, passeth through waterless places, seeking rest, and findeth it not. Then he saith, I will return into my house, whence I came out; and when he is come, he findeth it empty, swept, and garnished.

S. F. Mark 5:10–13.

The origin of demons is not revealed in the Scriptures. But it has been conjectured that they are disembodied spirits, perhaps of a pre-Adamic race or order of beings; or it may be, of the Adamic race, as some think. If they are disembodied spirits, this would explain the fact that they seek embodiment without which apparently they are unable to work their full measure of evil. May not these demons be the spirits of those who trod this earth in the flesh before the ruin described in the second verse of Genesis, and who, at the time of that great destruction, were disembodied by God, and left still under the power, and ultimately to share the fate of the leader in whose sin they acquiesced? Certainly one oft recorded fact seems to confirm such a theory: for we read that the demons are continually seizing upon the bodies of men, and endeavoring to use them as their own. And may not this propensity indicate a wearisome lack of ease, a wandering unrest, arising from a sense of incompleteness; a longing to escape the intolerable condition of being unclothed; for which they were not created—so intense that, if they can satisfy its craving in no other way, they will even enter into the filthy bodies of swine.

We find no such propensity on the part of Satan and his angels. They doubtless, still retain their ethereal bodies, for otherwise how could they carry on their conflict with the angels of God? They would be likely to regard with high disdain the gross and unwieldy tabernacles of men. Angels may, indeed, possibly enter human frames; not, however, from inclination, but only because such a course is absolutely necessary for the furtherance of some great conspiracy of evil. That the angels are not mere disembodied spirits seems clear from our Lord's words in Luke 20:34–36: "And Jesus said unto them, The sons of this world (age) marry, and are given in marriage; but they that are accounted worthy to attain to that world (age) and the resurrection from (Greek 'ek,' 'out- of') the dead, neither marry nor are given in marriage; neither can they die any more; for they are equal unto the angels; and are sons of God, being sons of the resurrection."

This would seem to imply that the angels are clothed with spiritual bodies, such as are promised to us. It may then, perhaps, be understood that while angels are spirits, having spirit or spiritual bodies, that all spirits are not angels. This distinction seems to have been made by the Jews according to Acts 23:9. "We find no evil in this man; but if a spirit or an angel hath spoken to him, let us not fight against God." This statement was made by the Pharisees concerning Paul at the time of his arrest in Jerusalem. In the preceding verse we are told of their opponents, the Sadducees, that they denied the existence of angels and spirits.

Demons are, therefore, an order of spirit-beings apparently distinct and separate from angels, and which, from the intimations of certain passages, seem to be in a disembodied state, having existed in some previous period and place in bodily form.

(4) Many in number.

Mark 5:9, R. V.—And he asked him, What is thy name? And he saith unto him, My name is Legion for we are many.

"A legion, in the Roman army, amounted in its full complement, to six thousand; but here the word is used as such words with us, and even this one, for an indefinitely large number—large enough however to rush, as soon as permission was given, into two thousand swine and destroy them." —JAMIESON, FAUSSETT, BROWN.

See further Luke 8:30, R. V.

See also Matt. 12:26–27, R. V.

Demons are so numerous as to make Satan practically ubiquitous or everywhere present through their representation.

2. Moral Nature.

(1) They are vicious and malicious—degenerate in character.

Matt. 8:28, R. V.—And when he was come to the other side into the country of the Gadarenes, there met him two possessed with demons, coming forth out of the tombs, exceeding fierce, so that no man could pass by that way.

S. F. Luke 9:39, R. V.

S. A. Luke 4:33, 36, R. V.

(2) Vile and malignant—debased in conduct.

Luke 9:39, R. V.—And behold, a spirit taketh him, and he suddenly crieth out; and it teareth him that he foameth, and it hardly departeth from him, bruising him sorely.

S. F. Matt. 15:22, R. V.

(3) Servile and obsequious—degraded in service—the service of Satan.

Matt. 12:24–27, R. V.—(See context)—But when the Pharisees heard it, they said, This man doth not cast out demons, but by Beelzebub the prince of the demons. And knowing their thoughts he said unto them, Every kingdom divided against itself shall not stand; and if Satan casteth out Satan he is divided against himself; how then shall his kingdom stand? And if I by Beelzebub cast out demons by whom do your sons cast them out? therefore shall they be your judges.

Demons are beings of a low moral order, degenerate in condition and ignoble in action, subject to Satan. They are represented in Scripture as belonging to his kingdom, and in direct and acknowledged opposition to the kingdom of our Lord.

D. S. Essentially demons are personal spirits, thought to be disembodied, morally base and vile.

III. Their Employment.

1. Taking possession of the bodies of human beings and beasts.

Mark 5:8, 11–13, R. V.—For he said unto him, Come forth, thou unclean spirit, out of the man. Now there was there on the mountain side a great herd of swine feeding. And they besought him, saying, Send us into the swine, that we may enter into them. And he gave them leave. And the unclean spirits came out, and entered into the swine; and the herd rushed down the steep into the sea, in number about two thousand, and they were drowned in the sea.

S. F. Matt. 4:24, R. V.; Matt. 8:16, 28, 33, R. V.; Acts 8:7, R. V.

Demons, when permitted, are capable of entering into physical bodies and bringing them under their evil control.

2. Bringing physical and mental affliction upon men.

Matt. 12:22, R. V.—Then was brought unto him one possessed with a demon, blind and dumb; and he healed him, insomuch that the dumb man spake and saw.

Mark 5:4–5, R. V.—Because that he had been often bound with fetters and chains, and the chains had been rent asunder by him, and the fetters broken in pieces; and no man had strength to tame him. And always, night and day, in the tombs and in the mountains, he was crying out, and cutting himself with stones.

S. F. Matt. 9:32–33, R. V.; Luke 9:37–42, R. V.

3. Producing moral impurity.

Mark 5:2, R. V.—And when he was come out of the ship, immediately there met him out of the tombs a man with an unclean spirit.

S. F. Matt. 10:1, R. V.; Eph. 2:2, R. V.

. A. II Peter 2:10–12, R. V.

Dr. Nevius in his great work on "Demon Possession and Allied Themes" suggests that, as a result of his years of experience in China and his study of the Scriptures, the conviction has come to him that there are five aspects or stages in the relations of demons to men.

First: Temptation in the form of spiritual suggestion. This mysterious influence from an unseen world, to which believers and unbelievers are constantly exposed, is referred to very frequently in the Bible, especially in the New Testament (Eph. 6:11, 12; I John 4:1).

Second: Obsession, which some regard as the first stage of demon-possession. This is demon control, the result of voluntarily and habitually yielding to temptation, or to sinful tendencies (Eph. 4:17-19). In this stage cases are often unpronounced in their character, leaving it difficult to determine whether they are to be classed with demon-possession, idiocy, lunacy, or epilepsy. In obsession, although fearfully under Satanic influence, they are perfectly free, follow the direction of their own wills, and retain their own personality.

Third: Crisis, or transition, the stage marked by a struggle for possession, in which the unwilling subject withstands and sometimes successfully resists (Matt. 15:22-28, R. V.; James 4:7; Eph. 4:26, 27).

Fourth: Possession, which may be designated, with regard to the subject as that of subjection and subserviency, and with regard to the demon, as that of training and development. The condition of the subject is most of the time healthy and normal, except in the paroxysm, which occurs in passing from the normal to the abnormal state. One chief characteristic of this stage is the addition of a new personality. To persons of this class alone is the term "possession" properly applied (Mark 9:17-27, R. V.; Mark 5:2-13, R. V.).

Fifth: Demoniac capability, in which the subject has developed capacities for use, and is willing to be used. He is the trained, accustomed, voluntary slave of the demon—in modern English phrase a "developed medium."

D. S. Demons in harmony with their nature and character are continually engaged in the work of subjugating men to the service of Satan and spreading both disease and defilement.

Study Questions on the Doctrine of Angels

1. Quote one passage proving the fact of the existence of angels as shown by the Old and New Testaments.
2. Distinguish between the title "sons of God" as applied to angels and "sons of the Lord" as applied to redeemed sinners.
3. Give nine characteristics of angels quoting one passage. Give D. S.
4. By what three things is it implied that angels were created holy?
5. Give the two different courses of action chosen by the angels, and quote one passage with each (See 2 and 3 under III).
6. Give D. S. showing the two contrastive results which have taken place in the experience and character of the good and the evil angels.
7. Give the nine-fold employment of good angels, and quote one passage.
8. Give the four-fold employment of fallen angels, and quote one passage. Give D. S.
9. What is the only source of reliable information concerning Satan?
10. Quote one passage under the Existence of Satan; give proofs from Scriptural reference to him and D. S.

11. Give gist of notes on Ezek. 28.
12. Give the five-fold description of Satan's original estate, with D. S.
13. Quote three passages of Scripture corroborating three proofs of the personality of Satan.
14. Describe in detail the character of Satan; quote one passage with one of them and give D. S.
15. Discuss the three titles of Satan which show his position as exalted, giving D. S.
16. Give the three-fold present habitation of Satan, with D. S.
17. Describe in detail the work of Satan and give D. S.
18. Give the six-fold description of the destiny of Satan, with D. S.
19. Give the five-fold course of the believer in relation to Satan, with D. S.
20. Discuss the meaning of the word "demons" and its use in the versions of our Scriptures.
21. Name the witnesses to the existence of Demons; quote one passage with each.
22. Give the four-fold description of the Essential nature of Demons.
23. Discuss from note under third point, the origin of demons.
24. Describe the moral nature of demons.
25. Give the three-fold Employment of demons.
26. Discuss Dr. Nevius' article on the five-fold relation of demons to men, and give D. S.

CHAPTER TEN

THE DOCTRINE OF LAST THINGS

(ESCHATOLOGY)

A. Second Coming of Christ.

This subject, which was so dear to the heart of the early Church and which was so prominent in Apostolic teaching and preaching, has in these days of modern thought and theology been relegated very much to the background. The teaching regarding the Second Coming of Christ has been in the history of the Church very much like the pendulum of a clock, swinging from one extreme to another. In the days when the Apostle Paul wrote his first and second epistles to the church at Thessalonica, the pendulum of this teaching was at one of these extremes, or tending that way. Some seemed to have decided that Christ's coming was so near that the only proper thing for them to do was to give up all work for their subsistence and wait for the sounding of the trumpet announcing the Lord's return; but Paul wrote the second epistle to regulate this pendulum of thought and direct their religious fervor into the proper channels.

After the first few centuries the pendulum began to swing back to the other extreme, and it seems that the religious world almost lost sight of this blessed hope of the Church. This was true during that period which is remembered as the dark ages, when popery and priestcraft reigned and even for some time after the Reformation. Then the teaching of the Second Coming began to be revived, the midnight cry was made amid the darkness of superstition and false teaching and the Church began to examine and trim her lamps, and prepare to meet the Bridegroom.

Then slowly the pendulum began to swing back to the old Thessalonian extreme of setting a definite time for the Lord's coming. This was true at least in some parts of the world. A sect arose, about 1840, known as the Millerites, who set a certain day upon which the Lord was to come. They made their robes and went out at the appointed time to wait for His coming, but they were doomed to disappointment.

The happy medium is to be found between these two extremes, and is to be secured through a careful study and unbiased interpretation of the Scriptures.

There are those who reject the doctrine of the Second Coming or refuse to teach or preach it because of its past association with extremism and fanaticism. These, however, have been associated with practically every doctrine of the Christian faith: Tritheism with the doctrine of the Trinity, Unitarianism with the Unity of God, Antinomianism with Justification, Perfectionism with Sanctification, and others which might be mentioned. The plain duty of the Bible teacher or theologian is to take these doctrines from the muck and mire into which they have been degraded and exalt them to the place and perspective given in the Scriptures.

I. The fact of it established by:

1. The testimony of the prophets.

Zech. 14:3–5—Then shall the Lord go forth and fight against those nations, as when he fought in the day of battle. And his feet shall stand in that day upon the mount of Olives, which is before Jerusalem on the east, and the mount of Olives, shall cleave in the midst thereof toward the east and toward the west, and there shall be a very great valley; and half of the mountain shall remove toward the north, and half of it toward the south. And ye shall flee to the valley of the mountains; for the valley of the mountains shall reach unto Azal; yea, ye shall flee, like as ye fled from before the earthquake in the days of Uzziah king of Judah; and the Lord my God shall come, and all the saints with thee.

Mal. 3:1—Behold, I will send my messenger, and he shall prepare the way before me; and the Lord, whom ye seek, shall suddenly come to his temple, even the messenger of the covenant, whom ye delight in; behold, he shall come, saith the Lord of Hosts,

Ezek. 21:26, 27—Thus saith the Lord God; Remove the diadem, and take off the crown; this shall not be the same; exalt him that is low, and abase him that is high, I will overturn, overturn, overturn it; and it shall be no more, until he come whose right it is; and I will give it him.

S. A. Jude 14, Isa. 11:1–9.

If the importance of a doctrine is to be judged by the place assigned to it and the emphasis given to it in the Scriptures, then certainly the Second Advent of Christ is one of the most important doctrines of the Christian faith. This prominence is especially noticeable in the Old Testament prophecy. In the Old Testament there are by far a greater number of predictions concerning the Second Coming than the first.

2. The testimony of John the Baptist.

Luke 3:3–6—See especially verses 4, 5—As it is written in the book of the words of Esaias the prophet, saying, the voice of one crying in the wilderness, Prepare ye the way of the Lord, make his paths straight. Every valley shall be filled, and every mountain and hill shall be brought low; and the crooked shall be made straight, and the rough ways shall be made smooth.

"The moment you enter the New Testament John the Baptist is heard speaking not of the First Advent but of the Second."—HALDEMAN.

3. The testimony of Christ.

John 14:2, 3—In my Father's house are many mansions; if it were not so, I would have told you. I go to prepare a place for you. And if I go and prepare a place for you, I will come again, and receive you unto myself: that where I am there ye may be also.

"When the starlight of Bethlehem, the mystery of the manger, and the apprenticeship of thirty years are passed and the Christ sets forth upon His mission His lips are full, not of the First Advent but of the Second." —HALDEMAN. He emphasized it in the Transfiguration, by spoken parable, and direct prophecy, together with His loving promise to His sorrowing disciples.

4. The testimony of the angels.

Acts 1:11—Which also said, Ye men of Galilee, why stand ye gazing up into heaven? This same Jesus, which is taken up from you into heaven, shall so come in like manner as ye have seen him go into heaven.

S. A. Rev. 1:1, 2; Luke 1:31, 32.

The angels who bore such faithful testimony to Christ's first advent, also bear witness to His second advent. If it be objected that the two men in white apparel may not have been angels, it may be replied that the entire book of Revelation which is concerned with the Second Coming of Christ and kindred events consists of Angelic testimony (Rev. 1:1, 2).

5. The testimony of the Apostles.

1) Matthew.

Matt. 24:37, 42, 44—But as the days of Noe were, so shall also the coming of the Son of man be. Watch therefore; for ye know not what hour your Lord doth come. Therefore be ye also ready; for in such an hour as ye think not the Son of man cometh.

(2) Mark.

Mark 13:26—And then shall they see the Son of man coming in the clouds with great power and glory.

(3) Luke.

Luke 21:27—And then shall they see the Son of man coming in a cloud with power and great glory.

(4) John.

I John 3:1-3—Behold what manner of love the Father hath bestowed upon us that we should be called the sons of God; therefore the world knoweth us not, because it knew him not. Beloved, now are we the sons of God, and it doth not yet appear what we shall be; but we know that, when he shall appear, we shall be like him; for we shall see him as he is. And every man that hath this hope in him purifieth himself, even as he is pure.

(5) James.

James 5:7—Be patient therefore, brethren, unto the coming of the Lord. Behold, the husbandman waiteth for the precious fruit of the earth, and hath long patience for it until he receive the early and latter rain.

(6) Peter.

I Peter 1:7, 13—That the trial of your faith, being much more precious than of gold that perisheth, though it be tried with fire, might be found unto praise and honour and glory at the appearing of Jesus Christ: Wherefore gird up the loins of your mind, be sober, and hope to the end for the grace that is to be brought unto you at the revelation of Jesus Christ.

(7) Paul.

I Thes. 4:13-18—But I would not have you to be ignorant, brethren, concerning them which are asleep that ye sorrow not, even as others which have no hope. For if we believe that Jesus died and rose again, even so them also which sleep in Jesus will God bring with him. For this we say unto you by the word of the Lord, that we which are alive and remain unto the coming of the Lord shall not prevent them which are asleep. For the Lord himself shall descend from heaven with a shout, with the voice of the archangel, and with the trump of God; and the dead in Christ shall rise first; Then we which are alive and remain shall be caught up together with them in the clouds to meet the Lord in the air and so shall we ever be with the Lord. Wherefore comfort one another with these words.

The Apostles magnified the Return of our Lord in their preaching and teaching.

D. S. The fact of the second coming of Christ is clearly established by the combined testimony of the prophets, John the Baptist, angels, the apostles, and Christ, Himself.

II. The Character of It.

1. Negatively considered.

(1) Not providential.

a. As death.

Death is the penalty of sin, but the Lord's coming delivers from sin and penalty (Rom. 6:23 and I Thes. 4:17). Thoughts and experiences of the one are painful; of the other, delightful (John 11:31 and Tit. 2:13). In the one event we look downward and weep; in the other, upward and rejoice (John 11:35 and Phil. 2:16). In one (death), the body is sown in corruption and dishonor; in the other, it is raised in incorruption and glory (I Cor. 15:42, 43 and I Thes. 4:16, 17). In one event we are unclothed; in the other, clothed upon (II Cor. 5:4). In the one, there is a sad separation of friends; in the other, a glad reunion (Ezek. 24:16 and I Thes. 4:13, 14). We enter into rest at death, but we are crowned at the Lord's coming (I Thes. 4:13 and Rev. 14:13).

Death comes as our great enemy; Christ as our great friend (I Cor. 15:26 and Prov. 14:27). Death is the king of terrors; Christ is the King of Glory (Job 18:14 and Psalm 24:7). Satan has the power of death; Christ is the Prince of life (Heb. 2:14 and Acts 3:15). In one event we depart to be with Christ; in the other He comes to us (Phil. 1:23 and John 14:3). Jesus makes a distinction between His coming and the believer's death. Christ and the apostles never

278

commanded the saints to watch for death, but repeatedly for the Lord's coming (I Cor. 15:51, 52).

"John 21:22 shows how utterly impossible it is to make Christ's Coming refer to death. (Jesus said unto him if I will that he tarry till I come, what is that to thee? follow thou me.) 'If I will that he tarry' evidently means 'If I will that he remain alive.' Now put Christ's Coming at the believer's death into these words and you get this nonsense: 'If I will that he remain alive until he dies what is that to thee?' "—TORREY.

b. As material progress.

This interpretation views the Second Coming of Christ as a process, contemporaneous with the advance of civilization, scientific invention and discovery. Every advance step in scientific investigation and invention according to this theory is the realization of Christ's return. The whole teaching of the Scripture makes impossible this interpretation.

c. As a historic event.

For example, it is not to be identified with the destruction of Jerusalem in A. D. 70, as some interpret. God's judgment upon Jerusalem is not the event referred to in the majority of the passages in which Christ's coming is mentioned. On the occasion of the destruction of Jerusalem those who slept in Jesus were not raised; living believers were not caught up to meet the Lord in the air, nor were their bodies transformed. Years after this occurred, we find John still looking forward to the Lord's Coming, Rev. 22:20; John 21:22-23. According to Rev. 20:5, 6 and other New Testament passages a reign of righteousness and peace is to follow immediately the return of Christ. This, however, did not occur at, or after the destruction of Jerusalem. The predicted events that are to accompany the return of Christ which were absent then have also been conspicuously absent from all other historic events since.

(2) Not spiritual.

a. As the Holy Spirit of Pentecost.

This was in a very real and important sense a coming of Christ (John 14:15-18, 21-23). But this coming of Christ is not that referred to in the passages cited above under the Fact of His Second Coming. This is seen by the following:

A large percentage of the promises concerning the Second Coming of Christ were made after the coming of the Holy Spirit at Pentecost, and pointed to an Advent still in the future.

Jesus does not receive the believer unto Himself to be with Him at the coming of the Holy Spirit. He rather, comes to be with believers (John 14:18, 21-23). At His Coming again, as mentioned in John 14:3, I Thes. 4:16, 17, He takes us to be with Him.

He does not at His Coming in the Spirit fashion anew the body of our humiliation (Phil. 3:20, 21).

There is no shout of the archangel or trump of God, no resurrection, no rapture in the clouds at this coming of Christ in the Spirit.

It was to be the work of the Holy Spirit when He came: to convict men of sin because they believe not on Christ as their Saviour,—but Jesus when He comes will destroy or banish sin; to convict men of their need of righteousness, —but Jesus when He comes will make righteousness universal; to convict men of judgment,—but Jesus at His coming will execute that judgment; to reveal Jesus as Saviour, during this age of Grace,—but Jesus at His coming will conclude the age of Grace. The Holy Spirit when He comes does not destroy death; but Jesus will abolish death at His coming. The Holy Spirit works unseen; but the coming of our Lord will be a visible event. The sign of the coming of the Holy Spirit was cloven tongues like as of fire; but the sign of the coming of Christ will be His own visible glory in the heavens.

The Coming of Christ in the Holy Spirit can in scarcely any particular be identified with the Second Coming of Christ as set forth in Old and New Testament promise and prophecy.

b. As in the conversion of the sinner.

None of the accompanying events of the Lord's return, as promised are then fulfilled. Christ does not take the converted sinner to be with Himself at this time, but rather comes to abide with and in the sinner thus converted.

c. As in the spread of Christianity.

The spread of Christianity is to be gradual without any of the phenomenal manifestations which are to accompany the return of our Lord, which is to be sudden and cataclysmic.

"New theology teaches that Jesus Christ will never come back to this earth in visible, bodily form. They say that the second coming is unseen, spiritual and continuous, that Christ is coming as fast as He can get into this world, that He came on Pentecost in the presence of the Holy Spirit, that He came at the destruction of Jerusalem, in judgment upon that city, and that He comes at death. The new theology declares that the apostles understood that Jesus Christ would come back in a visible manner, and in their own day, but in this, they say, the apostles were mistaken. Dr. Clark says, on page 399, 'Christian Theology,' in referring to the words of our Lord used in setting forth His coming, 'this language is borrowed directly from the prophets, ... who applied it to events on the earth, in which, of course, it could not be literally fulfilled.' The argument is, because the language was, as Dr. Clark says, 'borrowed,' therefore, it cannot be literally 'fulfilled.' This is another way of saying that the prophets of the Old Testament were mistaken and that Jesus perpetuated their mistake by using their misleading statements, either wilfully or ignorantly. But they reply, 'No, we do not teach that Jesus was mistaken, but that He used pictorial language to reveal a spiritual fact.' Such a mode of procedure would inevitably cause a misunderstanding on the part of the Apostles. And if this is the true interpretation, it is certain that He did cause a misunderstanding, for it is very evident that the Apostles believed Him to teach that He would literally and personally return to earth (Acts 1:9-11; 3:19-21; I John 3:2, 3). They believed in the possibility and rejoiced in the hope of our Lord's return in their day, but they also recognize the possibility of death intervening. They never positively affirmed that Christ's Second Coming was to occur during their life-time. 'Beyond the possibility of a doubt, our Lord intended His disciples to understand, that for some great purpose, and in some visible manner, and at some unknown future time, He would come back again.' "— AUTHOR UNKNOWN.

2. Positively considered.

(1) Personal and bodily.

Acts 1:11—Which also said, Ye men of Galilee, why stand ye gazing up into heaven? this same Jesus, which is taken up from you into heaven shall so come in like manner as ye have seen him go into heaven.

Jesus Christ will come again in person. He said "I will come again"; the Apostle Paul declared "The Lord, Himself, shall descend from heaven." Jesus Christ will come again in body. The angels announced "This same Jesus shall so come in like manner as ye have seen him go into heaven."

(2) Twofold.

The coming again of Christ is twofold; not two comings, but two stages in the one coming.

a. First stage—in the air—for His saints—the Rapture.

I Thes. 4:16, 17—For the Lord himself shall descend from heaven with a shout, with the voice of the archangel, and with the trump of God, and the dead in Christ shall rise first. Then we which are alive and remain shall be caught up together with them in the clouds, to meet the Lord in the air; and so shall we ever be with the Lord.

S. F. John 14:3.

The word "meet" in the original means "to meet to return with," as the Christians at Rome came out as far as Appii Forum to meet the Apostle Paul and return with him to Rome. The saints will be raptured to meet Christ in the air and after an interval, in which certain events will occur in the heavenlies, they will return with Him to the earth.

b. Second stage—to the earth—with His saints—the Revelation.

II Thes. 1:7-9—And to you who are troubled rest with us, when the Lord Jesus shall be revealed from heaven with his mighty angels, In flaming fire taking vengeance on them that know not God, and that obey not the gospel of our Lord Jesus Christ. Who shall be punished with everlasting destruction from the presence of the Lord, and from the glory of his power.

S. F. Col. 3:4. R. V.

S. A. II Thes. 2:7, 8.

It is this stage of Christ's return which will mark the beginning of His dealings with Israel and the nations, as Messiah and King.

(3) Visible.

Heb. 9:28—So Christ was once offered to bear the sins of many; and unto them that look for him shall he appear the second time without sin unto salvation.

S. F. Rev. 1:7; Matt. 24:26, 27; I John 3:2, 3.

Jesus Christ in His Second Coming shall be seen by the Church at the Rapture and by the world at the Revelation.

(4) Sudden.

Rev. 22:7-12, 20—Behold, I come quickly; blessed is he that keepeth the sayings of the prophecy of this book. And behold, I come quickly and my reward is with me, to give every man according as his work shall be. He which testifieth these things saith, surely I come quickly. Amen. Even so, come, Lord Jesus.

According to the testimony of the gospels, the Master laid emphasis upon the necessity of watching because of the suddenness which was to characterize His return.

(5) Imminent.

Tit. 2:13—Looking for that blessed hope, and the glorious appearing of the great God and our Saviour Jesus Christ.

S. F. Heb 9:28; I Thes. 1:9, 10.

S. A. Rom. 13:11.

By the term "imminence" in relation to the Second Coming of Christ we mean from the prophetic, not the historic point of view, that Christ might have come at any moment of any day during the past Christian era; and, from that same point of view, that He may come at any time in the future. From the historic point of view, however, Christ could not have come at any moment in the past for the reason that the events which have occurred during these passing centuries are a part of God's plan for this age, and, therefore, could not have been omitted. From the prophetic point of view, there were no events predicted to be fulfilled before Christ's Return for His saints, except those, which were mentioned as being contingent upon His continued absence, such as the arising of false teachers, the death of Peter, and the spread of Christianity, including the completion of the church, Acts 15:13–18.

(6) Near.

Luke 21:28—And when these things begin to come to pass, then look up. and lift up your heads; for your redemption draweth nigh.

S. F. Matt. 16:3; Matt. 24:33.

S. A. Matt. 24:3.

"The signs of Christ's Second Coming are now so striking and so numerous that they almost defy enumeration. The newspapers give us, daily, fresh signs of the close of this dispensation, and confirm the Bible in a remarkable manner."—E. E. HATCHELL.

a. Signs in the heavens.

Luke 21:25 (first clause)—And there shall be signs in the sun, and in the moon, and in the stars;

(a) In the moon.

Such remarkable changes have been noted in the moon for the last thirty years that it has been necessary to make new nautical and astronomical almanacs. It was determined in 1921 that the moon had deviated from its path by a distance of twelve miles. "Some unknown influences are acting on the moon, and we are at a loss to know what they are."—DR. CROMMELIN.

(b) In the stars.

In 1918 a new star of the first magnitude was discovered by several eyes at once, and promptly vouched for by Greenwich.

Other important discoveries in the heavens have followed in order, sufficiently often to keep the world aware of the signs "in the stars," which will increase, pointing to the coming of Christ and the end of the age.

b. Signs in the earth.

Luke 21:25 (last clause)—And upon the earth distress of nations, with perplexity; the sea and the waves roaring:

S. F. Matt. 24:6–8; Matt. 19:28.

(a) Earthquakes. (Matt. 24:7).

Earthquakes have never been so severe and frequent before.

(b) Pestilence. (Matt. 24:7).

The worst pestilence known in recorded history is that which swept the world in 1918 and 1919, and in India, alone, took a toll of 12,000,000 lives.

(c) War and Famines. (Matt. 24:7).

The worst war and also the worst famines, known to men have taken place within the last half of a century.

(d) Industrial unrest and lawlessness (II Thes. 2:7).

The whole condition of the world is abnormal. Industrial discontent and dissatisfaction are everywhere manifest.

(e) Multiplied transportation (Dan. 12:4; Nahum 2:4).

The increase of transportation, both national and international, is nothing less than phenomenal, whether viewed in relation to the individuals participating or to the means and methods used.

(f) Apostasy (I Tim. 4:1).

Every distinctive truth of Christianity is now openly denied and scoffed at, by many so-called "Christian" ministers and clergy. There are very few Theological Seminaries or Divinity Schools in any land that are loyal to the Christian faith as set forth in the New Testament.

(g) Commercial sign (Rev. 13:16, 17).

The amalgamation of banks, railway systems, and various business concerns, are preparatory to the regime which will be ushered in with the great Monopolist, the Antichrist.

(h) Political sign (Dan. 2 and 7).

The great alliances and groupings of nations which have characterized this century point the way to the eventual revival of the Roman Empire, and the organization of the greater part of the world under the domination of the Man of Sin. His kingdom will be a sort of super-League of Nations, with a compact political and military government.

(i) Jewish sign (Matt. 24:32–34).

"Since General Allenby entered Jerusalem on that never-to-be-forgotten day, December 9, 1917, the fig tree has been putting 'forth leaves' with amazing rapidity. Jews are returning to Palestine in great numbers."—HATCHELL.

A Jewish army has been formed, and the study of Hebrew is spreading among the Jews.

These signs have particularly, or primarily, to do with the second stage of Christ's coming in relation to Israel and the nations. But as there is only an interval of a few years between the two the near approach of the one involves the nearer approach of the other.

(7) In the glory and splendor of the divine Sonship.

Matt. 24:30—And then shall appear the sign of the Son of man in heaven; and then shall all the tribes of the earth mourn, and they shall see the Son of man coming in the clouds of heaven with power and great glory.

S. F. Tit. 2:13, compared with Ex. 19:9; Ex. 24:15; Ex. 34:5; Num. 11:25; Psa. 97:12; Matt. 11:5; Psa. 104:3; Isa 19:1; Acts 1:9–11; Luke 21:27; Rev. 1:7; Rev. 14:14.

S. F. Matt. 17:27; Mark 8:38.

The Lord Jesus Christ is coming in the clouds of heaven with all the glory of His Father and the holy angels.

D. S. Jesus Christ the Incarnate Son of God shall suddenly and personally come in visible and glorious manifestation for His saints in the air and with them to the earth.

III. The Purpose of It.

1. With regard to the righteous.

(1) The resurrection of the dead.

I Thes. 4:16—For the Lord himself shall descend from heaven with a shout, with the voice of the archangel and with the trump of God and the dead in Christ shall rise first.

S. F. I Cor. 15:22, 23.

(2) The transformation of the living.

I Cor. 15:51, 52—Behold, I shew you a mystery; we shall not all sleep, but we shall all be changed. In a moment, in the twinkling of an eye, at the last trump; for the trumpet shall sound, and the dead shall be raised incorruptible and we shall be changed.

There will be a generation of believers which will not see death but will participate in that mysterious change, when this mortal shall put on immortality and the body of our humiliation shall be fashioned anew, and conformed to the body of His glory.

(3) The rapture of all.

I Thes. 4:17 –Then we which are alive and remain shall be caught up together with them in the clouds, to meet the Lord in the air; and so shall we ever be with the Lord.

The risen ones and the transformed ones are to be united in the Rapture, caught up together.

(4) The judgment and reward for works.

II Cor. 5:10—For we must all appear before the judgment seat of Christ; that every one may receive the things done in his body, according to that he hath done, whether it be good or bad.

S. F. I Cor. 3:12–15.

(5) The consummation of the marriage relation between Christ and the Church.

Rev. 19:7–9—see especially verse 7—Let us be glad and rejoice, and give honour to him; for the marriage of the Lamb is come, and his wife hath made herself ready.

S. F. Matt. 25:1–10.

S. A. Eph. 5:25–32; II Cor. 11:2.

The Church is now the bride of Christ in espousal. This relation will reach

284

its culmination when the "marriage of the Lamb is come," which will be celebrated by the "Marriage Supper of the Lamb!"

(6) The establishment of the Bride in her home in the heavenlies.

Rev. 21:2—And I John saw the holy city, the New Jerusalem, coming down
from God out of heaven, prepared as a bride adorned for her husband.

S. F. Rev. 21:9, 10; John 14:2-3; I Thes. 4:17.

The future home of the bride of Christ is the place prepared in the Father's
house, and identified with the New Jerusalem, which John saw coming down
from God out of heaven.

2. With regard to the wicked.

(1) Will share in the tribulation experiences.

II Thes. 2:7-12—For the mystery of iniquity doth already work; only he who
now letteth will let until he be taken out of the way. And then shall
that Wicked be revealed; whom the Lord shall consume with the spirit
of his mouth, and shall destroy with the brightness of his coming. Even
him whose coming is after the working of Satan with all power and
signs and lying wonders. And with all deceivableness of unrighteousness in them that perish; because they receive not the love of the truth
that they might be saved. And for this cause God shall send them
strong delusion, that they should believe a lie; That they all might be
damned who believed not the truth, but had pleasure in unrighteousness.

S. F. Rev. 16:1-14; Rev. 3:10.

**(2) Those identified with the armies of the Antichrist destroyed from the earth at the
revelation of Christ.**

Rev. 19:19-21—And I saw the beast, and the kings of the earth, and their
armies, gathered together to make war against him that sat on the
horse and against his army. And the beast was taken and with him the
false prophet that wrought miracles before him, with which he deceived them that had received the mark of the beast, and them that
worshipped his image. These both were cast alive into a lake of fire
burning with brimstone. And the remnant were slain with the sword of
him that sat upon the horse, which sword proceeded out of his mouth;
and all the fowls were filled with their flesh.

S. A. Zech. 14:3-12; II Thes. 2:8; II Thes. 1:7-9; Matt. 24:21.

**(3) Those classified as the goat nations cut off in judgment—shut out from the Kingdom
—made subjects of eternal doom.**

Matt. 25:31, 32, 41—When the Son of man shall come in his glory, and all the
holy angels with him, then shall he sit upon the throne of his glory.
And before him shall be gathered all nations; and he shall separate
them one from another, as a shepherd divideth his sheep from the
goats. Then shall he say also unto them on the left hand, Depart from
me, ye cursed, into everlasting fire, prepared for the devil and his
angels.

(4) Perpetual judgment upon the openly wicked during the Kingdom age.

Psa. 101:5-8—Whoso privily slandereth his neighbour, him will I cut off; him
that hath an high look and a proud heart will not I suffer. Mine eyes
shall be upon the faithful of the land, that they may dwell with me;

he that walketh in a perfect way, he shall serve me. He that worketh deceit shall not dwell within my house; he that telleth lies shall not tarry in my sight. I will early destroy all the wicked of the land; that I may cut off all wicked doers from the city of the Lord.

S. A. Isa. 26:9; Psa. 72:4–6; Mic. 5:8–15.

(5) Resurrection of the wicked dead for the last judgment at the close of Christ's reign.

Rev. 20:12—And I saw the dead, small and great, stand before God, and the books were opened; and another book was opened, which is the book of life; and the dead were judged out of those things which were written in the books according to their works.

S. F. John 5:28, 29.

(6) Consigned to the place of final doom.

Rev. 20:15—And whosoever was not found written in the book of life was cast into the lake of fire.

S. F. Luke 12:4, 5.

Jesus Christ is coming again to judge the living nations and to punish and destroy from the earth the unbelieving and disobedient, and consign them to the place of final doom.

3. With regard to the Antichrist.

(1) His coming predicted.

I John 2:18—Little children, it is the last time; and as ye have heard that antichrist shall come, even now are there many antichrists, whereby we know that it is the last time.

S. F. I John 4:3.

S. A. II Thes. 2:3–12; II John 7; I John 2:22.

"The name 'Anti-christ' brings to us one of the most solemn and foreboding subjects contained in the Scriptures. A being spoken of as 'Anti-christ'—one opposed, absolutely opposed to Jesus Christ, and therefore also to God—shall come. The spirit of Anti-christ is already in the world, denying the coming of Jesus Christ in the flesh, either in the past or in the future. The spirit of Anti-christ, now possessed by many, will culminate in one person, the Anti-christ, who will deny both the Father and the Son. The many anti-christs doubtless were apostate Christians. That which constitutes the essential characteristic of Antichrist, or the anti-christian spirit, is the denial that 'Jesus Christ has come in the flesh,' or that 'Jesus is the Christ,'—a denial of the Incarnation."—ANDREWS.

The study of the subject of the Anti-christ is very important, but needs to be done most carefully. "Such study is frequently discouraged and discounted because of the strange theories as to who, or what, will constitute this Anti-christian power. Some contend that Anti-christ is a system of Atheism; others, of Anarchy; others can see nothing in this outbreak of wickedness but a manifestation, in its final form, of that great ecclesiastical system known as the Papacy. Many others hold that Antichrist is an individual, a literal man. The latter view is confirmed by the most obvious interpretation of the Scriptures.

"It is particularly important, in an age of phenomenal lawlessness and unrest, like the present, when everything is ripening for the reign of the Antichrist, that we should understand the Scriptures regarding this 'Man of Sin,' as he is called by the Apostle Paul. Sir Robert Anderson maintains that the predictions concerning the Antichrist are even more distinct and definite than those relating to the Messiah."—MANTLE.

a. His personality portrayed—magnetic and powerful.

II Thes. 2:3-4—Let no man deceive you by any means; for that day shall not come, except there come a falling away first, and that man of sin be revealed, the son of perdition. Who opposeth and exalteth himself above all that is called God or that is worshipped; so that he as God sitteth in the temple of God, shewing himself that he is God.

S. F. II Thes. 2:9.

As Christ is the express image of God, so it appears that Anti-christ is the culminating manifestation of Satan, "the prince of this world." His coming is "after the working (energy, or inward working) of Satan, with all power and signs and lying wonders, and deceivableness of unrighteousness."

"The Counterfeit Christ will be a marvellous scholar, and perfectly at home in every possible subject. He will be a scientist, having complete knowledge of the occult, with his hand on the forces of the unseen. He will be an orator, and possessing a silver tongue; men will hang upon his words with breathless interest. He will be a veritable king of finance, surpassing in skill the ablest financiers who have ever lived. He will be a military genius, putting all the greatest generals into the shade by his magnetism and strategy. Men will flock by thousands to his standard, and be proud to serve under his command. He will combine in one person the capabilities and attributes of the greatest orators, statesmen, diplomats, generals, and financiers who have ever lived, drawing to himself the homage and admiration of the whole world."—MANTLE.

See following references for corroboration of above:

Dan. 8:23-24; Ezek. 28:3; Dan. 7:20; Rev. 6:2; Rev. 13:2, 4; Rev. 17:17.

b. His character described—lawless and blasphemous.

II Thes. 2:3, 9, 10—Let no man deceive you by any means for that day shall not come except there come a falling away first, and that man of sin be revealed; the son of perdition. Even him, whose coming is after the working of Satan with all power and signs and lying wonders. And with all deceivableness of unrighteousness in them that perish; because they received not the love of the truth, that they might be saved.

S. F. II Thes. 2:8, R. V.

"His name exhibits him as the antithesis of the true Christ. The Lord Jesus was the Righteous One; the Man of Sin will be the Lawless one. The Lord Jesus was 'made under the law' (Gal. 4:4); the Antichrist will oppose all law, being a law unto himself. When the Saviour entered this world, He came saying, 'Lo I come to do thy will, O God' (Heb. 10:9); but of the Antichrist it is written 'And the king shall do according to his will' (Dan. 11:36). The Antichrist will set himself up in direct opposition to all authority, both Divine and human.

"Not only does 'anti-christ' denote the antagonist of Christ, but it tells of one who is instead of Christ. The word signifies another Christ, a pro-Christ, an 'alter christus,' a pretender to the name of Christ. He will seem to be and will set himself up as the true Christ. He will be the Devil's counterfeit. Just as the Devil is an anti-Theos—not only the adversary of God, but the usurper of the place and prerogatives of God, demanding worship; so the Son of Perdition will be antiChrist—not only the antagonist and opponent of Christ, but His rival; assuming the very position and prerogatives of Christ; passing himself off as the rightful claimant to all the rights and honors of the Son of God."—PINK.

(2) His entrance into covenant relationship with the Jews.

Dan. 9:27—And he shall confirm the covenant with many for one week, and in the midst of the week he shall cause the sacrifice and the oblation to cease, and for the overspreading of abominations he shall make it desolate, even until the consummation, and that determined shall be poured upon the desolate.

S. F. John 5:43.

S. A. Isa. 28:14–18.

The presumption is that he himself will be a Jew. "The Antichrist will be a Jew, though his connections, his governmental position, his sphere of dominion, will by no means confine him to the Israelitish people. It should, however, be pointed out that there is no express declaration of Scripture which says in so many words that this daring Rebel will be a Jew; nevertheless, the hints given are so plain, the conclusions which must be drawn from certain statements of Holy Writ are so obvious, and the requirements of the case are so inevitable, that we are forced to believe he must be a Jew (Ezek. 21:25–27, compared with Dan. 8:23–25, and 9:25. Ezek. 28:2–10, compared with Rev. 13:14; Dan. 11:36, 37; Matt. 12:43–45; John 5:43; I John 2:18).

"The Jews, having returned to Palestine, and with temple in Jerusalem rebuilt, will receive this Son of Perdition as their long-promised Messiah. In imitation of the true Christ Who will, at return to the earth, make a new covenant with the House of Israel and with the House of Judah, the Antichrist will make a covenant with the Jews. Under a seven years treaty, and in the guise of friendship, he will gain ascendancy in Jerusalem, only later to throw off the mask and break the covenant."—PINK.

(3) His covenant relationship with the Jews severed.

Dan. 9:27—And he shall confirm the covenant with many for one week, and in the midst of the week he shall cause the sacrifice and the oblation to cease and for the overspreading of abominations he shall make it desolate, even until the consummation, and that determined shall be poured upon the desolate.

S. F. Dan. 11:31; Matt. 24:15.

In the middle of the Seventieth Week of Daniel, the covenant, which has been made or confirmed by the Antichrist with "the many" of the Jews, will be broken. The identity of the False Messiah will then be revealed, and he will repudiate the promises formerly made with Israel. He will cause the Oblations or Temple worship to cease; so far as they pertain to the worship of Jehovah. He will then establish a new worship, the worship of the image of the beast, which in the final analysis is the worship of himself (II Thes. 2:4).

(4) His exaltation and worship as God.

Rev. 13:4–6, 12—And they worshipped the dragon which gave power unto the beast and they worshipped the beast, saying who is like unto the beast? who is able to make war with him? And there was given unto him a mouth speaking great things and blasphemies; and power was given

288

unto him to continue forty and two months. And he .opened his mouth in blasphemy against God, to blaspheme his name, and his tabernacle, and them that dwell in heaven. And he exerciseth all the power of the first beast before him, and causeth the earth and them which dwell therein to worship the first beast, whose deadly wound was healed.

S. F. Dan. 11:36; II Thes. 2:3, 4.

S. A. Isa. 14:12-17.

"The new religion which is formulated is then nothing less than the worship of the Antichrist. Having caused the sacrifices and oblations to cease in the temple which he had permitted the people to build, he seats himself in the Most Holy place. In the place where the Shekinah glory once shone forth, the Antichrist, with an audacity inconceivable, seats himself, demanding worship. Think of the brazen defiance of God, and the unspeakable blasphemy of such a procedure. This is the 'abomination of desolation standing in the Holy Place,' to which Christ referred in Matt. 24:15."—PINK.

(5) His headship over the armies of earth against Christ at Armageddon.

Rev. 16:13, 14, 16—And I saw three unclean spirits like frogs .come out of the mouth of the dragon, and out of the mouth of the beast, and out of the mouth of the false prophet. For they are the spirits of devils, working miracles, which go forth unto the kings of the earth and of the whole world to gather them to the battle of that great day of God Almighty. And he gathered them together into a place called in the Hebrew tongue Armageddon.

S. F. Rev. 17:8-14; Rev. 19:11-19.

"And then comes the grand finale. The heaven will open and from it will descend the King of kings and Lord of lords, seated on a white horse, with His eyes 'as a flame of fire' (Rev. 19:11, 12). Attending Him will be the armies of heaven, also seated on white horses (Rev. 19:14). Far from being appalled at this awe-inspiring spectacle, the Beast and the kings of the earth and their armies shall gather together to 'make war against Him that sat on the horse, and against His armies' (Rev. 19:19), (Zech. 14:3)."—PINK.

(6) His destruction and his final doom at the revelation of Jesus Christ.

II Thes. 2:8, R. V.—And then shall be revealed the lawless one, whom the Lord Jesus shall slay with the breath of his mouth, and bring to naught by the manifestation of his coming.

Rev. 19:20-21—And I saw the beast, and the kings of the earth, and their armies, gathered together to make war against him that sat on the horse, and against his army. And the beast was taken and with him the false prophet that wrought miracles before him, with which he deceived them that had received the mark of the beast, and them that worshipped his image. These both were cast alive into a lake of fire burning with brimstone. And the remnant were slain with sword of him that sat upon the horse, which sword proceeded out of his mouth: and all the fowls were filled with their flesh.

Jesus Christ at His return will destroy the Antichrist, or Lawless One. This destruction will be by means of the "breath of His mouth and the manifestation of His coming." "At last the Christ of God and the Christ of Satan will confront each other. But the instant the conflict begins, it is ended. The foe will be paralyzed, and all resistance cease."—PINK. This Man of Sin, now defeated and* deposed, is consigned to the place of final doom, the lake of fire.

4. With regard to Israel.

(1) To be restored to their own land.

Ezek. 36:24-28—For I will take you from among the heathen, and gather you out of all countries and will bring you into your own land. Then will I sprinkle clean water upon you, and ye shall be clean; from all your filthiness, and from all your idols, will I cleanse you. A new heart also will I give you, and a new spirit will I put within you; and I will take away the stony heart out of your flesh, and I will give you an heart of flesh. And I will put my spirit within you, and cause you to walk in my statutes, and ye shall keep my judgments, and do them. And ye shall dwell in the land that I gave to your fathers; and ye shall be my people and I will be your God.

S. F. Ezek. 22:19–22; Isa. 11:11–16.

(2) To restore the temple and its worship.

II Thes. 2:3, 4—Let no man deceive you by any means for that day shall not come, except there come a falling away first, and that man of sin be revealed the son of perdition. Who opposeth and exalteth himself above all that is called God, or that is worshipped; so that he as God sitteth in the temple of God, shewing himself that he is God.

S. A. Dan. 11:31; Ezek. 42–48; Matt. 24:15; Dan. 9:27; Isa. 66:1–3, 6; Rev. 11:1–2.

(3) To have a covenant confirmed with the Antichrist, which is to be broken.

Dan. 9:27—And he shall confirm the covenant with many for one week; and in the midst of the week he shall cause the sacrifice and the oblation to cease, and for the overspreading of abominations he shall make it desolate, even until the consummation, and that determined shall be poured upon the desolate.

(4) To pass through the great tribulation—the last half of Daniel's Seventieth week, a period of three and a half years.

Jer. 30:6, 7—Ask ye now, and see whether a man doth travail with child? wherefore do I see every man with his hands on his loins, as a woman in travail, and all faces are turned into paleness? Alas! for that day is great, so that none is like it; it is even the time of Jacob's trouble: but he shall be saved out of it.

S. F. Dan. 12:1; Matt. 24:15–22, 29.

S. A. Rev. 3:10; Rev. 7:14; Rev. 11:2; Dan. 7:25; Dan. 12:7.

(5) To be converted as a nation at Christ's return.

Isa. 25:9—And it shall be said in that day, Lo this is our God; we have waited for him, and he will save us; this is the Lord; we have waited for him, we will be glad and rejoice in his salvation.

S. F. Dan. 12:1; Matt. 24:15–22, 29.

S. A. Rom. 11:26; Isa. 66:8.

(6) To be missionaries to the nations.

Isa. 2:1-3—The word that Isaiah the son of Amoz saw concerning Judah and

Jerusalem. And it shall come to pass in the last days, that the mountain of the Lord's house shall be established in the top of the mountains and shall be exalted above the hills; and all nations shall flow unto it. And many people shall go and say, Come ye, and let us go up to the mountain of the Lord, to the house of the God of Jacob; and he will teach us of his ways; and we will walk in his paths; for out of Zion shall go forth the law, and the word of the Lord from Jerusalem.

S. F. Psa. 76:1, 2; Isa. 27:6; Zech. 8:13, 21-23; Rom. 11:12, 15.

(7) To be permanently established in the land.

Amos 9:15—And I will plant them upon their land, and they shall no more be pulled up out of their land which I have given them, saith the Lord thy God.

S. F. Ezek. 34:28.

(8) Israel and Judah to be united in one Kingdom under one King.

Ezekiel 37:21, 22, R. V.—And say unto them, Thus saith the Lord Jehovah: Behold, I will take the children of Israel from among the nations, whither they are gone, and will gather them on every side, and bring them into their own land: and I will make them one nation in the land, upon the mountains of Israel; and one king shall be king to them all; and they shall be no more two nations, neither shall they be divided into two kingdoms any more at all.

S. F. Zech. 8:13; 9:1, 10; 10:6-9; Ez. 34:23, 24; 37:24, 25; Jer. 30:9.

The Second Coming of Christ will have an especial reference to the Jewish nation. It will mean the removal of the veil from their eyes; their return from the nations where they have been scattered and their permanent establishment in the promised land. They will also play an important part in the dissemination of the truth.

5. With regard to the Gentile nations.

(1) Shall be separated by judgment.

Matt. 25:31-33—When the Son of man shall come in his glory, and all the holy angels with him, then shall he sit upon the throne of his glory; And before him shall be gathered all nations; and he shall separate them one from another, as a shepherd divideth his sheep from the goats. And he shall set the sheep on his right hand, but the goats on the left.

S. F. Zech. 14:1-4, 16-18.

This judgment is to determine what nations are to be included in, and excluded from the Millennial reign of Christ, and is to be based upon the treatment, by the nations, of the message and the messengers of the Kingdom (Matt. 25:40, 45).

(2) The saved nations shall go into the Millennial reign with Christ.

Matt. 25:34—Then shall the King say unto them on His right hand, Come ye blessed of my Father, inherit the kingdom prepared for you from the foundation of the world.

S. F. Zech. 14:16, 17; Isa. 19:23-25.

The saved nations are those who are the recipients of national salvation from the destruction which has been visited upon the lawless and disobedient, and who are granted entrance into the Kingdom Reign of Christ. It doubtless also includes their personal and eternal salvation, which has been obtained through the acceptance of Christ, not only as Messiah or King but also as Saviour.

(3) The wicked nations to be shut out from the millennial kingdom and suffer eternal doom.

Matt. 25:41, 46—Then shall he say also unto them on the left hand, Depart from me, ye cursed, into everlasting fire, prepared for the devil and his angels. And these shall go away into everlasting punishment; but the righteous into life eternal.

The doomed or the "Goat Nations" are those nations which will show their rejection of the King and the gospel of the Kingdom by their treatment of the heralds or messengers of the kingdom whom Christ calls His "brethren." These are the recipients not only of national but also individual condemnation and doom.

6. With regard to the Davidic or Millennial Kingdom.

"Millennium" (Latin) is the same as "Chiliad" (Greek), and both mean a thousand years. Both terms are used to refer to a future era of righteous government upon the earth, to last a thousand years.

(1) The period of it.

a. Beginning—marked by revelation of Christ and premillennial judgments.

II Tim. 4:1—I charge thee therefore before God, and the Lord Jesus Christ, who shall judge the quick and the dead at his appearing and his kingdom.

S. F. Matt. 13:41.

S. A. Matt. 25:31–46.

The Kingdom of Christ will be ushered in by a series of judgments, as a result of which sin and sinners will be removed from the earth.

b. Ending—marked by loosing of Satan and judgment of apostate nations.

Rev. 20:3, 7–9—And cast him into the bottomless pit, and shut him up, and set a seal upon him, that he should deceive the nations no more, till the thousand years should be fulfilled; and after that he must be loosed a little season. And when the thousand years are expired, Satan shall be loosed out of his prison. And shall go out to deceive the nations which are in the four quarters of the earth, Gog and Magog, to gather them together to battle; the number of whom is as the sand of the sea. And they went up on the breadth of the earth, and compassed the camp of the saints about and the beloved city; and fire came down from God out of heaven, and devoured them.

Men will be born during the Kingdom Age with evil natures as now, and also as now, render feigned or outward obedience to the rule of Christ. At the close of the Kingdom Age, therefore, when Satan is loosed for a little season he will find a following among those who come from the four corners of the earth. And he will lead them in an attack upon the camp of the saints, which doubtless refers to Jerusalem, where they will meet their doom; fire coming down out of heaven to destroy them.

(2) The character of it.

a. Righteousness.

Isa. 32:1—Behold, a king shall reign in righteousness, and princes shall rule in judgment.

S. F. Psa. 66:3; Psa. 81:15. R. V. (margin); Zech. 14:17–19.

The coming Kingdom of Christ will be a reign of righteousness. Righteousness will be compulsory during the Millennium and will therefore predominate. Sin and disobedience will be visited with summary judgment and punishment. This is in harmony with Isa. 26:9, which says, "For when thy judgments are in the earth the inhabitants of the world will learn righteousness." See also Zeph. 3:5.

b. Universal knowledge of God.

Isa. 11:9—They shall not hurt nor destroy in all my holy mountain for the earth shall be full of the knowledge of the Lord, as the waters cover the sea

S. F. Jer. 31:34.

The knowledge of God shall be disseminated throughout the earth. Jesus Christ, Himself, being the chief medium for its propagation (Isa. 2:3). The blinding power of Satan will be absent, so that men will have clear and correct conceptions of God and His will.

c. Peace.

Isa. 2:4—And he shall judge among the nations and shall rebuke many people; and they shall beat their swords into plowshares, and their spears into pruninghooks; nation shall not lift up sword against nation, neither shall they learn war any more.

S. F. Isa. 9:6, 7.

There can be no true peace except that which is based on righteousness. Universal peace, therefore, waits upon universal righteousness for its realization. This will come only with the coming of the Prince of Peace, of Whom it is said, "The sceptre of righteousness is the sceptre of thy kingdom."

d. Prosperity.

Isa. 35:1, 2—The wilderness and the solitary place shall be glad for them, and the desert shall rejoice, and blossom as the rose. It shall blossom abundantly, and rejoice even with joy and singing; the glory of Lebanon shall be given unto it, the excellency of Carmel and Sharon, they shall see the glory of the Lord, and the excellency of our God.

S. F. Isa. 51:3; Amos 9:13.

During the Millennial age the curse which has so long rested upon the animal and vegetable kingdom will be lifted, and the glad prosperity which greeted our first parents will again visit our sin-ravaged earth.

e. Longevity of life.

Isa. 65:20—There shall be no more thence an infant of days, nor an old man that hath not filled his days; for the child shall die an hundred years old; but the sinner being an hundred years old shall be accursed.

S. F. Isa. 33:24.

Length of life upon the earth will apparently be determined by obedience to law,—the law of Christ. Disobedience will bring death.

f. Universality of rule or scope.

Zech. 14:9—And the Lord shall be King over all the earth; in that day shall there be one Lord, and His name one.

S. A. Phil. 2:10.

Jesus Christ is coming again to sit upon the throne of His father David, to reign over the house of Israel and over the whole earth.

g. Universal language.

Zeph. 3:9—For then will I turn to the people a pure language, that they may all call upon the name of the Lord, to serve Him with one consent.

7. With regard to Satan.

(1) To be cast out of the heavenlies.

Rev. 12:7-9—And there was war in heaven; Michael and his angels fought against the dragon and the dragon fought and his angels, And prevailed not; neither was their place found any more in heaven. And the great dragon was cast out, that old serpent, called the Devil and Satan, which deceiveth the whole world; he was cast out into the earth, and his angels were cast out with him.

(2) To be confined to the earth.

Rev. 12:9, 12—And the great dragon was cast out, that old serpent, called the Devil and Satan, which was cast out into the earth, and his angels were cast out with him. Therefore rejoice, ye heavens and ye that dwell in them. Woe to the inhabiters of the earth and of the sea! for the devil is come down unto you, having great wrath, because he knoweth that he hath but a short time.

(3) To energize the Antichrist.

Rev. 13:2—And the beast which I saw was like unto a leopard, and his feet were as the feet of a bear, and his mouth as the mouth of a lion; and the dragon gave him his power, and his seat, and great authority.

S. A. II Thes. 2:9, 10.

(4) To be chained in the abyss for a thousand years.

Rev. 20:2, 3—And he laid hold on the dragon, that old serpent, which is the Devil and Satan and bound him a thousand years, And cast him into the bottomless pit, and shut him up, and set a seal upon him, that he should deceive the nations no more, till the thousand years should be fulfilled; and after that he must be loosed a little season.

(5) To be loosed for a little season when he shall deceive the nations.

Rev. 20:7, 8—And when the thousand years are expired, Satan shall be loosed out of his prison, And shall go out to deceive the nations which are in the four quarters of the earth, Gog and Magog, to gather them together to battle; the number of whom is as the sand of the sea.

(6) To be consigned to the lake of fire.

Rev. 20:10—And the devil that deceived them was cast into the lake of fire and brimstone, where the beast and the false prophet are and shall be tormented day and night for ever and ever.

D. S. The purpose of Christ in His second coming is manifold, including in its scope the righteous, the wicked, Israel, Satan and his confederates, the Gentile nations, and the Davidic kingdom.

IV. The Practical Value of It.

1. A doctrine of comfort for sorrowing saints.

I Thes. 4:13-18—But I would not have you to be ignorant, brethren, concerning them which are asleep, that ye sorrow not, even as others which have no hope. For if we believe that Jesus died and rose again, even so them also which sleep in Jesus will God bring with Him. For this we say unto you by the word of the Lord, that we which are alive and remain unto the coming of the Lord shall not prevent them which are asleep. For the Lord himself shall descend from heaven with a shout, with the voice of the archangel, and with the trump of God; and the dead in Christ shall rise first; Then we which are alive and remain shall be caught up together with them in the clouds to meet the Lord in the air; and so shall we ever be with the Lord. Wherefore comfort one another with these words.

S. F. Isa. 40:1, 9, 10, 11.

The comforting value of this doctrine lies chiefly in the threefold reunion, which will be effected by the return of our Lord. There will be the reunion of the body with the soul and spirit, thus making man again complete; a tripartite being, transformed and glorified. Living believers will be reunited with those who have departed this life, now raised from the dead—"caught up together." All believers will be reunited in visible manifestation with the risen and ascended Lord.

2. A blessed hope for the recipients of God's grace.

Tit. 2:11-13—For the grace of God that bringeth salvation hath appeared to all men. Teaching us that, denying ungodliness and worldly lusts, we should live soberly, righteously, and godly in this present world. Looking for that blessed hope, and the glorious appearing of the great God and our Saviour Jesus Christ.

S. A. II Peter 3:11-13.

"Hope is made up of desire and expectation. We may desire what we do not expect. We may expect what we do not desire. I might desire to be King of England, but never expect it. If I were a condemned criminal, I might expect to be hanged tomorrow, and not desire it. When I was a lad, the second coming of Christ was to me expectation without desire. But as I have learned the Scriptures, the desire has sprung up in my heart, so that it has become a real hope, desire with expectation; and now I can say from the depths of my soul, 'Come Lord Jesus, come quickly.' "—Dixon.

3. An incentive to a holy life including:

(1) Watchfulness.

Matt. 24:42-44—Watch therefore for ye know not what hour your Lord doth come. But know this, that if the goodman of the house had known in what watch the thief would come, he would not have suffered his house to be broken up. Therefore be ye also ready; for in such an hour as ye think not the Son of man cometh.

S. F. Matt. 25:13; Mk. 13:32, 37; Luke 13:35; Rev. 16:15.

295

(2) Sobriety.

I Peter 1:13—Wherefore gird up the loins of your mind, be sober, and hope to the end for the grace that is to be brought unto you at the revelation of Jesus Christ.

S. F. I Thes. 5:2–6.

S. A. I Peter 4:7.

(3) Patience.

Heb. 10:36, 37—For ye have need of patience, that, after ye have done the will of God, ye might receive the promise. For yet a little while, and he that shall come will come and will not tarry.

S. F. James 5:7–9.

(4) Mortification of fleshly lusts.

Col. 3:3–5—For ye are dead, and your life is hid with Christ in God. When Christ, Who is our life shall appear then shall ye also appear with Him in glory. Mortify therefore your members which are upon the earth; fornication, uncleanness, inordinate affection, evil concupiscence, and covetousness, which is idolatry.

S. F. I John 3:2, 3.

(5) Endurance of testing.

I Peter 1:6, 7—Wherein ye greatly rejoice, though now for a season, if need be ye are in heaviness through manifold temptations. That the trial of your faith being much more precious than of gold that perisheth, though it be tried with fire, might be found unto praise and honour and glory at the appearing of Jesus Christ.

S. F. I Peter 4:13.

(6) Abiding fellowship.

I John 2:28—And now little children, abide in him; that, when he shall appear, we may have confidence and not be ashamed before Him at His coming.

(7) Brotherly love.

I Thes. 3:12, 13—And the Lord make you to increase and abound in love one toward another, and toward all men, even as we do toward you. To the end He may stablish your hearts unblameable in holiness before God, even our Father, at the coming of our Lord Jesus Christ with all His saints.

The Second Coming of Christ in order to have practical value for the life that now is, must be first recognized as a sure hope. Heb. 6:18–20. It must also be realized as a living hope, i.e., a hope to which we have been "begotten again." I Pet. 1:3. It then becomes in daily life and experience, a blessed hope, Titus 2:13, at which time it exercises a practical influence and power over the life; it becomes a purifying hope, and this purification extends to every relationship and realm of life. "Every man that hath this hope in him, purifieth himself, even as He is pure." I John 3:3.

4. A motive to a life of faithful service, including:

(1) Fidelity.

Luke 12:42–44—And the Lord said, Who then is that faithful and wise steward, whom his Lord shall make ruler over His household, to give them their portion of meat in due season? Blessed is that servant, whom his Lord when He cometh shall find so doing. Of a truth I say unto you, that he will make him ruler over all that He hath.

S. F. Luke 19:12, 13; Matt. 25:19-21.

(2) Ministerial constancy.

II Tim. 4:1, 2—I charge thee therefore before God, and the Lord Jesus Christ, Who shall judge the quick and the dead at His appearing and His kingdom. Freach the word; be instant in season, out of season; reprove, rebuke, exhort with all long-suffering and doctrine.

S. F. I Peter 5:2-4.

(3) Soul-winning zeal.

I Thes. 1:5, 6, 9, 10—Paul, and Silvanus, and Timotheus, unto the church of the Thessalonians, which is in God the Father and in the Lord Jesus Christ; Grace be unto you, and peace, from God our Father and the Lord Jesus Christ. For our gospel came not unto you in word only, but also in power, and in the Holy Ghost, and in much assurance; as ye know what manner of men we were among you for your sake. And ye became followers of us, and of the Lord, having received the word in much affliction, with joy of the Holy Ghost. For they themselves shew of us what manner of entering in we had unto you, and how ye turned to God from idols to serve the living and true God. And to wait for his Son from heaven, Whom he raised from the dead, even Jesus, which delivered us from the wrath to come.

I Thes. 2:19, 20—For what is our hope, or joy, or crown of rejoicing? Are not even ye in the presence of our Lord Jesus Christ at His coming? For ye are our glory and joy.

S. F. I Cor. 4:3-5.

It is the servant who said in his heart "My Lord delayeth His coming," who also began "to beat the menservants and maidens, and to eat and drink, and to be drunken." Those servants who maintain an attitude of unceasing expectancy toward the Lord's coming will inevitably seek to be faithful to the tasks assigned. The unfailing incentive of Christ's return will produce devotion and constancy in life and action.

George Mueller, mighty in faith and unceasing in prayer, was stirred to action by the thought of the Lord's Return. He says, "When it pleased God in July, 1829, to reveal to my heart the truth of the personal return of the Lord Jesus . . . . . the effect it produced upon me was this: From my inmost soul I was stirred up to a feeling of compassion for sinners, and for the slumbering world around me, lying in the wicked one, and considered: 'Ought I not to do what I can for the Lord Jesus while He tarries, and to arouse His slumbering Church?' "

D. S. The return of our ·Lord constitutes a powerful motive and incentive for the cultivation of every Christian grace and the accomplishment of every good work.

B. The Resurrection of the Dead.

Resurrection is the impartation of life to that in which life has become extinct. The term Resurrection is never used in any instance in the Scriptures where the reference is only to the soul and spirit—where the body is clearly or specifically omitted. There are various attitudes toward this subject. There are those who altogether deny literal or bodily resurrection. Some seem to believe in the bodily resurrection of Christ alone, though not of the rest of the race. There are others who are confused on the subject, and, therefore, do not know what to believe.

While the Scriptures describe the impartation of new life to the soul in Regeneration as a spiritual resurrection, they also declare that, at the Second Coming of Christ, there shall be a resurrection of the body, and a reunion of the body with the soul and spirit from which, during the intermediate state, it has been separated.

I. The Fact of It.

If God formed man's body in the beginning out of the dust of the earth, is it not reasonable to believe that He can reform that body out of the dust of the earth? Is it not consistent to believe that when the original home of man's soul falls into decay that He will provide another for that being which has endless existence? When physical death came upon the human race it meant victory for sin. Shall sin continue to be victorious? If death continue its unbroken reign over the bodies of men, Yes. If there is no bodily resurrection from the dead, then sin through death remains unconquered. "But thanks be to God who giveth us the victory through our Lord Jesus Christ."

1. Taught in the Old Testament.

(1) By positive statement.

Job 19:25–27—For I know that my redeemer liveth, and that he shall stand at the latter day upon the earth. And though after my skin worms destroy this body, yet in my flesh shall I see God. Whom I shall see for myself, and mine eyes shall behold, and not another; though my reins be consumed within me.

S. F. Psa. 16:9–11; Psa. 17:15; Dan. 12:2.

"Now, how could a Redeemer stand without material feet? What could Job mean when he said, 'In my flesh shall I see God,' unless he expected to have a material body? How could he say 'mine eyes shall behold' except he expected to have material eyes to see with? It is quite certain that Job believed in a material bodily resurrection."—C. K. F., *Bible Scholar*.

(2) By plain figure.

Rom. 4:19, 20—And being not weak in faith, he considered not his own body now dead, when he was about an hundred years old, neither yet the deadness of Sarah's womb. He staggered not at the promise of God through unbelief; but was strong in faith, giving glory to God.

Heb. 11:19—Accounting that God was able to raise him up, even from the dead, from whence also he received him in a figure.

S. F. Gen. 15:5, 6; Gen. 18:1–16; Gen. 22:1–14, especially v. 13.

S. A. Num. 17:6–10.

The sterile condition of Abram and Sarai made the conception and birth of Isaac supernatural, and a practical resurrection, or coming out of death into life. This furnishes a figure or parable of the resurrection, which Abraham accounted God as capable of accomplishing, when he offered Isaac on Mount Moriah.

(3) By predictive prophecy.

Isa. 26:19—Thy dead men shall live, together with my dead body shall they arise. Awake and sing, ye that dwell in dust; for thy dew is as the dew of herbs, and the earth shall cast out the dead.

S. F. Hosea 13:14, Psa. 16:10, 11.

S. A. Dan. 12:2.

The resurrection of both Christ and men is a subject of Old Testament prophecy, though its mention is much more limited than other prophetic subjects.

(4) By practical demonstration.

II Kings 4:32-35—And when Elisha was come into the house, behold the child was dead, and laid upon his bed. He went in therefore, and shut the door upon them twain, and prayed unto the Lord. And he went up, and lay upon the child and put his mouth upon his mouth, and his eyes upon his eyes, and his hands upon his hands; and he stretched himself upon the child; and the flesh of the child waxed warm. Then he returned and walked in the house to and fro; and went up, and stretched himself upon him; and the child sneezed seven times, and the child opened his eyes.

S. F. I Kings 17:17-24; II Kings 13:20, 21.

The resurrection of the Old Testament differed from that of Christ and those of the future, in that they were not for the same purpose or with the same permanency,—they did not give immortality.

The Old Testament distinctly and definitely teaches the bodily resurrection of the dead.

2. Taught in the New Testament.

(1) By positive statement.

John 5:21—For as the Father raiseth up the dead, and quickeneth them; even so the Son quickeneth whom He will.

S. F. Acts 26:8, 22, 23; Acts 23:6-8; I Peter 1:3.

Jesus Christ in the plainest and most dogmatic language taught us to expect bodily life out of bodily death, and to expect that the physical bodies of men which had become the victims of bodily death would be raised from the dead, to be inhabited by their informing souls and rational spirits.

(2) By predictive prophecy.

a. As uttered by our Lord.

John 5:28, 29—Marvel not at this; for the hour is coming, in the which all that are in the graves shall hear his voice. And shall come forth; they that have done good, unto the resurrection of life; and they that have done evil, unto the resurrection of damnation.

S. F. John 6:39-40, 44, 54; Luke 14:13, 14; Luke 20:35, 36.

b. As presented by Paul.

I Cor. 15:22, 23—For as in Adam all die, even so in Christ shall all be made alive. But every man in his own order; Christ the firstfruits afterward they that are Christ's at His coming.

S. F. I Thes. 4:14-16; Phil. 3:11.

c. As recorded by John.

Rev. 20:4–6, 13, 14—And I saw thrones, and they sat upon them, and judgment was given unto them; and I saw the souls of them that were beheaded for the witness of Jesus and for the word of God, and which had not worshipped the beast, neither his image, neither had received his mark upon their foreheads, or in their hands; and they lived and reigned with Christ a thousand years. But the rest of the dead lived not again until the thousand years were finished. This is the first resurrection. Blessed and holy is he that hath part in the first resurrection; on such the second death hath no power, but they shall be priests of God and of Christ, and shall reign with him a thousand years. And the seas gave up the dead which were in it; and they were judged every man according to their works. And death and hell were cast into the lake of fire. This is the second death.

The predictions concerning future resurrection in the New Testament are plain and pointed. They deal with the subjects, the purpose, and the manner of it. Their meaning cannot be easily mistaken.

(3) By practical demonstration.

John 11:41–44—Then they took away the stone from the place where the dead was laid. And Jesus lifted up his eyes, and said, Father I thank thee that thou hast heard me. And I knew that thou hearest me always; but because of the people which stand by I said it, that they may believe that thou hast sent me. And when he thus had spoken he cried with a loud voice, Lazarus, come forth. And he that was dead came forth, bound hand and foot with grave clothes; and his face was bound about with a napkin. Jesus saith unto them, Loose him, and let him go.

S. F. Luke 8:41, 42, 49–56; Luke 7:12–15; Matt. 28; John 20; Matt. 27:52, 53.

If the practical demonstrations in the New Testament were of physical resurrection, which they undoubtedly were, then the predictions and promises of resurrection must involve and include the same.

D. S. In various ways the fact of the resurrection of the dead is clearly established by both the Old and New Testament teaching.

II. The Manner of It.

1. Literal and bodily.

I Cor. 15:22—For as in Adam all die, even so in Christ shall all be made alive.

S. F. Rev. 20:12; II Cor. 5:10.

S. A. Job 19:25–27; Psa. 16:9; John 5:28, 29 compared with John 5:25.

In the passage in I Cor. 15:22 the Apostle is speaking of physical death in Adam, and also a physical resurrection in Christ.

Rev. 20:12 and II Cor. 5:10 show the necessity of the raising of the body in order that judgment may take place according to things done in the body. The fruition of the hope, both of Job and the Psalms, requires a bodily resurrection. Acts 24:15 speaks of a resurrection of the just and the unjust—this can not refer to spiritual resurrection surely, if so, then in the future state, every justified man would have two spirits—the spirit he has here, and the spirit he would receive at the resurrection.

The Lord Jesus Christ in His resurrection body was capable of being seen, touched, and handled, of eating broiled fish and honeycomb (Luke 24:36–53). In this body He was seen to ascend into heaven (Acts 1:9–11). In it He was beheld standing at the right hand of God (Acts 7:55, 56). In it He is acting as the "one Mediator between God and man, Himself, Man, Christ Jesus" (I Tim. 2:5). In it He is coming again as the Son of Man (Matt. 25:31).

2. Universal.

John 5:28, 29—Marvel not at this; for the hour is coming, in the which all that are in the graves shall hear his voice, And shall come forth; they that have done good, unto the resurrection of life; and they that have done evil, unto the resurrection of damnation.

The dead will not all be raised at the same time; not to the same destiny; but all the dead will be raised—the resurrection will be all-inclusive.

3. Twofold. (Dan. 12:2; John 5:28, 29; Rev. 20:4, 5).

Acts 24:14, 15—But this I confess unto thee, that after the way which they call heresy, so worship I the God of my fathers, believing all things which are written in the law and in the prophets. And have hope toward God, which they themselves also allow, that there shall be a resurrection of the dead, both of the just and unjust.

(1) Resurrection of the just—to life.

Luke 14:14—And thou shalt be blessed; for they cannot recompense thee; for thou shalt be recompensed at the resurrection of the just.

S. F. I Cor. 15:22, 23; I Thes. 4:16; John 5:29 (First clause).

The resurrection of the just is really the resurrection of the justified or righteous, who have been made so on the ground of Christ's atonement. It is a resurrection unto life,—the more abundant life, freed from all the limitations due to sin, with criminal judgment forever passed.

(2) Resurrection of the unjust—to judgment.

Rev. 20:5 (first clause) But the rest of the dead lived not again until the thousand years were finished.

S. F. John 5:29 (last clause).

In contrast to the above this is the resurrection of the unjustified or unrighteous, those who have not been the recipients of the benefits of Christ's vicarious judgment and punishment, and therefore must face these for themselves.

"There has crept into the thought of man, and somewhat into the books that men write, the idea of a simultaneous resurrection of the just and the unjust. The Scriptures never speak of one simultaneous, universal resurrection. It is expressly said that 'all that are in the graves shall hear his voice, and shall come forth,' but two resurrections are immediately described (John 5:28, 29)."—Scofield.

D. S. All the dead will have a bodily resurrection—some unto life and others unto judgment.

III. The Characteristics of the Resurrection Body.

1. Of the believer.

(1) A redeemed body.

Rom. 8:23—And not only they, but ourselves also which have the firstfruits of tne Spirit, even we ourselves groan within ourselves, waiting for the adoption, to wit, the redemption of our body.

The believer's present body, which is called "the body of his humiliation" (Phil. 3:21) is not yet fitted for entrance into the kingdom of God (I Cor. 15:50). Paul's hope is' not for deliverance from the body, but the redemption of it (II Cor. 5:4).

(2) Identified with the body of the grave.

Job 19:25-27—For I know that my redeemer liveth and that he shall stand at the latter day upon the earth. And though after my skin worms destroy this body, yet in my flesh shall I see God. Whom I shall see for myself, and mine eyes shall behold and not another; though my reins be consumed within me.

S. A. Phil. 3:20-21 R. V.

Dr. Harry A. Ironside once, passing through his home city, saw a block of store buildings from which the firms had removed in order that the buildings might be completely remodeled. They had put signs in the windows which read: "Moved to such a number until repairs are completed." Dr. Ironside remarked to his wife that this was a striking picture of death for the believer. He then suggested as an epitaph for his tombstone, "Harry A. Ironside, saved by the grace of God, moved out until renovated and repaired."

Months afterward he again passed that way and saw these buildings completed. There were the same foundations and walls, the same buildings, occupied by the same firms, yet they were so altered and improved as to make a most marked contrast between the new and the old. So with the resurrection body of the believer. It will have a material relation to this body of our humiliation and yet will be gloriously fashioned anew, perfectly renovated and repaired.

(3) A God-given body.

I Cor. 15:38—But God giveth it a body as it hath pleased him, and to every seed his own body.

S. F. II Cor. 5:1-5.

The fact that we cannot conceive the nature of this body need not trouble us. Who without previous observation could ever imagine what would spring from an acorn or a grain of wheat? To each seed God gives its own body. We in our finite minds cannot conceive what our future body, subject to no waste or decay, can be; but we need not lose that heavenly hope that such a body will exist. "All flesh is not the same flesh." The kind of flesh you now wear may be unfit for your final estate, but there awaits you as suitable and congenial a body as your present familiar tenement. The bird has a body which fits him for the air; the fish lives with comfort in its own element. And the variety now existing does not exhaust God's resources. Are we not at the beginning of His works? May we not reasonably suppose that a truly infinite development and expansion await God's works?

(4) Similar to Christ's glorified body.

I John 3:2—Beloved, now are we the sons of God, and it doth not yet appear what we shall be but we know that, when he shall appear, we shall be like him; for we shall see him as he is.

a. Real.

Luke 24:39—Behold my hands and my feet, that it is I myself; handle me and see; for a spirit hath not flesh and bones, as ye see me have.

b. Recognizable.

Luke 24:31—And their eyes were opened and they knew him; and he vanished out of their sight.

S. F. Acts 7:55, 56.

c. Freed from earthly limitations.

John 20:19—Then the same day at evening, being the first day of the week, when the doors were shut where the disciples were assembled for fear of the Jews, came Jesus and stood in the midst, and saith unto them, Peace be unto you.

The resurrection body of the believer will be like his Lord's, not phantasmal, but real. And, like his Lord's, it will possess an individual identity with the body of this life and will therefore be capable of recognition. It will be fitted for the uses of the sanctified spirit. It will have many glorious characteristics which will differentiate it from "this body of our humiliation," and equip it for the higher service of the future.

2. Of the unbeliever—corrupt and mortal body suitable to the corrupt soul.

Matt. 5:29—And if thy right eye offend thee, pluck it out, and cast it from thee; for it is profitable for thee that one of thy members should perish, and not that thy whole body should be cast into hell.

S. F. Matt. 10:28; Rev. 20:12, 13; Rev. 21:8.

S. A. Gal. 6:7, 8.

The purpose and result of the resurrection of unbelievers namely, judgment and punishment, is about all that is given in the Scriptures. There is detailed information revealed unto us by the Spirit concerning things that God hath prepared for them that love Him (I Cor. 2:9, 10), but only the cold facts are given concerning the judgment and punishment of the wicked. The Scriptures are strangely silent on the subject of the resurrection of the unbeliever's body. But analogy would seem to indicate that the outward form will fitly represent the inward state of the soul, and thus will be corrupt and degraded as the soul which inhabits it. That the resurrection body of the unbeliever will be mortal is seen by the fact that it will be subject to death,—the second death.

D. S. The resurrection bodies of unbelievers will be characterized by mortality and corruption, while those of believers will be immortal, incorruptible and glorious.

IV. The Time of It.

1. In relation to believers—before the millennium.

Rev. 20:4—And I saw thrones, and they sat upon them, and judgment was given unto them; and I saw the souls of them that were beheaded for the witness of Jesus, and for the word of God, and which had not worshipped the beast, neither had received his mark upon their foreheads, or in their hands; and they lived and reigned with Christ a thousand years.

S. F. John 6:39, 40, 44; I Cor. 15:22, 23; I Thes. 4:15, 16.

This resurrection is called the "First Resurrection," and a benediction is pronounced upon its participants (Rev. 20:6). There seem to be two, at least, installments of this resurrection. One consists of those who were raised just prior to the Rapture at the coming of Christ for the saints. The other consists of the martyred dead, who are slain during the Great Tribulation, and who are raised prior to the establishment of Christ's Millennial Kingdom.

2. In relation to unbelievers—after the millennium.

Rev. 20:5—But the rest of the dead lived not again until the thousand years were finished.

S. F. Rev. 20:12–14.

The resurrection of unbelievers will take place at the end of this present dispensational order, after the Millennial reign of Christ, and just prior to the Great White Throne Judgment.

D. S. The resurrection of believers will take place at the coming of Christ for the Church and will be separated from that of unbelievers by the thousand year reign of Christ.

C. The Judgments.

The Scriptures present judgment as God's strange work, but while this is true, it is also His sure work. It is made certain by Divine appointment or ordination. It is made certain also by the very nature of things. The very nature of Divine justice demands judgment as a vindication of itself. The very nature of things as related to men, also requires it. Man's moral sense, or conscience, calls for judgment. The universal sense of, or belief in God, makes it necessary.

Judgment is not, however, to be identified with death. Death presupposes a judgment which has already taken place, of which it is the inflicted penalty. There are judgments depicted for the future which cannot with consistency and loyalty to the Scriptures be said to take place at death or to be identified with it. Jesus spoke of those who had already died as participating in a judgment, yet future (Matt. 12:41, 42; Matt. 10:15), showing that death and judgment were not identical, either as to fact or time.

There are those who hold the erroneous conception of a general judgment for all at the end of the world. This has no foundation either in revelation or in reason. The Scriptures show plainly that there are various groups to be judged and that various circumstances and conditions characterize these judgments. Reason cannot substantiate a belief in a general judgment, for there is no single basis upon which all can be judged. The ground of the judgment of one group cannot suffice for the others, for they have different responsibilities and obligations for which they are to be called to account.

I. The Meaning of Divine Judgment.

1. Negatively—not the ascertaining of guilt or merit.

Heb. 4:13—Neither is there any creature that is not manifest in his sight; but all things are naked and opened unto the eyes of Him with whom we have to do.

S. F. Luke 12:2.

God has perfect knowledge of all man's thoughts, words, and deeds, and therefore needs no evidence gained by examination or testimony.

2. Positively—manifestation, discrimination, and reward of character and conduct.

Rom. 2:5, 6—But after thy hardness and impenitent heart treasurest up unto thyself wrath against the day of wrath and revelation of the righteous judgment of God. Who will render to every man according to his deeds.

S. F. II Cor. 5:10, R. V.; Matt. 12:36; I Cor. 4:5.

Judgment gives God an opportunity for the display and demonstration of His righteousness and justice in relation to creatures, especially sinful creatures.

D. S. In His judgment of men, God does not need to be informed concerning their records, but only to make exhibition of them and administer proper awards and punishments.

II. The Fact of Them.

1. As taught in the Old Testament—the world to be judged in righteousness.

Psa. 9:7, 8—But the Lord shall endure forever, he hath prepared his throne for judgment. And he shall judge the world in righteousness, he shall minister judgment to the people in uprightness.

S. F. Psa. 96:12, 13.

2. As taught in the New Testament—man appointed unto judgment.

Heb. 9:27—And as it is appointed unto men once to die, but after this the judgment.

S. F. Acts 17:31.

There is to be a time of judicial reckoning and adjustment. Man is appointed unto judgment just as certainly as he is appointed to death, and the resurrection of Jesus Christ is God's assurance of that fact.

D. S. A time of reckoning and judgment is taught by both the Old and New Testaments.

III. The Personality of the Judge.

1. God.

Rom. 14:12—So then every one of us shall give account of himself to God.

S. F. Rom. 1:32; Rom. 2:2, 3, 5, 6; Psa. 96:13; Psa. 9:7, 8.

Future judgment will be executed by God, by whom all are held responsible, and to whom all are held accountable.

2. God in Christ.

Rom. 2:16—In the day when God shall judge the secrets of men by Jesus Christ according to my gospel.

S. F. Rom. 14:10–12; Acts 17:31; John 5:22, 23, 27; II Cor. 5:10; Acts 10:42.

Those passages which refer to God in the execution of future judgment are to be interpreted as meaning God, the Son, Who is to be "the Judge of the quick and the dead."

3. Saints as assistants.

I Cor. 6:2, 3—Do ye not know that the saints shall judge the world? and if the world shall be judged by you, are ye unworthy to judge the smallest matters: Know ye not that we shall judge angels? how much more things that pertain to this life?

S. F. Psa. 149:9; Rev. 2:26, 27; Rev. 3:21.

Judgment upon angels, kings, nobles and peoples, is an honor to be conferred upon the saints; instead of standing in the dock as criminals they will sit on the bench as associate judges.

D. S. The Father hath committed all judgment unto the Son; Christ will be the Executor of future judgment, assisted by the saints.

IV. The Order of Them.

1. The Judgment of the Cross.

(1) Satan judged and his authority potentially annulled.

Heb. 2:14 R. V.—Since then the children are sharers in flesh and blood, he also himself in like manner partook of the same; that through death he might bring to nought him that had the power of death, that is the devil.

S. F. John 12:31; Col. 2:15 W. T.; John 16:11; Rev. 12:11.

S. A. John 5:24.

That which was a seeming victory for the forces of evil was in reality their greatest defeat. By Satan's own weapon, death, Christ has provisionally brought him to nought. Christ paid the price of human redemption, and thus wrested the scepter of authority from the hands of Satan. Speaking anticipatively of the cross Jesus said "Now is the judgment of this world, now shall the Prince of this world be cast out." Looking on beyond the cross to the coming and work of the Holy Spirit, He said of Him, "He shall convince the world of judgment, because the Prince of this world hath been judged."

(2) The Adamic sin principle or nature judicially put to death.

Rom. 8:3.—For what the law could not do, in that it was weak through the flesh, God, sending his own Son in the likeness of sinful flesh and for sin, condemned sin in the flesh.

S. F. Gal. 2:20, R. V.

S. A. Gal. 5:13, 16–21, 24; Rom. 6:1–4.

God's plan of salvation embraces no schemes for the betterment of the old man. There is only one place for it and that is the cross, the place of death. Just as Christ was crucified for us and for our sins, so we—that is, the Adamic nature of sin within us—have been crucified with Him. Each one of these works is finished. That is a fact of God, eternal, unalterable, on which our faith is to rest for continuous victory and deliverance. Faith rests on the fact of God and the act of Christ and reckons that fact to be true because of the act. The believer has a two-fold union with Jesus Christ. He has a death-union with the Christ on the cross on the side of his old nature, and he has a life-union with

Christ in the glory on the side of his new nature. Both are to be reckoned real.

(3) Believers' sins substitutionally judged and punished.

I Peter 2:24—Who his own self bare our sins in his own body on the tree, that we, being dead to sins, should live unto righteousness; by whose stripes ye were healed.

S. F. Heb. 9:25–28 R. V.; Gal. 3:13; I Peter 3:18.

There will be no future judgment of the believer for his sins as crimes against God, for they have been already judged at the Cross. No judgment, no condemnation, and no separation are the emphatic declarations of Scripture (John 5:24, R. V.); (Rom. 8:1, 39). The weakest and feeblest believer is as free and immune from Divine judgment for sin as Christ, Himself. It can no more overtake them than it can reach Him. For us and Him it is forever past. For "as He is (beyond judgment) so are we in this world." We will be manifested before the judgment seat or "bema" of Christ for rewards, but not judged to reveal guilt or innocency or to determine destiny.

2. The present judgment of the believer's self-life.

I Cor. 11:31, 32—For if we would judge ourselves we should not be judged. But when we are judged we are chastened of the Lord, that we should not be condemned with the world.

S. F. I Cor. 11:28–30; I Cor. 5:3–5; I Tim. 1:19, 20; I John 5:16, 17; Heb. 12:5–11.

S. A. II Sam. 7:13–15; II Sam. 12:12–14.

There must be continually self-judgment—the discipline of self, going on in the believer's life, otherwise it will call for Divine discipline, the corrective and chastening judgments of God. God deals with us after our acceptance of Christ, not as subjects of a king, nor as criminals answerable to a judge, but as sons under the control and discipline of a righteous, wise and loving Father.

3. The judgment of the believer's works.

(1) The time of it—at the Return of Christ.

I Cor. 4:5—Therefore judge nothing before the time, until the Lord come, who both will bring to light the hidden things of darkness, and will make manifest the counsels of the hearts; and then shall every man have praise of God.

S. F. Rev. 22:12.

(2) The basis of it—believer's works.

II Cor. 5:10—For we must all appear before the judgment seat of Christ; that every one may receive the things done in his body, according to that he hath done, whether it be good or bad.

S. F. I Cor. 3:13–15.

The manifestation before the judgment seat of Christ will be "of every man's work." The examination will determine "what sort it is," whether it be good or bad, i.e., whether it is "gold, silver, precious stones," or "wood, hay and stubble," whether deserving of reward or loss of reward. The symbolism of the work which abides doubtless signifies that which is done for the glory of God, in connection with the redemptive purpose of Christ and in the guidance and power of the Holy Spirit; while that of the work which is burned signifies that which has been done in earthly wisdom and energy, by earthly means and methods, and for earthly aims and ends.

(3) The results of it.

> **a. Rewards to be received—described as crowns or chaplets.**

Rev. 22:12—And behold, I come quickly and my reward is with me to give every man according as his work shall be.

> (a) Crown of life for faithfulness.
>
> > aa. To those who live the martyr's life.

James 1:12—Blessed is the man that endureth temptation; for when he is tried; he shall receive the crown of life, which the Lord hath promised to them that love him.

> > bb. To those who die the martyr's death.

Rev. 2:10—Fear none of those things which thou shalt suffer; behold, the devil shall cast some of you into prison, that ye may be tried; and ye shall have tribulation ten days; be thou faithful unto death, and I will give thee a crown of life.

> (b) Crown of glory—for the faithful under shepherd.

I Peter 5:4—And when the chief Shepherd shall appear, ye shall receive a crown of glory that fadeth not away.

S. A. Heb. 2:9; John 17:22; I Peter 5:1–3.

> (c) Crown of righteousness—for them who love His appearing.

II Tim. 4:7, 8—I have fought a good fight, I have finished my course, I have kept the faith; Henceforth there is laid up for me a crown of righteousness, which the Lord, the righteous judge shall give me at that day; and not to me only; but unto all them also that love his appearing.

> > aa. The courageous soldier.
> > bb. The successful runner.
> > cc. The faithful steward.
>
> (d) Crown of rejoicing for the soulwinner.

I Thes. 2:19, 20—For what is our hope, or joy, or crown of rejoicing? Are not even ye in the presence of our Lord Jesus Christ at his coming? For ye are our glory and joy.

> > Comp. with Dan. 12:1–3.
>
> (e) Incorruptible crown—for self-mastery.

I Cor. 9:25–27—And every man that striveth for the mastery is temperate in all things. Now they do it to obtain a corruptible crown; but we an incorruptible. I therefore so run, not as uncertainly; so fight I not as one that beateth the air. But I keep under my body, and bring it into subjection; lest that by any means, when I have preached to others, I myself should be a castaway.

It is not necessary to contend for literal, material crowns. The rewards, however, will be literal and real, and exceed in value any merely material diadem or chaplet.

> **b. Loss to be sustained.**

II John 8—Look to yourselves, that we lose not those things which we have wrought, but that we receive a full reward.

S. F. I Cor. 3:15; I John 2:28.

Failure or negligence in relation to the believer's stewardship will cause him to suffer loss at the Judgment Seat of Christ.

The believer will be manifested before the judgment seat of Christ, and his works will be examined; the result of which examination will be; rewards for some, loss for others, but high and holy positions and privileges for all.

4. The judgment of Israel—preparatory for entrance into the kingdom.

Psa. 50:1-7—The mighty God, even the Lord, hath spoken, and called the earth from the rising of the sun unto the going down thereof. Out of Zion, the perfection of beauty, God hath shined. Our God shall come, and shall not keep silence; a fire shall devour before Him, and it shall be very tempestuous round about Him. He shall call to the heavens from above and to the earth, that He may judge His people. Gather my saints together unto me; those that have made a covenant with Me by sacrifice. And the heavens shall declare His righteousness; for God is Judge Himself. Selah. Hear, O my people, and I will speak; O Israel; and I will testify against thee; I am God, even thy God.

Comp. with Isa. 1:2, 24, 26.

S. A. Ezek. 20:30-44, Mal. 3:1.

"There is a future judgment predicted for restored Israel, preparatory to the re-establishment of the Davidic Kingdom. This is to determine who among the children of Israel found upon earth at the Lord's glorious appearing shall go into the kingdom. The rebels shall be purged out, and they shall not enter into the land of Israel."—Pettingill.

5. The judgment of the living nations.

(1) The place of it—on earth—in the valley of Jehoshaphat.

Matt. 25:31, 32—When the Son of man shall come in His glory, and all the holy angels with Him, then shall He sit upon the throne of His glory. And before Him shall be gathered all nations; and He shall separate them one from another, as a shepherd divideth his sheep from the goats.

S. A. Zech. 14:1, 2; Joel 3:2.

(2) The basis of it—attitude toward the message and messengers of the kingdom.

Matt. 25:40, 45—And the King shall answer and say unto them, Verily I say unto you, inasmuch as ye have done it unto one of the least of these, my brethren, ye have done it unto me. Then shall he answer them, saying, Verily I say unto you, Inasmuch as ye did it not to one of the least of these, ye did it not to me.

S. F. Joel 3:1-8, 19; Matt. 24:14.

"The basis of this judgment, by which the Gentiles will be tested, is their treatment of a third group, called by the King, 'My brethren.'. These, as will be seen in Joel's account, are Jews. Doubtless they are those Jews that shall have turned to the Lord after the catching away of the Church. At once upon their conversion, this Jewish Remnant, becomes God's evangelizing agency and begins the work of proclaiming the King's approaching advent 'in the clouds of heaven with power, and great glory' (Matt. 24:14, 30; Isa. 66:19)."—Pettingill.

(3) The results of it.

    a. The righteous to go into the kingdom prepared from the foundation of the world.

Matt. 25:34—Then shall the King say unto them on his right hand, Come ye blessed of My Father, inherit the kingdom prepared for you from the foundation of the world.

The nations, here mentioned, are doubtless those who have taken a favorable attitude toward the message and messengers of the kingdom, and who have shown that favorable attitude by their actions toward them in deeds of mercy.

That the righteous here cannot refer to the Church is seen from the following: These receive a "kingdom prepared from the foundation of the world;" the Church is blessed with all spiritual blessings in the heavenlies. These are "blessed of the Father"; the Church is in fellowship with the Father and the Son. These receive a "kingdom prepared from the foundation of the world"; the Church is chosen in Him from before the foundation of the world.

This result doubtless includes participation in the Millennial Kingdom with Christ as nations, and a share in the joys of eternal life, as individuals.

    b. The wicked to be shut out of the kingdom and suffer final judgment and doom.

Matt. 25:41—Then shall he say also unto them on the left hand, Depart from me, ye cursed, into everlasting fire, prepared for the devil and his angels.

S. F. Matt. 25:46.

The wicked nations by reason of their attitude and action in relation to those whom Christ calls His brethren shut themselves out of the kingdom of Christ and put themselves under an everlasting curse.

The wicked nations referred to in this judgment cannot consistently be identified with the wicked dead of Rev. 20. They appear before the Great White Throne; these wicked nations appear before the Son of Man as He sits upon the throne of his Glory. They appear as individuals for judgment; these as nations. They are raised from the dead to be judged; these are living upon the earth. They are judged according to the books of records and the book of life; these are judged according to their treatment of the "brethren."

6. The judgment of fallen angels—at a time called the "great day."

I Cor. 6:3—Know ye not that we shall judge angels? how much more things that pertain to this life?

S. F. Jude 6; II Peter 2:4.

The Apostle Paul declares that the Church shall participate in the administration of this judgment. She will herself have passed through the judgment of the "bema," and will then be identified with Christ in the future execution of His sovereign authority and justice.

7. The judgment of the Great White Throne.

Rev. 20:11—And I saw a great white throne, and Him that sat on it, from whose face the earth and the heaven fled away; and there was found no place for them.

(1) The personnel of the Judged—"The rest of the dead"—those not included in "the first resurrection."

Rev. 20:5, f. c.—But the rest of the dead lived not again until the thousand years were finished.

Those to whom justice is to be administered at the Great White Throne are those who failed to participate in "the first resurrection." These are the dead who "lived not again until the thousand years were finished." They are to be identified with those who are called "the unjust" and who are said to have a "resurrection unto judgment" (Acts 24:14; John 5:29).

(2) The basis of it.

a. According to the record of deeds in the books.

Rev. 20:12, 13—And I saw the dead, small and great stand before God; and the books were opened and another book was opened; which is the book of life; and the dead were judged out of those things which were written in the books, according to their works. And the sea gave up the dead which were in it; and death and hell delivered up the dead which were in them; and they were judged every man according to their works.

The books of record reveal the guilt of those judged. They contain the evidence upon which the verdict is rendered. Apparently there are degrees of guilt. Luke 12:47, 48.

b. According to the roll of names in the Book of Life.

Rev. 20:15—And whosoever was not found written in the Book of Life was cast into the lake of fire.

S. A. Rev. 20:12.

The final appeal in this judgment concerning those in question is the Book of Life. The Book of Life reveals the fact that no substitution has been made or redemption accomplished for those who have thus been found guilty.

(3) The issue of it—consigned to their final doom—cast into the lake of fire.

Rev. 20:15—As quoted above.

This is spoken of as the final judgment. It stands at the end of this present order of the ages. I Cor. 15:28.

D. S. The judgments of God begin with that borne by Himself in Christ on behalf of believers, continuing with that administered by them upon themselves, and including in its scope that meted out by Christ to the Church, Israel, the Nations, the Angels, and the wicked dead.

D. The Future Destiny of the Righteous and the Wicked.

What are we to believe concerning the present state of those who have died? The intermediate state of those who have departed this life has been a subject of much conjecture and speculation. Even the light which shines from Scripture does not seem to be as strong as some could wish. It is sufficient, however, to reveal the essential facts. There are two words to be considered in this connection, which play an important part in the Biblical teaching upon this subject. The two words are: "Sheol" and "Hades," the one a Hebrew word, the other, Greek. These two words have the same significance, i.e., they refer to same general place, the abode of the souls of the dead. In the authorized version these words are translated by various English words, such as "Hell," "the pit," and "the grave." These, however are not correct translations. Each of them has its

311

own Hebrew or Greek equivalent. The Revised Version has avoided this error by not translating the words "Sheol" and "Hades," but transliterating them into English.

In the Old Testament all those who died, both righteous and wicked, are represented as going to Sheol (Gen. 37:35; Psa. 9:17; Psa. 16:10). In the narrative of the Rich Man and Lazarus in Luke 16, Jesus lifts the curtain and reveals the fact that there are two compartments in Sheol or Hades. The one, spoken of as "Abraham's Bosom," was the abode of the righteous, and was at that time identical with Paradise (Luke 23:43, compared with Matt. 12:40). At the resurrection of Christ this part of Hades was emptied of its occupants, who were transferred to the Right Hand of God (Eph. 4:8–10 compared with II Cor. 12:2–4; Psa. 68:18; Zech. 9:11, 12). This new abode of the righteous is now called Paradise. It is to this place of Christ's presence that the believer takes his departure at death, and it is here, where he abides in conscious fellowship with Christ, that he remains until the resurrection of the just (Phil. 1:23, 24; II Cor. 5:6–8; I Thes. 4:14–17). That part of Hades or Sheol which was separated from Paradise by the Great Gulf is the abode of the souls of the wicked. This is the temporary prison where the criminals of the universe are held in confinement awaiting the Judgment of the Great White Throne.

Under this topic we are to consider the future destiny of the two classes, the Righteous and the Wicked—that destiny which has its beginning beyond this present earth-life and after the completion of this present world order.

I. Heaven in Its Relation to the Future Destiny of the Righteous.

According to certain traditional beliefs there are supposed to be seven heavens, but the Scriptures themselves refer to only three: the atmospheric heaven (Acts 14:17); the stellar heaven (Gen. 1:14); and the third heaven (II Cor. 12:2; Deut. 10:14).

There will be new heavens and a new earth. "The possibilities of the heavens being dissolved, the elements melted with fervent heat, and a new heaven and a new earth cannot be disputed (II Peter 3:10–13). In what sense are they new? It does not mean just brought into existence, but renovated, made fresh, and implies previous existence. Throughout Scripture, the reconstitution of the material world, by which it passes from the bondage of corruption into the liberty of the glory of the children of God, is taught, and the final seat of the City of God is set forth as being not a far-off misty heaven in space, but that new world which is the old. There are some noticeable absences from this new City—no sin, no Satan, no sorrow, no curse, no corruption, no mortality. Reverse the miseries of earth and you know some of the joys of Heaven. The former things are passed away.' "—KEMP.

1. The Scriptural fact of it.

Col. 1:5—For the hope which is laid up for you in heaven, whereof ye heard before in the word of the truth of the gospel;

S. F. I Peter 1:3–5; I Thes. 4:16, 17.

D. S. The Heavenly destiny of the righteous is a fact established not by human reason but by divine revelation.

2. The Character of it—a place.

The Scriptures designate a certain part of the universe called heaven as the future dwelling place of believers. They teach that heaven is a place.

John 14:2, 3—In my Father's house are many mansions: if it were not so, I would have told you. I go to prepare a place for you. And if I go and prepare a place for you, I will come again, and receive you unto myself; that where I am, there ye may be also.

S. F. I Thes. 4:17; Psa. 23:6; I Peter 1:3–5; Heb. 12:22; Heb. 11:10, 16.

The Believer's future home is described in some of the above passages and also in Rev. 21 and 22 as a city. Dr. Bonar speaks of it as being "well built, well lighted, well watered, well provisioned, well guarded, and well governed."

(1) A place of holy environment and associations.

Rev. 21:2—And I John saw the Holy City, new Jerusalem, coming down from God out of heaven, prepared as a bride adorned for her husband.

S. F. Rev. 21:3, 27; Rev. 22:15.

(2) A place of great beauty and splendor.

Rev. 21:18—And the building of the wall of it was of jasper: and the city was pure gold, like unto clear glass.

S. F. Rev. 21:19–21.

(3) A place of great joy and gladness.

Rev. 21:4—And God shall wipe away all tears from their eyes; and there shall be no more death, neither sorrow, nor crying, neither shall there be any more pain; for the former things are passed away.

S. F. Ps. 16:11.

(4) A place of holy delights and satisfactions.

Rev. 22:14—Blessed are they that do his commandments, that they may have right to the tree of life, and may enter in through the gates into the city.

S. F. Rev. 21:6; Rev. 7:16.

(5) A place of great light and glory.

Rev. 21:23—And the city had no need of the sun, neither of moon, to shine in it: for the glory of God did lighten it, and the Lamb is the light thereof.

S. F. Rev. 22:5.

3. The Inhabitants of It—Redeemed Men and Unfallen Angels.

Rev. 21:9, 10—And there came unto me one of the seven angels which had the seven vials full of the seven last plagues, and talked with me, saying, Come hither, I will shew thee the bride, the Lamb's wife. And he carried me away in the spirit to a great and high mountain, and shewed me that great city, the holy Jerusalem, descending out of heaven from God.

S. F. Rev. 21:2, 7; Rev. 22:3, 14.

Prominent among the occupants of the Heavenly City will be the Church; in fact, the title which is to be given this Holy City is "The Bride, the Lamb's Wife." There will probably be others of the Redeemed present, especially the Old Testament Saints. This is intimated by the names of the Twelve Tribes of Israel which are incorporated in the Gates of the city (Rev. 21:12).

313

Four descriptions are given of the inhabitants: "overcomers," identified with regenerate believers in I John 5:4, 5; "sons of God," those who have been made such by His regenerating grace, through faith in Christ Jesus; "servants," those who are such by consecration; and "the obedient," they that do his commandments, not to obtain their salvation, but as an evidence of it.

There are also angelic beings, which include the Cherubim and the Seraphim, as well as the angels, proper (Rev. 5:14; Isa. 6:1, 2, R. V.; Matt. 22:30). Pre-eminent, of course, among the inhabitants of Heaven are God upon His throne and the Lamb.

4. The Occupation of it—Doing the Will of God.

Rev. 22:3—And there shall be no more curse: but the throne of God and of the Lamb shall be in it; and his servants shall serve him.

S. F. Matt. 6:10.

(1) Rest.

Rev. 14:13—And I heard a voice from heaven saying unto me, Write, Blessed are the dead which die in the Lord from hence-forth: Yea, saith the Spirit, that they may rest from their labours; and their works do follow them.

(2) Worship.

Rev. 5:14, R. V.—And the four living creatures said, Amen. And the elders fell down and worshipped.

S. F. Rev. 5:11-13; Rev. 4:8.

(3) Service.

Rev. 7:15—Therefore are they before the throne of God, and serve him day and night in his temple; and he that sitteth on the throne shall dwell among them.

It may not be known just what or how many forms of service will be rendered. It is quite clear, however, that included among them will be judging and reigning with Christ (Rev. 2:26, 27; 3:21; II Tim. 2:12).

D. S. Heaven is a prepared place for a prepared people, with a program suited to both.

II. Hell in Its Relation to the Future Destiny of the Wicked.

By the term "hell," as used here, is meant the final abode and condition of the sinful. This is a subject upon which both Science and Philosophy must of necessity remain silent, while Revelation alone is allowed to speak as being authoritative.

The Greek word translated "hell," which is descriptive of this abode is "Gehenna"—"the name given to the valley of Hinnom, near Jerusalem in which the garbage of the city was cast and burned. At any time, day or night, the fires with their ascending smoke, could be seen in this valley. Jesus makes it the symbol of hell, 'Where the worm dieth not and the fire is not quenched.' "— DIXON.

1. The Scriptural Fact of It.

(1) Established by Reason.

a. The argument from the Principle of Separation.

This principle is operative in all realms of life. The dead are separated from the living—every cemetery and crematory are arguments for hell. Garbage is separated from wholesome food—every garbage can is an argument for hell. Refuse is separated from the things of value—every rubbish-heap is an argument for hell.

"Those who refuse life in God become 'refuse' in character sooner or later, and in the nature of things must be removed to a place apart."—DIXON.

b. The argument from the Principle of Natural Consequence.

Hell is the logical outcome of the sequence to a life of wickedness. Sin damns just as fire burns or water drowns or disease kills. S-I-N spells "hell" in this world and the next. The smoke of torment ascends here from the brothel, the dive, the saloon, the drunkard's home, the divorce court, the prison, the electric chair, the gallows, the madhouse, the gambling den, and the lives of men and women who are burning in the furnace of their own lusts.

c. The argument from the Principle of Restraint.

There are some who are restrained from criminality and lawlessness by the fear of punishment. To take away all penalty for disobedience to law is to open up the flood-gates of crime. "If there were more preaching of hell in the pulpit there would be less of hell in the community."—DIXON. The increase of suicides, murders, and other forms of crime has been due in no small measure to the removal of the fear of all future retribution.

d. The argument from the Principle of Governmental Obligation.

God owes it to his law and justice to visit punishment upon the sinner. Satisfaction to offended justices must be rendered. The penalty of broken laws must be paid. If this is not done for the sinner it must be done by him. A law without a penalty is a farce, as is also a penalty without its enforcement.

(2) Established by Revelation.

Matt. 5:29—And if thy right eye offend thee, pluck it out, and cast it from thee: for it is profitable for thee that one of thy members should perish, and not that thy whole body should be cast into hell.

S. F. Matt. 10:28; Matt. 25:46; Rev. 20:15.

D. S. The fact of hell is in harmony with reason and according to the teachings of Divine Revelation.

2. The Character of It—a Place.

Just as heaven is a place and has a definite location, so is hell. This is seen by the representation of its being inhabited. It is further shown by reason of the fact that the inhabitants are possessed not only of souls but of bodies. It may also be inferred by the description of the present abode of the wicked in Hades as "a place" (Luke 16:28), for it is from this location they are to be transferred to the place called "Gehenna." It is to be further said that all the descriptive terms that are used of hell denote locality.

(1) A place of unholy associations.

Rev. 21:8—But the fearful, and unbelieving, and the abominable, and murderers, and whoremongers, and sorcerers, and idolaters, and all liars, shall have their part in the lake which burneth with fire and brimstone: which is the second Death!

S. F. Rev. 22:15.

(2) A place of imprisonment and death.

Rev. 20:14, R. V.—And death and Hades were cast into the lake of fire. This is the second death, even the lake of fire.

S. F. Matt. 5:24, 25; Rev. 20:15.

(3) A place of sorrow and despair.

Luke 13:28—There shall be weeping and gnashing of teeth, when ye shall see Abraham, and Isaac, and Jacob, and all the prophets, in the kingdom of God, and you yourselves thrust out.

S. F. Matt. 25:30; 22:13; 24:51.

S. A. John 3:36.

(4) A place of conscious misery and torment.

Rev. 20.10—And the devil that deceived them was cast into the lake of fire and brimstone, where the beast and the false prophet are, and shall be tormented day and night for ever and ever.

S. F. Rev. 14:11.

S. A. Luke 16:24, 25.

(5) A place of darkness and degradation.

Matt. 25:30—And cast ye the unprofitable servant into outer darkness: there shall be weeping and gnashing of teeth.

Rev. 22:11, f.c.—He that is unjust, let him be unjust still: and he which is filthy, let him be filthy still.

3. The Occupants of it—the impenitent.

The Scriptures describe a motley crowd who are to be the inhabitants of this abode of the damned. These represent many and diverse forms and degrees of sin and wickedness, but all are guilty and condemned.

(1) Satan and his Angels.

Matt. 25:41—Then shall he say also unto them on the left hand, Depart from me, ye cursed, into everlasting fire, prepared for the devil and his angels.

(2) The Beast and the False Prophet.

Rev. 20:10—And the devil that deceived them was cast into the lake of fire and brimstone, where the beast and the false prophet are, and shall be tormented day and night for ever and ever.

(3) Wicked and Unbelieving Men.

Rev. 21:8—But the fearful, and unbelieving, and the abominable, and murderers, and whoremongers, and sorcerers, and idolaters, and all liars, shall have their part in the lake which burneth with fire and brimstone: which is the second death.

4. Duration—Eternal.

(1) Established by Reason.

a. The argument from endless being of the soul.

Man's creation in the image of God carries with it the necessity of endlessness of being, for this is a very essential element in the Being of God and therefore necessary in the being of man for the similarity indicated by the terms "image" and "likeness." As life is essential to being, so endless being implies

316

endless life. The Scriptures never represent the soul as being subject to death in the sense of its becoming extinct or passing into a state of unconscious existence. Since man has endless being, therefore he must spend eternity somehow, somewhere, and since the impenitence of the wicked precludes their restoration to God and release from punishment, therefore their punishment must be eternal. For the sin of the wicked thus becomes eternal sin and they become eternal sinners. See as illustration Mark 3:29.

b. The argument from the Infinite sacrifice of Christ.

"If anything less than eternal punishment be due to sin, what need was there of an infinite sacrifice to give deliverance from that punishment? Did Jesus shed His precious blood to deliver us from the consequences of our guilt, if those consequences be only temporary? Grant us the truth of an infinite sacrifice, and we argue from thence the truth of eternal punishment."— C. H. M.

(2) Established by Revelation.

Matt. 25:46—And these shall go away into everlasting punishment: but the righteous into life eternal.

S. F. Mark 3:29; John 3:36; II Thes. 1:9.

There are those who tell us that the Greek word "aionios" translated in the above passage "everlasting" means only an indefinite period of time, and does not mean "endless" or "eternal." This word occurs about seventy times in the New Testament, and should mean the same in each instance. "The word which is applied to the punishment of the wicked is also applied to the life which believers possess (Matt. 19:16), to the salvation and redemption in which they rejoice (Heb. 9:12), to the glory to which they look forward (II Cor. 4:17), to those mansions in which they hope to dwell (II Cor. 5:1), and to the inheritance which they expect to enjoy (Heb. 9:15). Moreover, it is applied to God (Rom. 16:26), and to the Spirit (Heb. 9:14). If, therefore, it be maintained that the word "everlasting" does not mean everlasting when applied to the punishment of the wicked, what security have we that it means everlasting when applied to the life, blessedness, and glory of the redeemed? What warrant has anyone, be he ever so learned, to single out seven instances from the seventy in which the Greek word "aionios" is used, and say that in those seven it does not mean everlasting, but that in all the rest it does? None whatever."—C. H. M.

D. S. Hell is a place prepared for the devil and his angels and becomes the eternal abode of those identified with him.

Study Questions on the Doctrine of Last Things

1. Quote one passage, giving the testimony of (a) Prophets, (b) John the Baptist, (c) Christ, (d) Angels, (e) One apostle, and name the other apostles who testify to the fact.
2. Discuss the negative consideration of the character of the Second Coming under (1) not providential, (a) as death, (b) as material progress, (c) as an historic event, (2) not spiritual, (a) as the Holy Spirit of Pentecost, (b) as in the conversion of a sinner, (c) as in the spread of Christianity.
3. Quote one passage showing the second coming of Christ to be personal and bodily.
4. Name the two stages of Christ's Coming and quote one passage with each.
5. Give four other descriptions of the Second Coming of Christ.
6. Discuss in detail the signs of the close of this dispensation.

7. Outline in detail the purpose of the Second Coming in regard to (a) the righteous, (b) the wicked, (c) the Antichrist, (d) Israel, (e) the Gentile nations, (f) the Davidic Kingdom, (g) Satan.

8. Outline in detail the practical value of the doctrine of the Second Coming.

9. Give the meaning of the Resurrection as found in the introductory note, mentioning that to which it has reference.

10. How is the fact of the Resurrection of the dead established:
(a) in the Old Testament, (b) in the New Testament? Quote one passage under the positive statement of each and give D. S.

11. Discuss the manner of the Resurrection of the dead as literal and bodily.

12. Quote one passage showing the Resurrection to be universal.

13. Discuss the two-fold aspect of the Resurrection of the dead and give D. S.

14. Give the description of the Resurrection body: (a) of the believer (four-fold), (b) of the unbeliever.

15. Discuss the time of the Resurrection in relation to both believers and unbelievers, and give D. S.

16. Discuss from introductory note the Judgments of God as being: (a) necessary, (b) distinct from death, (c) not to be regarded as one general judgment.

17. Discuss the meaning of divine Judgment, negatively and positively considered.

18. Quote passages under the fact of Judgments as found in both Old and New Testaments and give D. S.

19. Describe the three-fold personality of the Judge, giving D. S.

20. Discuss the Judgments in their order, as follows: (a) The three-fold Judgment of the Cross, (b) The Present Judgment of the Believer's self life, (c) The three aspects of the Judgment of the Believer's works, (d) The Judgment of Israel, (e) The three aspects of the Judgments of the Living Nations, (f) The Judgment of the Fallen Angels, (g) The three aspects of the Judgment of the Great White Throne.

21. Give D. S. under the Judgments and quote one passage of Scripture with each.

22. Discuss the meaning of the words "Sheol" and "Hades."

23. Describe the promised "new heavens and earth."

24. Quote one passage under the Scriptural fact of heaven and give D. S.

25. Describe the character of heaven as a place, in its five-fold aspect.

26. Discuss the inhabitants of heaven.

27. Quote one passage under each aspect of the occupation of heaven, and give D. S.

28. Discuss the use of the term "hell."

29. Discuss the Scriptural fact of hell as established: (a) by reason (four-fold arguments), (b) by Revelation, and give D. S.

30. Give the five-fold description of the character of hell.

31. Name the occupants of hell.

32. Discuss the arguments for the eternal duration of future punishment as established by: (a) reason (two-fold), (b) revelation.

33. Give D. S. and quote a passage of Scripture under proof from Revelation.

318

BIBLIOGRAPHY

Author   Name of Book

Andrews, S. J. . . . . Christianity and Anti-Christianity
Ashmore . . . . The New Trial of the Sinner—in Christian Review

Ballard . . . . The True God
Bancroft, E. H. . . . . Christian Theology
Beecher, L. to Bushnell . . . . . . The World's Greatest Sermons
Berry, G. R. . . . . A New Old Testament—Interlinear
Berry, G. R. . . . . A New New Testament—Interlinear
Biederwolf, W. E. . . . . Biederwolf's Illustrations, Vol. I
Bishop, G. S. . . . . Grace in Galatians
Bishop of Liverpool and
A. E. J. Rawlinson . . . . The Study Bible (St. Mark)
B I O L A . . . . The Fundamentals, Vol. I, II, III, IV
Brown, W. H. . . . . Christian Theology in Outline
Bullinger . . . . The Companion Bible

Champion, J. B. . . . . More than Atonement
Champion, J. B. . . . . The Virgin's Son
Collett, S. . . . . All About the Bible
Cooke, R. J. . . . . Doctrine of Resurrection

Davidson, A. B. . . . . The Theology of the Old Testament
Dick, J. . . . . Dick's Theology
Dixon, A. C. . . . . Present Day Life and Religion
Domer, I. A. . . . . System of Christian Doctrine
Drummond, H. . . . . Addresses
Drummond, H. . . . . Natural Law in the Spiritual World
Dwight, T. . . . . Theology

Edersheim, A. . . . . The Life and Times of Jesus
Evans, W. . . . . The Great Doctrines of the Bible

Fischer, G. P. . . . . History of Christian Doctrine
Fisher's . . . . Evidences of Christianity

Gaebelein, A. C. . . . . Gospel of Matthew, Vol. I
Gaebelein, A. C. . . . . God's Masterpiece
Goodchild, F. M. . . . . The Church. Its Nature and Purpose
Goodwin, H. M. . . . . Christ in Humanity.
Gordon, A. J. . . . . In Christ
Gordon, A. J. . . . . The Ministry of the Spirit
Gray, J. M. . . . . Christian Worker's Commentary
Gray, J. M. . . . . Primers of the Faith

Hall, W. P. ....A Remarkable Biblical Discovery
Haldeman, I. M. ....Christ, Christianity and the Bible
Harris, R. ....Origin of Doctrine of the Trinity
Harris, Samuel ....God, Creator and Lord of all, Vol I and II
Harrison, N. B. ....His in Joyous Experience
Hamilton, F. ....The Basis of Christian Faith
Hastings, J. ....The Great Christian Doctrines—Prayer
Hastings, J. ....Dictionary of the Bible
Hastings, J. ....The Great Christian Doctrines—Faith
Havergal, F. R. ....My King
Hodge, A. A. ....Outlines of Theology
Hodge, C. ....Systematic Theology, Vol. II

Inge and Goudge ....The Study Bible (Hebrews)

Jamieson, Faussett, and Brown .A Bible Commentary Vol. 1—Old Testament
Jamieson, Faussett, and Brown .A Bible Commentary Vol. 11—New Testament
Jones, E. G. and Welch, A. C. ..The Study Bible (Genesis)

Keyser, L. S. ....The Rational Test
Kohler, K. ....Jewish Theology

Lawson, J. G. ....Greatest Thoughts about Jesus Christ
Lawson, J. G. ....Greatest Thoughts about God
Lacordaire, Pere ....Jesus Christ, God, God and Men
London Bible and Tract Society Studies in the Scriptures—Series 5

Machin, J. R. ....The Virgin Birth
MacLaren, A. ....The Holy of Holies
MacLaren, A. ....The Expositor's Bible (Psalms)
Marsh, F. E. ....The Greatest Theme in the World
McClure, J. B. ....Pearls from Many Seas
McConkey, J. H. ....Article
McPherson, G. W. ....The Modern Mind and the Virgin Birth
McGregor, G. H. C. ....Article
Meyer, F. B. ....Christ in Isaiah
Meyer, F. B. ....Love to the Uttermost
Meyer, F. B. ....The Life and Light of Men
Meyer, F. B. ....The Way into the Holiest
Miley, J. ....Systematic Theology
Miley, J. ....Atonement in Christ
Miley, J. ....Systematic Theology, Vol. I
M'Ilvaine, C. P. ....Evidences of Christianity
Moffatt, J. ....The Old Testament
Moffatt, J. ....New Testament
Morgan, G. C. ....Purpose of Incarnation
Morgan, G. C. ....The Crisis of the Christ
Moule, H. C. G. ....The Expositor's Bible
Mullins, E. Y. ....The Christian Religion in its Doctrinal Expression

Neighbour, R. E. ....Sermons and Bible Studies
Newell, W. R. ....Old Testament Studies

Newell, W. R. ....Romans with Outline Lessons on the Acts
Norwood, F. W. & Barry, F. R. . The Study Bible (St. Luke)

Orr, J. ....Christian View of God and the World
Orr, J. ....The International Standard Bible Encyclopedia

Pardington, G. P. ....Outline Studies in Christian Doctrine
Patterson, A. ....The Greater Life and Work of Christ
Peake, A. S. ....Christianity—Its Nature and Its Truth
Peloubet, F. N. ....The Teacher's Commentary
Peloubet, F. N. ....Suggestive Illustrations
Pember, G. H. ....Earth's Earliest Ages
Pendleton, J. M. ....Church Manual
Pendleton, J. M. ....Christian Doctrines
Pepper, G. D. B. ....Systematic Theology
Phelps, A. ....The Still Hour
Pierson, A. T. ....The Scriptures—God's Living Oracles
Pierson, A. T. ....The Bible and Spiritual Life
Pierson, A. T. ....The Making of a Sermon
Pink. ....The Inspiration of the Scriptures

Rishell, C. W. ....The Foundations of the Christian Faith
Robinson, H. W. ....Christian Doctrine of Man
Rotherham, J. B. ....The Emphasized Bible

S. H. P. ....The God of Our Fathers
Saphir, A. ....Epistles to the Hebrews Vol. I and Vol. II
Scofield, C. I. ....Dr. C. I. Scofield's Question Box
Simmons, C. ....Scriptural Manual
Schecter, S. ....Some Aspects of Rabbinic Theology
Shedd, N. G. T. ....History of Christian Doctrine
Sheldon, H. C. ....History of Christian Doctrine
Simpson, P. C. ....The Fact of Christ
Smith, W. ....Dictionary of the Bible
Speer, R. ....The Man Christ Jesus
Stalker, J. ....Life of Christ
Stevens, G. B. ....Theology of the New Testament
Strong, A. H. ....Systematic Theology
Strong, A. H. ....The Great Poets and Their Theology
Stubbs, C. W. ....Christ of English Poetry
Symington ....Symington on the Atonement

Taylor, B. C. ....The Atonement Typified
Thayer ....The Analytical Greek Lexicon
Torrey, R. A. ....What the Bible Teaches
Torrey, R. A. ....The Higher Criticism and the New Theology
Townsend ....Collapse of Evolution
Tucker, W. L. ....His Son

Vincent, M. R. ....Word Studies in New Testament

Wakefield ....Article
Watt and McFadyen ....The Study Bible (Psalms)

321

Watt, G. .... The Name that Shall Endure
Watt, G. .... The Meaning of the Cross
Weymouth, R. F. .... New Testament in Modern Speech
White, W. W. .... The Resurrection Body
Winchester and Moffat .... The Study Bible (Romans)

Young .... Analytical Concordance

INDEX

323

324